THE LAST GENERATION OF THE
GERMAN
RABBINATE

THE MODERN JEWISH EXPERIENCE

Marsha L. Rozenblit and Beth S. Wenger, editors
Deborah Dash Moore and Paula Hyman, founding coeditors

THE LAST GENERATION OF THE GERMAN RABBINATE

German Refugee Rabbis in the United States, 1933–2010

CORNELIA WILHELM

INDIANA UNIVERSITY PRESS

This book is a publication of

Indiana University Press
Office of Scholarly Publishing
Herman B Wells Library 350
1320 East 10th Street
Bloomington, Indiana 47405 USA

iupress.org

© 2024 by Cornelia Wilhelm

All rights reserved
No part of this book may be reproduced or utilized in any form or by any means, electronic or mechanical, including photocopying and recording, or by any information storage and retrieval system, without permission in writing from the publisher.

First Printing 2024

Library of Congress Cataloging-in-Publication Data

Names: Wilhelm, Cornelia, author.
Title: The last generation of the German rabbinate : German refugee rabbis in the United States, 1933-2010 / Cornelia Wilhelm.
Description: Bloomington : Indiana University Press, [2024] | Series: The Modern Jewish experience | Includes bibliographical references.
Identifiers: LCCN 2023059523 (print) | LCCN 2023059524 (ebook) | ISBN 9780253070180 (hardback) | ISBN 9780253070197 (paperback) | ISBN 9780253070203 (ebook)
Subjects: LCSH: Jews, German--United States--History--20th century. | Jews—Germany—History—20th century. | Rabbis—Germany—History—20th century. | Rabbis—United States—History—20th century. | Jewish refugees—United States—History—20th century. | BISAC: HISTORY / Jewish | HISTORY / Modern / 20th Century / Holocaust
Classification: LCC E184.354 .W56 2024 (print) | LCC E184.354 (ebook) | DDC 973.0492/40430904—dc23/eng/20240313
LC record available at https://lccn.loc.gov/2023059523
LC ebook record available at https://lccn.loc.gov/2023059524

This book is dedicated to the refugees and their families and was written to honor their memory!

CONTENTS

Preface ix

Introduction: *Understanding the "Last Generation of the German Rabbinate"* 1

1. **German Jewry under Nazism:** *Changes and Challenges for the Rabbinical Profession* 21
2. **Rescue and Flight:** *Scholars and Students—And a Visa That Saved Lives* 45
3. **Flight and Rescue:** *Rabbis—And a Visa That Saved Lives* 83
4. **The Refugees' First Years in the United States:** *Employment, Settlement, Congregations, and the Encounter with American Society and American Judaism* 105
5. **Careers Lost and Found:** *Paths of Professional Success and Failure and the Making of the "Last Generation of the German Rabbinate"* 136
6. **Refugee Returns:** *Transatlantic Encounters and the Legacy of the "Last Generation of the German Rabbinate"* 179

Conclusion 208

Notes 217
Bibliography 263
Index 289

PREFACE

As a scholar of German-Jewish history, I have spent long periods of research on the campus of Hebrew Union College in Cincinnati in the American Jewish Archives. During these visits it crystallized to me, how the German refugees of the 1930s had been part of this college community and how their mark still resonated there.

For many years I wondered how their history could be written and presented as a solid empirical study which would also provide deeper insights to the realities of those who were forced to flee, a decision which turned their lives upside down, left them marked for life, but also secured their survival in a place that had become a new home for them. Our digital humanities database and this book may give the refugees and their families now the long-deserved visibility and recognition and will hopefully stimulate more research in this area.

All this work would have never been possible without the generous funding that I received from a number of organizations and foundations, most of whom have distributed public funds toward this project. I would like to underscore this fact, is important in this context and might be meaningful for the families of those who were forced to flee, that this project was funded by the German taxpayer. Therefore, I would like to thank the many funders in a special way:

The first enthusiastic funding came, - no surprise, - from the Jacob Rader Marcus Center of the American Jewish Archives on the campus of Hebrew Union College in Cincinnati, with one of their wonderful fellowships. This first opportunity to explore this topic in more depth was essential for the growth and conceptualization of all that followed. The Jacob Rader Marcus Center of the American Jewish archives have not only been a great resource for this work, but also an emphatic partner in this project form its very beginning.

Once the topic had been developed, it was generously supported by the German Research Foundation (Deutsche Forschungsgemeinschaft, DFG) and by the German Academic Exchange Service during my tenure as Distinguished DAAD Visiting Professor at Emory University from 2010 to 2016. Living and working in the United States allowed me not only to use libraries and archives there, but also to connect to many individuals and families in person which added to this project's depth and visibility in the United States.

After my return to Germany in 2016 I received generous funding from the Gerda-Henkel-Foundation, and from the Center for Holocaust Studies at the Institut für Zeitgeschichte in Munich to complete this manuscript and the database and am grateful for this opportunity to complete this work.

Currently a more comprehensive sophisticated digital research portal on the German rabbinate after 1933 is once again funded by the German Research Foundation in its priority program "Jewish Cultural Heritage" and allows us to provide a digital platform to analyze and research this group of refugees more intensely in the future.

Beyond the funding, it was a large group of scholars and colleagues who deserve special mention as ongoing mentors, supporters, and experts with a topic that had to be gradually uncovered and explored over time. Among them are Michael A. Meyer, Michael Brenner, Stephen Whitfield, Ismar Schorsch, Hasia Diner, Jonathan Sarna, David Jünger, Judah Cohen, Astrid Zajdband, Jonathan Magonet, Frank Mecklenburg, Raphael Thurm, Gary Zola, Dana Herman, Shuly Berger, Naomi Steinberger, Eric Goldstein, Deborah Lipstadt and the late Eli Faber and I want to underscore how indebted I am to them for their patience, wisdom, inspiration and collegial interest in my research.

Last but not least, I would like to thank the many individuals and family members, the refugees and their children, who all supported this work with stories, documents and memories and had time and great confidence to share such information with me. Among them are Abraham Lowenthal, Ismar Schorsch, Eli Faber, Gustav Buchdahl, Ralph Kingsley, Elizabeth Petuchowski, Elliott Bondi, Meta Bechhofer, Hillel Cohn, Yosef Schwab, Michael Leipziger, Norbert Weinberg, Hillel Cohn, Raphael Asher, Dan Wolf and Susannah Heschel.

This book is dedicated to the refugees and their families and was written to honor their memory!

THE LAST GENERATION OF THE
GERMAN RABBINATE

INTRODUCTION

Understanding the "Last Generation of the German Rabbinate"

History, Memory, Generational Structure, and the Building of a Legacy

After the Nazis seized power on 30 January 1933, more than 250 German rabbis, rabbinical scholars, and students for the rabbinate fled to the United States. While this was not the first time the United States had been the destination for German-Jewish migrations including its rabbinical leadership, the flight of these refugees from Nazism not only represented a heavy influx of migrants—the beginning of a special knowledge transfer—it also marked the end of German-Jewish history at the onset of the Holocaust.[1] Therefore, the presentation of its history appears in a number of larger research contexts such as the Holocaust, memory studies, migration history, the history of knowledge and related transnational relationships, and cultural transfers that resonated in both German and American Jewish history. Such histories cannot be fully understood without acknowledging what happened before and after the hasty departure of these refugees and through a long-term analysis of their lives.

In the following pages, I provide a short introduction to help readers understand the multiple settings, layers of action, and divergent religious and communal concepts in Germany and the United States that determined the flight and reorganization of German refugee rabbis and their cultural transfers and achievements as the last of a special kind—the "last generation of the German rabbinate."

A Special Historical Relationship: German and American Jewries

The historical connection to the nineteenth-century emigration of German Jewry to the United States made it attractive and promising for the German rabbinate as a place of refuge. After the influx of the first wave of German-Jewish immigrants, who arrived in the United States after 1830, American Jewry developed an inherently modern and pluralistic Jewish identity that exceeded even the progressivism of German Jewry at the time.[2] While these two Jewish communities developed in different societal frameworks, each maintained a close "cousinly" relationship and a vital exchange of knowledge and scholarship, especially with American Reform and Conservative Jews, whose existence was directly affected by nineteenth-century German-Jewish migration. This existing close relationship made the United States uniquely attractive to the German rabbinate as a place of refuge during Nazism and motivated American rabbis and rabbinical seminaries to launch a spectacular and highly effective rescue effort of their German colleagues.

History: A New Rabbinate, *Wissenschaft des Judentums*, and Judaism's Encounter with Modern Society

Since the nineteenth century, German and American Jewries had been uniquely committed to the model of a modern rabbinate that emerged in the postemancipation era in German-speaking Europe and completely undermined the particularistic, traditional, premodern Jewish community and traditional rabbis' leadership, scholarship, and jurisdiction therein. Rather, the states' enforcement of Jewish emancipation went hand in hand with the rise of Haskala, the Jewish enlightenment, and triggered a process in which Jewish individuals and communities were actively preparing for a future as Jews within society.

In the newly founded Kingdom of Bavaria, emancipation legislation in 1813 for the first time required that a modern rabbi obtain a doctorate at a secular university to expedite his new role in society and the community. Here the modern "German" rabbi had emerged as an employee (*Beamter*) who not only needed the approval of the Jewish community but was also subject to a training and selection process involving state and secular knowledge. Consequently, the rabbinate experienced a radical change and a new level of professionalization in line with the changing times. The modern rabbi was to be the driving and defining force in the changing relationship between Jews and society and in the process of the social and religious integration of Jews in society at large. Therefore, the new rabbi was also to be a role model for his congregants and was expected to speak high German, not Yiddish.

The new rabbi was to rely on secular knowledge to represent the Jewish community in society, participate in public and religious discourses as an intellectual beacon of the community, gain the respect of the wider world, and provide a new type of guidance to his congregants. His role was not considered to be political; it was mainly the rabbi's scholarly qualities grounded in *Wissenschaft des Judentums* ("academic study of Judaism") that made Judaism subject to critical inquiry, and it was his training as a pastor (*Seelsorger*) and religious teacher in the community that changed his duties and shifted the tasks dramatically while Jews as citizens fell under the jurisdiction of the state. Unlike his historical precursor, who acted primarily as a legal expert and communal authority, the modern German rabbi served his community as mediator, spiritual leader, social worker, scholar, and representative in society.

The transformation of the rabbinate created a Reform movement in Judaism in Germany in the 1840s, which drove the process and tried to make Judaism fit for a new role in society. The Reform movement argued that Judaism itself was subject to history, which meant that change was needed to help keep Judaism attractive to a new generation of Jews and in line with contemporary requirements. This idea paved the way for a revision of Jewish practice and forms embracing Enlightenment thought, modern scholarly analysis, and intense intellectual exchange with the non-Jewish world.

Accordingly, a rabbi's professional training shifted from instruction in traditional yeshivot to modern rabbinical colleges, which combined *Wissenschaft des Judentums* with modern secular study at a state university, and where—at least in Germany—a doctorate was essential for rabbinical ordination. These standards were maintained in the three modern rabbinical colleges that emerged in Germany in the nineteenth century: the Jüdisch-Theologisches Seminar in Breslau (1854), the Hochschule für die Wissenschaft des Judentums (1872) in Berlin, and the Orthodox Rabbinerseminar (1873) in Berlin. The standards were also upheld in many smaller but similar and often related institutions in central Europe that followed the model of the new German seminaries, such as the Israelitisch-Theologische Lehranstalt in Vienna and the Jewish Rabbinical Seminary in Budapest.

Wissenschaft des Judentums represented a new critical and scholarly approach to Jewish studies. Under the lens of *Wissenschaft* (science), Judaism was confronted and challenged by modern history, modern philosophy, the sciences, and religious philosophy. This give-and-take with the secular world drove Judaism's historical transformation and stood front and center in a newly designed form of dual-track rabbinical education.

Since many of its founders felt that Wissenschaft was inseparably rooted in the intellectual context and culture of German-speaking central Europe and could not be separated from German language and thought,[3] its study introduced generations of American rabbis to central European culture and prompted many to travel to Berlin and Breslau, where modern Jewish scholarship was centered until 1938.

The rise of National Socialism threatened this modern Jewish school of thought because Nazi ideology completely rejected the idea of the social inclusion of Jews; thus this modern Jewish leadership was a special target of Nazi atrocities. Yet the last German rabbis and scholars were quite aware of the difficulty of transferring the core of this academic culture into a new English-speaking environment, where it could survive and flourish as modern Jewish studies. The term *Wissenschaft des Judentums* is used throughout this book as it is the old-world model of a concept that has turned into modern Jewish studies in the English-speaking world since the Holocaust. Even though the two are closely related, the discipline of modern Jewish studies, unlike *Wissenschaft des Judentums*, has become an essential part of the curricula of many American universities and has developed into an academic discipline on equal footing with other fields. Wissenschaft was never incorporated into the German state university system as an independent academic field before the Shoah—even though some of its elements were part of larger fields, such as Oriental studies—because the state rejected the idea of equating it with Christian theology and of training Jewish rabbis at state universities

During the Nazi era, the German rabbinate was symbolic of the rabbis' leadership and Judaism's connection with society at large and was therefore attacked as part of the larger plan to reverse a process that had been occurring since the early nineteenth century. The Nazis worked to eliminate this unique Jewish leadership because they were instrumental in helping the Jewish communities in Germany confront exclusion and persecution, obtain or maintain a proud sense of Jewishness, and deal with the growing plight of German Jews. Ironically, many of the rabbinate used the Nazi attacks to spread a feeling of Jewish ethnic pride, resulting in an outcome quite unintended by the Nazis.

The Focus of This Study

This book presents a long-term analysis of the biographies and life cycles of a Jewish elite that accounted for approximately one-third of the German rabbinate at the time. It aims to determine how persecution, forced migration, and the flight of more than 250 individuals and their families from Germany alone affected their lives and careers. In particular, the younger members of this group made a considerable impression intellectually, socially, and theologically on American Judaism and American Jewish congregational and organizational life in the postwar world.

Little is known about how the rabbinical profession has dealt with the challenge of Nazism and the rising tide of systematic exclusion from society. The existing literature often ends at or just before Nazism or focuses on individuals or a specific community. Much of what we know today is found in postwar scholarly records of the rabbinate's testimony of the end of an era. Surprisingly, even the literature on the *Kristallnacht* pogrom does not discuss the effects on rabbis or Jewish communities in depth—a large piece missing in the analysis of this fateful event.[4] This study begins by exploring the effects of Nazism on the rabbinical profession and its schools, teachers, and students. It explains the rise of a new political rabbinate in a post–First World War generation that became the backbone of Jewish communities and whose new and vast secular activities dramatically affected the profession of the rabbi. It also examines the social and intellectual backgrounds of this new generation of rabbis. While some came from Germany and struggled with assimilation, many others came from a traditional setting in eastern Europe and hoped to become "German rabbis" in Berlin and Breslau.

The refugees' forced flight from Germany is often considered the history of a group that was not quite involved in the Holocaust. This is because, unlike their east European cousins, a relatively large number of German Jews were able to flee Germany before 1941, when east European Jewry was overrun by German troops and confronted with an unprecedented genocide under German occupation in Poland. A closer look at German-Jewish life experiences—available in the online database German Refugee Rabbis in the United States after 1933 (Ludwig-Maximilians-Universität München) and analyzed in this book—reveals that German Jews were intensely involved in the events and effects of Nazism. They were the first to be struck by this movement and had more time than their east European cousins to deal with exclusion and persecution in a place and culture they called home.[5]

A close examination of the rabbis' roles in German-Jewish communities after 1933 underscores that rabbinical leadership in the communities was targeted by Nazi persecution, and many of the rabbis endured the situation as long as they could. Their many different experiences, including the destruction of synagogues long before November 1938, are an essential part of this book.

That the rabbis' colleagues and friends abroad, especially in the United States, were well informed and concerned about the events in Europe is proof of the professional and private networks in the profession and its scholarly centers. While some studies discuss the supposed inactivity of American Jews before and during the Holocaust, a closer look at the rescue of the German rabbinate challenges this view and shows how this unique effort to save lives and knowledge preserved a valuable tradition. This research reveals an unprecedented, well-organized, and coordinated effort by America's rabbis and religious bodies to use all legal administrative options to facilitate and enhance the rescue of their European colleagues and families and help them continue their careers in America. While some aspects of these endeavors are known in relation to the American Reform movement and the role of the Jewish Theological Seminary (JTS), the systematic evaluation of personal records in this study provides a larger and much more cohesive picture across the religious spectrum and also explains how American rabbinical colleges were affected and challenged.

Jewish people of this period have long been regarded as only German or American Jews, with no attention paid to transnational networks and identities that transcend national frameworks. But it is these networks—friendships, schools of thought, intellectual circles, schools, religious groups, teachers and students, rabbis, synagogues, congregants and their leaders—that make this history and experience observable, nuanced, and clear. Tracing these networks allows us to identify refugees' efforts to reorganize, commemorate, confront, and take action in a completely changed Jewish post-Holocaust world. In an increasingly global world, a growing interest in the historical profession in migration studies and the "cultural turn" in the writing of history has underscored that this transnational perspective opens up new ways to understand the complex multidimensional networks of refugees. This book looks beyond what the rabbis experienced in one country—Germany or America—and provides a cohesive perspective on their multicultural background, cultural connections, communications, memories, and varied identities.[6]

How this trajectory affected the intellectual and communal leadership of German Jewry, the heart of German Judaism, is the focus of this book. It presents the history of German refugee rabbis in the United States, the country that not only accepted the largest number of German refugee rabbis and thus facilitated a spectacular rescue by American Jewish seminaries and research centers but also gave them the best opportunity to continue their careers *within* American Judaism. Due to the long-standing special relationship between German and American Judaism, the latter offered a unique opportunity to allow continuity for a distinctly modern German-Jewish leadership through the integration of the refugees into the world of American Judaism and its religious movements.

This unique cultural transfer is not described in most existing studies. But only a closer look at individual experiences allows us to understand how the integration into American Judaism progressed, how difficult it was, and what stimulated a vivid cultural transfer. The encounter with American Judaism came at a high price, and older rabbis and scholars in particular had difficulties adapting. In this book, a variety of documents underscore that these new beginnings were complex transformations that came with challenges in the rabbis' professions, in the social and professional networks, and in a congregational structure that was completely new to them.

Books such as Steven Lowenstein's remarkable *Frankfurt on the Hudson* do not explore the individuals who ventured into American Judaism but rather focus on a minority of older rabbis who continued their careers in German-Jewish communities in immigrant neighborhoods like Washington Heights within American ethnic religion,[7] a phenomenon that lasted only a generation or two and focuses on the refugees in their ethnic and religious enclaves.[8]

The younger and vital majority of refugees, including students who graduated after their flight to the United States, were overlooked as a group that was driving this cultural transfer. To understand their complex story, this book traces the sometimes global path a large and diverse group of 200–250 individuals took after 1933 before settling in the United States.

Exploring the group as a whole is a methodological challenge in itself. The collection of prosopographical details on their individual experiences, hopes, thoughts, struggles, and interactions in the processes of flight, rescue, relocation, and coping with their past was necessary to write this book and evaluate their actions. It provided unknown details about the rabbis' experience of Nazism, their flight, the role of their seminaries, and their first years in the United States. Most importantly, the collection provided the long-sought, long-term perspective on their careers and personal, political, and intellectual encounters.

This perspective emphasizes that they played a distinct role in American Jewry's postwar renaissance by highlighting the necessity of harboring and nourishing the substance of Judaism in the modern world and encouraging American Jews to learn more about their Jewish identities.

It also reveals that Germany was always on their minds,[9] for better or worse, and that for many, the cultural transfer did not end in the United States but in reconstructing Jewish life in Germany and in confronting their history.

Memory: Reasoning over the Holocaust, Going Back, and Late Renewal

The refugees took many years and much spatial distance to reestablish their lives and careers. Only after they had reconstructed the foundations of their lives and reached midlife did they have the time, opportunity, and desire to reflect on and historicize their experiences in an effort to make sense of their personal past and the German-Jewish experience as a whole. This process was difficult and painful because it involved a direct and often very emotional confrontation with a divided Germany and German population after the Second World War. Nevertheless, these encounters provided a unique opportunity to come to grips with the Nazi past,[10] personal and material loss, and flight and displacement, and thereby to seek answers to unaddressed questions and understand why German society broke apart and failed to stand up for its Jewish minority in the 1920s and 1930s.[11] As Rabbi Leo Baeck predicted soon after the Shoah, the answers to these questions could only be found in a dialogue with the Germans,[12] and many of the refugee rabbis pioneered an exchange with postwar West Germany[13] and Germans, an exchange that frequently touched sensitive areas on both sides and required care and expertise. The emerging dialogue between Germans and Jews on moral and social questions of the past, their attempt to build a future together, and the return of these religious leaders to Germany in the postwar years created a unique bond in German American and German Jewish relations, which was undoubtedly part of West Germany's uniquely close postwar relationship with the United States. Their exchanges initiated a new understanding between both groups that was difficult and painful at the beginning but that opened up new and satisfying opportunities for cooperation and a brighter future on both sides.[14]

This book explores how the German refugee rabbinate in the United States took on a special mediating role as ethnic brokers of a transatlantic exchange of history and memory that managed to support an incomplete but highly symbolic "return" to Germany. This return was particularly important and visible among liberal Jews, especially those who had joined the American Reform movement and pioneered the encounter.[15]

The Jewish identity of the Reform movement was rooted in a special way in German culture, and the destruction of German Jewry and its institutions had shaken its intellectual and theological roots during and after the Nazi period. In fact, Nazi persecution shifted the center of modern Judaism from Europe to the United States after 1938; when the modern German rabbinical seminaries were closed in Germany, many of the German rabbis emigrated, and those who stayed with their communities perished in the Shoah. Therefore, the founding of the Abraham-Geiger-Kolleg at the University of Potsdam in 1999, which reinstituted the study of modern Judaism on the European continent just outside of Berlin on the initiative of former refugee rabbis in the American Reform movement, may be regarded as the pinnacle of a mutual rapprochement and celebrated as a belated "victory over history." This helped clear the way for the successive founding of the Zacharias Frankel College of the Conservative movement in 2013 and also a new modern Orthodox Rabbinerseminar in 2009 in Berlin—all of which consciously connected to the tradition of the schools in Berlin and Breslau.[16]

Not only did the lasting connection of the former refugees and their American Jewish religious institutions to the European continent seventy years after the Shoah mark the return of modern Jewish learning to its historical homeland; it also celebrated the integration of *Wissenschaft des Judentums* into a university program of *Jewish theology*—a construction that was the first of its kind in Germany. Abraham Geiger had unsuccessfully demanded an inclusive setup for the training of the modern rabbinate in the nineteenth century to give modern Jewish rabbinical training equal standing with the study of Christian theology at German state universities.

Related, but Different: Synagogue and Community in Germany and the United States

To understand the challenges the refugees met, readers must fully grasp the structural differences between German and American Judaism and those of their synagogues and communities, which essentially defined the rabbis' tasks as well as their religious affiliations. While its relationship with American Judaism was close, American society provided a uniquely liberal environment for religious movements, including Judaism, which had long embraced American pluralism. In Germany, religions and their mutual relationships were still impacted by the effects of the Middle Ages and the Reformation, the separation of religion and society was incomplete, and a modern civil society struggled with hierarchical structures and the absence of pluralism. This was reflected in the religious movements, in both their structure and role in society.

Wissenschaft had created a new pluralism in modern Judaism with competing schools of thought in early nineteenth-century central Europe. In addition to Reform Judaism and positive historical trends within the larger orbit of German liberal Judaism, there was an Orthodox Judaism that was open to taking on an active role in society. This created a particular type of German Orthodoxy because it was both modern and Orthodox and emphasized the unique model of *Torah im Derech Eretz* (Torah with the way of the land). Because of their outward modernity and identification with German culture, German Orthodox Jews were not always accepted in a traditional Orthodox Jewish environment and struggled to continue their careers elsewhere. Nevertheless, it should not be overlooked that many of the students of the Berlin Rabbinerseminar preserved the memory of their alma mater after the Shoah and established brilliant careers, particularly in the state of Israel.

In Germany, parts of Orthodoxy and (radical) Reform also struggled with the communal organization of the *Gemeinde*, a Jewish communal superstructure that had emerged from the traditional European Jewish kehillah and united all Jews in a locality under one roof. The Gemeinde incorporated the synagogues of all the various religious movements and Jewish institutions, like hospitals and schools, which were maintained and administered by the group, usually under a liberal majority. This required religious compromise to guarantee cohesion, but it did not always satisfy radical Reform or Orthodox perspectives and sometimes triggered secession from the Gemeinde and the formation of separatist congregations.

The Gemeinde also affected the mainstream aspects of the German Reform movement. Although this progressive movement had emerged in the German lands early in the nineteenth century, it was apparent by the middle of that century that the development of the German Reform movement would face challenges within the Gemeinde. Both the need to enforce Jewish cohesion among Orthodox and Liberal Jews therein and the conservative social and political development of German society added to this and did not allow the Reform movement to develop along similarly radical lines as in the United States. Therefore, in Germany, the Reform movement developed into the prevailing so-called liberal Judaism and leaned far more toward Conservative Judaism than its American cousin, which turned into a uniquely progressive Reform movement in the United States.

The relative absence of politics in the lives of rabbis in Europe helped maintain a kind of peace within the multifaceted Gemeinde, where different identities were forced to compromise to find common ground as one community. Here the rabbi, qualified by his Jewish and secular scholarship, served as pastor and spiritual and intellectual leader to the community. Granted, he was also a representative of the Gemeinde in non-Jewish society, but he did not have quite the same standing as a Christian minister in society and rarely maintained close social or professional contacts with Christian colleagues. Instead, he represented a minority that had suffered from a new form of antisemitism since gaining full emancipation in 1871. Based on that situation, the rabbi was indeed a mediator between a minority group and society and a role model and leader in this process.

Since the Gemeinde was large and well established and was staffed and funded by the state's collection of taxes (as were other religious groups), the rabbinate was far less burdened than its American counterpart by organizational and business tasks and did not have to worry about raising funds for the community. As a consequence, the rabbi maintained his independence as a leader of the community and enjoyed a reputation of dignity and honor. He also represented a distinct form of masculinity. This was illustrated by Leo Baeck's demand that German rabbis were to maintain posture and dignity especially when humiliated, as was the case during the pogrom of 9 November 1938. Their leadership style resonated in their sermons, which demonstrated their intellectual capacities and potential for religious abstraction, sometimes to a degree that alienated their congregants from religious feeling and community. After 1933, their daily experience was affected by social exclusion and the crumbling of community while they witnessed the rise of innovative trends in Judaism, such as Zionism and a romanticized view of eastern European Jewish cultures—two trends that would shape a new generation of rabbis who came of age in the 1920s and profoundly change the profession.

In the United States, the nineteenth-century offspring of the German Reform movement, which had been transplanted to the United States by that century's German-Jewish migration, quite literally found its land of promise. Here the initial goals of the German Reform movement materialized into a uniquely progressive and socially involved dynamic modern Judaism that corresponded with American modernity and individualism and exceeded the expectations of its European founders.

The extreme progressivism of the American Reform movement was supported by the independent congregation in the United States. The adoption of that structure in the establishment of Jewish community and religion was backed by many German immigrant rabbis arriving in the first wave from Europe in the nineteenth century because they saw the "free community" or congregation as a way to preserve a hence-unknown liberty of conscience for the individual Jew. This liberty was nonexistent in Europe, where any reforms to the Gemeinde were severely hampered by social integration, religious compromise, and pressures from both the old Jewish establishment and the national governments/states, which rarely permitted secession to those who did not conform to religious compromise.

America was an appealing option for many German Orthodox Jews. Separatist Orthodox communities in Germany gravitated to American religious setting; the congregations enjoyed the pluralism and were able to exist as independent communities and replicate the kahal (local governing body) outside any of the existing religious movements.

American freedoms deeply affected the American Jewish congregation and its rabbinate, and this impacted the refugees' experiences, professional transformations, and standing in the synagogue. Under the influence of American individualism, the congregation, as a much smaller entity than the Gemeinde, was supported by families or individuals who deeply identified with what both the congregation and the rabbi, as their representative, stood for in the public sphere. In the highly democratic American religious arena, laypeople possessed a previously unknown self-awareness that challenged a rabbi's leadership and authority far more than was the case in Europe.

The American rabbi was the public face of the congregation and part of the larger local community; he was accepted among the other religious leaders and had a responsibility to present his congregation in this context. Because the congregation lacked the manifold services and institutions of a Jewish Gemeinde, secular Jewish organizations took on an important role in the organization of Jewish life. These organizations included the B'nai B'rith, the American Jewish Committee, the American Jewish Congress, the Zionist Organization of America, the National Council of Jewish Women, the Jewish Federations, and many others. In fact, these secular organizations constituted the linchpin of American Jewish life, as they also embraced those Jews who were not members of a congregation. American rabbis therefore had to maintain a relationship with these organizations and demonstrate serious participation in society. Besides the fact that the American Reform movement propagated a strong societal engagement by its religious leaders, this context resulted in far more political and societal roles of American rabbis than was the case in central Europe.

Definitions: The "German" Rabbinate, the Role of the Seminaries, and Generation-Building

In the course of conducting research for this book, it became obvious that the history of the forced migration of German rabbis to the United States could not be separated from the history of the colleges and seminaries. They were not only the centers for modern rabbinical training in central Europe; they were also the cradle and later the hubs of the negotiations for the rescue of graduates, students, and faculty. Therefore, this book discusses the migration of faculty from the rabbinical colleges, for they were sometimes ordained rabbis who had chosen a scholarly career over a community rabbinate. Their stories highlight how the seminaries were changing under Nazism as they faced increasing financial and political pressures, how they helped support Jewish scholars who had lost their positions at state universities and offered them career prospects, and how swiftly faculty positions were vacated and passed on to new colleagues due to increasing emigration. The situation offered some young scholars who were rare specialists in their fields a chance to advance in their careers to a professional level that would otherwise have been more difficult to reach. One scholar was the Talmudist Alexander Guttmann, who was appointed to a full professorship at the Hochschule at age twenty-eight, barely older than his students.

The book also examines the rescue of students, many of whom could finish their studies only after immigrating to the United States. Their rescue was facilitated by mentors such as Ismar Elbogen, Leo Baeck, and Jacob Hoffmann, who supported their placement at American colleges and yeshivot with countless letters of recommendation and empathetic support. Like the faculty of the rabbinical schools in Germany, these students were an essential part of the organic fabric of centers for rabbinic education.

Community rabbis also found that their careers were expedited by the crisis. Advanced students graduated quickly to fill the urgent need for chaplains, teachers, and rabbis; recent graduates moved into full rabbinical positions without working as a teacher or assistant rabbi because emigration vacated many posts and their services as pastors, social workers, and spiritual leaders were in great demand. This provided them with unusual opportunities and in fact enhanced a development that had been underway since the end of the First World War. It created a new type of rabbi: young, dynamic leaders in modern Judaism who were engaged not only in Wissenschaft and scholarship but also in Zionism, politics, and a completely new way of constructing a Jewish community.[17]

The seminaries played a key role in selecting candidates for emigration and paving the way for those who were willing to emigrate. After all, a large majority of refugee rabbis and scholars depended on receiving nonquota visas that were available only to clergy or scholars. Thus their hopes of escaping Nazism rested on offers and invitations from the respective modern American rabbinical seminaries and the associated movements in American Judaism, which trained and hired American scholars and the rabbinate.[18] Long-existing contacts and a good working relationship facilitated the exchange between German seminaries and their American counterparts, primarily the Hebrew Union College (HUC) in Cincinnati (1875), the Jewish Institute of Religion in New York (1922), the Jewish Theological Seminary of America in New York City (1886), Dropsie College (1907–1986), and Yeshiva College (1928) in New York City.

The definition of the "German rabbinate" at the center of this study must be understood in its widest possible framework. It embraced scholars of Wissenschaft, many of whom were not officiating but ordained rabbis—students, and rabbis serving a Gemeinde or Jewish institution. Of course, this included

German citizens who were trained in Germany at one of the flagship seminaries mentioned above. Nevertheless, citizenship cannot be the only defining criterion for "the *German* rabbi." Whereas the label "German rabbi" was more or less a cultural self-description, citizenship was a matter not of choice but of political borders, many of which were highly contested, discussed, and reversed after the First World War.

After 1919, borders were redrawn, thereby excluding multiethnic areas that had formerly belonged to the lost empires of Prussia and Austria-Hungary. These were areas in which a large number of officiating rabbis had been born as Prussians or Austrians. They were deeply rooted in German culture, especially in the bourgeois middle class, but their places of birth suddenly turned into newly emerging nation-states, such as Poland, Czechoslovakia, Romania, or Russia, which classified them as foreigners if they had not acquired German citizenship in the meantime.[19]

After 1919, this restructuring may have been the reason why, in the 1920s and 1930s, over half of the students in the German rabbinical seminaries did not possess German citizenship but were officially "east Europeans" who were attracted by modern "German" Judaism and modern German scholarship. Many of them, irrespective of citizenship, had grown up in a German cultural context reaching as far east as Bukovina. To complete their education, some of them may have been attracted to the schools in Berlin and Breslau by a curiosity to explore Western, specifically German, cultures of knowledge and academia, which at the time were famous for their dedication to scholarship and critical method.[20]

In this book, the definition of the "German rabbinate" is expanded to include these cultural backgrounds, diverse citizenships, educational backgrounds, and the training of those rabbis who could, in the widest sense, be considered part of the group: in short, everyone who—irrespective of their citizenship—obtained their rabbinical training at one of the German rabbinical seminaries, who officiated in Germany (even if they were not German citizens or trained at a modern German rabbinical seminary but resided in Germany and served a German synagogue), and who were Orthodox students and rabbis with German citizenship but did not attend a modern German seminary.

Since legacy, memory, and generational self-identification as the "last generation of the German rabbinate" also include those who are referred to in the literature as "the second generation" (those who emigrated as children with or without their parents and received their education in the United States at one of the modern rabbinical seminaries),[21] their data and experiences were also included in the group of "German refugee rabbis." Although they constitute a specific subgroup and were not German trained, they have the core features of the ethos of the "German rabbinate," such as their commitment to earning a doctorate as a prerequisite for the rabbinate, their dedication to scholarship and teaching, and a strong cultural affiliation to their tradition. Their biographical data highlights how devoted they continued to be to the German-Jewish community and German culture. A significant number found partners within the refugee community and continued to speak German, which was essential for their access to German culture, their Jewish scholarship, and a meaningful exchange with postwar Germans. They participated in the generation-building process and throughout their lives identified with a specific memory of the German Nazi past, which continued to play an essential role in their private and professional lives. They remained quite conscious of their experience with and connection to a lost Jewish culture and tradition, even though their American identity was never in question.[22]

This identification was the result of a generation-building process that started with their hurried flight from Germany and launched their displacement. Generations are more than mere age cohorts that share several similar experiences or one particularly dramatic experience that shapes the lives of those who associate with a specific generation. For the generation-building process, collective communication of shared experiences and one's role therein are essential. A number of events and social and political contexts in the postwar world have provided frameworks in which these rabbis could reflect on, discuss, and cope with their shared biographical experiences, roles, and events, including their own rescue and survival. Plenty of frameworks existed for communication crucial to the generation-building process, and they usually allowed the refugees to share their firsthand knowledge as victims of Nazism in a way that was unique and meaningful for their later lives and that permitted them to speak with special authority.[23]

In their careers, the rabbis frequently benefited from their shared expertise with Nazism during this period. This expertise was in high demand, both in the United States and postwar Germany for reasons that are explored in detail in the second half of this book. Segregation and the emerging American civil rights movement created one such framework, providing a wide, popular, and certainly important projective surface to connect the past with the present. Others included the growing demand for interfaith dialogue, the discussion of ethnic diversity in the United States after the Second World War, and the effort to contribute to a timely and meaningful sense of Jewish identity and Judaism to which the individual community member felt connected. For some rabbis, Jewish theology as such provided a framework by which they can understand

and seek answers for the Holocaust and amalgamate it into their autobiographical experiences or to engage in Holocaust education and commemoration; others undertook difficult trips back to Germany and initiated a dialogue with the postwar German population as they thought it necessary to search for answers where the destruction had begun.

All of the refugees, rabbis, scholars, and students of the former Berlin and Breslau seminaries used burials, commemorations, anniversaries, and their new rabbinical organizations to build or reflect on their image as a special generation, one with a shared past and unique legacy. After all, these spaces and events connected them to a specific time and place. One such occasion was the burial of Ismar Elbogen, the former rector of the Hochschule für die Wissenschaft des Judentums (Higher Institute for the Academic Study of Judaism), who died in New York in 1943. His funeral was attended by an overwhelming number of his former students and colleagues who gathered to honor him five thousand miles away from Berlin, where these relationships had been formed. The event marked the end of an era: the Hochschule had become history. At the time, it enhanced the communication of the past, one's role therein, and the future. In like fashion, memorial volumes about the seminaries, a community, or an institution such as the Hochschule—some of which were even labeled to be the work of "the last generation"—signal where and how communitization, or the formation of a special community, occurred hand in hand with Americanization. This is also true for many of the autobiographical writings and memoirs, as they present an additional medium by which communitization took place.[24] In this process, the (destroyed) seminaries turned into "generation objects" that represented the social formation of their professors, students, and graduates and connected them into a collective.

The refugees' American institutional counterparts served a similar function in the respective movements of American Judaism because they corresponded to the former German seminaries with regard to their history and tradition and provided a haven where the refugees felt stable and could transition into American Judaism. They became centers for the Americanization of the refugees as well as for the reconstruction of their lives and careers and provided a platform where they could continue their scholarship. *Wissenschaft des Judentums* stood at the center of their identities and may perhaps also be regarded as a generation object because it provided them with a strong intellectual realm to express themselves and combat obscurity in exile. The centrality of Wissenschaft in this process explains the return of modern Jewish learning to German universities; the founding of the Hochschule für Jüdische Studien (Higher Institute for Jewish Studies) in Heidelberg and more recently the Abraham-Geiger-Kolleg in Potsdam held special significance for this generation when they launched these projects.

The former refugees' return to Germany as visiting professors, leading faculty, or community rabbis and their fundraising or institutional support signaled that this last generation was a bridge between the past and the future. Even though the refugees were the last of the graduates and students of the destroyed seminaries, elements of the German-Jewish tradition, liberal Judaism, Wissenschaft, and the spirit of modern Judaism were not extinct but were reinstitutionalized by them in the United States and, later in their lives, in Germany. For those forced to leave Germany in the 1930s, this marked a personal victory over Nazism. When they looked back at their biographies, they could feel satisfaction and find some sort of closure. The historicization of one's biography, which typically begins at midlife, corresponds with the database findings, which state that the cohort known as the "last generation of the German rabbinate" was born after 1895/1900. It must be noted that only the younger refugees had the time to build careers and reflect on their histories, and the way they built their careers and lives in the United States with respect to their past is significant and has played an important role in society.[25]

Method: Managing and Analyzing Data of the Group and Sources

This book examines, distinguishes, and analyzes the personal lives and professional development of these different groups of German refugee rabbis from a transatlantic perspective and also as a whole—instead of focusing merely on one period of their lives, be it persecution, emigration, or postwar integration into American Judaism—by using an extensive collection of data gathered from a web-based database called German Refugee Rabbis in the United States after 1933 (MIRA).[26] The database structures these refugee life cycles into several segments, exploring the specifics of their migration, careers, and personal lives to evaluate and compare the individual biographies, analyze the commonalities and differences of their life cycles, and use this information to explore the generational structure and the generation-building process within this larger group of refugee rabbis. This collection of quantitative data gives us a comprehensive overview of this relatively large and diverse group of refugees and their paths of travel and professions before, during, and after emigration, and it plots their migration paths on an interactive map. Thus it becomes obvious that this is not just a transatlantic but a global migration, which took the refugees not only westward to Great Britain and the United States but also eastward to Palestine and even to Asia, the Pacific Islands, and Australia before they settled in the United States. The database research emphasizes how Great Britain was a special European haven for Jewish refugees and how it contributed to the wide dispersion of the rabbis by forced internment in other Commonwealth nations such as Australia or Canada. This systematic quantitative evaluation and collection of data provides a balanced judgment about a group whose social significance varies and for whom there are not always records or biographical data to track their paths. Part of the collected data has been made accessible in an online database hosted by the University of Munich to stimulate further research on this refugee group and the German rabbinate. I hope that in the future, the database will be expanded to include additional regions and upgraded qualitatively with regard to its digital potential, resources, and analytical instruments.[27]

To evaluate the group of refugee rabbis as a whole, it is essential not to overlook the less visible individuals, those who left the profession after they emigrated and those who were older and died soon after their resettlement in the United States. Without considering them, the well-documented biographies of individuals with outstanding careers may falsely be considered typical for the group as a whole.

It is striking that this group made a major effort to document their experiences in autobiographical writings, memoirs, survivor interviews, websites, memorial volumes, and even films. These records are an important resource, allowing us to not only reconstruct their past but also to see how they tried to preserve history and memory. With this documentation, these people directly linked the past with the present and created a special legacy as "the last generation of the German rabbinate" many years after their forced migration and the Holocaust.[28] The second part of this book focuses on the analysis of these records, exploring the postwar lives and careers of the refugee rabbis, the construction of "a last generation of the German rabbinate," and the rabbis' return to Germany in the postwar era.

In addition to the systematic collection of prosopographical data in the database mentioned above and the autobiographical publications, this book relies on a vast array of original records from a number of German and American archives, particularly those of the three major rabbinical seminaries in the United States, which were key to the rescue process: the American Jewish Archives on the campus of HUC in Cincinnati, the Archives of the JTS, the Archives of Yeshiva University, and the American Agudah Israel in New York, from which I used papers pertaining to individuals, the college administration, their presidents' correspondence, and their publications. In addition, I have greatly benefited from the holdings of the Leo Baeck Institute in New

York City, which permitted me to use the papers of individuals and the collection of the New York–based Research Foundation for Jewish Immigration. This collection was compiled under the guidance of Herbert Strauss, a former student of the Hochschule für die Wissenschaft des Judentums, who was a professor of history at City College before returning to Berlin to become the director of the Center for the Study of Antisemitism in 1982. Based on his research experience and work on German refugees, Strauss launched a research project with a group of scholars at the Institut für Zeitgeschichte (IfZ) in Munich in the 1970s and managed to reconstruct the biographies of a vast number of "intellectual émigrés" in the early 1980s. This group published its results in the multivolume *Biographical Dictionary of Central European Emigres*, one of the first groundbreaking works on the history of refugees from Nazism. The questionnaires and interviews this research project collected proved to be an extremely valuable source of information and guided my research far beyond what the published materials had provided. These records informed me in detail about the flight and resettlement until the late 1970s of a large number of rabbis. Because the Research Foundation for Jewish Immigration partnered with the IfZ on this project, the materials could be examined in the archives of the IfZ. Over the years, I returned many times to this rich resource for research in German contemporary history and was fortunate that the institute's newly founded Center for Holocaust Studies was able to sponsor my work during my tenure as a senior research fellow there during the summer of 2019.

I have reviewed the papers of the Cultural Department of the Political Archive in the German Foreign Office in Berlin and the records of German missions in the United States after 1949. Consular officers and diplomats were involved in organizing the visits of major Jewish leaders to West Germany after 1949 and co-organized the visitor programs of specific German cities from the 1960s onward. Several smaller collections were examined, such as the Joseph Asher Papers at the Bancroft Library of the University of California, Berkeley, the archives of the United States Holocaust Memorial Museum in Washington, DC, and a remarkable number of digitized materials and Holocaust testimonies, which are publicly available through research libraries or the internet.

Finally, I want to stress the importance of the digital database MIRA, which is currently undergoing an intense update into a sophisticated research portal and a massive expansion with more features, updates, visualizations, and analytical tools after the project received additional funding in the Priority Program "Jewish Cultural Heritage" by the German Research Foundation (DFG). It aims to provide a modern, user-friendly, and sustainable resource that will hopefully stimulate more work in this field of research. With quick links to archival materials, library resources, and finding aids, the database facilitates access to materials that highlight the history of this transnational group of refugees. I also hope that it will help in the analysis of the persecution, flight, and memory of these German-Jewish refugees, who have received little attention from historians until recently but whose stories have been passed on to the twenty-first century, thanks to my colleagues Gerhard Schön and Christian Riepl at the Center for Digital Humanities of Ludwig-Maximilians-Universität München.

ONE

German Jewry under Nazism

Changes and Challenges for the Rabbinical Profession

The Nazi seizure of power on 30 January 1933 heralded the spread and intensification of state-approved antisemitism that destroyed the integration of Jews into German society. Sanctioned and encouraged by the Nazi state, this sentiment was then transformed into "scientific knowledge," codified into exclusionary legislation, and implemented as systematic persecution, thereby generating insecurity, economic hardship, social exclusion, constant fear, and legal arbitrariness in the German-Jewish community. The integration that German Jews had achieved in Germany's middle-class society after a long and complicated process to attain full emancipation from the Napoleonic era to 1871 was now under deconstruction. The effort to undermine the social status and access of Jews to the German middle class was felt in the modern German rabbinate, who had historically been a key element and role model in the process of social integration.[1]

A Profession under Duress and Germany's Rabbinical Seminaries

Scholars of *Wissenschaft des Judentums*, many of whom were ordained rabbis, were among the first to be affected by anti-Jewish legislation when the Law for the Restoration of the Professional Civil Service (*Gesetz zur Wiederherstellung des Berufsbeamtentums*) was passed on 1 April 1933. This so-called restoration removed all Jewish scholars from the dominant German state university system and impacted many Jews in middle-class professions such as civil servants, educators, doctors, and lawyers, all of whom lost their state certifications. There was no legal basis for similar measures directed against other state employees, but they were nonetheless affected, even if their discrimination was based solely on the pressure from the dominating Nazi employee organization, National-sozialistische Betriebszellenorganization (NSBO), in large state businesses or administrations.[2] Jews faced exclusion not only from the state legislation but also from their professional organizations, which failed to show solidarity with their members. In fact, these organizations eagerly "Aryanized" themselves and quickly withdrew support for "Jewish" colleagues, many of whom were seen as unwelcome competitors in their respective fields.

This outright racialization of German society was not limited to its universities, which were, in fact, a hub for the rising generation of Nazi supporters. Since the emancipation period, education and self-improvement had been central elements of German-Jewish ideals, advancement into the middle class, and participation in society. But the growth of a young and dynamic Jewish middle-class elite was suppressed in April 1933 by the establishment of quotas to curtail Jewish access to higher education and restrict access to match the ratio of Jews in the German population.[3] Four years later, in April 1937, Jewish students were banned from obtaining a doctoral degree,[4] and beginning in December 1938, Jews were prohibited from all access to universities.[5] While the German states and communities had enacted several such measures long before the passing of a federal law on 21 April 1933, many Jews were broadly affected by these exclusions. Quotas prevented them from pursuing their studies and completing their degrees, regardless of their progress. This in turn impacted their ability to enter their respective professions and pursue their desired careers.

The lack of professional prospects enforced by educational quotas and the changing role of the Jewish community from a primarily religious center to a network of solidarity, ethnic support, and cooperation in an increasingly dangerous and hostile environment attracted many nonreligious Jews to these communities. The rapid growth, shifting responsibilities, and concerns of the communities led to an increasing demand for leadership and organization by social workers, rabbis, teachers, and chaplains (*Seelsorger*). The pressures of Nazism changed the nature and role of the religious community, or Gemeinde,[6] as well as the professional profile of the rabbi, which had previously been that of a politically neutral religious leader, immersed in *Wissenschaft* and intellectual advancement.

The first signs of change to the rabbinate and community were felt as early as the 1920s. Influenced by Martin Buber, Franz Rosenzweig, and political Zionism, German Jews sought ethnic cohesion and an inspiring experience of Jewishness, Judaism, and the Jewish tradition. They preferred communal warmth over religious rationalism. At the time, a new, youthful generation of rabbis emerged who demonstrated that a timely Judaism and Jewish identity could help modern Jews solve everyday problems and answer questions. These rabbis reached out particularly to the young generation as religious leaders and social activists in their communities.[7] As such, they inspired a new professional style. Challenged by the growing social rejection of Jews, the reorganization of swelling communities, the training and preparation for the emigration process, the necessity of social work, and a high demand for pastoral care, the need for qualified personnel was such that the "private" ordination of the first female rabbi, Regina Jonas, by Rabbi Max Dienemann[8] was tolerated on 27 December 1935.[9]

Joining the rabbinate was not an easy professional choice during the Nazi period, but it still represented a promising career option for male Jewish adolescents who were academically ambitious and willing to take on a specifically *Jewish* leadership position. In addition, the seminaries continued to provide funding for students with little means.[10]

Interest in the professions of rabbi and teacher surprisingly rose significantly among young men and women during the Nazi regime, despite the threat of Nazi measures. The profession was a last resort for young Jews seeking an academically trained job. It offered the chance for a middle-class career and perhaps even prominence and leadership within the Jewish community. The profession gave young Jews agency to develop leadership within society and community, an opportunity young men and women may have found compelling. The daily confrontation with stereotypes and exclusions based on their "Jewishness" drove a growing number of these young people, many of them secular Jews who never went to services, to attend lectures and study groups at the Hochschule, where they hoped to learn more about Judaism and find a sense of belonging and a spiritual encounter with Judaism.[11]

As a result, the Hochschule continued to attract a small but increasing number of both laypeople and students pursuing careers in the rabbinate, students who were attending lectures in Wissenschaft des Judentums, and those pursuing careers as Jewish teachers. While many of the younger students, including a growing number of young women, were seeking job security and a middle-class future, many were driven by a serious desire to confront their previously neglected identity as Jews.[12] With support from the Reich Association of Jews in Germany (Reichsvereinigung der Juden in Deutschland) and Jewish organizations abroad, the seminaries could still provide financial aid to registered students who were unable to support themselves or pay their tuition.[13] This was an important consideration for families whose breadwinner had lost employment during the Nazi period, and it added to the appeal of rabbinical studies as a career option.

It is noteworthy that many of the students at all three seminaries were not German citizens, a fact that sometimes protected them from some of the Nazi atrocities.[14] Other times, however, it made them a special target of Nazi atrocities, as in the case of the 17,000 Polish Jews who were forcibly deported across the border on 28 October 1938. The young Abraham Joshua Heschel, a Polish citizen, was among those whose life and academic future were considerably impacted by this event.[15] Otto Toeplitz discussed their situation at length in his memorandum and reported that many of the students had been born outside of Germany, a claim that is confirmed by reports on the Orthodox Rabbinerseminar stating that over 50 percent of its students were from eastern and east-central Europe.[16]

Similar numbers of students with a foreign citizenship were also recorded at the Breslau Jüdisch-Theologisches Seminar.[17] Behind this attraction may have been a deeper connection to German Jewry than might be anticipated because the majority of these students had been raised in areas that belonged to Germany or Austria until 1919 when they fell (back) to Poland, Czechoslovakia, Rumania (now Romania), Hungary, Russia, and other newly emerging nation-states in eastern Europe. This process changed their citizenship but not necessarily their cultural affinity and connection to German Jewry or their curiosity about German culture. This means that their socialization and cultural affiliation in the ethnically mixed Polish or Czech areas after 1919 continued to be German.

At the time, these students were attracted to German society and scholarship either because both were perceived as dynamic and modern or because both still provided access to a culture they cherished.[18] Among these individuals were men as prestigious as Alexander Guttmann, Henry Guttmann, Leo Baerwald, Nahum Glatzer, Joseph Breuer, Marcus Breger, Ralph Neuhaus, Max Nussbaum, Ismar Elbogen, Alexander Altmann, Jacob Hoffmann, Hans Enoch Kronheim, Ezekiel Landau, Cuno Lehrman, Samuel Atlas, and Wilhelm Weinberg.[19] Others coming from farther east were said to have been attracted to the idea of studying modern Jewish thought along with secular studies at German universities. This was an experience that sparked their curiosity about Jewish Wissenschaft and modern scholarship such that they joined one of the seminaries as either registered or unregistered students while also pursuing secular studies at the universities of Berlin or Breslau. Some may have belonged to a cohort of young Orthodox eastern Europeans who experienced the German occupation during the First World War with awe and admiration. They had encountered modern Orthodox German-Jewish officers as Jewish peers and "liberators" from Czarist suppression and thereby realized that the secular modern world offered them a place in society.[20]

Post–First World War Disillusionment with Assimilation and Tradition: A New Generation of Rabbinical Students and Young Rabbis

These experiences triggered an intensive exchange and mutual curiosity for intellectual, religious, and artistic models unavailable or long lost among German and east European Jewish intellectuals.[21] Both developments greatly affected the German rabbinical colleges and led to a significant increase in east European enrollment after the First World War. Thereby arose an elite of dynamic and curious young intellectuals who had been active in the Zionist or youth movements and searched for a renewal of Jewish life.[22]

Just like those of their east European cousins, the backgrounds and motivations of German-born students to join the rabbinate changed in the 1920s.[23] The German adolescents were deeply affected by a number of experiences. On one hand, they were confronted with growing antisemitism, which had manifested during the war and dominated German society and the political debate throughout the Weimar Republic. It became a core element of the undemocratic political right. On the other hand, the cultural trend toward peoplehood as a leading motif in German identity not only shaped non-Jewish Germans; it also influenced Jewish culture and society and helped Jewish youths maintain their spirits and self-respect by developing a type of ethnic pride. Rather than immerse themselves solely in academic Jewish study, they were interested in finding answers to the current social and political situation facing Jews in Germany. This resulted in a growing interest in Zionism and ethnic Jewish identity and provided a counterbalance to the rising German nationalism, which increasingly excluded Jews from participation in society. During these years, many young German Jews grew up in Zionist youth movements, enjoyed new forms of community, and were enthused by the fresh, lively, dynamic, and political experience of Jewish community.

These trends also affected the rabbinical colleges, where a newly emerging generation of rabbis, including Max Nussbaum and Joachim Prinz, confronted their teachers with Zionist ideas. These openly political attitudes, especially Zionist ones, created generational conflict. Not only were the older members averse to politics in the pulpit, but they also rejected Zionism in particular. Although the support for Zionism had grown substantially in the 1920s, only a few years earlier, in 1907, the "Cohn Affair" had shaken the Berlin Jewish community and led to the dismissal of Zionist Emil Moses Cohn as rabbi there.[24] Thus the style of preaching among ardent young Zionist rabbis such as Prinz and Nussbaum was sometimes considered inappropriate by the rabbinical establishment. They did indeed bear messages of upheaval because they increased enthusiasm and emotions in an otherwise highly Protestantized Jewish service dominated by a rational sermon among their congregants.[25] Both men personified this new and very dynamic generation of rabbis; thus it is worthwhile to explore their backgrounds and motivations a little more closely. Most of those who associated with Prinz and Nussbaum, including Prinz's brother-in-law Max Gruenewald (Grünewald), were born around 1900 or later and pursued support for an ethnic renewal among German Jews of all types within Judaism. They were dedicated to a rabbinate that sought to establish a new Jewishness by reconnecting congregants with Jewish tradition, religion, ethnic identity, socialism, and a sense of social responsibility that would guide their lives and reenergize their communities from within.

As a Romanian citizen, Max Nussbaum was considered one of the "foreign" students at Breslau and Berlin. He grew up in a middle-class family in Suceava in the Bukovina, which, at the time of Nussbaum's birth in 1908, was part of Austria-Hungary and only became Romania after the First World War. Some members of the Jewish population there had long felt a cultural connection to the German-speaking world, and Nussbaum was raised in a family steeped in (Austrian) German bourgeois culture. The same is true for Joachim Prinz, who was born in Burkhardtsdorf, Upper Silesia,[26] a province of Prussia (bordering the Polish province of Posen) in 1902.

Nussbaum grew up in an ethnically mixed area, where the long-gone multiculturalism of eastern Europe still prevailed and Jewish life was rich and exhibited multiple east European influences stemming from the Socialist Bund movement, Zionist groupings, and the surrounding Hasidic communities. The town included a variety of synagogues and communal organizations from traditional Orthodoxy to a Reform temple, but the Nussbaum family's religious background was linked to one of the Hasidic communities of the area. Family photographs show Moshe (Max) at a young age in a traditional caftan. His father was a strict traditionalist and religious observant who studied the Talmud regularly and served as a shohet, a Jewish ritual butcher, in his community.[27] Accordingly, young Moshe received a traditional Jewish education, rejected the Romanian language, and spoke Yiddish but was equally versed in German, the official language at the schools he attended before 1918.

As a teenager, however, Nussbaum broke away from the strict religious traditionalism of his family after conflicts with his father. He acquired a secular education in the nearby Jüdisches Ober-Realgymnasium in Stroginetz, where he learned modern Western languages,[28] joined the Zionist youth group Ziona, and met students of different religious backgrounds, such as Roman Catholic and Greek Orthodox. In this environment, Moshe changed his first name to Max. Once he completed his secondary schooling, he moved on to the University of Cernauti (Czernowitz), where he started studying philosophy.[29]

In the fall of 1928, after two semesters, Nussbaum decided to enroll in rabbinical studies at the Jüdisch-Theologisches Seminar in Breslau and the University of Breslau, where he was ordained in 1933. During this time, he studied modern Jewish Wissenschaft as well as modern West European literature, French, and theater. This provided him with cultural and practical talents he would later use as a gifted speaker and excellent performer as a rabbi known for his familiarity with Western culture. He spent one year at the University of Würzburg to work on his dissertation on Immanuel Kant, Karl Marx, and the social philosophy of Max Adler because a doctorate was a prerequisite for rabbinic ordination.[30] By 1934, he was ready to launch his career as a rabbi of the Berlin Jewish community, where he officiated first as teacher, then preacher, and finally as community rabbi.

Like Nussbaum, German-born Joachim Prinz had a middle-class background, but unlike him, Prinz came from a highly assimilated family. His father not only believed in classic Prussian ideals but demonstrated authoritarian behavior himself. This eventually destroyed his relationship with his adolescent son, who increasingly rebelled against bourgeois morals and attitudes. Instead, Prinz found a fatherly supporter and friend in Rabbi Felix Goldman of Oppeln, the town where Prinz grew up.

With Goldman's guidance, Prinz developed an interest in Judaism that provided an alternative environment to the stiffness and emotional distance of his family home. Under the influence of Zionism and the rich and exciting new Jewish culture of eastern Europe, the young Prinz found a spiritual home and the warmth of a father figure in Rabbi Goldman, which helped him channel his rebellious, socially dynamic, and politically active ideals into a new Judaism challenging the establishment. The new, lively, and very political Jewish identity and the idea of Jewish ethnic pride spoke to the feelings, problems, and questions of a younger generation of contemporary Jews.[31]

In 1921, Prinz embarked on his rabbinical studies at the Breslau seminary, where he followed the path for rabbinical ordination and acquired a doctorate at the University of Giessen in 1927.[32] In 1926, he moved to Berlin, where he started preaching and serving as a rabbi at the local Friedenstempel, a synagogue outside the communal organization of the local Jewish Gemeinde that typically embraced Jewish life across synagogues and other local Jewish organizations, like a kehillah. Organized like an American-style, independent congregation, the Friedenstempel was not subject to the Gemeinde's pressures to make theological compromises to maintain peace among its congregants and members within the communal superstructure. This situation provided unusual freedom to the young rabbi, who left the discipline of the usual Jewish establishment and Gemeinde, quickly building himself a reputation.

Prinz developed into a Jewish rebel in the pulpit by claiming that a rabbi should have full freedom of conscience, that it was his *duty* to speak up in political matters, and that he should feel free to do so without fear of repression from his peers (something Cohn had experienced). He rejected the existing models of the rabbinical profession and criticized the view that *preaching* alone was the essential task of the rabbinate. Instead, he insisted that the rabbi's main task was to serve as a *teacher* to his congregants, to actively link their contemporary experience to Jewish tradition not only by stressing the historical connection between modern Jews and their rich Jewish past but also by showing how this past and this tradition could motivate Jewish answers to contemporary questions and a Jewish future.[33]

With this approach, Prinz, who was fully ordained by 1929, targeted the youth in particular by offering programs, books with a new outlook on Judaism,[34] youth bibles, Jewish histories,[35] and games,[36] all of which were tailor-made for younger Jews, thereby making Jewish tradition more accessible and evoking further curiosity among those considered to be the future of German Jewry. Celebrated by the younger generation as a role model and leader and by the older generation as a dynamic rabbi, Prinz broke with the existing style of the rabbinate.[37] He became a trailblazer for others in this young cohort of rabbis who sought to reach out not only to the youth but to the whole Jewish family and ignite a new interest in Jewish identity by way of tailored programs for families and the young. This changed the synagogue from a stiff, distanced experience to one lively with political undertones that featured youth camps, youth services, and youth congregations, in cooperation with specially trained youth rabbis, such as Prinz's brother-in-law in Mannheim, Max Gruenewald.[38]

Prinz's dedication to providing Jewish solutions to the growing political and societal crisis was expressed in a number of publications, such as *Wir Juden* (We Jews), which first appeared at the end of 1933. This book criticized Jewish assimilation, declared it a failure, and demanded that German Jews open their eyes to the realities of Nazism. Jews, Prinz argued, should adopt a new understanding of Jewish identity, one that acknowledged that Jews were a nation, had a state, and could choose immigration to Palestine rather than adhere to what he declared to be the historical failure of Jewish liberalism.[39]

Prinz was not the only one making this argument. His older colleague Emil Moses Cohn, an establishment outsider who had also built a career as a

Durch Wüstensand ins Heilige Land. Chessboard game in "Jüdischer Kinderkalender," edited by Emil Cohn. Berlin: Jüdischer Verlag, Jg.1 1927-Jg. 6.1936 (the title changes): Leo Baeck Institute New York (LBI), call number r 162.

playwright and writer, criticized the predominant modern Jewish identity in 1923 in his book *Judentum, ein Aufruf an die Zeit* (Judaism, a call on the times).[40] Like Prinz, he denounced the highly rationalized understanding of Judaism as influenced by the European Enlightenment and the similar perception of God, which he claimed had destroyed history, tradition, religious feeling, peoplehood, community, and love of God. He suggested a return to a feeling of Jewish nationhood, piety, and an active Jewish lifestyle in line with religious ideals. He claimed that this change would revive and enhance the Jewish experience even in the twentieth century.[41]

Liberal Jews, like Prinz, were not the only ones dissatisfied with the dominant German-Jewish identity that was still rooted in the ideal of assimilation and that rejected the idea of a Jewish nation. Among German Orthodox Jews, similar dissatisfaction was growing, as the case of Simon Schwab illustrates. Schwab was born in 1908 in Frankfurt. He was raised in the so-called Breuer Yeshiva, Frankfurt's prominent Orthodox secessionist community (*Austrittsgemeinde*), and he was educated at the yeshivot of Mir and Telz. Like his liberal colleagues, he strongly criticized opening German Orthodoxy to secular life.

His book *Heimkehr ins Judentum* (Returning home to Judaism) attacked assimilation, Jewish liberalism, the idea of Jewish life in exile, and the belief in emancipation and political Zionism. Already under the impact of Nazism, Schwab argued that the hopes of German Jewry in the early nineteenth century never materialized and that contemporary Jewry had to acknowledge the failure of both the concept of a modern Jewry and the idea of German Jewry as such. Jews were now facing God's punishment through Nazism.

Intermarriage, assimilation, and Torah-less lives among German Jews were proof to Schwab that they had lost their connection to God as His people. Schwab demanded that German Jews abandon these engagements and distractions to instead strengthen their spiritual relationship with God by changing their lives in favor of dissimilation, a pious lifestyle, and dedicated study of the Torah, Jewish law, and the Jewish people.[42] Schwab was not alone in his criticism.

In public debate, the Hirschian modern Orthodox approach to *Torah im Derech Eretz* was criticized for its failure to maintain cohesion under one intellectual roof due to the split between the Hildesheimer and Hirschian schools of thought, and it caused a significant setback among German Jews. Young Orthodox scholars, rabbis, and even teachers looked eastward to complete their education or to learn from the Lithuanian yeshiva experience.[43] The young and dynamic Samson Raphael Weiss, who was born in 1910 in Emden and studied at the universities of Breslau, Berlin, Zurich, and Prague, was a perfect example of this new curiosity for traditional Jewish learning.

After studying at a number of leading European universities, Weiss joined the yeshiva in Mir (Lithuania) for a different perspective on Jewish knowledge, received his ordination there in 1934, and earned a doctorate at the University of Dorpat (Estonia) in 1938. The new perspectives he gained in eastern Europe formed him and resonated among his students and peers at the Israelitische Lehrerbildungsanstalt (ILBA) in Würzburg, where he started teaching in 1934.

He consciously left behind the detached, competitive, and hierarchical academic atmosphere of German universities and introduced a new style of teaching at ILBA that he claimed to have adopted at Mir, where the rabbis lived and studied with their students in a symbiotic relationship and offered fatherly guidance to yeshiva students in solving personal *and* academic problems.[44] Weiss generated great enthusiasm at ILBA through his presence and leadership as a rabbi, professor, and dean. He set an example as a brilliant youthful scholar who tore down hierarchical walls between faculty and students by, among other things, inviting them to his home on Shabbat evenings.

A number of his students were motivated to follow their role model and experience the unknown world of the east European yeshivot. The excitement brought about by this new type of educator spread; by 1937, seven of Weiss's students were studying at the yeshiva in Mir, and by 1938, twenty students wanted to continue their Talmud studies there but were prohibited from leaving by German authorities.[45]

Nazism and the relative helplessness of the Jewish religious establishment during this crisis reinforced the criticism of modern German Orthodox thought and initiated a push for renewal. These reactions signaled, already in the 1920s, that a new and vigorous generation of rabbis was emerging across all religious groups of Judaism in Germany. This generation was dedicated to using new ways to change their congregants' relationship with Judaism and the Jewish leadership. Their new identity and criticism of the assimilationist, Protestantized, and unpolitical forms of German Jewry, as they had crystallized during the nineteenth century, stood at the center of the newly emerging Jewish leadership, their treatises, appearance, and services.

By 1933, if not earlier, it became clear to these rabbis that the ideas of social acceptance and inclusion had been wishful thinking. The day-to-day experience of contemporary reality proved to German Jews how fragile their integration was, how easily it could be destroyed, how many of them had lost the connection to Judaism as a guiding force in their lives, and how much they needed special guidance to again develop a meaningful *Jewish* identity.

Jewish Renewal from the Pulpit

It was becoming increasingly apparent to German-Jewish families that they were facing social exclusion, the loss of their jobs, and the arbitrariness of Nazi power in their everyday lives. Denied their identity as Germans, they turned to their religious communities, the Gemeinde, to find spiritual, psychological, and practical support. This assistance took many forms, including social services, schooling for children, support for the emigration process, vocational training, and chaplaincy of the rabbis.[46] It was important for people to understand that the community would provide a network of solidarity and sociability and a place of inclusion rather than exclusion, even if they had not previously been active and explicitly religious members of the community. Besides practical support, they sought to learn about their Jewishness because it had suddenly taken on a determining role in their lives and prompted many questions. In this climate, this new generation of rabbis saw it as their calling to live up to the challenges of the times and carry their ideals into a new community life.

Joachim Prinz describes quite vividly how the degraded and humiliated members of his congregation were attracted by the new self-image he provided them in his synagogue and services as their rabbi. In his autobiography, he claims that his goal was to undo the verbal, graphic, and legal assaults of Nazism on these individuals, people who were being stripped of self-respect because of their Jewishness, even though religion often did not play a large part in their assimilated lives. Prinz claimed that he gave answers, community, self-respect, and humanity back to them by providing access and information on "their own nobility, [which] went back thousands of years—a nobility of love and not hate, of humanity and not brutality. There are a thousand variations on this topic, and I used them all in the four long years under the Hitler regime."[47] Thus the teaching of Jewish history, religion, and philosophy turned into an essential vehicle to bring the essence of Judaism to the increasing numbers of congregants in the synagogue. Their desire to leave Germany and incorporate a new Jewish identity into their lives was underscored by the strong Zionism of Prinz's teachings.[48]

While the existing literature highlights Joachim Prinz as an outstanding personality in this profession, which he may have been, I question whether parts of his strategy and arguments to raise the spirits of his community were as singular as he portrayed them. He may have been the first to use new forms and messages in the synagogue, but other rabbis in his age cohort, including Orthodox ones, demonstrated similar engagement as preachers and teachers in an effort to reach the Jewish youth,[49] and they made comparable arguments from the pulpit, even if they did not have the oratorial skill and the unique, youthful glamour of the young and dynamic Prinz. Prinz made a name for himself in Berlin, the capital city that stood out in Germany for its large Jewish population and well-organized Jewish life. This framework and Prinz's personality gave this young Jewish leader a unique platform and the tools to present himself as an alternative to the establishment.

Among the liberal rabbis, only one of Prinz's colleagues could match his reputation at the time, the Romanian Max Nussbaum. Due to his foreign citizenship, Nussbaum had a special status and was somewhat protected from Nazi atrocities compared to his German-Jewish colleagues.[50] Nussbaum was young, handsome, and eloquent. He had a PhD from the University of Würzburg,[51] had been ordained in 1934, and had married the attractive and well-educated German Jew Ruth Offenstadt-Toby in 1938. This newcomer to the profession earned a reputation as an outstanding speaker on the bimah (synagogue platform) during his tenure as a young rabbi at the Rykestrasse synagogue in Berlin.

Nussbaum was not quite the rebel against the establishment that Prinz was, but his style and way of preaching were different from those of his predecessors. He stood out because he gave very political sermons. For Nussbaum, the bimah was a stage spotlighting his elegant appearance, knowledge of Western culture, theater, and the arts, and familiarity with traditional Judaism. Since many of his sermons survived the Nazi period, we know the details of his arguments made at the pulpit—which resembled Prinz's line of argument—making Nussbaum a preacher who would be long remembered by his congregations.

Nussbaum highlighted the meaning of community in Jewish history and the eternal validity of the Jewish religion. A sermon presented at the *Shavuot* holiday reminded his listeners that the nature of religion and its eternal truths were universal and not restricted to a specific historical period. He argued that it might have been a mistake in Jewish history to have disassociated religion from life in a way that made religion seem superfluous and no longer able to provide answers to current questions. Religion, he claimed, had been left behind in the past several hundred years. But in times marked by a return to all things Jewish, it was important to not neglect religion, to ask questions, and to explore the contribution religion could make to addressing current problems.[52]

After this prelude, Nussbaum asked: How meaningful did the Shavuot holiday remain as a festival of the Torah and the book? He then described the development of literature in European societies and explained the exceptionally important collective nature of Jewish identity by citing a number of Jewish religious texts, including the Bible—all of which underscored the collective nature of the Jewish people. He claimed that this collective spirit was not just mere citation or dogma; it had shaped and molded the cultural output of Jews throughout their history. Consequently, he concluded "that not just a commandment of the Torah [that] determines this community, but that the Torah is the living embodiment of the collective spirit inherent to the Jews in its totality" and was part of an ongoing negotiation. He stressed that the message should be revealing to contemporary Jews... and emphasized that the exodus from Egypt and the revelation at Sinai—although already nine thousand years past—had still relevance for them *today*. It was then, when the conversation between the Jewish people and the Torah began. Nussbaum underscored in his sermon "[that] if Shavuot is to make any sense in their times, it was the reception of Torah based on that new spirit [and active participation] in the community."[53]

Many of Nussbaum's sermons relied on a somewhat secular framework that he used to *always* stress the depth of Jewish history, tradition, or religion and connect it with the present.[54] He sought solutions to current Jewish problems and tried to prepare the young generation spiritually for the difficulties they were facing and those he anticipated.[55] Jewish knowledge and "substance," he claimed, had never been so important to preventing the abuses Jewish people suffered in the current situation.[56]

A major topic of his sermons was peoplehood, which he argued would change not only non-Jewish lives but also those of Jews because this concept could provide a Jewish state and mark the beginning of a new era for the modern Jew.[57] Like many of his younger colleagues, he criticized the *Galut*[58] as well as the assimilationist development German Jewry had taken since the Enlightenment as one that believed in rationalism and science and applied these ideas to their understanding of Judaism.[59]

Based on the allegory of Abravanel, Nussbaum pointed out that the rejection and persecution currently experienced could be a chance for Jews to return to Judaism,[60] a trope that he also presented in the historical framework of peoplehood and tradition, calling on the Jewish people to embrace their Jewish heritage immediately.[61]

Thus, under Nazism, innovative religious services, a joint religious study based on the academy-like model of the *Lehrhaus*, and the sermon became weapons to actively shield Jews against the current onslaught, to demonstrate Jewish strength, and to empower the Jewish people through an understanding of their history, identity, and community. To gather for Shabbat or attend High Holy Day services was to make a political statement. So, too, was the sermon, especially under the leadership of a younger generation of rabbis who had left behind the nineteenth-century ideal of an "unpolitical" German rabbinate.

Demonstrations of Jewish resilience and self-awareness angered the Nazis and made religious services and rabbis the targets of surveillance, chicanery, and arbitrary harassment. Of the 250 refugee rabbis recorded in the database German Refugee Rabbis in the United States after 1933, almost all reported harassment as students in public schools by classmates or teachers, or as adults in the workplace or public locations. Rabbis were under constant surveillance, had denigrating encounters with Nazi storm troopers or secret police, and were victims of numerous staged libel cases and physical attacks. The first to be targeted were often the Orthodox Jews because they were usually visibly different in their dress and hairstyle.

Nazism's Effects on Rabbinical Education and the Rabbinate

Many of the students who tried to enter the rabbinate experienced growing rejection in the public education system. Besides being harassed by classmates and teachers, they were no longer allowed to pursue their studies there. Such legislation also affected seminary students. Not only were many of them unable to train for a doctorate at German state universities; those who did manage to write a dissertation faced growing difficulties in fulfilling the doctoral requirement of publishing their dissertation in Jewish studies.

In Germany, receiving a doctoral degree depended on successfully publishing a dissertation. As more and more Jewish publishing houses closed or were "Aryanized" and censorship of the print media grew stricter, it became increasingly difficult, and at times impossible, for these young graduates to find a publisher for their dissertations. This prevented many of the young scholars from obtaining their well-earned degrees as well as the important certification and full accreditation they needed to emigrate. Technically, completing a doctorate was necessary even for ordination into the rabbinate, although the high demand for young rabbis gradually reduced the need for such formal qualifications. However, students such as Abraham Joshua Heschel who were pursuing a scholarly career were seriously affected by the circumstances. He completed his dissertation in 1935 but could not prove to the faculty that the necessary two hundred copies had been printed. He could not receive his official degree without proof of publication, and he could not emigrate until he had received his degree.[62]

Long before the pogrom of 9 November 1938, the chicanery of local Nazi groups eroded the social, legal, and professional standing of rabbis, particularly the Orthodox rabbis, teachers, and shohets, and triggered confrontations and destroyed any hopes for being able to compromise with the authorities.

Simon Schwab was accused of making a libelous statement about Adolf Hitler during a religious service in 1936. He was able to disprove this with great effort by explaining to the Gestapo agent in the synagogue that he had not said anything about "Hitler" but that the agent had misunderstood Schwab's pronunciation of the German word *Vermittler* (mediator).

Teacher, cantor, and shohet Justin Fränkel lived in the Franconian university town of Erlangen, near Nuremberg, a hotbed of antisemitism at the time. He had come to the attention of local Nazis long before the NSDAP seized power. His torturous relationship with them (a result of false accusations for years) culminated in 1937 when local authorities accused him of ritual murder. He was arrested and held in detention for six months by the Gestapo, then set free due to lack of evidence. All this time, his wife had been preparing for their emigration, which ultimately took them to Cincinnati, Ohio.

Rabbi Ernst Appel of Dortmund also had frequent encounters with Nazi authorities, who regularly spied on him even outside his services, so he increasingly spoke Hebrew to evade their interference.

Between 1933 and 1938, most of the German rabbis felt compelled to stand by their communities in their darkest hour. The rabbis' presence, leadership, and perspective were essential to ease the effects of Nazi exclusion and persecution in their communities in a spiritual, economic, and social way. Rabbis and the Gemeinde were key in helping their congregants to survive and prepare for emigration because the communities became centers for economic support, retraining, and preparation for the emigration process. The German-Jewish leadership enforced a policy that ordained rabbis must stay in the line of duty while students were being evacuated to sympathetic institutions abroad. For the older generation, though, it was an essential part of their obligation to the profession to minister to the needs of their brethren.

Emigration was increasingly on the minds of rabbis and their congregants—and several of them, such as Simon Schwab, Max Grunewald, Max Vogelstein, Hans Enoch Kronheim, and Emil Moses Cohn, undertook a number of exploratory trips to find possible destinations for emigration. Of particular interest to the refugees were Palestine, Switzerland, and the United States. After two visits to Palestine in 1935 and early 1938, Cohn, a committed Zionist, decided to build a life in the United States, mainly due to the difficulties he expected to face in Palestine pursuing a career as a liberal rabbi, but also because of the problems he anticipated in continuing his work as an author in the Hebrew language.

Simon Schwab visited Palestine in the late fall of 1935, as did Max Grunewald in 1938; his family stayed in Palestine during the war. Joachim Prinz, who also made an exploratory trip to Palestine with his wife in 1934, claimed in his memoirs to have returned to Germany because his community needed him.

Switzerland also ranked high as a potential refuge because it offered the possibility of continuing one's career in a neighboring European country where German was spoken. This would have made the transition much easier for the refugees and given them good career options. Unfortunately, Switzerland had very restrictive immigration laws and practices because it bordered on Germany, and a closer look revealed a rather traditional and strong Orthodox community there. Not all of the rabbis mention that their journeys to Switzerland were exploratory trips for possible future emigration, but their accounts highlight the great interest they had in Jewish community life in Switzerland, which suggests that this was the reason that rabbis such as Simon Schwab and Joachim Prinz made the trip.

Before 1935, however, few German rabbis considered leaving Germany, and immigration to the United States was not yet a prioritized goal. Emigration to an overseas country was considered to be a long-term situation, and the decision to leave for good meant financial and cultural challenges for a profession deeply embedded in the cultural fabric of central Europe, including the German language and Wissenschaft. Only gradually did the United States become the preferred immigration destination as rabbis faced growing pressures and threats of expulsion and arrest, witnessed how their communities were falling apart by mass flight, and learned that staying was becoming increasingly dangerous and options for emigration were dwindling.

Many of these men chose the United States over all other immigration destinations, mainly for professional reasons and the freedoms they were guaranteed there to practice their specific ethnic religion, but also because organized help was available from the United States and Great Britain, as will be explained in chapter 2.

Even Orthodox rabbis turned to the United States as their preferred immigration destination because they could continue their professions as modern Orthodox rabbis there. The American congregation allowed many of those who were separatists outside the Gemeinde to maintain their religious individualism, and many hoped to continue their scholarly work in the academic institutions of American Jewry. This was the determining factor that prompted Max Gruenewald to leave his family in Palestine and accept a research fellowship at the JTS in New York in 1938.

Finally, not all attempts to leave Germany were successful, as was the case with the first attempt to relocate the Hirschian neo-Orthodox kehillah of Frankfurt. Rav Joseph Breuer's early decision to leave Frankfurt in the fall of 1933 to become the head of the Jewish community in Fiume near Trieste, which at the time belonged to Italy, failed unexpectedly.[63] He could not set up a yeshiva according to the Hirschian principles there—an essential element of the Frankfurt kehillah—because he was unable to raise the necessary funds for the project in Fiume. Disillusioned, he returned to Frankfurt in 1934 to reconsider his family's emigration and plans for financing the reorganization of the yeshiva. He stayed in Frankfurt until *Kristallnacht* triggered the final and very hasty second emigration of the Breuer family from Germany to the United States.

Emigration: Plans for the Relocation of the German Rabbinical Seminaries

The events of this time and the crisis experienced by German Jewry greatly affected the Jewish seminaries for rabbinical training in Berlin (the Hochschule für die Wissenschaft des Judentums and the Orthodox Rabbinerseminar) and Breslau (Jüdisch-Theologisches Seminar). Since their founding in the nineteenth century, these schools promoted the training of a *modern* Jewish rabbinate, which embraced both secular study at state universities—primarily in history, philosophy, or Semitic languages—and the modern Wissenschaft des Judentums at the seminary.

This dual-track education of secular and Jewish studies, enhanced by a doctorate from a state university, was not only expected as an academic qualification for the rabbinate but was also a central qualification enabling the modern German rabbi to represent and lead his community in society at large.[64] This concept and its ultimate goal fell prey to Nazi legislation, which restricted the access of rabbinical students to state universities until all access was completely denied.

In addition, Jewish seminaries faced serious restrictions in status and funding. In June 1933, the Hochschule für die Wissenschaft des Judentums was forced to change its name to *Lehranstalt* (educational institution), which indicated a significantly lower academic standing compared with a Hochschule, an accredited institution of higher learning. It also lost its status as a "corporation under public law" (*Körperschaft des öffentlichen Rechts*), which lowered its legal standing *and* its ability to receive state funding under the same conditions as a German state university and as an accredited educational institution. From then on, the Hochschule received regular funding only from the Reich Representation of German Jews (Reichsvertretung der deutschen Juden),[65] an organization of Jewish self-governance imposed by Nazism. The Hochschule came under increasing financial pressure and had to find ways to offer programs that would substitute for the secular education formerly obtained from state universities.[66]

The task of developing a complementary curriculum on non-Jewish subjects *within* the Hochschule to supplement the Jewish studies curriculum became the task of the Arbeitskreis für allgemein-wissenschaftliche Vorlesungen (Working Group for Scholarly Lectures on General Subjects). The members of the working group were Ismar Elbogen, Arthur Lilienthal (secretary general of the Reich Representation), Otto Toeplitz (former professor of mathematics at the University of Bonn), Martin Buber, and Ernst Kantorowicz (both from the Mittelstelle für Jüdische Erwachsenenbildung/Center for Jewish Adult Education).[67]

It was technically illegal to organize and hire scholars to teach at the Hochschule, but such positions provided an opportunity for many of the young Jewish professionals who were no longer permitted to teach at state universities to support themselves while still in Germany and to eventually emigrate from an accredited institution of higher learning. Among the scholar recruits were Arnold Metzger (philosophy), Hans Friedländer (philosophy), Fritz Kaufmann (philosophy), Hans Liebeschütz (history), Arnold Berney (history), Eugen Taeubler (Täubler) (history), and Moses Goldhagen (history). Sociology was taught by Franz Oppenheimer, Paul Eppstein, and Friedrich Caro; philology and literature were covered by Ernst Brumach, and Semitic languages were taught by Franz Rosenthal.[68]

The massive pressures and efforts to handle the difficulties imposed on the seminaries by Nazism are illustrated in the "Memorandum betreffend einige Punkte der Ausbildung der Rabbiner in der Lehranstalt für die Wissenschaft des Judentums" (memorandum on several points regarding the education of rabbis at the Lehranstalt für die Wissenschaft des Judentums) by Otto Toeplitz.[69] This memorandum emphasizes the problems faced by the rabbinical seminary, reveals the faculty's concerns about living up to the growing need for outstanding Jewish leadership, and shows the Jewish leadership's determination to address the challenges of the times. Under the current circumstances, stressed Toeplitz, the rabbinate was challenged to excel in humanity and intellect. He pointed out that people's need for spiritual guidance had almost doubled the demand for rabbis and chaplains, even though the size of the Jewish community had decreased by a third of what it had been in 1933 because of emigration. Moreover, rabbis and members from small and rural communities were increasingly moving to urban centers or leaving the country altogether. This left small communities without a Jewish spiritual leader and overburdened urban centers with new and challenging social duties that were difficult to master with the existing communal structures and staff.

In an effort to find solutions to these problems, Toeplitz refused to give up core qualifications just to increase the number of students because he believed that academic excellence in the profession was needed more than ever. While the working group discussed ways to expedite the training of rabbis, Toeplitz defended the *Abitur* (secondary education diploma needed for university entry) as an entry qualification for German students, and no one in the faculty of the Hochschule questioned the dissertation as an essential qualification for the rabbinate.

To make up for the lack of access to secular knowledge at state universities, the study time at the Hochschule was increased. While students usually spent two years studying full time at a secular university and five years at the Hochschule, the new curriculum allowed them to attend the Hochschule for seven years under the assumption that two years were dedicated to secular studies. The strict selection of the personal and intellectual qualifications for the profession among the candidates was upheld by the faculty precisely *because* of the growing everyday challenges.[70]

There is no detailed information on the impact of Nazism on the Orthodox Rabbinerseminar in Berlin and the Jüdisch-Theologisches Seminar in Breslau, but the problems there were likely similar to those at the Hochschule.[71] These Jewish institutions were still suffering from the events of the Depression years after 1929. Under the pressure of Nazism, the Breslau seminary reduced the number of students admitted, arguing that it would be irresponsible to train more students for what seemed to be a doomed rabbinate as Jewish communities crumbled. The students in Breslau considered immigrating to Palestine, therefore modern Hebrew classes were in great demand, and the Breslau seminary helped transfer students to partner teacher seminars in Jerusalem.[72]

The increasing importance of Berlin to Germany's Jews and the city's strong and ever-growing Jewish community during this time of crisis marginalized both the seminary and Breslau, a city that had once been home to the third-largest Jewish community in Germany and was a vibrant center of modern Judaism. However, in light of decreasing student enrollment in 1933, it was discussed whether the historic seminary in Breslau should be closed to maintain enrollment at the two major institutions in Berlin instead.[73]

The established rabbinate was desperately needed in Germany's Jewish communities, and rabbis were reminded to stay there as long as possible.[74] Meanwhile, the rabbinical seminaries turned into important hubs for the scholarly and economic survival of Jewish scholars and students for the rabbinate, many of whom learned that these institutions could use their scholarly networks to help the emigration process. In fact, the rabbinical seminaries made plans to evacuate their institutions, but they were too late, or they struggled to find support and a match in scholarly cultures outside of central Europe.

The Orthodox Rabbinerseminar in Berlin was still financially strained by the Depression and shaken by the retirement and emigration of some of its core faculty members, so its members explored the possibility of relocating the institution to Palestine in the hopes for a brighter future. The idea took form in September 1933 when Meir Hildesheimer, son of Esriel Hildesheimer and the driving force behind the plan, traveled to Palestine on an exploratory trip.

His plan to rescue the entire institution was strongly opposed by traditional Orthodoxy, particularly by the leading east European establishment under Rabbi Grodzensky of Vilna, the leaders of the Va'ad Hayeshivot and the Agudah Israel, the president of the Council of Torah Sages, and the leading rabbis in the Yishuv (the Hebrew word for settlement, used to refer to the land of Israel before 1948). They feared that a modern Orthodox institution for rabbinical training that included secular studies would seriously undermine the predominance of traditional Orthodoxy and erode the existing structures of religious life in Palestine.[75] Having witnessed the growing influence of modern Orthodox thought in the 1920s and early 1930s and noticing that the plan was supported by the rapidly growing modern city of Tel Aviv, the religious establishment, backed by the Lithuanian religious leadership, defeated it out of fear of permanent religious competition in the Yishuv.[76] Unfortunately, this also destroyed the prospect of a successful and timely rescue of the institution. As a result, students and faculty left Germany gradually and individually, thus weakening the chances for the continuation of this school of thought.[77]

In Berlin, the failure of the relocation plan of the Rabbinerseminar resulted in a gradual but steady decline of the seminary, which increasingly depended on the support of the Reich Representation and its neighbor, the Hochschule in Berlin's Artilleriestrasse. From 1937 on, both schools joined forces to provide lectures in secular studies of the general department in the Hochschule because there was no longer access to secular universities. After addressing concerns about the appropriateness of some of the content of these lectures for the students of both seminaries, this measure was put into practice.

As the political and social pressures became almost unbearable in 1938, plans were developed for the evacuation of the Hochschule as an institution. The first plan was suggested in October 1938 and deliberately adopted the "University in Exile" (a university composed of refugee scholars) model of the New School for Social Research in New York as an example to save Wissenschaft

Group portrait including Leo Baeck (seated far right), Ismar Elbogen (standing to his left), and other faculty and students in the reading room of the library of the Lehranstalt für die Wissenschaft des Judentums for commencement, Artilleriestraße 14, Berlin, 1938: LBI: AR 730, F 1959.

des Judentums and reorganize scholars and institutions in the United States and Palestine. The Hebrew Union College (HUC) in Cincinnati and its president, Julian Morgenstern, played leading roles in implementing this plan, but it was nevertheless undermined by administrative, financial, and political circumstances. Of the twenty-five scholars the exile plan intended to save, HUC managed to invite nine scholars from Germany, eight of whom were brought to Cincinnati in a difficult rescue effort that generated endless discussions with American immigration authorities.[78]

The exile plan was undermined by the pogrom of 9 November 1938, which led to a forced closure of all rabbinical colleges in Germany and hampered their function as safe havens for this Jewish elite. *Wissenschaft des Judentums* lost its framework, its last remaining employers, and its educational centers. Only the Hochschule was able to resume activity in January 1939. It continued to operate to a limited degree until June 1942 and became a center to support the profession at large, including the persecuted community rabbinate during its last years.

The circumstances forced the seminary to expedite the ordination of its advanced students who were already officiating or serving in the communities as teachers, the lowest rank in the rabbinate, perhaps equal to that of an assistant rabbi. Since the majority of rabbis had been arrested during the pogrom and were released only on the condition that they would soon leave Germany, few rabbis returned to their communities and synagogues. Students who had not yet received ordination could neither replace them nor emigrate because they lacked the necessary official degrees and qualifications to be rabbis in Germany or to make a living elsewhere. Consequently, there were formal reasons the seminaries supported the decision to award "emergency ordinations": only fully ordained community rabbis could obtain a nonquota visa for clergy, which would provide them with a safe haven and chance for a profession.

A second attempt to transfer the Hochschule was made after the pogrom in November 1938. Jewish studies scholar Herbert Loewe of Cambridge University played the leading role. He suggested moving the institution with the faculty, the student library, and other scholars to Cambridge in the United Kingdom. He presented his idea to Leo Baeck during one of Baeck's visits to the United Kingdom in late 1938 or early 1939 and proposed that the institution be reestablished as a "Jewish Academy." Loewe had for years been a key contact for German émigré scholars in the United Kingdom and provided a detailed scheme for the rescue of Wissenschaft.

To avoid a rejection similar to that experienced by German Orthodoxy in Palestine from the (Orthodox) British Chief Rabbi Joseph Hertz, the plan for the Jewish Academy underscored that the project was not an exclusive transfer of *liberal* Judaism but would also include conservative scholars and institutions from such places as the Israelitisch-Thelogoische Lehranstalt in Vienna and the Jüdisch-Theologisches Seminar in Breslau.[79] Ruth Nattermann points out the role played by historian Eugen Taeubler, the former head of the Gesamtarchiv der Deutschen Juden (Central Archive of German Jewry) and a confidant of Leo Baeck, in the discussion about this planned Jewish Academy. He seemed interested in expanding the plan to include branches of the academy in Jerusalem and New York. None of these plans ever materialized, however, because the outbreak of the Second World War on 1 September 1939 prevented any large-scale transfers of Jewish refugees and property to Britain.[80]

Between 1939 and June 1942, the Hochschule was threatened by final closure on a daily basis, and life there reflected the rapid emigration and subsequent replacement of its faculty and students.[81] The number of full-time enrolled students during this period was low. Among those students were Ernst Ludwig Ehrlich, Nathan Peter Levinson (Lewinsky), Herbert Strauss, and Wolfgang Hamburger. They worked very closely with the few professors still left in Berlin, such as Leo Baeck, with whom they developed a close relationship. In the absence of intact synagogues and community centers, the Hochschule—still a signpost of a fading, if not dying, era—became the last hub for community activity and shared study. It assumed the role of a *Lehrhaus* more than a rabbinical seminary and also attracted community members who were not all studying for the rabbinate. It became a center that helped Jews from all backgrounds find community and consolation by studying Judaism in extremely troubled times.[82]

The rescue of scholars and students preceded the mass flight of the communal rabbinate in Germany, which would represent the largest cohort of surviving refugee rabbis globally. Like in Germany, American seminaries stood at the center of the three religious movements in Judaism, trained the rabbinate, and linked the rabbis' professional organizations with the congregations and religious movements in American Judaism. They were the central agencies driving the placement of graduates and rabbis.[83]

This structure and the seminaries' centrality to the relationships among active scholarship, training, and the rabbinical profession as well as their close transatlantic relationship made them essential to the rescue and placement of German rabbis.

Only with the aid of these seminaries were German and American Jews able to benefit from a loophole in the US immigration legislation, the so-called nonquota visa. These individual visas were available outside of the existing national quota system of the US immigration law, which limited the options for regular immigration, as "the right to refugee status" had not yet been established under US immigration law.[84]

Hence the nonquota visa offered a unique chance for those rabbis who sought to relocate under pressure: this temporary entry permit was available for students, scholars, and clergy visiting the United States if the respective institutions of higher learning, congregations, or religious organizations could prove the availability of adequate funding and the need to fill a specific position because of a substantial growth of congregants. This legislation put rabbinical seminaries and leadership front and center in the rescue of "the last generation of the German rabbinate."

Under these circumstances, the rabbinical seminaries used their international networks to facilitate the emigration and immigration of their scholars, their students, and the rabbinate. It was in this order that opportunities abroad were sought for these three groups, an emigration that launched a historical knowledge transfer from Europe to the United States. Chapter 2 discusses how American Jews—scholars, students, and rabbis—tracked the events in Germany, how they developed ways to aid their German peers, what motivated them to help, and how successful they were in this unique rescue operation.

TWO

Rescue and Flight
Scholars and Students—And a Visa That Saved Lives

The Emerging Crisis

Long before the Nazis seized power in January 1933, it was apparent to American Jewry and its religious movements that nationalism and antisemitism had been on the rise globally and that many Jewish communities, particularly those in central and eastern Europe, were at the brink of a crisis. Jewish solidarity and action were needed. Thus, during its November session in 1932, the Central Conference of American Rabbis (CCAR) appointed William Rosenau, a German-born, American-educated rabbi in Baltimore, to chair a newly appointed Special Committee on World Jewry to explore if and to what degree Jewish organizations and representations should and could take action.[1] The committee sought to present a resolution to national Jewish organizations globally in order to prepare a platform for this plan. The ideas from these diverse organizations were to be presented and discussed at the next meeting of the CCAR in June 1933 in Chicago.[2]

The CCAR was not alone in its concerns about the state of Jewish communities abroad. In early March 1933, the conservative Rabbinical Assembly answered Rosenau's letter and pointed out that a similar project, a Committee to Study the Organization of Jewish Public Opinion in America, had just been launched by the Rabbinical Assembly, and cooperation was being considered.[3] The Union of Orthodox Jewish Congregations of America, the Orthodox counterpart to the Reform and Conservative organizations, advocated political action on the part of the American Jewish Congress and the American Jewish Committee.[4]

These exchanges formed two competing approaches to action: on the one hand, a World Jewish Conference composed of national Jewish organizations worldwide and led by the American Jewish Committee, the American Jewish Congress, and B'nai B'rith in the United States; on the other hand, a Zionist World Congress. Zionist groups argued that the Zionist World Congress scheduled for 1934 in Geneva would provide a sufficient global representation of Jews.[5] Personal correspondence between Stephen Wise—a leading Reform rabbi who supported Zionism, a political rabbinate, and the idea of a World Jewish Congress (WJC) as the democratic representation of Jews globally— and William Rosenau—the outspoken anti-Zionist who supported a venture led by the assimilationists—showed the degree to which American Jews were conflicted, even within the American Reform movement, over how to best assist their European brethren.[6]

At the June 1933 Milwaukee meeting of the CCAR, the conference project was postponed due to difficulties coordinating the plan. Nevertheless, the meeting minutes show that the CCAR was already quite aware of the persecution of "Jewish" scholars in Germany and decided to provide $1,000 for rabbis and scholars in need.[7] The funds were to be made available by the Joint Distribution Committee (JDC), an organization that had gathered experience and developed networks to provide aid to European Jewry since the beginning of the First World War, when many Jewish communities in eastern Europe were suffering from the war's effects and aftermath.[8] This aid, however, was intended to help individuals still in Germany and excluded the first refugees who were starting to arrive at America's shores.

Aware that the new Nazi legislation and the anti-Jewish Law for the Restoration of the Professional Civil Service were driving Jewish professors and scholars out of the country and that liberal and leftist intellectuals were also being chased out of Germany, Jewish seminaries worked on behalf of numerous scholars they intended to bring to the United States. Most refugees were not yet seeking to rebuild their lives in the United States but were instead exploring professional opportunities for exile in Europe. Some experts in the field of Jewish studies turned to American rabbinical seminaries because these scholarly institutions were centers of narrow fields of study and highly specialized knowledge. In the absence of modern Jewish Studies Departments at American universities, it seemed logical to rely on Jewish seminaries that embraced *Wissenschaft des Judentums*.

Jewish Knowledge at Stake

American seminaries were aware that a unique collection of expert knowledge in the field of modern Jewish studies was at stake. The dispersion of the European scholarly community and particularly the leading experts in Jewish studies, several of whom were also ordained rabbis, could potentially shift the center of Jewish learning from Europe to wherever these scholars could find employment. As early as 1933, Cyrus Adler, president of the Jewish Theological Seminary (JTS) in New York and Dropsie College in Philadelphia, and Julian Morgenstern, president of the Hebrew Union College (HUC) in Cincinnati, sensed that the emerging humanitarian crisis was a unique opportunity to recruit scholars who might otherwise not consider continuing their work in the United States.[9] From the onset of the crisis, both leaders helped refugee scholars find employment[10] and provided guidance to individuals exploring the American job market in their field by directing job seekers from Europe to a volunteer clearinghouse established at 270 Madison Avenue and headed by philanthropist Fred Stein.[11]

This clearinghouse was the nucleus of the executive committee of the Emergency Committee in Aid of German Scholars (ECAGS), which was in its formative phase in May and June 1933.[12] The initiative was launched by Stephen Duggan, director of the Institute of International Education, which had assisted students and scholars fleeing from the Bolshevik Revolution in Russia decades earlier.[13] The institute worked with the Rockefeller Foundation and philanthropists Abraham Flexner and Fred Stein to launch a concerted effort by the American community of higher learning to aid German refugee scholars. This refugee aid committee was composed of legal scholar Abraham Flexner, securities analyst and philanthropist Fred Stein, and Felix Warburg, who supported the project with his philanthropist wife, Frieda Schiff.

The project quickly grew into a communication center for open positions and expertise sought among refugees from Europe. The newly founded ECAGS facilitated communication between American colleges and universities and the refugees in the hiring process. It brought together a vast number of American professional organizations, universities, and educational societies to assist in the rescue and recruitment of these scholars.[14]

Supported by the Rockefeller Foundation, the project offered limited three-year contracts for refugees and made these appointments affordable for American universities by arranging compensation far below the salaries of comparable American experts in these fields and by having European refugee scholars hired for short periods to avoid long-term obligations for tenure track positions. The temporary arrangements gave the refugees what they needed to quickly obtain the so-called nonquota visas as professors or fellows. These visas were issued outside the regulations for immigrant visas in the US national quota system. Thus these institutions provided an attractive alternative for refugees to enter the United States relatively quickly. Refugees avoided a lengthy and difficult admittance process, and their immigration status could gradually be adjusted after they entered the United States.[15]

Besides the ECAGS, which worked directly with American universities, a so-called University in Exile was conceptualized by Alvin Johnson, director of the New School of Social Research. He had been in discussions with numerous German social scientists affected by the Nazi legislation through his participation in an ongoing scholarly project, the *Encyclopedia of the Social Sciences*,[16] and was acutely aware of the events in Germany. Johnson suggested organizing and funding the University in Exile to transfer the leading scholars of the modern German social and political sciences to the United States by issuing nonquota visas and providing temporary positions for them.[17]

Edwin Seligman, an economist at Columbia University who had been coeditor of the *Encyclopedia* with Johnson, discussed with Cyrus Adler the possibility of including scholars of Jewish studies in the plan to set up the University in Exile project. Enthusiastic about the idea of aiding German Jewry, Adler promised to approach the Guggenheim Foundation about changing its program from supporting American students' travel abroad to offering research fellowships to German scholars to pursue their studies in Germany or elsewhere, including America.[18]

In January 1934, Cyrus Adler approached Stephen Duggan for help recruiting new faculty for the JTS and Dropsie College. Potential candidates were Alexander Sperber, a lecturer of biblical Greek and Aramaic at the University of Bonn; Leo Rosenzweig, a philosopher who had found refuge in Palestine; Jacob Klatzkin, a Zionist publicist and editor of the *Encyclopedia Judaica* who had been recommended to Adler by Albert Einstein; and Julius Lewy, an Assyriologist at the University of Giessen, whose availability he praised as the "chance of a century [in] getting a man of his type."[19] Aware of the economic value of some fields versus others, Adler made a case for Jewish studies at large and pointed out that the idea of a University in Exile focused on social scientists and economists but not on those who were the first victims of Nazi racial cleansing and who had the hardest time finding new employment, such as scholars in Jewish philosophy and Semitic languages. Adler urged Duggan to give them appropriate attention in the emergency rescue effort because they had been largely overlooked.[20]

The Rescue of Scholars in Modern Jewish Studies

By the fall of 1934, Adler had hired Alexander Sperber and Julius Lewy with the support of the ECAGS. Adler received $3,000 from the newly formed executive committee of the ECAGS and followed the recommendation of Prof. William Foxwell of Johns Hopkins University, who mentioned the two men as being unique experts in their fields. An additional $1,000 from the Rockefeller Foundation allowed Adler to invite Lewy, who held a visiting professorship at Johns Hopkins University for the fall of 1934, to teach at the JTS in the spring semester of that year. Alexander Sperber's visiting position at the JTS started in the academic year 1934/35, but Sperber stayed at the seminary until he was offered a permanent position on the JTS faculty in 1938 at a salary of $2,500 a year.[21]

Other scholars were not as lucky. Saving Aramaic scholar Eugen Mittwoch was not a priority to the seminary, and although Adler tried to assist his German colleague anyway, he was not successful.

A decisive criterion in the decision to invest in the rescue of German scholars was their ability to teach and communicate with students in English and share their thoughts in the classroom. This task was difficult for most of them, not only because of language challenges but also because they were not used to the style of teaching and academic culture in the United States. The older scholars in particular were challenged, and there was no time for them to successfully master the difficulties. The ECAGS and leadership of the Jewish seminaries were aware of this, and it was frequently a reason for declining to hire a scholar in need.[22]

Another major criterion for the selection of candidates at the seminaries was whether their specific skills corresponded to a particular college's curriculum development. Even brilliant scholars were rejected on this basis but were helped to continue their work and eventually find employment elsewhere. Such was the case of Guido Kisch, a legal scholar and expert on medieval Jewish law who had difficulty finding a position at an American law school due to the vast differences between the legal systems of the United States and Germany. He could not be hired to the JTS faculty because he had not been trained in rabbinical studies or any other area that would contribute to the seminary's curriculum. However, he was assisted in obtaining a two-year research fellowship from the American Academy of Jewish Research in 1934, with funds granted by the ECAGS but largely raised by the JTS.[23]

In the meantime, rabbinical organizations joined the Special Committee Representing the CCAR and the Rabbinical Association of the JTS of America, which approached American rabbis and congregations for solidarity and financial aid to ease the plight of rabbis, teachers, and the religious communities in Germany.[24]

The CCAR also contacted other religious groups through Rev. Everett Clinchy, founder of the National Conference of Christians and Jews, including the Quakers (Religious Society of Friends), to discuss with them their experience as suppressed minorities and learn strategies to successfully fend off religious persecution.[25] In response, Henry J. Cadbury,[26] Hollis Chair of the Harvard Divinity School, accepted an invitation to attend the CCAR meeting on 13 June 1934 and address the convention with a talk on the Quaker experience and strategies to deal with religious persecution. After all, Cadbury had experienced discrimination because of his religion during the First World War when he publicly criticized America's entry into the war and then lost his teaching position at Haverford College, just outside of Philadelphia.[27] This episode illustrates that, at the time, Nazi persecution was completely misunderstood as a form of *religious discrimination* rather than *racial persecution* of the Jews in Germany. Its severity was also thoroughly underestimated.

At the same CCAR convention, it was resolved to contact the Orthodox Rabbinical Council of America and coordinate activities on behalf of German Jewry with this group and Conservative rabbis.[28] In the meantime, as the issue of refugee aid became more pressing, a new plan for a *Jewish* University in Exile developed among Jewish institutions of higher learning. In 1938, HUC put forth a plan to support a "Jewish College in Exile" by hosting about twenty-five scholars in its dormitory and library for up to three years. The refugees could use the library and continue their work with the college faculty. Julian Morgenstern, president of HUC, displayed great ambition with his plan, which transformed the college into a global center of modern Jewish learning and provided a new home for modern Jewish *Wissenschaft* in America while its corresponding European centers were being destroyed by the Nazis.[29]

Ismar Elbogen, former rector of the Hochschule in Berlin, arrived in the United States early in November 1938 after the dramatic effort of four seminaries[30] to raise the funds for a research position for him, compensated with $4,000 annually, which allowed him to obtain a nonquota visa. Since Elbogen did not hold a university position in Germany but "only" the position of *Rektor*, or administrative head, of the Hochschule (which had been degraded to a *Lehranstalt* under Nazism), his rescue could not be financed by the ECAGS. Its aid was restricted to assisting professors at accredited universities only.

Raising the funds for a scholar as eminent as Ismar Elbogen was a financial challenge for the four seminaries—HUC, the JTS, Dropsie College, and the Jewish Institute of Religion (JIR)—and their rabbinical organizations and congregational unions. The JTS had already tried to rescue Elbogen by awarding him an honorary degree and inviting him to take part in the celebratory bestowal in New York City in the spring of 1937. But Elbogen declined the invitation and thus missed the opportunity designed to facilitate his emigration.³¹ Elbogen, no doubt, had a close relationship with the conservative modern seminary in the United States, for the school's more conservative theological outlook was perhaps even closer to what German liberal Judaism represented. Elbogen also had a warm relationship with the leadership of the JTS, Alexander Marx, Louis Finkelstein, and Cyrus Adler, representing the JTS and Dropsie College. All three men worked tirelessly with HUC to make Elbogen's emigration possible when he finally felt the need to leave Berlin at the end of 1937.³²

Elbogen was by then sixty-five, and both his age and experiences during his last months in Germany had left their mark on him. Therefore, the seminaries offered him the fellowship ($4,000 annually) with no obligations to teach or conduct research.³³ On his arrival at the end of October 1938, Elbogen chose to reside in New York City until his death in 1943. He was an influential presence at the JTS, which became an important institution for him, conveniently located as it was next to the libraries of Columbia University and the Union Theological Seminary.³⁴

Once in the United States, Elbogen became a central figure in the execution of the plan to save world-class scholars in modern Jewish studies from Nazism and to commit them to positions at HUC. In the weeks after Elbogen's arrival, one of his primary tasks was to prepare for Julian Morgenstern a list of candidates to be considered for temporary employment or a fellowship by HUC.³⁵ Since Elbogen had been somewhat "the nestor" of the Hochschule in Berlin for thirty years,³⁶ he was very familiar with German scholars, students, and rabbis in both the Liberal and Conservative factions of German Jewry. Thanks to this background, he played a vital role in the exchange of information and testimonies on scholars, students, and rabbis who sought help leaving Germany. Even amid his own difficult flight, he tirelessly helped students and faculty get admitted to one of the US seminaries and set up to continue their work.³⁷

When Elbogen arrived in Cincinnati, four German refugees were already affiliated with HUC, making it the institution with more scholars than any other Jewish seminary in the United States.³⁸ Among them was Julius Lewy, professor of Semitic languages and Oriental history from the University of Giessen. Lewy accepted a position at HUC as a visiting professor and was then offered a permanent appointment in 1936, but this was only after an odyssey of visiting professorships at the Sorbonne and at Johns Hopkins University in the fall of 1933, the JTS in the spring of 1934 with the support of an ECAGS grant, and again at Johns Hopkins in the fall of 1935.³⁹

Michael Wilensky, a cataloger from Lithuania, arrived at HUC in Cincinnati in 1937 with an invitation for one year, but he stayed until his retirement.⁴⁰

Legal scholar Guido Kisch spent time as a visiting scholar at the JIR in New York under the guidance of Stephen Wise in 1937.[41]

Last but not least, musicologist Eric Werner joined the faculty of HUC in Cincinnati as a visiting scholar based on a nonquota visa, but he ended up staying permanently.[42]

Among the scholars suggested by Ismar Elbogen were Talmudist Alexander Guttmann,[43] art historian Franz Landsberger,[44] theologian and philosopher Albert Lewkowitz, historian and cartographer Isaiah Sonne, historian Eugen Taeubler, philosopher of religion Max Wiener, director of the Oriental Department of the Prussian State Library Walter Gottschalk, philosopher of religion Abraham Heschel, and expert for Semitic languages Franz Rosenthal. HUC added to its faculty Jewish studies scholar Arthur Spanier.[45]

The two youngest and least established invitees, Heschel and Rosenthal (both recent graduates), were offered positions as research fellows with a stipend of $500 per year including room and board at HUC; the others were given positions as research professors with salaries of $1,800 for two years and the option to extend their tenure if their services were needed.[46]

The Rabbinical Seminaries and the Hurdles of the American Immigration Administration

While the rescue of Elbogen revealed some of the problems present in the framework of immigration administration, more difficulties emerged around HUC's efforts to rescue the abovementioned nine scholars. The State Department refused to consider the refugees' former employers, all highly accredited German institutions of Jewish higher learning, as "universities." The Hochschule für die Wissenschaft des Judentums, the largest seminary, was particularly disadvantaged by the fact that the Nazis had degraded the Hochschule (university) to a *Lehranstalt*. To receive a nonquota visa, scholars had to be from an institution of higher learning classified at the level of university. In addition, American bureaucrats were less than creative in interpreting the academic standing of others who had been employed by one of the many institutions of higher learning that existed independent of the German university system but that were quite typical for the German scholarly community, such as academies of sciences, museums, state libraries, and independent research institutes.

Morgenstern's correspondence with the invitees, their relatives, and the immigration authorities describes the problems they faced: Arthur Spanier, who taught at the Hochschule (*Lehranstalt*) and was a Hebraica librarian at the Prussian State Library, was arrested and sent to a concentration camp after *Kristallnacht*, where he was told that he would be set free only if he could prove that his immediate emigration was organized. As a result, he urged Morgenstern to offer him an appointment. With the support of Elbogen, Jonah Wise, and Elbogen's sister, who resided in New York, the funding for Spanier's salary of $2,000 could be offered. However, the attempt to extend an invitation was denied by the US State Department because Spanier had not taught at an accredited German university but had "only" been employed at the Prussian State Library and the *Lehranstalt*; the department even based its argument for rejection on the recent degradation of the Hochschule.[47]

This interpretation also limited the chances of several other scholars selected for a position and involved Morgenstern in endless negotiations with the State Department, which refused the admittance of research fellows and at times even demanded that the appointments on a nonquota visa would have to be for a tenured position rather than a temporary appointment.

American authorities questioned the eligibility of the University in Exile in applying for nonquota visas. After all, they argued, the institution only represented a research institution without a student body, so the existing legislation was therefore not applicable.[48] Just a few weeks later, the State Department suggested that HUC should only be allowed to invite professors on a nonquota visa if they were appointed "as regular members of its faculty," provided they qualified for these positions according to the law.[49] Such arbitrariness in the handling of immigration cases, all of which represented urgent pleas for assistance, undermined not only the arrival of those who had been invited but also the survival of the project as a whole. It was not until Julian Morgenstern had held countless meetings with the head of the Visa Division of the State Department, Ava Warren, in Washington, DC; received the assistance of the office of Congressman Taft of Ohio;[50] and had a conversation arranged by Assistant Secretary of State George Messersmith on 20 September that the legal framework in which nonquota visas could be issued was explained in detail. Still, the initiative was not successful in all cases.

Arthur Spanier was denied a visa based on the fact that he did not hold a teaching position but was instead a scholar employed at the Prussian State Library.

Albert Lewkowitz, a philosopher, taught at the Jüdisch-Theologisches Seminar in Breslau and could have expected to be given a nonquota visa following due process. But he did not have the time required to deal with the bureaucratic hurdles. He and Spanier relocated to the Netherlands, where his documents were destroyed in a German air raid. New documents were requested from the

German authorities, but he did not receive them before the US consulates in Germany were evacuated in the summer of 1941.

As a librarian, Walter Gottschalk shared a fate similar to that of Spanier. His application was rejected because he was not employed by an institution of higher learning as defined by the State Department.

Max Wiener, who was both an eminent scholar in the philosophy of religion and an ordained rabbi, did not want to depend on a nonquota visa as a scholar because he believed he would be more successful in obtaining a visa if he applied as an assistant rabbi of a congregation in Syracuse, New York. After entering the country on a nonquota visa as a rabbi, he decided that he did not want to serve there in that capacity and thus did not fulfill the requirements for his admission for this type of visa. Instead, he headed to HUC in Cincinnati to pursue his research and was redirected to a congregation in Fairmont, West Virginia. He soon abandoned this place as well, only to end up as an assistant rabbi of Congregation Habonim in New York City in an insignificant position far below his qualifications, though it allowed him to also work as the editor of the scholarly journal *The Reconstructionist*.

Art historian Franz Landsberger had been imprisoned in the Sachsenhausen concentration camp during *Kristallnacht* and turned to Morgenstern with an urgent plea to help him leave the country. He received a temporary invitation to the University of Oxford from his colleague Gilbert Murray, which allowed him to leave Germany. From England, he departed for the United States and arrived at the end of August 1939 on a nonquota visa from HUC just days before the outbreak of the Second World War. Landsberger stayed in Cincinnati with a permanent position until his death in 1964.

Isaiah Sonne, a medieval scholar, had already obtained a nonquota visa for Palestine when HUC's invitation reached him. The proposal to hire him had faced some serious opposition from faculty at HUC, which undermined the college's plan to extend an offer earlier. As compensation, the college intended to provide him with research funding for Palestine, but in the end, he managed to secure a position teaching in Cincinnati.[51]

Abraham Heschel's emigration also illustrated a variety of problems caused by the State Department, progressing persecution, and the outbreak of the Second World War. In June 1938, while he was still living in Frankfurt am Main, Heschel registered with the American consulate in Stuttgart for a regular quota visa for immigration.[52] He did not hear from the consulate until ten months later, in April 1939, but he had been expelled to Poland in October 1938 and was residing in Warsaw. He was informed that his case "could not be examined earlier than in 9 months."[53] He learned from Morgenstern that problems related to his lack of teaching experience at an accredited university in Germany, where Jewish scholars had been banned from teaching at state universities since April 1933, were complicating his application to immigrate to the United States. Heschel managed to leave Poland in mid-July 1939, just weeks before the German invasion of Poland, and found temporary shelter in England.[54] It took until 21 September 1939 before Morgenstern, after many trips to Washington, could finally extend an invitation to him as an "instructor in Bible for an indeterminate period,"[55] which allowed Heschel to obtain a visa from the US consulate in London.

Once the Second World War began, the American consulate in London stopped issuing visas for the United States. Morgenstern advised Heschel to travel to Dublin to receive the necessary visa there.[56] Without hesitation, Morgenstern wrote to the American consulate in Dublin to inform the visa department that all paperwork for Franz Rosenthal, who was by then residing in London like Heschel, had been completed.[57] Finally, Heschel learned that the Visa Department of the American consulate in London had resumed its work. He received his nonquota visa on 31 January 1940 from this office. He left almost immediately and arrived in New York City on 21 March 1940.[58]

The emigration of Eugen Taeubler, a Jewish classicist and historian of ancient Rome, and his wife, Selma Stern-Taeubler, one of the first German women to become a historian, proved similarly complicated. The State Department's visa division and the Consulate General in Berlin caused problems concerning the issuance of nonquota visas, but in addition, irrespective of the persecution of Jews in Germany, the couple found it extremely hard to leave Berlin, where they were at home emotionally and intellectually, and to relocate to the United States. Cutting old bonds, both professional and private, and giving up central Europe where they had been part of an academic culture they knew they would lose, posed a challenge for them. However, in May 1941, they arrived in the United States and settled in Cincinnati, where Eugen Taeubler taught until 1953. Stern-Taeubler, who had earned her doctorate at the University of Munich in 1913 and continued to work on a second book to advance her career, found a position as archivist, for which she was greatly overqualified, in the newly established American Jewish Archives.[59]

The last professor to arrive in Cincinnati was Samuel Atlas, an expert on the Talmud and Jewish philosophy. He found a temporary teaching position in England where Morgenstern's invitation had reached him in May 1941. At the time, US immigration authorities were increasingly worried about the loyalties of refugees entering the United States, and considerations about the nation's security prolonged the processing of immigration cases. Once again, it was Morgenstern's

German Refugee Scholars at HUC in Cincinnati: (*from left*) Samuel Atlas, Abraham Joshua Heschel, Michael Wilensky, Eugen Täubler, Julius Lewy, Julian Morgenstern, Alexander Guttmann, Isaiah Sonne (hidden in image), Eric Werner, Franz Landsberger, and Franz Rosenthal: AJA, hucpc240cin.02.

tireless work that enabled Atlas to join the faculty of HUC in early 1942, shortly after the United States entered the war. In Atlas's case, Morgenstern brought his frustration with Ava Warren to the attention of Secretary of the Treasury Henry Morgenthau, who intervened and personally monitored the processing of Atlas's visa until it was issued by Undersecretary of State Sumner Wells.[60]

While HUC was rescuing scholars, an act that transformed the college for years to come, its conservative cousin, the JTS in New York City, felt that German colleagues would not fit in with its curriculum and hired only a few of them. The only cases exempted from this criterion were those of Julius Lewy, who taught there during the spring semester of 1935, and Alexander Sperber, who arrived as a visiting scholar during the academic year 1934/35.[61] Nevertheless, JTS president Cyrus Adler helped Guido Kisch obtain funding from the ECAGS and American Jewish organizations including the JDC, the American Jewish Committee, and B'nai B'rith for a fellowship at the American Academy of Jewish Research.[62]

Aside from Lewy, Kisch, and Elbogen, Max Gruenewald, a former rabbi in Mannheim, developed a close relationship with the JTS and resided there for several years in the dormitory, living on a fellowship provided by the college. This was not an unusual setup; for shorter periods, the seminary hosted rabbis and students who had no other way of supporting themselves, but the complex case of Max Gruenewald demonstrates that Jewish seminaries dedicated enormous energy to rescue, visa, and fundraising efforts for their colleagues abroad and were personally quite involved in their fates. This is vividly underscored by the involvement of provost Louis Finkelstein in Gruenewald's case. Finkelstein was a close friend and colleague of Gruenewald's father-in-law, Dr. Saul Horovitz of the Jüdisch-Theologisches Seminar in Breslau. Together, they edited the *Sifre*, a halachic commentary on the fifth Book of Moses.

Gruenewald visited the United States from late 1936 to early 1937 on behalf of the Reich Representation, for which he worked after April 1936. He claimed that the goal of the trip was to secure affidavits for especially endangered German Jews.[63] After his return to Germany, Gruenewald experienced serious harassment by the Gestapo, which had spied on his activities in the United States. He decided to leave Germany with his wife, a medical doctor, and his son in August 1938. The family arrived in Palestine in August 1938, but Gruenewald could find neither a position as a liberal rabbi nor an opportunity to continue his scholarly work.

Many of Gruenewald's colleagues experienced the difficulties that modern rabbis encountered in Palestine when they explored it as a potential destination for emigration.[64] None of them, not even ardent Zionists, found liberal or modern Orthodox congregations, and all of them struggled with Hebrew, missed the intellectual climate of central Europe, and felt they could not make a living on the salaries paid in the Yishuv to immigrant rabbis.[65]

Legal scholar Heinrich Kronstein, who had befriended Gruenewald and permanently relocated to the United States in 1936, highlighted Gruenewald's dilemma and lack of prospects to Cyrus Adler in December 1937.[66] He asked if there was any way to assist him and his family, but the JTS could only offer them residence in a men's dormitory, a rather unsuitable place to house a family.[67] With no alternatives, Gruenewald accepted the offer of a fellowship at the JTS, which was to bring him to New York City for one year starting in the spring of 1939.

On 13 January 1939, Louis Finkelstein asked the American Consul in Tel Aviv what was necessary to issue a visitors' visa to Gruenewald as a guest of the seminary dormitory with room and board.[68] By May 1939, just months before the outbreak of the war, Gruenewald started his fellowship in New York City, leaving his wife and child in Palestine in anticipation that the separation would only be temporary.[69] While the refugee rabbi embarked on his research, the seminary tried to involve him in some religious functions, in working with the refugees, or in a congregation to acquaint him with American Jewish religious life and develop his English.[70] After one year, Gruenewald wanted to return to Palestine for a time while Finkelstein tried to extend his visitor's visa in February 1940. The plan was to have Gruenewald renew his visa during his stay in Palestine, but the ship Gruenewald had sailed on was recalled to the United States just after it arrived in Lisbon due to Italy's entry into the war. This left Gruenewald without the proper paperwork on a ship that returned to the United States in June 1940. He was placed under arrest on Ellis Island for three weeks and was denied entry into the country.

Gruenewald received another research fellowship for the academic year 1940-41 at the JTS,[71] but before he could accept it, Louis Finkelstein was forced to explain the situation to the US immigration authorities and tried to initiate Gruenewald's admission process. Early in July, Gruenewald's brother Ernst, a resident of Long Island, contacted the Hebrew Sheltering and Immigrant Aid Society of America asking for their advice and support in his brother's case. Max Gruenewald's readmission was granted for only sixty days after he applied for a visa waiver at the State Department on the condition that his brother pay a departure bond of $500.[72] Gruenewald managed to extend that period and moved back into the JTS dormitory.

In March 1941, he traveled to Cuba to apply for an *immigration* visa to the United States from there, a process used by many of the refugees to change their visa status from temporary to permanent as immigrants to the United States. Louis Finkelstein personally provided an affidavit of support for Gruenewald.[73]

After the United States entered the war, new regulations forced Gruenewald to file his application once again in July 1941. Under the Alien Registration Act (Smith Act), the German refugee rabbi was forced to confirm his political loyalty and submit newly issued affidavits for the application of his immigrant visa under the quota. At the same time, the JTS tried to support Gruenewald with continuing fellowships, but the school was financially challenged by the support it gave to a growing number of German refugees. Only the aid of the American Academy of Jewish Research and some private donations secured Gruenewald's room and board at the JTS during the war.

Frustration with his situation and the desire to reunite with his family drove Gruenewald to finally accept a position in Milburn, New Jersey, as substitute rabbi when Melvin Kieffer, the congregation's rabbi, left to serve as a chaplain in the US Army. By 1946, he would become the full-time rabbi of this congregation and be able to reunite with his family.[74]

Bernard Revel—president of Yeshiva University, its college for general studies (Yeshiva College), and its Orthodox rabbinical school, the Rabbi Isaac Elchanan Theological Seminary (RIETS)—also reached out to the Emergency Committee in November 1933 requesting its cooperation. Specifically, he wanted suggestions for German refugee scholars to add to Yeshiva University's faculty and financial support to fund these appointments.[75]

His primary interest lay in securing support for philosopher Leo Rosenzweig, whom he considered suitable to teach at RIETS.[76] Revel hired Rosenzweig, who was residing temporarily in Palestine. His case was discussed by the Emergency Committee in 1934 but was ultimately turned down due to a lack of funding. The university was encouraged to reapply for support from the Emergency Committee on Rosenzweig's behalf at a later time. This effort was obviously successful because Rosenzweig was negotiating in the fall of 1936 to teach a class on "Problems of Jewish Philosophy" at Yeshiva College, a class he apparently did teach in the spring semester of 1937.[77]

Yeshiva College received a long list of scholars recommended by the Emergency Committee to add to the liberal arts college faculty and who were already in New York City. Among them were Klara Deppe, Dr. Marie Munk, Dr. Anna Berger, Dr. Felix Salomon, Dr. Erich Gutkind, Dr. Leo Cahn, Dr. Erwin Hirschfeld, Klaus Liepmann, Dr. Heinz Steinhaus, and Dr. Leo Rosenzweig.[78]

Yeshiva University Archives reveal that Erich Gutkind, an unusual and somewhat esoteric scholar of several disciplines, was appointed, but there is no proof in the college's administrative correspondence that any of the other scholars were hired by Yeshiva University. Perhaps it was the special endorsement from Rabbi De Sola Pool of the Sephardic congregation Shearith Israel in New York City that pointed to Gutkind's unique spiritual usefulness for American Orthodoxy and thus made him a strong candidate for the college. Or, it might have been his active engagement and communication with the college's registrar, Jacob Hartstein, and his willingness to serve as a speaker for Yeshiva University Speaker's Bureau. In this way, he could demonstrate his teaching skills, mastery of English, and multidisciplinary value, making him a successful candidate not only for hire but also as someone to be referred to Columbia University's library for additional employment.[79] Yeshiva University likely employed Gutkind for two years, perhaps with a grant from the Emergency Committee. His name is on the faculty list of Yeshiva College for the 1936 spring term, and he discussed with registrar Jacob Hartstein the two courses he wanted to offer in the spring and fall semesters of 1937, namely, a two-semester seminar on the contemporary problems of philosophy and a two-semester seminar on Kant and Hegel.[80]

Outside of RIETS, Yeshiva University hired several German refugee scholars, including legal scholar and judge Bruno Birnbaum, who was offered a permanent position as chair of political economy in 1934, and Rudolf Kayser, who was appointed as chair of German language and literature. As the son-in-law of Albert Einstein, who had a close relationship with Yeshiva University, Kayser also received the support of the eminent physicist for this appointment.[81]

Revel was also interested in employing a young Orthodox professor of the Berlin Rabbinerseminar, Dr. Max Landau, an expert on modern and medieval history who had been recommended by both Ismar Elbogen and Jehiel Jacob Weinberg, the rector of the Berlin Rabbinerseminar.[82] Landau had sought employment at Yeshiva University in May 1939 just after the institution was shut down by the Nazis. He relocated to Warsaw and was on the run from Nazi persecution. His correspondence ended suddenly with a letter dated 26 June 1939 and addressed to philanthropist Harry Friedenwald in Baltimore, who was obviously willing to sponsor Landau's emigration with an affidavit or loan. Unfortunately, a tragic road accident took Landau's life.[83]

Considering the unique relationship of German Orthodoxy to modern secular thought, it may also have been difficult to integrate a large number of scholars into the Rabbinical Department of the college. Yeshiva University was approached by the Rabbinerseminar after *Kristallnacht* in 1938 for admission of students and temporary work permits for its faculty, but it is unclear how much of a response, if any, that urgent plea received. No evidence exists of a reaction, and the lack of archival resources hinders any attempt to definitively answer this question.[84] At the time, Yeshiva University was still struggling with a lack of finances as a result of the Depression, so it might also have been difficult to launch a large-scale rescue in the brief window of time that was available then.

Esriel Erich Hildesheimer approached Alexander Marx of the JTS several times about a position in the library of that institution, but he never reached New York City.[85]

Surprisingly, the only rabbinical scholar from Germany for whom Yeshiva University issued visa application papers for a teaching position was Rav Joseph Breuer of the Frankfurt Kehillah. A former student of his, Jacob Salomon, had already settled in New York City and had contacted Bernard Revel on Breuer's behalf after the Breuer family had fled to Antwerp and were exploring their options for further emigration. Joseph Breuer and his family finally did receive a nonquota visa through Yeshiva University, although it is unclear why he taught at the Yeshiva Torah Vodaas instead. David Kranzler and Dovid Landesman explain that Breuer received "affidavits" from Yeshiva University and entered the United States on a nonquota visa for rabbis, a fact confirmed by the Breuer family.[86] Kranzler and Landesmann also explain that Breuer was ready to start teaching at Yeshiva University but feared that there might be some sort of internal opposition to his joining the faculty. Revel had asked him to take some time first to settle with his family before making that decision. Revel then died unexpectedly, which ultimately led Breuer to abandon the idea of teaching at Yeshiva University. Instead, he started teaching at Yeshiva Torah Vodaas, whose director, R. Shraga Feivel Mendlowitz, showed great interest in hiring him to fulfill the obligations that came with Breuer's nonquota visa.[87]

For American Orthodoxy, the exodus of German Jewry was only the beginning of a crisis and rescue effort that did not end in central Europe. Unlike the Reform and Conservative movements in Judaism, Orthodoxy's centers of study and rabbinical learning were still mostly in Lithuania and Poland and not seriously threatened before the beginning of the Second World War. But once the war began, the Nazis rapidly and brutally gained control of eastern Europe, destroying centers of Orthodox Jewish learning there. However, a small minority of the students and religious leaders of these schools were able to flee and reestablish themselves elsewhere. Nazism and the Holocaust forced a process of Jewish knowledge transfer to take place. The fates of these people and the history of the postwar reconstruction should be examined in a complementary analysis of the migration of European Jewry in the context of the Shoah because a larger view of the two European traditions may provide insight into the rescue and knowledge transfer involved in this migration that exceeds the scope of this work.

The rescue and employment of "German" scholars and rabbis was only a prelude to a second phase of scholarly rescue from Poland, Lithuania, and Russia. This involved the Orthodox movement in one of the most notable international rescue efforts of the war, known as the *Vaad Hatzalah*.[88] In this initiative, any differences between "rabbis" and "scholars" paled because in traditional Judaism, the rabbi is still a traditional scholar and, in this respect, has little in common with the new modern German rabbinate. That is why this rescue effort is not covered in this book, even though it represents a missing piece in the larger picture of research on the rescue of European rabbis, their scholarly institutions, and the transfer of knowledge during and after the Second World War.[89]

At the time, modern German Orthodoxy clearly did not belong to the Orthodox mainstream in the United States. It stood out due to its small size, ethnic background, cultural identity, commitment to *Bildung*, and strict encounter with modernity.[90] Even though a number of the leading intellectuals in the American Orthodox movement had studied at the Rabbinerseminar in Berlin and had close links to Germany (such as Alexander Marx of the JTS, Leo Jung, and Joseph Soloveitchik), the ethnic background of the refugees and their cultural involvement in modern Western society complicated acceptance of the German Orthodox rabbinical leadership outside German refugee congregations in the United States despite the efforts of Yeshiva University to expand its services as an Orthodox scholarly institution.[91]

At Yeshiva College, the continuing commitment to east European Jewish scholarship became apparent when the *Yeshiva College Quarterly* announced in December 1941 the appointment of Polish scholars to its faculty, including the chief rabbi of Vilna, Yitshack Rubinstein,[92] and the head of the Yeshiva at Grodna, Rabbi Moses Shatzkes.[93] Both men had been trapped by the German invasion of Poland and were able to leave Vilnius only once that city fell back under Soviet control.

After a venturesome flight via the Soviet Union and Japan, Rubinstein and Shatzkes eventually made it to the United States in 1941, where they both started teaching at Yeshiva University. Such activity may have benefited from the new financial independence Yeshiva College gained from a fund provided by the motion picture industry in 1939, which allowed the college to invest in fellowships for students.[94] The numerical relationship became increasingly striking between the modern German rabbinate and the east European rabbinical refugees, of whom many were stranded in Canada on their flight from Nazism.

This helps us understand the role German scholars and rabbis played in American Jewish Orthodoxy. By late 1941, 451 east European rabbis and scholars were stranded in Canada, where they tried to establish a "Yeshiva in Exile," a project that involved almost double the number of German refugee rabbis in the United States and that needed the support of Orthodox Jewry far beyond that of American Jewry alone. It found perhaps its largest supporter in the British Chief Rabbinate, a topic that has so far been largely neglected in the existing research.[95]

Besides Yeshiva University, smaller American yeshivot were also affected by the influx of German Orthodox rabbis and scholars, including the Yeshiva Torah Vodaas in Brooklyn. This school not only educated and graduated a number of refugee students[96] after 1945; it also had a strong relationship with the Orthodox refugee community. One person very active in this regard was Rabbi Joseph Breuer. As the former head of the Frankfurt Kehillah, he set up Kahal Adass Jeshurun as a modern Orthodox kehillah in Washington Heights and taught for two years after his arrival at Yeshiva Torah Vodaas. The school's head was Rabbi Shraga Feivel Mendlovitz, who was familiar with and supportive of the Hirschian philosophy of *Torah im Derech Eretz*. He was genuinely dedicated to broadening Orthodox Jewish education[97] and introduced new models for institutions of Orthodox Jewish education, such as Aish Dosh, Torah U'mesorah, and Beis Medrash Elyon. This may have been what brought him together with Joseph Breuer, who was at the time energetically exploring the situation of American Jewish schooling and American public schools to set up the Yeshiva Rabbi Samson Raphael Hirsch in the United States. By the fall of 1939, the periodical *Mitteilungen* of Kahal Adass Jeshurun announced that the former Frankfurt Yeshiva had started the process of reinstituting itself "*in Anlehnung an die Brooklyner Jeschiwa 'Thora Wedaas.'*" This meant that Breuer had carved out a curriculum for the children of his community within the Brooklyn-based Yeshiva Torah Vodaas. They would be provided an education within an established and *licensed* educational framework, which Breuer continued to supervise as long as the community did not have an accredited yeshiva.[98]

This refugee community's dedication to education is apparent in that one of Breuer's first initiatives after immigrating to the United States was to set up a so-called *Schulverein* (school association) for the congregation members in September 1939. The association prepared and financed the reestablishment of the former education system, in which rabbis Dr. Philipp Biberfeld, Goldschmidt, Dr. Rothschild, Dr. Ullmann, and Joseph Breuer were employed as teachers, in a religious school called Nachlas Zwi.[99] The setup of the Nachlas Zwi in 1939, the Beth Jacob Schule for girls in 1940,[100] the opening of the Yeshiva Rabbi Samson Raphael Hirsch in 1944,[101] and the Reka Breuer Teacher's Seminary for girls in 1963[102] were essential for the survival of this ethnic religious group, which did not want to merge with American Orthodoxy or adopt its schooling system.[103]

Kahal Adass Jeshurun's educational system not only provided jobs for teachers and rabbis in the community; it also became the backbone of their cultural and religious independence because it allowed them to educate the next generation according to their ideals of *Torah im Derech Eretz*, which explicitly expressed their openness for an encounter with the secular world. This reflected the widespread opinion that the existing Jewish parochial schools were unsatisfactory. However, the fact that the Yeshiva Rabbi Samson Raphael Hirsch was designed and set up as a *public school* providing a broad range of secular subjects besides religious training was just as indicative of this as the community's commitment to the education of girls.

In his 1940 exchange with Leo Jung, Joseph Breuer explained his vision of a "Work Yeshiva," a yeshiva that would be dedicated to the vocational training of crafts not included in the American trade school system while also providing religious education for its youth. How intensely the community studied the American school system is apparent in its publications. In the *Mitteilungen* of Kahal Adass Jeshurun, Jacob Breuer, son of Rabbi Joseph Breuer, analyzed in detail the American school system and American Orthodoxy's yeshivot to defend, define, and distinguish Kahal Adass Jeshurun's own path in Jewish education and to explore how to best set up its own educational system in this new environment.[104]

Since modern German Orthodoxy did not correspond ideologically or ethnically to the American Orthodox movement or its congregations due to its commitment to secular education and the education of girls, there are no analyses of the role of German Orthodox scholars and rabbis in the literature. Yet an analysis like this should consider their impact on the Orthodox education system in the United States. While many of the German Orthodox rabbis struggled to continue their careers as leaders of American congregations, the refugees had a major impact on the development of a modern Orthodox education system, the establishment of schools for girls, and the design and creation of explicitly modern, innovative approaches to American Jewish Orthodoxy, which were in great demand at the time.

Beyond Yeshiva University, smaller colleges and yeshivot also benefited from the social capital the refugees could invest in American Orthodoxy, and they played a hence-unknown role in the rescue of German (and likewise east European) Jewry. The records of the ECAGS clearly show how many of the new, small institutions of Jewish learning were interested in the "brain drain" from Germany. They all approached the ECAGS for support. One of these institutions was the Brooklyn-based Mesifta Talmudical Seminary, whose exact status in the larger American education system was explored by Betty Drury to properly answer its grant application.[105] Finally, the Baltimore-based Ner Israel Rabbinical College, founded in 1933 by Rav Yaakov Y. Ruderman, hired German Orthodox leaders, although it is not known whether this was facilitated by a grant from the ECAGS.[106]

The first refugee rabbi appointed on a nonquota visa at Ner Israel Rabbinical College was Samson Raphael Weiss, who arrived in the United States in late 1938. Just before his emigration, he earned a PhD from the University of Dorpat in Estonia. Besides his graduation from a secular university, he had also acquired traditional Jewish knowledge in Lithuania and attended the notable Yeshiva Mir, where he received his *Smicha*, a traditional ordination, in 1934. During his secular studies in Germany, he made a name for himself as a leader in the Zionist Orthodox Jewish youth movement "Ezra," where his charismatic leadership and dynamic style were much appreciated. He was appointed professor and then dean of the Israelitische Lehrerbildungsanstalt (ILBA; Israelite Teacher Training Seminary) in Würzburg in 1934.

At the ILBA, Weiss found a region and institution where he could develop his innovative style of leadership and dedication to a new style of teaching. His teaching and administrative style held a unique fascination for the students during the Nazi period and dissolved the formal barriers between professor and student, which were typical for German institutions of higher learning at the time. It was his experience at the Yeshiva Mir that defined his personal and warm style of leadership and instruction and motivated many students to follow their role model and explore the world of traditional yeshivot in Mir.[107]

Among those he inspired was young Herman Naftali Neuberger, who was not formally enrolled at the ILBA but attended some of Weiss's classes in Würzburg to prepare for the Yeshiva Mir in 1935.

Neuberger immigrated to the United States in March 1938 when the opportunity arose for him through a cousin in Baltimore.[108] Subsequently, he was introduced to the newly founded Ner Israel Rabbinical College in that city, which hired him as a leading administrator. Neuberger was quickly promoted to the top levels of the college's administration and was referred to as its "executive secretary" in the summer of 1939.[109] Neuberger advanced as a masterful administrator and architect of the college's infrastructure and growth and was also ordained by the college in 1943.

Personally affected by the refugee crisis, Neuberger understood that the ECAGS was providing funds that could be used to rescue many of his peers from Würzburg and elsewhere in Germany. Like the other leading administrators of American rabbinical seminaries, the young man discussed with the State Department the conditions under which his institution could hire German scholars or invite students to Baltimore. He struggled with the State Department's lack of recognition for the newly founded and, at the time, still relatively unknown Ner Israel Rabbinical College as an accredited institution of higher learning.[110]

Ultimately, Neuberger rescued several people, including his former teacher Samson Raphael Weiss and twenty-three students from the ILBA in Würzburg (their immigration is discussed later in this chapter).[111] To save Weiss, Neuberger applied for two nonquota visas for Weiss and his wife, Leni Carlebach, a student whom Weiss married while he was teaching at ILBA. Weiss arrived at Ner Israel Rabbinical College at the end of 1938 and taught there until 1940. The two-year period of his employment and the fact that he had a nonquota visa suggest that he was hired with help from the ECAGS, which facilitated the distribution of nonquota visas for clergy.

Weiss had been teaching not at a university in Germany but at a teachers' seminary and therefore, strictly speaking, would not have qualified for this visa. However, in 1936, he was promoted to the position referred to as *Studienprofessor*. Although this was actually a mere promotion to a teacher in the seminary and not to a full professor at a university, the word "professor" in his documents enhanced his chances to immigrate with a nonquota visa. This situation was quite different from the difficulties experienced by some of the liberal professors of the *Lehranstalt* and other high-ranking academic institutions, but it demonstrates that the State Department was struggling to understand the German education system and its research and scholarly institutions.[112]

Unlike Weiss, who left Ner Israel after his initial two-year contract on the nonquota visa, Herman Naftali Neuberger continued his lifelong career as executive director and later vice president of Ner Israel Rabbinical College and married Ruth Kramer, the sister of Rabbi Ruderman's wife. During his tenure at the college, Simon Schwab, who found a pulpit at Baltimore's Shearith Israel congregation, joined the faculty of Ner Israel Rabbinical College as a professor of the Talmud and taught at the Baltimore Beis Yaakov School for Girls. According to Schwab's account, the support of his congregation and particularly the Strauss family in Baltimore secured a large number of affidavits for Jewish refugees who emigrated from Germany to Baltimore.[113]

The Rescue of Rabbinical Students from Central Europe

Besides the rabbinate and (ordained) scholars associated with the four seminaries, the students of these institutions were an essential part of a transatlantic migration. They can be classified into two general groups. The first are those who were enrolled first at German seminaries and then sought to continue their studies in the United States because they felt their prospects were less than promising in Germany, their families had immigrated, or their immigration was organized by the seminaries. The second group is made up of children who emigrated with their parents or family and trained for the rabbinate at the American Jewish seminaries *after* they came to the United States. For the new immigrants, yeshivot and seminaries that supported students during their studies may have provided a welcome opportunity for their sons to gain access to graduate education and a career in the Jewish world.

Although these people were raised and educated in the United States, their lives were dramatically shaped by their refugee past and by a German-Jewish identity that was still very much alive in their family environment. Recent publications explore the generational belonging of this second generation of refugees, their relationship with the first generation, and the impact of their refugee experience on their work and careers.[114] Such scholarship focuses on "historians" and their memories and identities as a group. It is not surprising that this group also includes individuals associated with the history of modern Judaism, the rabbinate, and the Jewish seminaries in the United States because the academic study of history plays an essential role in the interpretation of modern Judaism. This cohort of the last generation of the German rabbinate will be explored in more detail in the following chapters, along with refugee rabbis from Germany.

The most prominent and best-documented transfer of rabbinical students to the United States is the case of the five men who were sent from the Hochschule in Berlin to HUC in Cincinnati in the summer of 1935. The prominence of this case may be related in part to the outstanding careers these students embarked on later in their lives and the way they shaped the American Reform movement in the postwar era. But it may also be rooted in the accessibility of documentation in the American Jewish Archives at HUC in Cincinnati. Conscious of what they owed to the lucky choices they made in 1935 and the opportunities provided by their alma mater, the Hochschule in Berlin, and HUC, these students left records documenting their lives and specifically their rescue that are available in the American Jewish Archives. Therefore, their stories have been well researched.[115]

Wolli Kaelter, Alfred Wolf, Leo Lichtenberg, Herman Schaalman, and W. Gunther Plaut were selected at the Hochschule for five fellowships to complete their studies in Cincinnati. HUC gave them this opportunity to cover their tuition at the University of Cincinnati, just as the Hochschule had once offered fellowships to students from Cincinnati in the 1920s. The American institution decided to return the favor during the Nazi regime when the Hochschule was experiencing extraordinary pressures; it was a gesture that spoke to the close personal and intellectual relationship these two seminaries had developed since their founding in the 1870s.[116]

While the fellowship agreement stipulated that the students eventually return to Germany after they completed their degrees and rabbinical ordination, the HUC board of governors farsightedly left open the option for them to stay in the United States if conditions did not permit a return. Two of the five students, Kaelter and Plaut, were selected by Ismar Elbogen[117] and Leo Baeck,[118] who left three other fellowships open for applications from the student body. The opportunity garnered little interest among students of the Hochschule at the time, even though Elbogen continued to actively urge students to apply.

One of the students Elbogen appealed to was Herman Schaalman, who had no interest initially and little or no understanding of the opportunity a fellowship at HUC offered him. Only after Elbogen had contacted Herman's father in Munich and emphatically stated that Herman should seize this chance did the student submit an application.[119]

Wolli Kaelter's selection was not met with enthusiasm either. His mother, the widow of Rabbi Robert Raphael Kaelter in Danzig, was hesitant but consented when Wolli suggested making a commitment for only one year.[120]

The case was different for Alfred Wolf, who was actively looking for an opportunity to leave Germany and had discussed this option with his parents just when the fellowship announcement was made.[121]

Little is known about Leo Lichtenberg, who also joined the group, or Heinz Schneemann, who withdrew his application at the last minute when he, Schaalman, Wolf, and Lichtenberg were forced to decide who would fill the three open positions for students.[122] The passing of the Nuremberg Laws only a few months later illustrates how lucky this group of men were to have been a "brand plucked from the fire," as it is described in the literature.[123]

Their stay in Cincinnati was highly successful, even though they found it hard to adjust to American Jewish standards and forms. Although they stood out as German refugees, they successfully pursued their studies.

By 1939, W. Gunther Plaut, the most advanced among the students, was already ordained. Kaelter and Lichtenberg followed, with ordination in 1940, as did Schaalman and Wolf in 1941.

In the summers of 1936 and 1937, Schaalman, Kaelter, Wolf, and Plaut were able to return to Germany. They consulted with their families about their futures because their temporary residence in the United States allowed them to save their families through immigration at a time when immigration to the United States based on a strict national quota system was almost impossible. Plaut was able to bring over his seven-year-younger brother, Walter, to study at Franklin and Marshall College starting in 1937.

Wolli Kaelter, Alfred Wolf, and Herman Schaalman also visited their parents and friends, even at the risk of not being allowed to return to the United States from their summer vacations in Germany.[124]

Wolli Kaelter applied for American citizenship during a visit to Germany in the summer of 1936. While he was in Danzig, press reports on German politics alerted his fellow HUC student and friend Lou Silberman, whose family had originally come from Wreschen, Germany. Silverman's family provided the necessary affidavit for citizenship for Kaelter, who could then sponsor his mother and brother Hans.[125]

In 1938, W. Gunther Plaut and Herman Schaalman traveled from Cincinnati to Havana, Cuba, where arrangements for their necessary "change of status" had been made. Like other students and exchange visitors who came to the United States on a temporary visa, they knew that this document would not permit them to take out "first papers"; that is, to apply for citizenship and sponsor family members to follow them. Accordingly, they sought to change their visa status to that of legal permanent residency, which would allow them to file first papers for American citizenship so they could stay permanently and then initiate the process of sponsoring their family members as immigrants to the United States. For that purpose, they had to leave the United States. Since going back to Germany in 1938 was too dangerous and the US consulates were flooded with Jews applying for immigration visas, they decided to travel to Cuba via Miami to apply for permanent resident status.

The "band of five" were not the only students to arrive in Cincinnati from Germany. In 1936, Ernst Lorge, a student at an early stage of his studies at the Hochschule in Berlin, was awarded a fellowship by the United Jewish Youth Movement to continue his education in the United States. Lorge had been exploring several venues for coming to the United States and had been in touch with the National Committee in Aid of Jewish Ministers to see whether he could be enrolled at the JTS in 1935.

Cecilia Razovsky's correspondence with the JTS on his behalf[126] highlighted the problem posed by his lack of an American bachelor of arts, the degree required to enter the JTS, and expressed concern about his proficiency in English; therefore, his application was rejected.[127] Lorge was nineteen at the time. Although he only had the German degree of *Abitur*, he was able to eventually enroll at the University of Cincinnati and HUC, where he quickly earned a bachelor of arts degree before moving on to graduate studies and finally graduating in 1942 with a Master of Hebrew Letters. HUC continued his initial fellowship from the World Student Service with a fellowship from the college, and he was ordained shortly after he graduated in 1942. Lorge also managed to help his parents join him in the United States.[128]

HUC extended special guidance and empathy to these young men and their family members, some of whom were well known to the college faculty because the fathers were also rabbis and no strangers to the college leadership. For example, Lorge's father, Moritz, was a graduate of the Hochschule and had been a district rabbi of Sobernheim near Bad Kreuznach, a fact mentioned in a communication from Julian Morgenstern on the colleges' responsibilities toward refugee students.[129]

In the spring of 1938, shortly after the annexation of Austria with its dramatic impact on the Jewish community of Vienna, Samuel Krauss, professor at the Israelitisch-Theologische Lehranstalt in Vienna, received an offer from HUC for two fellowships for Austrian students.[130] The students were Joshua Haberman (Habermann) of Vienna and Nachum Norbert Müller. Since Müller was denied a visa to the United States for unknown reasons and therefore could not accept the fellowship, another student was nominated, David Lanner. Lanner also had to decline from participating in the program because of his advanced status as a student. It is unclear if a substitute was ever nominated to replace him.[131]

The generosity HUC offered to central European students dramatically changed the ethnic composition of its student body, of which 15 percent were German-speaking students. But they were not the last refugee students to come to this campus, even though Julian Morgenstern in 1938 noted the college's intention to halt the enrollment and support of refugee students for a few years before the next arrivals.[132]

A second group of former students of the Hochschule arrived in 1941 and included Ernst Conrad, Walter Plaut (younger brother of W. Gunther Plaut), Nathan Peter Lewinski (Levinson), and Steven Schwarzschild.

Ernst Conrad lost his father, a liberal rabbi, at age eight and had been placed in an orphanage as a teenager while his mother worked as a matron at a Jewish home for the elderly. He arrived in Cincinnati early in 1939 without any family. His admission seems to have been part of a decision to extend special support to the son of a colleague who deserved special assistance within the larger college family. Conrad had been studying at the Hochschule since 1938 and left Berlin after the *Kristallnacht* pogrom of 9 November and the resulting closure of the Hochschule. In 1947, he graduated from the University of Cincinnati and HUC and was ordained as a rabbi of the American Reform movement.[133]

The next arrivals were Walter Plaut and Nathan Peter Lewinsky, who changed his name to Levinson after arriving in the United States. Levinson had been one of the last students of the Hochschule before he left Berlin with his parents on an unusual path via Siberia early in 1941 and entered the United States in Seattle, Washington, on 18 April 1941.[134] While he initially tried to gain admittance to the JTS in New York, where the family settled, he—like many German students—struggled with the seminary's admission regulations, which required a BA. Since he did not yet possess a bachelor's degree, he could not be accepted into the program in New York. His plans to study for the rabbinate were finally realized after his mother found out that a seminary in Cincinnati, HUC, admitted students without a bachelor of arts degree due to the pressures imposed on the college by the general draft.[135] In the fall of 1941,

Nathan started his studies on the campus of HUC, where he graduated in 1948 shortly after Walter Plaut, who was ordained in 1947.[136]

Steven Schwarzschild, who also attended classes at the Hochschule in Berlin in the 1930s and had to hastily leave the city after *Kristallnacht* in early January 1939, arrived in New York City in the spring of 1939, where he first attended American high school to earn the necessary diploma. With this document, he was admitted to HUC in Cincinnati to continue his studies for the rabbinate. He was ordained in 1948.[137]

Two other young men who began studying for the rabbinate before departing from Europe found their way to HUC, both under difficult circumstances and somewhat delayed plans. Wolfgang Hamburger, whose mother was not Jewish, was among the last students of Leo Baeck in Berlin and was ordered to forced labor in 1941. With the support of his mother, he followed Baeck's advice to leave the capital of Berlin and hide in Stettin, a small town on the Baltic coast. There Hamburger managed to survive until liberation in 1945. He was among the first Jewish preachers in postwar Berlin and enrolled as a student at the reopened Humboldt University in 1946. The following year, he left Berlin for the United States where he continued his studies at HUC and the University of Cincinnati. He graduated and was ordained in 1952.[138]

Joseph Ansbacher was born in Heilbronn and raised in an Orthodox family with a father who served as an Orthodox rabbi in Wiesbaden. In 1939, he and his parents left Germany for Britain. While living in London, he attended Etz Chaim Yeshiva and the London School for Jewish studies, where he was ordained. In 1940, he was interned to Australia on the ship *Dunera* and served throughout the war in the Australian Army as a chaplain.[139] Immediately after the war ended, he traveled to London to visit his parents, who had stayed there throughout the war. It was during this visit that he met Leo Baeck, who recruited him for a special mission in the rabbinate and an exploratory trip to Germany in 1946 for the World Union for Progressive Judaism (WUPJ) and acquainted him with HUC in Cincinnati. Although Ansbacher had an Orthodox training and family background, these intense experiences in the war and postwar era and the encounter with Baeck motivated him to seek a future in the liberal rabbinate. He relocated permanently to the United States via England and eventually arrived in Cincinnati to attend HUC in 1947. At that time, Ansbacher changed his name to Asher.[140]

Like HUC, the JTS was challenged by the volume of applications for fellowships to the rabbinate from German students. It was also contacted by the ECAGS about placing students there who sought the opportunities offered in the United States. As a result, the seminary appointed Rabbi Herbert Parzen as chairman of the Committee in Aid of Foreign Students of the Rabbinical Assembly, the Conservative rabbinical organization.

Unlike the Reform movement, which had a robust connection with Germany historically, the Conservative movement was more conscious and skeptical of the cultural differences between the German and the American rabbinate. Therefore, the seminary suggested and sometimes explicitly demanded that already ordained and established German rabbis undergo additional qualifications for the American rabbinate before being placed in an American synagogue. Preparations included taking additional classes in homiletics (the art of preaching or delivering sermons), which was a key qualification in the modern rabbinate where expectations differed considerably between German and American congregations. Younger graduates were sometimes required to earn an American doctorate in divinity to have long-term prospects in the American rabbinate. The minutes of JTS faculty meetings note that Rabbis Ernst Appel, Leo Ginsburg, and Oscar Adler, all established rabbis in Germany, were attending additional homiletics classes at the JTS.[141]

By 1937, the seminary was accommodating several students from Germany, including Bert Woythaler. Woythaler was originally from Danzig and had studied a few semesters at the Hochschule in Berlin before he immigrated to the United States in 1936. His enrollment at the JTS may have been arranged through the Hochschule, where his advanced Jewish training distinguished him from his peers. He had been privately tutored, which may have qualified him to continue studying at the JTS. The administration obviously found a way to bypass his lack of a bachelor of arts degree.[142] Among others who applied for admission in 1937 were Hans Lewkowitz, a student at the Jüdisch-Theologisches Seminar in Breslau, and Leon Wind, originally from Turka in Poland.[143]

The Refugee Students as a Challenge for the Seminaries in Cincinnati and New York

All German and other European students encountered serious admission problems at the JTS because the school considered itself a graduate institution and therefore required a bachelor of arts degree from its applicants. Since neither that degree nor an equivalent existed in the German (and many other central European) university system at the time, European refugee students could not be admitted to the JTS in a timely or simple manner.[144] To evaluate its applicants' qualifications, the JTS had them take an examination prepared in New York and administered by the students' European professors or teachers abroad. In Breslau, professor Isaak Heinemann, faculty chairman of the

Jüdisch-Theologisches Seminar, performed this task for students from the Jüdisch-Theologisches Seminar; Rabbi Lewin of Turka did so for Polish student Leon Wind.[145]

These were the circumstances under which not only Leon Wind but also Manfred Rösel (born in 1916 to Isaak Rösel, rabbi of Tilsit) and Helmut Galliner (born in 1910 to Rabbi Julius Galliner of Berlin) were admitted. Galliner had made an exploratory trip to New York in 1937 and seized the opportunities offered by his father's close relationship with the seminary in New York.[146] He applied to the rabbinical school at the JTS, although he had not pursued this career and never intended to become a rabbi. In November 1937, he was admitted to the JTS as a "special student."[147] This was the preliminary status of most refugees because the JTS felt they needed special preparation for a successful career in the American rabbinate, meaning special language training and courses to help them understand their future role as rabbis in the United States. By January 1938, however, Galliner asked to be admitted as a regular student, a move that was rejected and that complicated matters between him and the seminary.[148]

While the JTS seemed more hesitant to admit refugee students in the mid-1930s, the faculty minutes show that by 1938, the applications of German and other European students dominated the meeting discussions. The faculty repeatedly tried to obtain solid information on the applicants before they considered their applications or even permitted them to take the admissions test.[149]

Early in 1938, German-born and German-trained chief librarian Alexander Marx, who had many contacts in Germany, presented the applications of three German students at the JTS in New York:[150] Ernst Blau, who had been teaching a course on library research with Abraham Heschel in the Frankfurt *Lehrhaus*;[151] Reinhold Herz, a rabbinical candidate from Speyer who had experienced humiliation and degradation by Nazi authorities since 1933;[152] and Hans Grunewald.[153] The growing number of applications overburdened the seminary, and the faculty rejected Blau because it was felt that he would not be able to pass the entrance exams. Consideration of Grunewald's application was made dependent on an admittance test.[154]

In Europe, German Jews desperately tried to exploit the loophole that a nonquota visa presented for their youth. Even Leo Baeck intervened on behalf of two students who had just completed their *Abitur* and only planned a career in the rabbinate. But even his vocal support was rejected at the JTS because neither student met the formal qualifications, such as a bachelor of arts degree.[155] In May 1938, Sigmund Szobel, a former student of the Orthodox Rabbinerseminar in Berlin, arrived in New York to continue his studies at the

JTS. His application was facilitated because of his depth of traditional Jewish knowledge and a brother who sponsored him.[156]

The admission policies of the JTS were strict and did not reflect the empathy and transnational sense of "family" directed toward European students at HUC at this time. From 1938 on, the JTS faculty minutes indicate a growing number of rejections. Among them were the applications of Rabbi Egon Loewenstein, who had traveled as far as Chile, and an advanced student from Breslau named Franz Rosenthal, who also studied at the Charles University of Prague.[157] The wave of applications from students in central Europe kept the JTS busy and raised questions of admittance and rejection that the seminary tried to coordinate with other institutions of Jewish higher learning in the country. In May 1938, the minutes show that a request was made to explore whether the other seminaries had developed a formal policy regarding the admission of German students, who were flooding the rabbinical schools with their applications.[158] By June 1938, the faculty meeting decided to inform nine pending foreign applicants "that the Seminary cannot at present consider the admission of any more foreign students," including Dr. Oscar Adler,[159] Dr. Asher Bombach, Hans Lewkowitz from Breslau, Jakob Stahl, Karl Weiner,[160] Dr. Hermann Reinitz, Dr. Josef Babad (community rabbi of Vienna), David Lanner, and Nachum N. Müller (these last two students of the Israelitisch-Theologische Lehranstalt in Vienna who had been previous candidates for HUC).[161]

By the late fall of 1938 but before the pogrom of 9 November, Gertrude Adelstein, secretary of the JIR, voiced her concerns over the growing number of applications from Germany and Austria that were overwhelming HUC and JIR and over the future job prospects of the graduates, if admitted. She explained that the college had not presented a definite policy on refugee students due to the complexity of their cases and underscored that HUC felt it should consider each case on its own merits rather than develop a rigid and perhaps unsuitable general policy that might not be in the best interest of each student.[162] Yeshiva College did not respond to these concerns, and no respective communication was preserved, so we do not know what attitudes dominated the admission policies in the largest of the Orthodox seminaries at the time.[163]

In June 1938, the JTS faculty admitted Rabbis Solomon Geld of the Jüdisch-Theologisches Seminar in Breslau and Kurt Klappholz of the Rabbinerseminar in Berlin as postgraduate candidates for a Doctorate of Hebrew Letters (DHL) at the JTS in New York. The faculty once again stressed that graduates of German seminaries would be admitted not as regular students but as "special students." The application of Dr. Alexander Scheiber of Budapest was rejected, as was that of Dr. Hermann Reinitz. Reinitz had been admitted ten years earlier but turned down the opportunity, which was considered a mark against him in 1938.[164] Rabbi Curt Arndt's application was referred directly to the provost, Louis Finkelstein.

Arndt's story highlights the difficulties faced by applicants who were officially admitted and should have had easy access to a nonquota visa. With little to no support from officials because he had left his peers in Germany and studied in Italy, Arndt corresponded with Louis Finkelstein for more than four years about his immigration to the United States.

Arndt was born in Germany and began his rabbinical studies there, but he left Germany after the Nazi government came into power. He completed his studies at the Collegio Rabbinico in Rome. Late in 1938, after the formation of the German-Italian Axis, Arndt was under increasing pressure to leave Italy quickly. But where could he go? He certainly could not return to Germany. While he was desperately exploring possibilities to be accepted as a regular student by the JTS and to obtain a nonquota visa to continue his career in the United States, the JTS issued him a statement that should have allowed him to apply for a nonquota visa in Italy in December 1938. The American consulate in Naples, however, informed him that he had to wait "his turn" in accordance with quota limitations. Not only was this inaccurate information, (Arndt had already been admitted to the JTS and was applying for a nonquota visa) staying in Italy put his life at risk.

In early 1940, Arndt's letters appeared among the correspondence of Louis Finkelstein. He explained that he relocated to Bournemouth, England, because of the consular information from Naples and his precarious situation in Italy. He was staying with a relative there and working through the US consulate in London to obtain his visa. The correspondence stops until later in 1940 when Arndt's letters reappear in the Finkelstein correspondence.

At this time, he was an inmate of a Canadian internment camp in Ottawa just across the New York state border. Although the camp was close to the US border, it was impossible to make the crossing due to immigration restrictions. Finkelstein patiently continued the correspondence, but Arndt could not understand why his admission at the JTS would not remain valid for three years and that the outbreak of the Second World War had changed the situation regarding the seminary and his position. Arndt never received the nonquota visa.

With the help of Alexander Burnstein and the National Committee in Aid of Jewish Ministers, he was finally released from the internment camp in May 1942. It had been a painful experience for an observant Jew, and he eventually found employment as a rabbi at the Spanish-Portuguese Synagogue in Montreal, a position that improved his situation and reinstituted him as a rabbi.[165]

Arndt's formal admission was recorded in the faculty minutes of 23 November 1938 along with the admissions of Werner Lampel[166] and Heinrich Kraus[167] as special-status students. Kraus's brother was prepared to support him, but none of these men ever arrived at the JTS. Multiple factors may have contributed to their decision not to pursue careers in the United States. In Arndt's case, tragic historical circumstances and an uninformed or unwilling consular officer who blocked Arndt's emigration from Italy led to his change of plans.

There might have been other reasons why these students never arrived at the seminary in New York City. The high volume of applications and unused admissions suggest that the seminaries and students in Germany and Austria knew that the opportunities offered by nonquota visas for students of American seminaries could expedite their plans to leave Germany, but they applied at multiple institutions and might have had a variety of preferences and options, or their plans did not materialize for personal, financial, or administrative reasons.

Sometimes, the reasons were dramatic, as in the case of Rabbi Fritz Kempner. He was considered for admission in January 1939, but his application was forwarded to Alexander Burnstein for his advice because Kempner either had a degree or was close to completing one. This extra consideration stalled the process. In the meantime, Kempner continued to officiate at the synagogue on Heylstrasse in Berlin-Schöneberg until 1942. He never made it to the United States. His biographical record shows that he was deported to Auschwitz on 29 November 1942.[168]

Even those who had faced harrowing situations experienced rejection. Luitpold Wallach, a recent graduate of the Hochschule, had been arrested in Dachau after *Kristallnacht*. His admission to earn a DHL at the JTS was rejected.[169] He subsequently applied successfully for a visa as a community rabbi, led several American congregations until 1948, and then switched to an academic career and became a successful medievalist.[170]

While the college almost categorically rejected applications from foreign students and graduates from mid-1938 to 1939, it did admit two candidates on 15 May 1940: Elihu Kushelevsky and Julius Eidenbaum.[171] These two men were probably the last students admitted by the seminary before the war and the onset of the Holocaust prevented Jews from emigrating from central Europe.

A closer look at the admissions and graduation charts of German seminaries and the faculty minutes of the Jüdisch-Theologisches Seminar in Breslau suggest that after 1935/36, German seminaries understood that the opportunities for their students in Germany were decreasing, despite the fact that rabbis were urgently needed. After the passing of the Nuremberg Laws, faculty and seminary leadership explored alternatives for their students abroad, even though these students were not prepared for the US environment and did not recognize American Judaism as a developed Jewish culture.

An essential problem for students of modern Jewish Wissenschaft was that fewer and fewer of them could complete their doctorates at German universities. Even though the seminaries gradually dropped the PhD as a prerequisite for ordination, these young men felt incomplete as modern rabbis without this qualification because the degree was part of their professional ethos.

Several of them may have followed Harry May's example and traveled to German-speaking universities outside of Germany, such as in Prague, to complete their degrees. After studying for ten semesters at the JTS in Breslau, Harry May could not continue his secular studies due to the restrictions from the Nuremberg Laws.[172] One solution would be to continue his work at the Charles University in Prague, but if May completed his PhD there, he would not be allowed to return to Germany—especially to Breslau—to finish his rabbinical studies. A similarly modern Jewish seminary did not exist in Prague.

In August 1938, he applied for admission to the JTS in New York and was supported by the local HICEM office, a global Jewish aid organization.[173] He was also backed by a number of influential friends such as Dora Magnus, sister-in-law of Max Warburg, and Elisha Friedman.[174] Friedman warmly spoke on his behalf to the college leadership, stressing his qualities and potential as a rabbi.[175]

Cyrus Adler responded to May's request for admission by stating that many (young) men were seeking refuge under the wings of the JTS in New York and their number was growing due to the increasing Nazi terror in Czechoslovakia and Italy. Willing to provide aid but keenly aware of the limited means available to a college that could not predict the number of refugees hoping for admission, Adler concluded that only a small number of applicants could be admitted. However, he also mentioned the increasing efforts to work with the National Coordinating Committee for Aid to Refugees and Emigrants Coming from Germany (NCC)[176] and the British Chief Rabbi to provide refuge to rabbis fleeing central Europe and place them in English-speaking countries.[177] In September 1938, Harry May received an answer from Joseph B. Abrahams of the JTS referring him to the Rabbinical Assembly Committee in Aid of Foreign Students led by Rabbi Herbert Parzen, who successfully obtained May's visa and placement. By 1941, May was a rabbi in Sedalia, Missouri, near his brother-in-law Rabbi Karl Richter, who had found a pulpit in Springfield, Missouri.[178]

While the JTS leadership was aware of the language and acculturation problems of the refugee students who flocked to the seminary from central Europe, it was obvious that these problems could usually be fixed by thorough training or retraining provided by the seminary.

One student, however, was in a class by himself when it came to misusing the loophole the nonquota visas provided to rabbinical students. Helmut Galliner was the son of Julius Galliner, a prominent Berlin rabbi and scholar who belonged to the Berlin Jewish establishment. On a trip to New York in 1937, Helmut explored the possibilities for immigration and contacted the JTS. Encouraged by his father and able to use his name to open doors, Helmut applied at the JTS in October 1937 as a "special student" to the rabbinate for the study of Hebrew, Jewish literature, and history—yet all he really wanted to do was complete his training as a librarian, which he had begun in Berlin.[179] Hoping that he could benefit from the ability to receive foreign currency transfers from Germany, work part-time in the college library, and live reasonably in the dormitory, Galliner was admitted as a special student on 19 November 1937. He was expected to take courses on the Talmud, the Bible, Hebrew, the Midrash, and other subjects.

At this point, he asked to be admitted as a regular student rather than a special one and was told by Louis Finkelstein that this decision would be made after his first semester.[180] The JTS offered him a scholarship for room and board in the dormitory of the seminary,[181] and Galliner proceeded to submit these materials for a visa application at the American consulate in Berlin. On 15 December 1937, the consulate informed him that to receive a nonquota visa, he must be admitted as a "regular student," and the college was to specify the contributions it made to him with its "scholarship."[182]

On 29 December 1937, Louis Finkelstein presented a new letter to Galliner, confirming that Galliner had been admitted, detailing what the scholarship covered, and explaining that only after the first semester would the college faculty make a decision on Galliner's status and whether he could be a candidate for the rabbinate and advance to the status of "regular student."[183] With the hasty intervention of Ismar Elbogen, who was still at the Hochschule in Berlin, and Eugen Mittwoch, who sent a cable to Louis Finkelstein[184] underscoring the urgency of the matter and suggesting that Alexander Sperber at the JTS could provide more information on the applicant,[185] the seminary finally admitted Galliner as a "regular student."[186]

Galliner arrived in New York City on the *Queen Mary* in March 1938 with a nonquota visa for one year. Since this visa did not grant him permanent immigration status, Galliner, like many others, traveled to Havana, Cuba, in November 1938 to apply for a permanent visa for the United States. To facilitate the process, he received a loan from the seminary[187] and help from Joseph

Abrahams, Louis Finkelstein's secretary, who referred him to some relatives in Havana. But in February 1939, Finkelstein complained about Galliner. Although he had been admitted as a regular student and was expected to study for the rabbinate, it was reported that Galliner was not attending any courses and seemed to be disinterested in the rabbinical profession. Louis Finkelstein was quite upset and vocal about what he thought should be done: even if Galliner chose to attend his courses, he should not be permitted to do so under the current conditions. Finkelstein suggested to Cyrus Adler that he put Galliner on the payroll of the library instead.[188]

Cyrus Adler approved the cancellation of Galliner's scholarship, and one week later, Alexander Marx announced that Galliner had returned from Havana and resumed work in the library with the understanding that this position would allow him free room and board in the dormitory.[189] The new regulation forced Galliner to work forty hours a week for his room and board and put him under quite a bit of financial pressure.

In April 1939, he again explored his status at the JTS but was informed that since he was a permanent resident of the United States, he would be required to work for his room and board.[190] By this time, Marx intervened on Galliner's behalf because he felt the punishment by the seminary's leadership went too far and put Galliner under impossible financial pressure during the summer when the college did not provide food.[191] This interference once again forced the seminary to provide small subsidies to Galliner.

The tension culminated early in 1940 when Galliner wrote a letter to Finkelstein stating that he no longer considered himself to be a student of bibliography, expressing his conviction that he had advanced to the level of a full-time staff member under Alexander Marx, and requesting a salary adequate to this position.[192] In March 1940, Finkelstein answered Galliner to clarify his status at the seminary, once again underscoring the unpleasant relationship Galliner had with the seminary.

First, Finkelstein offered to reconsider his status as a student should Galliner be willing to continue his studies for the rabbinate. Second, Finkelstein clarified how unrealistic Galliner's hope was to eventually be offered a permanent position in the library and advised him to make other plans for his career. By offering his assistance in discussing Galliner's options, Finkelstein took on the role of a concerned father figure, pushed the young man to move forward with his life, and once again offered Galliner one last scholarship, if only to help him support himself.[193]

It is unclear who provided the funds for this final scholarship for Helmut Galliner in his last year at the seminary in the academic year 1941–42, but the extensive communication between Louis Finkelstein and Frieda Schiff Warburg suggests that she may have done so, just as she previously supported the seminary's efforts to save German refugee rabbis and students. Finkelstein made it very clear to Galliner that he was to use this last year of support to leave the college and provide for himself in the future.[194]

Soon after that exchange, Galliner found employment contributing to the *Universal Jewish Encyclopedia*, but the salary was so small that he could not afford housing. He struck a deal with the JTS that allowed him to pay a low rent to live in the dormitory until 7 June 1942.[195] It was not until September 1942 that Helmut Galliner removed his belongings from the dormitory and moved on to another institution.[196]

Unlike other American seminaries, Yeshiva University was likely not part of the larger initiative to admit German students during the prewar years. One reason may have been the strained financial situation of the newly emerging academic institution and its RIETS after the Depression years. Due to missing records in Yeshiva University's archives in the admissions department, its registrar's Hartstein Collection, and the Bernard Revel papers, information on the applications and acceptance of students from Germany is sparse. Other sources do, however, indicate how hesitant the institution was toward modern German Orthodoxy for ideological reasons. The Rabbinerseminar reached out to colleagues in New York to find ways and means for an organized transfer of faculty and students in 1938, but this attempt failed.[197] Even though former students and faculty managed to immigrate to the United States, few of them benefited from a nonquota visa obtained by Yeshiva University, which would have facilitated direct immigration to the United States. Instead, it seems that some of them were ordained so they could obtain a nonquota visa as a rabbi (Alfred Jacobs, Max Kapustin, Kurt Klappholz, Eric Löwenthal).

A high percentage of the former students of the Rabbinerseminar who could be identified for this study came to the United States only after they had found preliminary refuge either in Great Britain on the emergency visa of the Religious Emergency Council of the Chief Rabbi (Immanuel Lewy, Victor Moses Shulwass, Ephraim Carlebach, and Joseph Hirsch Dünner) or had relocated to the United States from Palestine after a short stay there (Hermann Dicker).

Finally, some were admitted by the JTS in New York, as was the case for Sigmund Szobel; others turned to the Conservative movement for a future in the rabbinate, reflecting a trend that was also noticeable in the placement of modern Orthodox rabbis from Germany: the modernity of the German Orthodox movement had a hard time fitting into prevailing American Orthodox congregations for reasons of religious outlook and ethnic background, which often did not match the community's expectations and preferences. Therefore, some of the students and young rabbis found a new home with a Jewish training that was considered an advantage in the Conservative movement of American Judaism.

Unlike German-trained rabbis in the Orthodox spectrum, a second generation of German refugee students, those who fled as children and grew up in the United States, found a home and intellectual and financial support at Yeshiva University, which prepared the way for their academic careers. This group includes such people as Leon Feldman, Walter Würzburger, Manfred Fulda, and Ib Nathan Bamberger. Their numbers and names have not yet been researched in the university's histories,[198] but a thorough study of who and how many of the postwar students at RIETS came from German refugee families would be revealing. A closer look at smaller yeshivot, such as Yeshiva Torah Vodaas in Brooklyn as well as other local yeshivot regarding the admittance of German refugee students would also be helpful and is an area that has been overlooked because it was thought that no contact existed with modern German Orthodoxy.

These institutions, however, hired German scholars like Joseph Breuer, educated a number of young German refugees for the rabbinate, and provided an education for the sons of economically challenged refugee families who qualified for a career in Jewish organizations, like Henry Siegman—despite his controversial attitude toward parts of the community later as president of the American Jewish Congress.[199]

Hans Steidle's work on Jakob Stoll and the last years of the ILBA in Würzburg[200] reveals that the institution's director, Jacob Stoll, presented invitations from the Mesifta Talmudical Seminary in New York to a number of students who were arrested during the pogrom night of 9 November 1938 and detained in Dachau. While it is unconfirmed that these students could have used that invitation to escape, it is clear that this Orthodox community nonetheless had its own channels to facilitate its students' emigrations.

The ILBA's most important US contact was young Herman Neuberger at Ner Israel College in Baltimore, who exploited the potential of the nonquota visas for students and brought many of his former fellow students at the ILBA to Ner Israel. Several of them were later ordained as rabbis. Among them were Eric Levi, Jacob Wiener, Avraham Zentman, Meir Steinharter, Hans Ney,

"א גרופע דייטשע ישיבה בחורים אין דער באלטימארער ישיבת, נר ישראל."
Jewish American, Family Magazine and Gazette 37, no. 36 (7 July 1939): 1. Yeshiva University, Gottesman Library, Special Collections, courtesy of Shulamith Berger.

Irwin Mayer, Ludwig Fleishman, Naftali Henry Carlebach, Ernst Neumann, Lou Steinhouser, Ludwig Bodenheimer, and Ib Nathan Bamberger, a great-grandson of Seligman Baer Bamberger. Ib Nathan arrived at Ner Israel after his family had managed to survive in Denmark and Sweden. He went on to continue his studies at RIETS of Yeshiva University.[201]

THREE

Flight and Rescue

Rabbis—And a Visa That Saved Lives

The Communal Rabbinate: Uneasiness before 1938

As early as 1934, the American Reform movement had been concerned about the events in Europe, particularly in Germany. A committee of the Central Conference of American Rabbis (CCAR) was preparing to raise funds and support the immigration and placement of German refugees. The committee began to explore what was necessary to create positions for refugee rabbis and how to raise funds for these temporary positions.

The spiritual leaders who fled to the United States at that time were seeking immediate shelter from persecution or trying to avoid imminent arrest, or they were expelled, like Joachim Prinz in mid-1937. Most were seen as political figures in their environment and played a significant role in public. But in 1937, the German Nazi state was still enforcing the emigration of Jews and trying to eliminate any Jewish leadership that generated resilience and inner strength among Jews. Such leadership was a prime target because it protected and guided the weaker members of the community.

Most of the aid these early refugees in the rabbinate received from American institutions came from friendships with leading American rabbis or scholars who either had a close connection with German Jewry and its seminaries or had long shared a common ideological interest, such as Zionism. These friendships facilitated the process of finding employment and obtaining a nonquota visa to enter the United States, as there was no centralized administration or committee to coordinate that process at the time. Rabbis Stephen Wise and Leo Jung had been born in central Europe, had a cultural background there, spoke German, and had studied either in Vienna, where Wise was ordained, or in Berlin, where Jung had attended the Rabbinerseminar. In like fashion, both Zionism and family relationships connected the refugees and their rescuers, but few German refugees were in a position to benefit from these types of support or aid.

Among the first rabbis to read the writing on the wall was Joseph Breuer. He was the spiritual and intellectual leader of the strong and economically well-situated separatist Hirschian Orthodox community in Frankfurt, which was organized as part of the Israelitische Religionsgesellschaft and included an established kehillah and multiple educational and religious institutions that operated independently from the local *Einheitsgemeinde*.

A towering leader of German separatist Orthodoxy, Breuer was the perfect target for the Nazis. He was confronted with libel charges by Nazi authorities as early as the spring of 1933 when, during the purges of communists, his yeshiva was accused of harboring members of this political opposition. Breuer may have felt more exposed to Nazi terror than his colleagues under the protection of the Gemeinde.

Due to these accusations and the growing antisemitic mood in Germany, Joseph Breuer opted for emigration and accepted a position as a rabbi of the Jewish community in Fiume (Rijeka) on the Adriatic coast. The territory had been designated as a free port for landlocked Hungary after the First World War before it was integrated into Italy in 1924. As a result, the city had a small Hungarian-Jewish community that wanted Breuer, a native of Hungary, to become its leader and establish a yeshiva. This destination seemed to fulfill the promises of a temporary home for the Breuer family and the students who followed their rav for rabbinical training. Over time, the rabbi planned to relocate to Palestine, but he was unable to acquire the immigration visa.

Faced with disappointments and insufficient financial resources for establishing the yeshiva and witnessing the rise of a local fascist movement, Breuer realized that Fiume might not live up to its initial promises. The rav decided to return to Frankfurt after consulting with his brother Isaac, who still resided in Germany and was convinced in 1934 that Adolf Hitler and the Nazi Party were a temporary phenomenon and would not cause any serious long-term harm.

Breuer's return to Germany was meant to be temporary. He intended to find a more suitable long-term option for his large family. Perhaps one of the few Jewish refugee families that voluntarily returned to Germany, the Breuers resettled in Frankfurt in 1934, where the rav resumed his duties in the yeshiva and continued to plan for a relocation of the school. Quite similar to the rabbinic leadership of the three seminaries in Berlin and Breslau, Breuer felt he had a responsibility to provide his students with assets that would facilitate their emigration, such as semicha (ordination), letters of recommendation, and information that would help them relocate and continue their professional lives outside Germany. In doing so, Breuer utilized his contacts through the Yeshiva Samson Raphael Hirsch and his former students.

Simon Schwab, the district rabbi of Ichenhausen in rural Bavaria, was another target of Nazi harassment. After studying at the Yeshiva Samson Raphael Hirsch in the Frankfurt secessionist community led by Rav Joseph Breuer, Schwab pursued his rabbinical training as one of the first German-Jewish students who chose to study at east European yeshivot instead of modern Orthodox seminaries or yeshivot. In the 1920s, he studied at the yeshivot of Telz and Mir in Lithuania before returning to Germany to take a position in Darmstadt; he then moved to the rural Bavarian town of Ichenhausen to become the district rabbi.

Enthused by the traditional forms of Jewish learning in eastern Europe and convinced that the Enlightenment and emancipation were not beneficial for Jews, Schwab sought to establish a traditional yeshiva in Ichenhausen, the first of its kind after traditional yeshivot had disappeared from Bavaria in the nineteenth century as a result of the educational requirements for a modern rabbinate. While the yeshiva was being planned and organized between 1933 and 1934, Schwab met with little objection, but once the yeshiva opened its doors in 1934, the local Hitler Youth targeted it with demonstrations, a poster campaign, and threats of violence. The yeshiva closed on its second day when Schwab was forced to send home his students after a warning from the local police chief that the Hitler Youth was planning a pogrom targeting the yeshiva and its students.[1]

In 1935, even before his experience in Ichenhausen, Schwab was considering finding a position in Palestine. He made an exploratory trip there that year and was offered a position by a congregation in Haifa. However, as he stated in an interview with the Research Foundation of Jewish Immigration in 1971, he could not accept the offer because the salary was so low he could never have supported his family. Then, during visits to Switzerland in the summer of 1936, Schwab met Rabbi Leo Jung,[2] spiritual leader of the prestigious Jewish Center in New York and one of the first academically trained Orthodox English-speaking rabbis in America. Jung listened closely to Schwab's reports on the political situation and growing persecution in Germany. After Schwab said that he was thinking about leaving Germany, Jung advised him to contact Dr. Nathan Adler, a distant relative of Schwab and an influential lay member of Congregation Shearith Israel in Baltimore. There, a pulpit had been vacant for three years, and the local Orthodox congregation was searching specifically for a *German* Orthodox rabbi. Schwab quickly contacted the lay leadership of Shearith Israel, submitted his paperwork with recommendations, and was invited to meet the congregation and give several talks in Baltimore.

He received an unexpected offer to take on the pulpit of Shearith Israel late in September 1936, which allowed him to settle with his entire family in Baltimore by the end of 1936.[3] His passport, which had been seized by Nazi authorities after his first trip to the United States, was "graciously" returned to him for the purpose of emigration *only*, which indicated how Jewish emigration was being enforced by the Nazi state at the time.

Among the small number of rabbis who left Germany before 1938 was Joachim Prinz. In his autobiography, he explained how his situation deteriorated under constant Gestapo surveillance and that even a "well-meaning" "Gestapo-friend" could no longer shield him. While the Berlin rabbi had not anticipated *expulsion* as his fate, he claimed that he had prepared for emigration in 1936 during a trip to the United States and had also visited Palestine with his wife in 1934.

While in the United States in 1936, Prinz met with his wife's uncle, a successful investment banker, and his Zionist colleague and friend Stephen Wise, who introduced him to American Judaism and American society. He was ultimately able to secure an affidavit from his wife's relative for a regular quota visa and a contract with the United Palestine Appeal for a lecturing engagement. This would ensure that he could support his family after they arrived in the United States at the end of July 1937.[4] As in Schwab's case, the Nazis had seized Prinz's passport in early 1937 after his return from the United States and explained to the young rabbi that it would be returned *only for the purpose of emigration*.[5]

Max Koppel arrived in the United States shortly after Prinz in August 1937. A graduate of the Jüdisch-Theologisches Seminar in Breslau,[6] Koppel had officiated in Hirschberg, Silesia, and Berlin before his emigration. He traveled to the United States in 1936 to visit relatives and must have obtained an affidavit for emigration from them.[7] To make a living, he first taught German language classes and organized services only on the High Holy Days. By 1938, he was able to launch the Conservative refugee congregation Emes Wozedeck in Washington Heights. He continued to minister to this congregation until his tragic death in 1974 when he was murdered by a burglar in his apartment.[8]

Max Vogelstein, a rabbi from Coblenz, took a different route. He traveled first to Cuba and then to the United States in 1938. While it is unclear if he went to Cuba to obtain a visa, the trip must have facilitated his emigration because he left Germany permanently for the United States in 1940.

Playwright and author Rabbi Emil Moses Cohn held a pulpit in a small secessionist congregation in Berlin-Grunewald that was not part of a Gemeinde. He was a forceful and charismatic man with a strong devotion to culture and the arts and a robust social conscience, which was increasingly linked to his Zionist convictions. A prominent author and artist who spoke to Jews and non-Jews and used sermons, plays, and books to express his powerful messages and progressive humanist thoughts, Cohn stood out among the German-Jewish rabbinate and soon attracted the attention of the Nazi apparatus.

As early as 2 April 1933, he was taken into custody for the first time, albeit briefly, and accused of communist activities and connections. Since these accusations could not be proven, he was allowed to return to his rabbinate and family the same day. As a prominent voice of German Jewry, he continued to be on the radar of the authorities and was again arrested in December 1935 and charged with instigating subversion, treason, and acts against the government. The accusations were derived from a public talk he gave titled "The Commandment of This Hour" (*Das Gebot der Stunde*) in a synagogue in Köpenick, Berlin, which was considered offensive by the police monitoring the event. As a result, Cohn was sent to the Plötzensee prison in Berlin where he was held in investigatory custody until he was released and tried in a special court (*Sondergericht*) in June 1936. This time, his former political engagement on the side of the pro-German separatist movement in the Ruhr area in the early 1920s and a friend's testimony helped him avoid further consequences and ultimately set him free.

However, only weeks later, in early September 1936, he was arrested again, a sign that the intention was to silence him permanently. Accused of spreading "treasonous" content in his Rosh Hashanah sermon in which he quoted and repeated a central passage of the Haggadah stating that God would liberate Jews from outward suppression, he was once again jailed. Cohn was aware that a trial would most likely result in being sent to a concentration camp from which he might never return. Thus he lost all hope of continuing his ministry and cultural activities in Germany and applied for a two-day parole, supposedly to attend his son's upcoming bar mitzvah.

To everyone's astonishment, this parole was granted to him. After having given his blessing to his son, Cohn used this rare opportunity to cross the border into the Netherlands that night and lived in Amsterdam until late in 1938. Cohn no longer saw a future for himself and his family in Europe. At the same time, he was aware of the professional and cultural problems he might encounter as a rabbi and writer in Palestine, and his wife did not want to settle there permanently. So he accepted an invitation from his Zionist friend Stephen Wise and Albert Einstein to give a lecture tour in the United States, which provided entry on a nonquota visa.

From the beginning, he planned to not return to Germany and to use this visa to stay with his family in the United States. In 1938, one of his daughters had married a German refugee in San Francisco and settled there. Cohn spent his first year of emigration, 1939, at the New Synagogue in New York, familiarizing himself with American Judaism and society. In 1940, he changed his immigration status on a visit to Cuba, where he—like many others—took out his first papers and began the process of obtaining citizenship. He was subsequently able to bring over the rest of his family legally.[9] His wife and two other children entered the United States successfully in New York City in 1940.

The Communal Rabbinate: Growing Despair

Memoirs, interviews, and family members' recollections illustrate how difficult it became even for Jewish leadership to deal with social exclusion, economic pressures, and constant surveillance. In 1937 and 1938, these issues greatly concerned congregations and the rabbinate as a profession at the center of a community under duress. The situation affected the health and resilience of the rabbi, his family, and their private life.

Martha Appel, the wife of Rabbi Ernst Appel, who officiated in Dortmund, provides detailed insight into the everyday challenges of the rabbinate and its encounters with Nazi spies and police and explains how Jewish life became almost unbearable. Her recollections illuminate how the policies crushed not only congregants but also the rabbis, who had to perform their duties under almost impossible circumstances after 1935/36.[10]

Confronted with and challenged by humiliation, pain, and misery at home and in the community, Ernst Appel's health deteriorated. His doctor told him to avoid stress and go on a vacation. Still feeling a strong sense of belonging, Ernst did not want to give in to his wife's urgings to leave Germany. When they finally took a short vacation in April 1937, they were surprised by a forced lockdown of the local B'nai B'rith lodge and the confiscation of the financial property of their lodge. Both of them were arrested as leading B'nai B'rith members, which they were. The Appels had long been active in this prominent German-Jewish organization as board members.

As a result of these experiences, Ernst finally gave in to Martha's desire to leave Germany. In May 1937, the family fled to the Netherlands with no notice; from there, they obtained affidavits from relatives and visas to enter the United States in November 1937.[11]

At the local level, the legal situation of Jews in Germany deteriorated in 1937. Wolf Gruner observed this in Berlin, which had become a center for the internal migration of Jews from small towns and villages. People fled to the community because it was large and well organized and could shield its members more effectively than other communities in Germany. But even in Berlin, individuals could not be protected from the arbitrary cruelty of the Nazis, a circumstance that spurred emigration to a hence-unknown degree that year.[12]

The tension between the Jewish community and Nazi authorities became more tangible after the 1936 Olympics in Germany. During 1937, pressures on Jews increased, and it was no accident that Jewish leaders like Schwab, Prinz, and Cohn were forced to leave the country that year. The following year brought a steady expansion of anti-Jewish measures and an increase in Nazi atrocities, which foreshadowed the coming expulsion, removal, and destruction of the Jewish population and increasingly legitimated a new level of brutality against Jews in Germany. The annexation of Austria in March 1938, the cruelty experienced by the Austrian Jewry, and the annexation of the Sudetenland from Czechoslovakia in September 1938 underscored that Germany was expanding its influence and wanted to expel the country's Jews by force.[13]

Violence and intimidation had threatened the physical existence of communities and synagogues long before the pogrom of 9 November 1938[14] and was facilitated and encouraged by the newly passed Law on the Redesign of German Cities (Gesetz über die Neugestaltung deutscher Städte),[15] which legalized the elimination of Jewish facilities from urban spaces in the fall of 1937.

The Communal Rabbinate: Physical Assault

A chain of events began in Munich and Nuremberg, two prominent centers of Nazi activity where local antisemites and party members were encouraged to eradicate any signs of a proud and integrated Jewish presence. These two centers were often referred to as the "capital of the [Nazi] movement" (Munich) and the "city of the Reich party assemblies" (Nuremberg). When the cities became hubs of the Nazi movement and state-enforced antisemitism, Jewish communities experienced an extraordinary degree of chicanery and humiliation.

Therefore, when the main synagogue in Munich—a majestic building representing the integration of the community late in the nineteenth century—had its fiftieth anniversary in 1937, neither the community nor the rabbi felt that it was a time to celebrate.[16] Their magnificent home, which was once Germany's third-largest synagogue and known for its tasteful design, had been labeled an architectural eyesore by the German authorities. Senior rabbi Leo Baerwald feared that any celebrations of the synagogue's anniversary might cause repercussions, so the festivities were toned down and overshadowed by concerns about the future. One year later, on 7 June 1938, Hitler visited the adjacent building housing the local artists' association and declared that the synagogue was an obstacle to inner-city traffic (and inappropriately close to the party headquarters) and ordered that it be removed.[17]

Within less than a month, the synagogue was demolished. The last service witnessed the pain and frustration of a community that felt this indicated a loss that went much further than the removal of a building. The event was attended by a large number of Germany's rabbis, who had gathered in Munich for a meeting of the German rabbinical association and closely followed the destruction of this monument to Jewish presence in Munich.[18]

At almost the same time, on 15 June 1938, the Jewish community of Nuremberg learned that its main synagogue on Hans-Sachs-Platz would suffer the same fate because its "oriental" architecture conflicted with the German architecture of the city and was not in line with the newly passed Law on the Redesign of German Cities.[19]

In Dortmund, the synagogue on Hiltropwall succumbed to the ambitions of the local NSDAP *Kreisleiter* (county leader), who seemed to be copying the measures taken in Bavaria. In an effort to turn Dortmund, rather than Bochum, into the capital of the local *Gau* (regional administration), it was argued that the synagogue on Hiltropwall should be razed to make way for an air raid bunker in the future capital. As a result, the synagogue was torn down, starting on 21 September 1938, leaving the community with no safe place to assemble.[20]

A similar desire to make Kaiserslautern the capital of the local *Gau* determined the fate of its synagogue, which happened to be located along the future main parade avenue, then named Dr.-Frick-Strasse. Once again, at the end of August 1938, an ambitious mayor ordered the destruction of the synagogue. The demolition began, and the building's remnants were finally blasted away on 10 October 1938, less than a month before the pogrom of 9 November 1938.[21]

The events shook all Jewish communities and the rabbinate nationwide, as they proved that Nazism was not aiming for "only" segregation, nor would it respect or even allow separate Jewish spaces. Instead, these acts demonstrated the fragility of the Jewish presence in Germany, how far the Nazis would go, and that the goal was to rid the country of the Jewish population.

Another significant act undermining the status of Jews in Germany was the so-called *Polenaktion* (Polish action), the forced expulsion of Polish nationals residing in Germany to Poland, which began on 27 October 1938. At the time, approximately seventy thousand Jewish-Polish nationals were living permanently in Germany; due to the overtones of exclusion in German citizenship legislation, their naturalization was difficult, if not impossible.[22] They continued to represent a legally vulnerable "foreign" minority, even though many of them were socially well integrated into German society and were long-term residents.

Jewish-Polish nationals were also threatened by antisemitic policies in Poland, specifically a decree passed on 6 October 1938 that required them to have their foreign residence endorsed by Polish authorities by 30 October 1938. If they did not comply, they could lose their Polish citizenship rights. The fact that the Polish government was extremely restrictive with its endorsements left many Polish Jews in Germany in a precarious position regarding their citizenship status and residence and provided a pretext for the Nazis to take action against this minority in Germany.

Starting on 27 October, Nazi authorities raided Jewish communities and arrested some seventeen thousand Polish citizens living in Germany. While this measure did not directly affect German-Jewish nationals, the dramatic expulsion of this many Polish Jews from Germany certainly resonated, especially since the Polish authorities' refusal to admit them to Poland created a humanitarian crisis whereby they were stranded for weeks in a no-man's-land between Germany and Poland near the city of Zbaszyn.

The treatment and broad rejection of these Jews by both countries affected German-Jewish community members indirectly. Many were married to Polish citizens or had relatives in Poland. The German rabbinate and its institutions were shaken. Many of the seminaries' foreign faculty members, students, and graduates were trapped in Zbaszyn for several weeks because they had a Polish passport. These included Hebrew professor Moses Sister of the Hochschule, Abraham Joshua Heschel, and Erwin Zimet.[23]

In mid-1938, the correspondence of American seminaries noted the rising numbers of rabbis from countries affected by Nazism, such as Austria and the so-called Sudetenland, who were seeking assistance for immediate emigration in addition to their colleagues from Germany proper. This included scholars like Professor Kaminka, who had temporarily relocated to Tel Aviv, and Professor Samuel Krauss, both of Vienna.[24] On 17 August 1938, the Orthodox Rabbinical Association of Germany officially turned to Cyrus Adler, begging for help with their members, many of whom were forced to emigrate for several reasons, including the fact that they were increasingly unable to support themselves.[25]

The dramatic course of events drove home the realities the rabbinate encountered as Jewish leadership during those years. While many officiating rabbis were convinced until 1936 or 1937 that their place was with their communities, the timeline of events highlights how the Nazi authorities were increasingly focused on eliminating the rabbinate as the backbone of Jewish communities. Targeted rabbis were those who spoke out fearlessly, who were well known in their larger Jewish and non-Jewish communities, and whose voices were heard widely. Rabbis in small towns and rural communities with usually smaller communities had a much harder time withstanding the pressure of Nazi intimidation and experienced less backing as an excluded minority.

This led to an internal migration to larger cities and especially to Berlin, which was a Jewish hub before the onset of mass emigration. Even during *Kristallnacht*, some rabbis fled from their assigned pulpits as their synagogues were being destroyed and sought shelter or support in the capital or went underground there.[26] Due to the growing number of refugees, more pulpits were vacated and needed new leaders. These positions were filled by new graduates, often barely or hastily ordained. They advanced quickly in their careers by taking positions for which they would have waited for a long time under "normal" conditions. These new responsibilities so early in their careers challenged them accordingly. A sense of urgency accompanied this erosion of Jewish communities, which is well described in a number of autobiographical and biographical recordings.[27]

The events did not go unnoticed by the American Conservative and Orthodox rabbinical seminaries. Cyrus Adler, president of the JTS and Dropsie College, approached Rabbi Simon Greenberg, president of the Rabbinical Assembly, about organizing efforts with the respective Reform and Orthodox rabbinical associations and coordinating their work on behalf of the German refugee rabbis.

It was suggested that Greenberg also work with British Chief Rabbi Joseph Hertz in London. Hertz had created an emergency council to aid religious leaders, students, and scholars seeking shelter in Britain or its dominions, since Britain had become the central European hub for the rescue of Jewish refugees in Europe. Adler reminded his colleague to also consider the availability of rabbinical positions in Britain, the British dominions, and South America and negotiate possible training accordingly.[28] In the United States, Adler alerted the CCAR, the United Synagogue of America, and the Union of Orthodox Rabbis to the crisis and urged them to cooperate with the National Coordinating Committee (NCC) to form a special committee to aid rabbis and religious functionaries in a larger national framework.[29]

The first meeting of the steering committee took place on 13 October 1938, before *Kristallnacht*, with Gustave Falk, Herbert Parzen, Samuel Cohen, Samuel Grinstein, Leo Jung, and Rabbi Jacob Hoffmann as representatives of the

American rabbinate and Samuel Kohs, Cecilia Razovsky, and Robert Dolins as representatives of the NCC, a joint venture of Jewish and non-Jewish organizations to aid refugees from Nazi Germany.[30]

The meeting participants defined the type of person and qualifications they were looking for to coordinate the project. Among other things, the person needed "a good command of Yiddish, German, and English" and should have a unifying personality that could bring the three religious movements together. He did not have to be a rabbi.

Rabbi Jacob Hoffmann, once the Orthodox rabbi of the Frankfurt Gemeinde, was invited to represent the German rabbis. He had just arrived in the United States in 1938 after his expulsion from Germany as an "enemy of the state"[31] and stressed that most of the refugees might be Orthodox rabbis because they encountered the strongest persecution. He proposed to set up a central fund supporting those congregations that were willing to hire a refugee rabbi, especially if they could not finance a position themselves.

All of the committee members voted that Cecilia Razovsky[32] become part of the committee because she had served as the head of the immigration division of the NCC and brought with her a lot of expertise in working with the administration and aiding teachers and rabbis. She agreed to support and advise the rabbis once they entered the United States, approved the establishment of a central fund, and stated that she was already working on securing positions for rabbis in the US.

Leo Jung expressed concern about the placement of the younger, less experienced refugees, who he felt were more like "teachers" than "rabbis." Thus a committee was formed to discuss measures for training these refugees to meet American standards. To explore the options for their placement, Rabbi Herbert Parzen suggested using the reports prepared by students of the JTS on small-town communities where they had temporarily officiated during the High Holidays in areas that could not otherwise afford a full-time spiritual leader.[33]

The next meeting of that committee, which became known as the Special Committee Meeting to Consider Problems of Refugee Jewish Religious Functionaries, took place on 24 October 1938 and addressed how to deal with the growing number of refugees, including rabbis, cantors, and religious teachers, all of whom could apply for a nonquota visa to the United States.[34] Present at this meeting were representatives from each of the American Jewish movements: Rabbi Gustave Falk of the Union of American Hebrew Congregations, Rabbi Samuel M. Cohen of the United Synagogue of America, and Rabbi Samuel Grinstein of the Union of Orthodox Jewish Congregations. Once again, Rabbi Jacob Hoffmann represented the German rabbinate.

At this meeting, Rabbi Herbert Parzen, born in 1896 in Prussian Poland and educated in the United States,[35] was appointed chairman of the special committee. He explained that the duties of his future secretary would be to serve as an intermediary among the NCC, national lay and rabbinical organizations, and the refugee rabbis. This person would also develop positions for the refugees, select suitable applicants for specific congregations, and organize meetings in which the representatives of the three American Judaism movements could interview them. Like the chairman, the secretary was expected to possess a working knowledge of Yiddish and German and have the support of all three religious groups engaged in the project.

In addition, the committee decided that applicants for positions in the United States must be interviewed *in person* by each of the religious movements representatives, attend courses in English and on the requirements and expectations of the American rabbinate, and, if necessary, sign up for additional training to enable them to continue their work in the United States.[36]

Kristallnacht: Emergencies at Home and Abroad

As the special committee was being set up, *Kristallnacht* (Night of Broken Glass) occurred on 9 November 1938 and thus added a new and unexpected urgency to these preparations. One day after the pogrom, Cyrus Adler interviewed thirty-eight-year-old rabbi Alexander Burnstein of Newark, New Jersey, for the position of executive secretary of the special committee. Burnstein was born in the Ukraine but educated in the United States, satisfied the language requirements, and was willing to move to New York City. He was extraordinarily dedicated to this position and quickly developed a scheme to facilitate and structure his work.[37]

Kristallnacht expedited the existing crisis because of the mass atrocities carried out against Jewish businesses, institutions, synagogues, Jewish archives, and rabbis. Although it has been well documented that the event was intended to demonstrate the Nazis' willingness to use violence to rid themselves of all Jewish presence in Germany, it is unclear why there is so little research on the rabbinate as a target in the events of that night. After all, synagogues and communities came alive mainly through the presence and support of the rabbis who actively conducted and led community life, strengthened the perseverance of the congregation, and tried to ameliorate the social, economic, and psychological effects of the Nazi regime on their congregants. In fact, rabbis at the time were maintaining the communities as safe havens for Jewish sociability and centers where Jews in Germany could develop practical solutions to their problems.

The impact of the pogrom on Jewish communities can only be fully understood if that event is also considered as the night that targeted rabbis and thus caused a mass flight of the rabbinate. *Kristallnacht* not only destroyed Jewish communities physically but also lashed out against a large portion of their leadership, crushed community spirit, and thus broke the backbone of Jewish resilience. The destruction of Germany's synagogues, the systematic elimination of Jewish leadership, and the elimination of safe havens and retreats for community and solidarity were soon to facilitate the onset of the Shoah.

The backdrop of the pogrom was the assassination of German diplomat Ernst Eduard vom Rath in Paris by a young Polish Jew, Hershel Grynspan. This act was used as grounds for the massive reaction of the Nazis. Grynspan's parents had been victims of the so-called *Polenaktion* only two weeks earlier, and his act was promoted as one of *Jewish* revenge against German national representatives abroad. Subsequently, the Nazi Party portrayed the pogrom as a spontaneous reaction, a rising up of the *German people* against the "*Jewish* crime."

The pogrom of 9 November resulted in the deaths of over one hundred people in a single night, left many victims injured, and destroyed over seventy-five hundred businesses and most of the synagogues in Germany. Over thirty thousand Jewish men were arrested and "disappeared" in camps and prisons without warrants or any other information on their whereabouts for weeks. Recent research indicates that a large part of the German public, including the official police and fire departments, watched the atrocities performed against Jews, even if fewer Germans than anticipated actively participated. Regardless, the German people did not rise up to stop the carnage the Nazis were inflicting on their neighbors.

The atrocities were carried out with stunning rigidity and brutality and are documented in the archives of the Institut für Zeitgeschichte in Munich, where a database contains information about the postwar trials of Germans who perpetrated crimes against Jews during the Nazi period.[38] This pogrom, finally, was the moment when the rabbinate experienced firsthand how far German society had collapsed. They saw how formerly well-respected Jewish citizens, religious leaders, institutions, and businesses received *no* support from their fellow citizens and witnessed how German society had become a racially *exclusive* community, the social fabric of which held no solidarity with those labeled racially different.

The destruction of the synagogues undermined the community, triggered mass flight, and left those who stayed with little or no protection. Employees of the communities and their families were confronted with ruined facilities and the loss of income. Most of the officiating rabbis were arrested, and many of the advanced seminary students went into hiding or tried to cross the border.[39]

Even for those more fortunate, the situation was dangerous, as in the case of Erich Löwenthal, a young Orthodox rabbi from Berlin who went into hiding during the pogrom. Löwenthal was offered a job by the Swiss congregation Agudass Achim of Zurich just days after the pogrom, on 16 November 1938. But he experienced unexpected challenges: the *Swiss* authorities refused to allow him to cross the heavily guarded border into their country.[40] Only with the assistance of German-born Gisela Warburg Wyzanski, a Zionist leader of the youth organization Aliyah with whom he was friends, was Löwenthal able to reach the United States six months later.[41]

Meanwhile, rabbis were fleeing with few possessions and no plans for long-term stays abroad. If they were lucky, their families could stay behind and arrange for a more organized transfer of their household and departure. Alfred Kober of Cologne described how he was prevented from entering the synagogue to save objects.[42] Almost all rabbis were freed from detention only on the condition that they leave Germany immediately, as Manfred Swarsensky graphically described in his account of his circumstances. On his release from Sachsenhausen concentration camp, Swarsensky had to promise not to share his experiences with anyone in Germany and state in writing that he had entered protective custody voluntarily to escape the "rage of the German people" (*Wut des deutschen Volkes*) and that no harm was done to him.[43]

Rabbi Leo Trepp of Oldenbourg, also imprisoned in Sachsenhausen "with his congregation," explained how shaken he was from his experiences at the camp. While he was imprisoned, his wife contacted the British chief rabbi, whom she happened to know. When Manfred Swarsensky was released and forced to leave Germany within two weeks, the two men obtained temporary visas from the Emergency Council of the Chief Rabbi.[44]

Many rabbis left without their families, relying on their wives to organize visas for them and other family members.

Walter Jacob, the eight-year-old son of Augsburg's rabbi Ernst Jacob, recalls the circumstances of his father's arrest and release in late December 1938 and the responsibilities his mother took on during this crisis. When Ernst Jacob returned from the concentration camp, he was not only shaken by what he had experienced during his arrest in Dachau; he was also forced to leave Germany immediately.

He obtained one of the emergency visas provided by the Emergency Council of the British Chief Rabbinate and left for London. His family stayed in Augsburg until they received permission to leave Germany, a process that involved extensive paperwork and emigration tax payments. Since leaving Germany at the time also meant leaving behind any access to bank accounts and resources, they required time to plan their departure and did not leave to reunite with Ernest in London until the spring of 1939.

The following nine months in England were difficult. Unsettled, in transit, foreign, and unable to make a living due to their status as refugees, the family used the time to learn the English language. Once their immigration number came up, they embarked on a ship to New York, where they spent their first months on Long Island for the orientation phase of their new life in the United States.

While Jacob's autobiography is not very specific about the visa the family obtained, they likely received a regular quota visa because he recalls that they had to wait until their number "came up" late in 1939 and mentions a relative who met the family on arrival, an indication that the immigration was facilitated by the affidavits of family members who were already in the United States.[45]

Rabbi Hans Enoch Kronheim from Bielefeld was in the United States when the pogrom occurred and was informed by his wife, Senta, to stay in America. Kronheim was forced to quickly find a position and make preparations for his wife and two daughters, who finally arrived in Jamestown, New York, in June 1939 with the aid of the United Synagogue of America.[46]

Rabbis caught during the pogrom experienced horrific humiliation and loss. In the Silesian town of Oppeln (Opole), Rabbi Hans Hirschberg was forced by Nazi storm troopers to set his own synagogue on fire that night—a traumatic experience.[47]

Emotional trauma resonated in the memories of many rabbis and their children. Ismar Schorsch underscored this when discussing his father Emil's experience of witnessing the complete destruction of his synagogue in Hanover.[48]

Jewish schools, seminaries, and yeshivot were closing, including the Samson Raphael Hirsch Yeshiva in Frankfurt am Main, where Rav Joseph Breuer had been taken into custody on the morning of November 10 and put in a holding center called the Festhalle in Frankfurt. Here the victims of the pogrom were herded together to await further action. The fifty-six-year-old rav was unexpectedly fortunate because one of the guards, a SA officer (storm trooper), knew him and shouted that he was to step forward as a man over age sixty. Subsequently, Breuer joined the group of seniors who were not deported to Buchenwald or Dachau but were ultimately released, which enabled Breuer to relocate with his children Jacob, Samson, and Meta to Antwerp where his daughter Hanna Schwalbe lived. Once his wife had hastily made travel arrangements for herself and her remaining children Edith and Sophie, the family was reunited.[49]

From Antwerp, the Breuers immigrated to New York City with all their underage children; the older children could not be included in their father's nonquota visa. The Breuer family received assistance from a former student of the Breuer Yeshiva, Jacob A. Samuel, who had relocated to the United States and promised to help Breuer get an affidavit. On 28 January 1939, the family traveled by ship to Le Havre, France, and turned their backs on Europe. In their possession was a nonquota visa obtained through Yeshiva University, where Samuel had approached its president, Bernard Revel, for assistance.[50]

Emil Fackenheim describes in his autobiography how he found the Hochschule closed on the morning of 10 November 1938. After returning to his family's home, where he learned that his father had been imprisoned, he was arrested and taken to Sachsenhausen. He reports that he experienced intense humiliation in Sachsenhausen until he was released on 8 February 1939. The Gestapo had made clear to him that his choice was to either leave Germany in six weeks or return to Sachsenhausen.[51]

Some German rabbis, like the Orthodox Hartwig Naphtali Carlebach, fled to eastern Europe to look for solidarity and safe haven among east European colleagues in traditional yeshivot, such as the Yeshiva Mir. But the decision to go east often put them in an even worse situation once the Nazis started the Second World War in 1939. While Carlebach managed to escape to the United States from Lithuania in 1939, others were unable to leave before the Nazi invasion and could only escape east, if at all, via Shanghai. From there, some reached the United States and other countries after 1945.[52]

In Wilhelm Weinberg's case, fleeing eastward from Nazism was just a prelude to an extremely difficult and dangerous flight that covered nearly the entire globe. After staying in several countries in eastern Europe, he crossed into the Soviet Union and ultimately into central Asia (Kyrgyzstan), where he survived the Shoah under communism while hiding the fact that he was an ordained rabbi.

Weinberg was born on 3 April 1901, in Dolina, Galicia, and arrived in Berlin to study for the rabbinate at the Hochschule in 1932. It might have been his political activism in the Zionist movement that got the attention of the Nazi Party because he soon ran into serious trouble with the police. After a trip to Zurich in June 1935, he was harassed, arrested, and sentenced to one year and nine months for foreign currency violations. When he was released from prison, he left the country and returned to Austria, where he received his ordination from the Hochschule in absentia. This is evidence that the faculty there did their best to give students the most support possible, even under almost impossible circumstances.

Only after 1945 could Weinberg finally return to the German-speaking part of central Europe, where he used to feel at home. He joined the flow of so-called Displaced Persons and ministered to them in the American occupation zone in Hallein near Salzburg and in Frankfurt am Main, where he served as the first postwar chief rabbi of Hesse until he left Europe for the United States in 1951.[53]

Apparently, rabbis with a foreign citizenship, such as the Romanian Max Nussbaum, were barely noticed and could stay longer in Germany for that reason. Nussbaum was neither arrested nor bothered during the pogrom, and he left Berlin with his wife only in 1940.[54]

This experience was confirmed by Salamon Faber, an advanced student at the Jüdisch-Theologisches Seminar in Breslau, who witnessed the pogrom and the closing of the seminary in that city. He told his son Eli Faber that he was not touched because of his foreign citizenship and could actually assist his fellow German students and professors at the seminary.[55]

While the American rabbinate was hastily preparing to deal with the emergency in the German rabbinate, the mass exodus was met with reservations by the German-Jewish leadership. Leo Baeck, who had supported the emigration of young rabbis, stated that he had expected different behavior from his mature colleagues.

In an April 1939 letter to Ismar Elbogen, he explained that the Hochschule had resumed its work as well as it could under the circumstances. The goal, he stressed, was to conclude "in honor." To achieve that, the Hochschule sought ways and means to publish completed scholarly works, provide students with diplomas, and carry on with honorable conduct and attitude in this already doomed enterprise. Baeck bitterly criticized the majority of the rabbis, claiming that they had not only failed their duty but that many of them had just disappeared after *Kristallnacht* or their imprisonment afterward. In his eyes, only a very few had demonstrated leadership and actually returned to their communities, as did Manfred Swarsensky and Max Dienemann.[56]

The Work of the Committee on Refugee Jewish Ministers of the NCC

The pogrom directly affected the work of the newly founded Committee on Refugee Jewish Ministers (CRJM), which, under the developing emergency conditions and only four weeks in office, changed its original goal of finding permanent positions in the American rabbinate for refugee rabbis to creating short-term positions. This would save lives and give German colleagues time to acclimate to the American rabbinate.

Alexander Burnstein, executive secretary of the CRJM, petitioned for this change of strategy because he was receiving "dozens and dozens of pleas and cablegrams from the very best Rabbis, who are still abroad and most of whom, seemed to be jailed in concentration camps."[57]

As a solution, Burnstein proposed joining with British Chief Rabbi Joseph Hertz, who, in close proximity to Nazi Germany, was confronted with the plight of German Jewry, particularly German rabbis. Having set up an Emergency Council of the Chief Rabbi, Hertz's office worked with the Central British Fund for German Jewry, the largest central aid organization on behalf of German Jewry, based in London. Directly confronted with the rising flood of refugees from Germany, the council developed a plan with the British Home Office to offer German refugee rabbis a special visa that would provide them with temporary shelter in Britain for one year.

These emergency visas allowed refugees to find long-term homes in areas such as the United States or the British dominions. Burnstein suggested that American Jewry approach the American government and immigration authorities to reach a similar deal to free Jewish prisoners from Nazi concentration camps, a suggestion that never materialized because the US immigration bureaucracy was growing increasingly reluctant to issue visas as the crisis expanded.[58]

Nevertheless, Burnstein drummed up solidarity among his American colleagues. He persuaded them to use their influence and prestige inside and outside their congregations in support of hiring refugee rabbis and explaining to their congregations that this support would not only free these men from concentration camps but would also allow them to receive a special nonquota visa to enter the United States. American rabbis were to spread this information among smaller congregations that might not have a permanent rabbi but would hire a refugee under the circumstances.

An attached survey form discussed what type of minister, cantor, ritual butcher, choir leader, and organist could be hired; which funds were available in the congregations to support the project; and in what ways the special committee could help them take responsibility for a refugee from Germany.[59] The importance and success of this grassroots support are evident in the fact that by mid-January 1939, the British Chief Rabbi's Religious Emergency Fund had succeeded in providing emergency visas for 112 rabbis and teachers, 26 cantors and ritual butchers, and 130 yeshivot students, many of whom were waiting to settle permanently in the United States after an interim stay in Britain.[60]

Under pressure to function and produce positions for refugee rabbis, the American committee adapted its structure and changed its name to the CRJM.

To enable the committee to respond more quickly to problems and requests, an executive committee was created consisting of Dr. David de Sola Pool, Dr. Benedict Glazer, Rabbi Gustave Falk, Rabbi Samuel M. Cohen, Rabbi Samuel Grinstein, Cecilia Razovsky, and Dr. S. C. Kohs. Rabbi Dr. David de Sola Pool, president of the Synagogue Council, presided over the new executive committee as chairman. This new committee was to support Alexander Burnstein in his ongoing business. Efficiency and a systematic approach were Burnstein's main concerns amid the ongoing crisis. He dedicated a great deal of his time to confer with several major leaders of American Jewry on how to organize the exchange of information on opening pulpits between congregations and the executive committee, which expanded to include Dr. Julian Morgenstern, Dr. Felix A. Levy, Rabbi Max Currik, Dr. Cyrus Adler, Rabbi Simon Greenberg, and Dr. Leo Jung.

Based on the first exchanges and placements, Burnstein decided to start working with rabbis who were already in the United States and gather information about their experience and needs to help them find positions. By systematically recording this data, he gained a better understanding of their training, backgrounds, and qualifications. To classify the refugees' experience and knowledge for placement purposes, Burnstein recommended establishing examining boards to rate their qualifications. In addition, he suggested setting up a working relationship with the appropriate rabbinic organizations to explore what these professional organizations might offer to this special group of job seekers.

The significance of his work is proven by the numbers he listed in his correspondence. By 16 January 1939, he had interviewed 52 candidates, and there were "at least 150" newly arrived cantors, teachers, shohetim, rabbis, mohelim, and organists. Their information was collected on registration cards and distributed to the examining board before the arrivals were interviewed by the board and classified for specific positions. At this time, Burnstein made 13 placements, received 120 responses from congregations, was in the process of confirming 62 additional positions, and was heading the negotiations for an additional 14 openings in congregations.[61]

Across the United States, the CRJM executive committee worked with communities, congregations, and rabbinical associations as well as a nationwide network of local committees of the NCC for Aid to Refugees and Emigrants Coming from Germany.

The NCC was a national nondenominational organization, initiated in 1934 by the League of Nations High Commissioner for Refugees and headed by Professor Joseph Perkins Chamberlain. A number of leading Jewish organizations were represented, including the National Council of Jewish Women, the Jewish Social Service Association of New York City, and the Young Men's Hebrew Employment Service. Non-Jewish groups were represented as well, such as the International Migration Service and the Emanuel Federated Employment Service.[62] The NCC quickly mobilized greater support among Jewish and non-Jewish organizations and arranged for the placement of many refugees. The committee tried to facilitate immigration for three hundred refugee rabbis for whom Jews in Britain had managed to secure temporary emergency visas there.

Burnstein knew that the refugees depended on his aid because Jewish organizational life had largely broken down in Germany. He felt it was his responsibility to bring over as many of these colleagues of the approximately 650 synagogues of Germany at the time.[63] Conscious of the obligations of his position and the centrality of the American effort to aid their German colleagues, Burnstein demonstrated great empathy for these refugees, their situation, and their plight. Their experiences troubled him personally and prevented him from sleeping at night, a circumstance he shared with Cyrus Adler.[64] Feeling strongly for the German refugees, he stressed that his task was well worth the effort based on what the German Jewry was experiencing.[65] Burnstein's personal correspondence with Cyrus Adler illuminates how emotionally involved in the project that senior leader of the American Jewry was as well and how much he cared about every detail Burnstein reported to him.[66]

On 20 February 1939, Burnstein shared his first success by presenting a list of twenty-three placements he had arranged for German rabbis; he then continued to submit similar lists on a regular basis.[67] He may have gotten some information on available positions from lists annually prepared and circulated by the United Synagogue of America, which provided detailed information on congregations. This was one way the United Synagogue helped congregations meet their needs and solve such problems as hiring a rabbi.[68] By the beginning of 1939, the circle of refugees was widening as Burnstein's letters reveal: Rabbi Solomon Feuerstein of Prague, Czechoslovakia, and Dr. Kalman Friedmann, former chief rabbi of Florence, Italy, also approached the committee as they began to feel the Nazi influence in their areas.[69]

While small congregations welcomed the opportunity to hire a rabbi under Burnstein's program but often lacked the necessary funds, the more prominent and wealthy congregations, such as the well-known Reform Temple Emanu-El in New York, were hesitant to hire a refugee from Germany for fear of the resistance they could face among the socially exclusive lay membership. Burnstein's office managed both problems by, on the one hand, providing the necessary funds to congregations that needed financial support to hire a refugee and, on the other, by actively promoting the acceptance of refugees among other prominent Reform congregations, such as those led by Abba Hillel Silver in Cleveland or Louis Mann in Chicago, who had already started to create positions for refugees.[70]

Besides challenges among the Jewish communities, the rescue efforts faced administrative resistance in the State Department, even though or precisely because this type of immigration was a privilege and an exception to the rule, which was frequently underscored in how these applications were processed.

The case of Eugene Horovitz, who was trapped in Britain on a temporary visa, demonstrates how paper walls often blocked the way of several rabbis. Having found a position in a small congregation in Wilkes-Barre, Pennsylvania, with the committee's assistance, Horovitz was denied the nonquota visa because the congregation members could not explain why they wanted to hire a rabbi at that time and why they could not continue meeting without a rabbi as before.

Edward S. Maney, the American consul in charge, demanded documentation on the congregation's financial ability to properly support a rabbi and a statement that the rabbi would be filling a need, as indicated, for example, by a growing membership or the recent resignation of another rabbi.[71] Horovitz's case was not the only one in which consular staff created problems, as few of the rabbis who had received a placement based on Burnstein's lists were actually hired for the positions. These lists and available personal recollections and stories document instead that after the initial appointment, the visa process posed a significant challenge for refugees. Even though the nonquota visa provided a loophole, the visa process included plenty of bureaucratic ways for refugees to fail.

Other hurdles for the placement and the successful transition into American Jewry were the language barrier and a lack of familiarity with American Jewish congregations and the American rabbinate. The modern rabbi was expected to present a meaningful and articulate sermon at the pulpit, a task that few of the refugees were able to master upon arrival. Many had barely any command of English.

Therefore, an essential tool for the new arrivals from Germany was the English-language courses at the Teacher's College of Columbia University, organized by the CRJM. At the same location, the committee prepared lectures on the challenges and expectations the refugees would encounter in American Judaism. The speakers were prominent American rabbis such as Leo Jung, Max Arzt, Benedict Glazer, and David de Sola Pool.[72]

Besides rabbinical associations, religious movements, and seminaries, the CRJM continued to work with the NCC and its mostly Jewish member organizations. The NCC's main goal was to remove as many refugees as possible from the New York area to prevent a concentration of refugees that might trigger anti-Jewish sentiments.

A key personality in setting up efficient aid for the refugees continued to be Cecilia Razovsky. She mobilized Jewish organizations and groups to support and work with the new arrivals in their local chapters beyond the service of merely providing general information. Some of these organizations included the National Council of Jewish Women, HIAS, B'nai B'rith, and the Zionist Organization of America. They joined forces to help the new arrivals and their families learn English, find a job, locate an apartment, and deal with their visa situation. Those with temporary visas especially depended on informed assistance to avoid deportation to Germany. Others were trying to bring over family members from Europe or elsewhere. Razovsky served as an experienced and engaged liaison to the State Department and traveled to Washington from New York City to settle cases on an almost weekly basis.

From 1938 on, the exclusively Jewish-sponsored National Coordinating Committee Fund supported the work of Jewish organizations dealing solely with the overwhelming numbers of new refugees and spent over $813,000 that year for that purpose. This was just the beginning of a complete reorganization of the efforts on behalf of refugees, and it launched the replacement of the NCC with the newly founded National Refugee Service (NRS), a Jewish aid organization that was created to handle the ever-growing emergency. The NRS continued to support the rising numbers of refugees from Germany, Austria, and parts of Czechoslovakia until the flow ebbed in the fall of 1941 when the expansion of the Second World War and the ramifications of the Holocaust stopped emigration from central Europe for the duration of the war. When the war ended in 1945, the NRS was challenged by the next wave of immigrants, displaced persons, the refugees from war-torn countries in eastern Europe.[73]

FOUR

The Refugees' First Years in the United States

Employment, Settlement, Congregations, and the Encounter with American Society and American Judaism

While emigration saved the lives of rabbis and scholars from Germany, their arrivals and early years in the United States were not necessarily celebratory. They experienced a difficult phase of transition and adaptation while seeking a place in both American society and American Judaism, and they encountered a new global Jewish context in which Europe, the former center of their lives, no longer played much of a role. Their efforts to adapt and reconstruct their lives were accompanied by worries about what they had left behind: their loved ones, ties to their old and increasingly dispersed communities, the course of the Second World War, and the increasingly dire information about the fate of Europe's Jews.

While some of the rabbis enjoyed private or institutional support upon their arrival, many came to the United States with unrealistic expectations of life in general and of their profession and American Jewish religious life in particular. They had to deal with a loss of status, community, and cultural context. An essential part of the refugees' new beginnings was *becoming American* in a legal sense. They needed to fix the loss of citizenship and nationality caused by Nazi racism, a humiliation they encountered in several stages starting in 1933. Since being stateless meant being vulnerable, with no protection of a nation or consular services and with limited agency as aliens in the United States, refugees needed to become American citizens to build a future, find opportunities, and resume careers or begin new ones.

Age, social capital, and access to professional networks helped to determine how quickly German refugee rabbis felt settled in the United States, as did their ability to connect with American Jews, an American congregation, and the American rabbinate. Their success in these endeavors depended on *when* the refugees experienced displacement and *how* they negotiated their complex transnational identities, backgrounds, skills, and knowledge with the contemporary needs, trends, and challenges of American Judaism.

The Challenges of Cultural Integration: Rabbinical Students and American Seminaries

The youngest of the refugees, the rabbinical students, initially reacted to the religious forms of American Jewry with awe, as Wolli Kaelter, W. Gunther Plaut, and Richard Damashek state in their publications. When Kaelter, Plaut, Alfred Wolf, Leo Lichtenberg, and Herman Schaalman arrived in Cincinnati, they were the only ones wearing head coverings, and they experienced a broad rejection of Zionism and a strong commitment to ethical universalism inside and outside the synagogue.[1] The splendor of the newly built campus of the Hebrew Union College (HUC) in Cincinnati impressed them. It differed substantially from the simple and functional building of the Hochschule and signaled a high degree of social acceptance and pride.

Their first meeting with college president Julian Morgenstern confused them not only because it took place in the college gym—which established an unexpected dedication of a professor to athletics—but also because Morgenstern was naked and wet when he stepped out of the pool to greet them with no reservations whatsoever. The students were then invited to Nelson Glueck's home, where they were offered bacon and eggs for breakfast, a dish that was customary at HUC but shocking for the guests from Berlin.[2]

Both the scholars and American rabbis at this college appeared to be shockingly different from what the students were accustomed to. Rabbi David Philipson told them to *never* wear hats or yarmulkes for services or elsewhere, a custom they were reluctant to give up because it was part of their Jewish identities. Rabbi Mort Cohen and particularly his wife, Sally, overwhelmed them with their style and behavior because both the rabbi and rebbetzin differed from their European counterparts, who had a spiritual and unpretentious appearance. Cohen was described by Kaelter as having a physique and appearance resembling that of Mexican American film star Ramon Novarro, which departed from the outward appearance of a modest scholar. Sally had an even greater effect on the group: they had never seen a rebbetzin (wife of a rabbi) who drove a car, let alone on the Sabbath, which is what she did when she picked them up for services. Kaelter described Sally Cohen and their trip to the synagogue as a rebbetzin beyond everything he had ever experienced, as "a buxom blonde, who looked like Jean Harlow and invited us to her lovely car for a ride to the temple. . . . The radio was blaring in her car."[3]

Plaut described the encounter in his autobiography, relating the awe the boys felt when they met Sally. They came to understand that in America, the wives of rabbis could be profoundly different from the efficient and unassuming rebbetzin they knew in Germany.[4]

> Ah America, what a great, marvelous and frightening land you are! How many surprises you harbor! I had seen rabbis' wives before, but none of them looked remotely like Sally. Furthermore, I did not know a single rabbi who owned a car, let alone a rebbitzin [sic!] who would drive one. Last but not least, this was Sabbath and none of us rode on the day of rest. Whatever our background, it was simply not done at the Hochschule.
> Sally discerned our embarrassment. "When in Rome, do as the Romans do," she quoted—and what was there left for us, but to follow her?[5]

The band of five stood out as "Germans"[6] among the student body of HUC during the late 1930s, and they all belonged to the Gate Club, a German refugee club in Cincinnati.[7] Their stories and the recollections of Joshua Haberman and Nathan Peter Levinson underscore that their transition into student life at HUC and the University of Cincinnati went smoothly and was ultimately successful, despite setbacks like comments on their comparatively "Orthodox" religious practices and the academic expectations they had to fulfill.[8]

They learned English quickly during their studies, though they might have struggled with a German accent for a while. They worried about their families abroad, but Kaelter was able to bring over his mother and brother, and Plaut helped his brother Walter and his parents immigrate to the United States.[9]

Herman Schaalman was reunited with his family in the United States, and Joshua Haberman welcomed his parents in 1940 in New York, two years after his sister had joined him and found a job in Cincinnati with HUC's support.

The college also assisted and at least partially advised the other students in the naturalization process and helped them sponsor the rescue of close relatives. Friendships with fellow students and their families generated empathy and active support. HUC student Lou Silberman befriended "the Germans"—perhaps due to curiosity about his own German background—and talked his family into providing an affidavit of support for Kaelter's naturalization.[10]

The college family in Cincinnati provided a new and lifelong support system for the newcomers because the social fabric in and around HUC was highly inclusive and very supportive. Academically, the refugee students worked hard and were soon successful. Plaut, the oldest, graduated and entered the American rabbinate in 1939. His fellow students from Berlin followed him soon after.

After a trip to Cuba in the summer of 1938 to take out first papers for citizenship,[11] Plaut prepared for his ordination to the American rabbinate. At that time, he took another step that reinforced his sense of belonging in the United States: he fell in love. His serious romance with a young American woman, Elizabeth Strauss, a native of Cincinnati, led to their marriage in 1938 and a family of his own.[12]

The other students soon followed in his footsteps: Kaelter married Sarah Shapiro in 1938, Schaalman wed Lotte Stern in 1941, Wolf took Miriam Jean Office as his wife in 1940, and Lichtenberg tied the knot with Hilde Levor in 1939. Finding a spouse and starting a family positively affected their lives, especially if they were also able to reunite with some members of their German families. Their early arrival as well as the institutional and personal support they received from HUC in the process of immigration were key to the successful rescue of their family members.

Not everyone enjoyed the same advantages. The group's teacher, Abraham Joshua Heschel, arrived in Cincinnati in March 1940 after a difficult flight via London. He entered the country on a visitor's visa that did not allow him to sponsor family members. His status could not be changed as quickly as was necessary. Heschel learned in 1943 that his mother and sister had been killed in the Warsaw Ghetto, and he suffered greatly from that news.[13]

Both the students' recollections and the correspondence on their admission and arrival underscore that their professors, especially Julian Morgenstern, felt a special responsibility for the new arrivals from Germany. Morgenstern and other faculty members had lived in Berlin or knew the students' fathers. Some professors were obliged to the young men based on the recommendation of their former rector, Ismar Elbogen. Others simply felt a deep connection to the young men's German background and great sympathy for them.

HUC in Cincinnati advocated commitment to tradition and modern Judaism, both in scholarly interests and in private relationships between the refugees and their American hosts and counterparts. The unique German history of Cincinnati as a city and the friendly openness of the American Midwest may have added to the climate of familial acceptance and integration, something that did not exist in the other two rabbinical seminaries in New York.[14]

A closer look at their research projects and rabbinical theses shows that these refugees proudly studied topics related to the nineteenth-century history of the German Reform movement, an area in which their fluency in German and background in European history helped them excel.[15] They took on these topics not to avoid reading English literature but because they were interested in the common roots of the American Reform movement and liberal Judaism in Germany. This was acknowledged and valued in Cincinnati, and they were encouraged to make these academic contributions as an expression of being part of the extended family.[16]

For the students, this was an important signal. It highlighted that modern Judaism, even though it had different features and forms in the United States, was also welcomed and practiced in this country, and they could feel that same welcome and sense of belonging in America with their Jewish identities intact. This inclusiveness may also have been nurtured by their course of study and research, in which the recognition of a common past and the pursuit of a joint approach to the study of Judaism played a role. Also important was the presence of their German (refugee) professors, many of whom had also transferred to Cincinnati.

The presence and reputation of the German refugee scholars on campus provided a special context to the students who—as this fact demonstrated—did not come from the periphery of modern Judaism but from its center in the heart of Europe. Even though they had left this world behind and might have been seen as greenhorns, their origins gave them prestige, standing, and distinction in this new country. Their integration benefited from this situation, as did their motivation to take advantage of the opportunities they received as a lucky minority rescued from the Shoah. Fully aware that they were witnessing the end of an era and were an integral part of the process, they noted that they also had a future in American Judaism, which enhanced their acculturation.

In the 1950s and 1960s, HUC welcomed many German refugee students to its growing campus system. In 1950, a second campus was created in New York City through the merger with Stephen Wise's Jewish Institute of Religion, and in 1954, the college launched a campus in Los Angeles. In all of these institutions, "the second generation" made a lasting impact and often attended several campuses during their academic careers.

In Cincinnati, many of the young men in this group were part of the student body from the 1930s to the 1960s. Their numbers continued to grow and provided the college with a strong German-Jewish flavor. Among those who attended the Cincinnati campus were Herman Schaalman, Alfred Wolf, Wolli Kaelter, Alfred Lichtenberg, W. Gunther Plaut, Walter Plaut, Joshua Haberman, Ernst Lorge, Nathan Peter Levinson (Lewinsky), Alexander Schindler, Jakob Petuchowski, Joseph Asher (Ansbacher), Steven Schwarzschild, Alfred Gottschalk, Albert Friedlander (Friedländer), Bernhard N. Cohn, Walter Jacob, Robert Lehman, Ralph Kingsley (Kissinger), Gustav Buchdahl, and Frank Fisher (Fischer). Bernhard Cohn and Alfred Gottschalk also studied on the

New York campus, and Gottschalk and Hillel Cohn stayed on the Los Angeles campus of HUC, which housed twenty-three students. While some of them immigrated with their parents, others were rescued by family members (such as Walter Plaut, whose older brother W. Gunther was studying at HUC) or international student organizations (such as Ernst Lorge), or they were saved by international aid organizations (such as Jakob Petuchowski).

Petuchowski did not arrive in the United States until after the war. He had been saved by a *Kindertransport* ("children's transport") and had spent the war and immediate postwar years in Britain, where he studied with Leo Baeck and Arthur Löwenstamm in London. Coming from an Orthodox family with a long lineage of rabbis and comfortable in a German-Jewish milieu, he came to the United States in October 1948 to study at HUC for the rabbinate. He was ordained in 1952 and obtained a doctorate at the college in 1956. For several years after his ordination, he served as a rabbi. After completing his dissertation, he was offered a position as a professor of rabbinics (later theology and liturgy, then Christian-Jewish relations) at HUC in Cincinnati, where he joined the growing number of German-Jewish faculty members and was known for his dedication to scholarship in theology and Christian-Jewish relations.

Like Petuchowski, Joseph Asher came from an Orthodox background and arrived in the United States after the war. He had fled with his mother and father, Jonas Ansbacher, an Orthodox rabbi trained at the Breuer Yeshiva, to Britain. There he continued his religious education at the Orthodox Tree of Life Yeshiva and received his ordination in 1940. Interned to Australia for the duration of the war, he joined the Australian Forces, where he served as military chaplain. As in Petuchowski's case, Asher's encounter with Baeck during a visit to see his family in the immediate postwar years in Britain likely sparked his interest in modern Judaism and motivated him to move to the United States with his Australian wife, Fae, in 1947 and attend HUC.

There, he familiarized himself with Reform Judaism and stayed until 1948, when he started taking on small pulpits in the United States. For a long time, he and Fae felt a sense of displacement after the family's travels and dispersion on an almost global scale.[17] They were not sure where they belonged or where they should put down roots, and they even considered going back to Australia.

Most of the young men in this second generation had much easier access to American Judaism, the American congregation, the English language, and the mentality of the congregants. Growing up in American public schools, attending British or American universities, or officiating in the Australian Army, they were fluent in English at the beginning of their academic careers, or they learned it during their studies at the seminaries. Although they all may have stood out as "Germans" due to their background and culture, they mastered cultural assimilation and the transition into American Jewry.

The seminaries were an essential transmission belt of their cultural transformation and a door opener for their careers. Here they were introduced to American academic and professional culture, taught the knowledge and skills needed in the American rabbinate, and given access to social capital, group belonging, and lasting friendships, all of which were essential for building a successful future in the American rabbinate. Some of them, like Asher, Petuchowski, and Jacob, came from families with a long-standing tradition in the rabbinate and were motivated to continue this tradition. Others may have been attracted by an affordable graduate education in an institution where their history and background as Jews were known and respected and where they could immerse themselves in American Judaism—not as Germans or Americans but as Jews.

Even though they were working intensely on their American careers, these young men upheld the ethos of what it meant to enter the rabbinate in Germany. This included a strong identification with *Wissenschaft*, which was often reflected in their interest in teaching at colleges and universities. Their knowledge of Judaism was often deeper than that of their fellow students due to their European or family background, where such knowledge was cultivated and passed on to the next generation from an early age. But they were also shaped by the worldly and sometimes extremely progressive outlook that distinguished German Jewry. This also affected their rabbinate and their decision to earn a doctorate, which was a prerequisite to enter the rabbinate at German seminaries but was not necessary for a career as an American rabbi.

At HUC, more than at other colleges, this group's presence in and impact on the religious movement, the college, and the rabbinical organization resonated in a unique way, as their future careers demonstrated. At HUC, their cultural differences and hybridity did not make them outsiders; rather, they were a group with an *essential* role and impact, a remnant of the historical relationship the college and the Reform movement had with their center in Germany. Driven by a youthful desire to understand their history, fate, and survival, many of these young students found leadership positions in American Judaism and pondered the future of modern Judaism in its new American home.

Cultural Encounters and Scholarship at the American Rabbinical Schools

The experiences of acceptance and integration of older German refugee scholars on campus were quite different from those of the younger students. By 1941, there were ten German refugee professors on campus: Samuel Atlas, Abraham Joshua Heschel, Michael Wilensky, Eugen Taeubler, Julius Lewy, Alexander Guttmann, Isaiah Sonne, Eric Werner, Franz Landsberger, and Franz Rosenthal, in addition to historian Selma Stern-Taeubler, who worked in the American Jewish Archives.

While the students acclimated fairly quickly to the differences between the academic cultures, between the Hochschule and HUC, and between liberal Judaism and Reform Judaism, the German refugee scholars struggled with the integration process and Americanization. Their lack of proficiency in English was much harder on them than it was for the students, whose youth helped them learn the language more quickly and easily. These men found their status as professors and scholarly role models undermined by being unable to teach efficiently or find the right words. Even worse, some of them, such as Michael Wilensky, were mocked for their inability to express themselves properly.[18]

The refugee scholars knew that the college had not only saved their lives but also welcomed them, however, they were frustrated by Americans' indifference to the Second World War and the fate of Jews in central Europe, an issue of special concern to them that isolated them from American society.[19]

Except for Heschel and Rosenthal, the refugee scholars had held advanced, if not eminent positions in Germany. In America, their role was reduced to that of a visiting professor, limited in tenure and compensation. In fact, the refugees did not even officially belong to HUC faculty as long as they held temporary contracts, which meant that they were not allowed to attend faculty meetings or contribute to faculty decisions. This painful and degrading experience underscored the degree to which their careers had been affected.[20]

Their identities never completely changed; they were scholars and teachers at home in the German university system, highly immersed in Wissenschaft, and much less concerned about skillful teaching. In ongoing complaints against the college's standards, they expressed their frustrations with a student body from the American South and Midwest that was much younger, less academically advanced, and deficiently educated in Judaism.[21] Many students from Germany could only be admitted to study in Cincinnati, instead of at the Jewish Theological Seminary (JTS) in New York, because they did not have a BA degree. This fact proves that their criticism reflected two sides of the same coin and may have saved the lives of a number of students from Germany.

The "chalk and talk" teaching methods at HUC were antiquated, stiff, and unappealing to many of the students.[22] As Wolli Kaelter recalled, "Subjects, rather than students were taught."[23] This caused frustration among students and graduates who complained that they were not properly prepared for their role as rabbis in the communities. Except for Samuel Cohon, a professor of theology, none of the faculty members had ever held a pulpit. Yet it would be wrong to blame the situation exclusively on the refugee scholars because all students, including the refugees, complained bitterly about the situation. It is possible that the refugee students were particularly aware of the problem because they had been instructed in practical rabbinics in the German seminaries.

The presence of the German refugee scholars, however, added to the strong *scholarly* ambitions of the college and its identity as a research college rather than a place to educate rabbis. The recruitment of the refugees used funds that could have gone toward younger colleagues who might have taught practical rabbinics or changed the relationship between students and faculty as a German *Seminarrabbiner* (seminary rabbi) would have done. A *Seminarrabbiner* was typically a young faculty member with experience as a rabbi and scholar who ministered to the student body and served as the students' mentor.[24] This triggered a college-wide discussion in 1943 on the value of more *practical* rather than *scholarly* training in HUC's curriculum, and it was decided to hire someone who could serve as a mentor and confidant to the student body, ease the concerns about practical preparations for leadership in Jewish communities, and inspire students to want to teach and live Judaism.[25]

Many of the refugees were accustomed to living and working in large urban centers in Berlin or other European cities, so acclimating to Cincinnati was difficult. Samuel Atlas and his wife spent a lot of time in New York City.

Abraham Joshua Heschel was estranged from both American Reform Judaism and Cincinnati. The city was located in the Midwest, bordered the American South, and lacked any connection to a vibrant Jewish community outside the strongly assimilated German-style college community, where he did not fit in ethnically or theologically.[26] Because he depended on his scholarship to build a future for himself, he stood out as being eager to please yet reluctant to attract negative attention.[27] Like Atlas, he was looking for a position in New York, stayed there frequently, and maintained a close relationship with Louis Finkelstein, chancellor of the JTS, and Jacob Hartstein, registrar of Yeshiva University. After landing a position at the JTS in 1945, Atlas moved to New York in 1951 to continue teaching at the newly established New York campus of HUC-Jewish Institute of Religion.

A rivalry between Heschel and Atlas developed during their time in Cincinnati and involved much more than their mutual interest in relocating to New York City, one of the few US cities with a lively Jewish community and a broad variety of ethnic and theological backgrounds that was comparable to the cultural and intellectual life of European metropolises. Both men wanted to live and work there, but the older and more experienced Atlas held the more prestigious position at HUC. Nevertheless, the JTS hired the young Abraham Heschel rather than Atlas when a position opened up. At HUC, both men had competed for the same set of courses—philosophy and the Talmud—which they taught based on their very different approaches to Judaism.

Atlas was born in Lithuania, received a traditional Jewish education at the Slobodka Yeshiva, and taught at the Institute for Judaic Studies in Warsaw before moving to London. Unlike Heschel, who had a traditional Hassidic background and upbringing and continued to gravitate toward Hassidism and Jewish Orthodoxy, Atlas was an Orthodox Jew who strictly held a neo-Kantian rationalist perspective that Heschel rejected. Heschel negated the rationalist theology of Herman Cohen that Atlas upheld, and this became a source of conflict between the two men once Henschel published his dissertation.[28]

Conflict among the scholars was not limited to teaching matters and scholarly prospects. After a period of adjustment, almost everyone at HUC was concerned about their scholarly future, their academic status, their prospects, and especially their income.

Alexander Guttmann, professor of Talmud and rabbinics at HUC in Cincinnati and a full faculty member, complained to Julian Morgenstern in October 1942 about the college's disregard of his experience and prior academic status with regard to his salary. When he was hired as a full professor, he had been promised a salary of $3,000 a year with an annual raise of $300 until a maximum of $6,000 a year was reached. Guttmann argued that he had received "by far the lowest salary paid to full professors" and that his experience and status at the Hochschule were being ignored.[29] He claimed that he could not make ends meet with this salary and asked Morgenstern to submit his request for an "adjustment" of $300 to "approach the living standards of the other members of the College faculty" to the board of governors at HUC at their next meeting.[30]

Morgenstern submitted Guttmann's request, but the board of governors did not share Guttmann's view and rejected his request for an adjustment of his salary.[31] Guttmann was not the only one dissatisfied with his salary, as we learn from Morgenstern's correspondence. Other faculty members approached him for a raise because they felt their salaries did not properly reflect their actual value and qualifications as scholars.[32]

The refugees' correspondence with Julian Morgenstern reveals even deeper conflicts not only with the college faculty but also among the refugees themselves. These conflicts originated from past irritations and affronts in the German (academic) culture. Emigration and other factors, such as the Shoah, the democratic American environment, and academic culture, distorted old hierarchies and gave new agency to those who had been suppressed in the Old World. In other cases, the new environment gave them a more promising framework and value system with which to hurt a former "enemy" and pay back the insult.

In March 1947, Eugen Taeubler gave Julian Morgenstern a memorandum for the board of governors in which he vehemently protested against "calumnies" regarding Eugen Taeubler's person that were supposedly being spread by his colleague and fellow refugee Julius Lewy.[33] Taeubler, who belonged to the German academic establishment until 1933, informed the college of imminent legal action against Lewy for defamation and slander. In this memorandum, Taeubler details his concerns about Lewy, who had referred to Taeubler in a lecture given in 1942 or 1943 as a person suffering from a "lack of character" and as someone who "a few years ago ... was an ardent worshipper of Hitler, today he probably adores Roosevelt." Even worse, Taeubler argued, Lewy had tried to systematically set students and faculty against him by stating that he, Taeubler, defended known Nazis. He stressed that this type of behavior was a danger to the entire college and that Lewy should be reported to the FBI.

According to the memorandum, Lewy claimed that in Germany, Taeubler had only associated with the social classes of Junkers[34] and military leadership and prided himself on his connection with these Prussian elites. He stated that Taeubler also prided himself on having been the only Jew to have received an answer from the "Führer" and had only left Germany shortly before facing deportation. Lewy complained about Taeubler's recommendations to students to return to Germany after the end of the Second World War and claimed that Taeubler had been against the promotion of Jewish professors during his tenure in Germany.[35]

In the second part of the memorandum, Taeubler took an unequivocal stand against Lewy's accusations, stressing that he had only met with German colleagues who were anti-Nazis, such as Hermann Ranke[36] and Hajo Holborn.[37] He also stated that his contact with those he called "Junkers" was limited to his military service during the First World War, where he had met one such aristocrat in the army. This person later enrolled at the University of Berlin, and Taeubler met with him once a semester.

Taeubler prided himself on developing a plan for the evacuation of a large number of Jews to Palestine and submitting the plan to the Reich Chancellery, meaning to Adolf Hitler himself, through contacts he had with a professor at Heidelberg University. While he received an answer from the Reich Chancellery that Hitler was interested in the project and that the plan was referred to the Minister of the Interior, Taeubler never received an answer from that department. He stressed that he never recommended to students to return to Germany and explained that he stayed in Germany until the last minute only "because he considered his work essential."

Finally, he turned to Lewy's accusation that he had prevented the promotion of Jewish professors. This was most likely the basis for the strained relationship between Lewy and Taeubler and the resulting antagonism. Taeubler, who was professor ordinarius (chair) at the University of Heidelberg, was involved in hiring and promotions, which included processing Lewy's application for the position of chair at the University of Giessen. Taeubler explained that the faculty did not want to fill the position again in 1927, but decided to permit an "associated professor"[38] to fill this position. Lewy, at the time a *Privatdozent*[39] in Giessen, was considered. As part of the hiring process, Taeubler served as an external reviewer and claimed that he had recommended Lewy as professor *extraordinarius*, an advanced but still untenured rank of a professorship.[40]

While Taeubler stated that he had fulfilled his collegial duties and thus demonstrated an appropriate measure of loyalty with his recommendation, Lewy may have hoped for a stronger promotion from a fellow Jew and a scholar in his field so that he might advance to a tenured full professorship or even chair at the University of Giessen. Both Lewy's accusations and Taeubler's explanations in his statement point to a conflict in which Taeubler's loyalty as a fellow Jew was questioned and his social standing, class, and elitism were attacked. Taeubler made it clear in the memorandum that he was defending his "honor" and his position in the hierarchical German university system—a system in which his position was far higher than that of his colleague Lewy, who was eight years older than Taeubler.[41]

This episode shows that the refugees did not necessarily start anew in their American environment but continued to be plagued by old rivalries, confrontations, habits, and identities that were related to their former lives and shaped their hybrid identities. The new American environment, the Second World War, and a different academic culture at a *Jewish* college may have turned this old world upside down and inspired Lewy to challenge Taeubler on the grounds of what he called his "German" values and a self-understanding that no longer fit into the new American environment.

This assumption is reinforced by an official letter of apology Julius Lewy wrote to Julian Morgenstern on 22 April 1947,[42] in which he stated: "Although certain remarks of Dr. Taeubler's had demonstrated to me that the environment to which he had been exposed... had left their imprint on his way of thinking, I did not intend at all to depict him as a man who consciously advocated Hitlerite doctrines or to suggest this to anyone else." He stressed that he regretted the misunderstandings and suspicions that had troubled Taeubler over the past six years and said he would do all he could to end the animosities.[43] Nevertheless, Morgenstern's efforts to mediate the situation between the two men failed, and Taeubler never accepted the apology.[44]

Taeubler's strong attitude and arrogance can be seen in other contexts; for example, in a complaint to the historian and director of the American Jewish Archives, Jacob Rader Marcus. In a letter dated 8 October 1950, Taeubler wrote on behalf of his wife, Selma Stern-Taeubler, a highly qualified historian. Selma, who had found a position as a historian in the American Jewish Archives under Marcus, did not speak for herself. Instead, her husband complained for her, expressing his concern about how Selma's position at the institution was described.

Selma had been listed in the most recent college catalog as an "archivist of the business manager," a title that indicated an administrative responsibility rather than a scientific or scholarly one and completely minimized her qualifications as an advanced historian. In a letter to Jacob R. Marcus, Taeubler took this as an unbearable degradation and an affront to his wife and *his* "consent, to follow your [Marcus's] wish and accept your [Marcus's] offer," which he felt completely ignored Selma's actual qualifications as a highly advanced historian.[45]

While at first, Taeubler seemed to be making a case for the acknowledgment of his wife's high qualification as historian, a second look at his words reveals the double standard he was applying. Taeubler diminished his wife by referring to her in the third person and stressing that she needed *his consent* to accept the position in the first place—a position he considered his wife to be overqualified for. This assessment of her qualifications might have been accurate, but his statement also underscored the double standards of a classic bourgeois view on the "appropriate" gender roles to which he adhered, even though they did not match the advanced scholarly achievements of his wife.

Similarly detailed information on the integration of refugees, their challenges, and their (cultural) flaws is not available from the JTS or Yeshiva University because these colleges simply did not accept as many students and faculty as HUC did. For several decades at HUC, about a third of the faculty had a refugee background and the college continued to attract students from German refugee families.

Institutions like the JTS, located in a metropolitan environment far from any sort of German ethnic enclave and the rescue effort, were far more conscious of the potential for cultural clashes between Germans and Americans in the profession and therefore focused strictly on graduate studies.

The JTS demanded from the beginning that refugee rabbis undergo additional training for the American rabbinate in courses designed exclusively for new arrivals. Alternatively, younger rabbis could earn a doctorate at the JTS to acquaint themselves with the prevailing academic spirit as well as the new standards of the American rabbinate under the guidance of the JTS.[46] While the JTS in New York provided an important framework for the refugees in which they could find a home for their professional development, the seminary did not offer the depth and intensity of involvement experienced by the Reform movement and HUC's German counterpart, the Hochschule, which was looked on as HUC's sister organization to which special ties existed.

While some German refugees, such as Max Gruenewald or Julius Galliner, experienced a close relationship with the JTS, this was usually the result of an existing friendship or personal relationship. For example, Louis Finkelstein maintained a close personal and professional friendship with Saul Horovitz of Breslau (Gruenewald's father-in-law) and Julius Galliner (Helmut's father) at the Hochschule. Alexander Marx also cultivated a friendship with Julius Galliner and knew Esriel Erich Hildesheimer, the librarian of the Rabbinerseminar in Berlin, who was looking for a library position at the JTS. But these relationships did not involve the whole institution, as was the case at HUC.

Louis Finkelstein supported both Max Gruenewald and Julius Galliner's son Helmut and even provided an affidavit for Gruenewald. At the same time, he did not hesitate to criticize Helmut Galliner, who proved to be a difficult guest at the JTS. Finkelstein assisted many others, but none of the refugees' records depicted the spirit of a college family on that campus.

"The Germans" were never as large a group at the JTS as they were in Cincinnati, nor did they have a similarly lasting impact on the institution. Rather, as a minority, they were directed to comply with Americanization and the expectations of the institution. This is underscored by the experience of Max Gruenewald, who mentioned an "anti-German sentiment" in New York City, a city far more cosmopolitan in character than Cincinnati.

Gruenewald enjoyed great loyalty from the seminary, but at one point, the institution could no longer provide him with a fellowship. He had to support himself by working for other organizations, such as the American Friends of Hebrew University or the World Jewish Congress. He also received short-term funding from the Academy of Jewish Research in January 1944.[47] The JTS permanently stopped supporting him, thus setting an example that the seminary expected these men to establish a life outside the seminary; namely, to find a pulpit. In June 1944, Gruenewald finally confirmed that he had found a congregation in Millburn, New Jersey.[48] He was accepted as a substitute rabbi on weekends until the congregation asked him to substitute for his predecessor, Rabbi Kieffer on a full-time basis since the latter did not want to return to his congregation after his service in the army. Joachim Prinz, Gruenewald's brother-in-law, who officiated in Newark, New Jersey, had brought the position to his attention.[49]

There were far fewer second-generation students at the JTS than at HUC. Among them were Bernard Wechsberg, Bert Woythaler, Ludwig Nadelman, Sol Landau, Ismar Schorsch, Pessach Schindler, Hermann Dicker, Michael Leipziger from Sao Paolo, and Norbert Weinberg. Their assimilation went smoothly, and their careers were likewise promising.

This was especially true in the case of Ismar Schorsch, who was not only an outstanding scholar of modern Jewish history; he also rose to become the chancellor of his alma mater, the JTS. The ethnic and religious background of this group did not resonate in the same fashion at the seminary. The JTS understood itself as an *American* academic institution with links to many traditions in the Jewish world, and German-speaking central Europe did not play quite the same role as it did in the Reform movement. This was true even though Schorsch's career in particular as a historian during this movement underscores that intellectual history and historical Judaism continued to be central to the academic and intellectual identity of the movement.[50]

A lack of family spirit may have been even more true at Yeshiva University, which was situated next to the largely Orthodox German refugee community in Washington Heights in Manhattan. Despite its proximity to this community, the university had few exchanges with the refugee congregations and their leaders, especially in the university's Rabbi Isaac Elchanan Rabbinical Seminary (RIETS). The school was more focused on recruiting and rescuing rabbinical leaders from Lithuania for its faculty because these activities better fit the college's theological goals and orientation. Ironically, like the relationship of HUC in Cincinnati, RIETS was family for Lithuanian Orthodox scholars and essential to the Orthodox movement, whose reliance on the school's assistance in saving their lives and knowledge was similar to the role played by HUC.

This does not mean that Yeshiva University was not assisting its German brethren or ignoring their plight. The university hired several German refugee scholars as faculty for Yeshiva College. Max Landau from the Rabbinerseminar was considered, but he died in an accident before he could be rescued by RIETS. Bernard Revel assisted Joseph Breuer, for whom Yeshiva University is said to have requested a nonquota visa for the whole family.[51]

As an institution, however, Yeshiva University felt an obligation toward and interest in aiding sages of the traditional yeshivot in eastern Europe, the centuries-old heart of European Jewish knowledge, rather than assisting the modern Orthodox minority from Germany, which was uniquely tied to its German cultural context and did not easily fit into the larger Orthodox mainstream, intellectually or ethnically.

A study on the intellectual and social integration of Orthodox European Jewish refugees at Yeshiva University or the smaller yeshivot in the New York area would no doubt contribute to the research on the Jewish knowledge transfer from Europe to the United States during and after the Shoah, but there is nothing on this topic in the historiography of European and American Jewish history.[52]

The spirit of family that united refugees from Nazism with American institutions seems to have also played an important role at Ner Israel Rabbinical College in Baltimore. This institution had close ties with the Yeshiva Slobodka and the Yeshiva Mir, two yeshivot that deeply influenced Rabbis Samson Raphael Weiss and Herman Naftali Neuberger of Würzburg. Both men were helped by their new institution to bring twenty-three students from Würzburg to Ner Israel Rabbinical College.

Surprisingly, the second generation was almost as significant among Orthodoxy as it was in the Reform movement because of their intellectual leadership. Over fifteen young men born in Germany were educated for the rabbinate in American Orthodox institutions. Five of them—Leon Aryeh Feldman, Norbert Weinberg, Manfred Fulda, Walter Würzburger, and Shlomo Kahn—studied at RIETS, while two—Jacob Wiener and Herman Neuberger—attended Ner Israel Rabbinical College.

Ludwig Nadelman attended Yeshiva College, where he earned a BA, then switched to the JTS for rabbinical school. The other students attended smaller yeshivot in New York or were ordained by a local Orthodox rabbi.

Aaron Rabenstein received his *Smicha* (traditional ordination) from Eliezer Silver in Cincinnati. Unlike their older peers, who had been educated and ordained in Germany, these young men were at ease in the American Orthodox movement and had no trouble leading American Orthodox congregations.

Manfred Fulda continued his career at RIETS, where he was hired in 1956 as an expert on Gemara (the second part of the Talmud). Walter Würzburger was born in Munich, obtained a PhD at Harvard University, and combined Orthodox thought with a secular presence and scholarly spirit while promoting a stronger societal engagement of American Orthodoxy.

Born in Berlin, Leon Feldman attended the Adass Jisroel School there and a special program of the Rabbinerseminar until he graduated with *Abitur* in 1939. In April of that year, he fled to the United Kingdom. From there, he was deported to Canada and arrived in the United States in 1944, where he started his education at the New School for Social Research and RIETS. He was dedicated to the promotion of Jewish education and taught at Yeshiva University and Rutgers University, where he launched a Jewish studies program. Like Würzburger, he obtained doctorates from prominent secular universities—in history from Columbia University and theology from the University of Amsterdam—and established himself as a highly educated Orthodox pioneer by orchestrating theological principles with contemporary challenges.[53]

From Gemeinde to Congregation: The Communal Rabbis

Just as the first achievements made by students and scholars in American culture depended on their acceptance to and socialization at American rabbinical colleges, so, too, was the success of the rabbis' first years in the United States dependent on how they dealt with American Judaism and its congregations and members.

Accustomed to living within a Gemeinde (Jewish community), the refugee scholars struggled with the highly individualistic American congregation, the political role of the American rabbi, and the rabbi's administrative and business responsibilities, for which the refugees had never been trained. In a poorly staffed congregation dependent on powerful laymen, the rabbi's standing was undermined. Intellectual strength and scholarship were not very important; they were often not even welcome. The rabbis' job security depended on pleasing and successfully representing their congregation, an obligation that undercut their authority as independent spiritual leaders, a role they had been trained for. Many were angered by this.[54] In addition, they were confronted with ethnically diverse congregations and the role ethnicity played in American Judaism, an issue they were unfamiliar with and one that challenged them more or less, depending on the religious movement they joined.

Many of the refugee rabbis struggled to relaunch their careers in the United States. They discovered that to lead an American congregation, it was crucial to master English to meet the congregation's expectations of social and political leadership and to conduct the service and deliver the sermon with dignity.

Language and cultural adaptation were major hurdles in the refugees' careers, especially those over age fifty, such as Leo Baerwald, Jehuda Leo Breslauer, Hartwig N. Carlebach, and Siegmund Hanover. These rabbis found careers outside of American Judaism within the world of "ethnic religion" (imported religion of immigrants preserving the religious rituals and forms from their home country) in congregations founded by refugees in the United States.

Most of these congregations stood outside the three movements of American Judaism.

Only the Reform movement was likely to admit refugee congregations. These refugees, often members of the rabbis' former German communities, were grateful that this vital part of their lives could be transplanted to America because it provided essential emotional and cultural support and community at a time of displacement, as historian Steven Lowenstein describes in his study on Washington Heights in Upper Manhattan.[55]

Most German refugee congregations preferred not to live in ethnic communities because of their ideal of social integration. But in cities with a dense refugee population, separate neighborhoods like Washington Heights in Manhattan naturally emerged. Here refugees shared an Orthodox identity and lifestyle, came often from small-town Germany—mostly from the German south— and clustered in an ethnic neighborhood that allowed them to reinvent themselves and deal with Americanization at their own pace. Living in an ethnic enclave facilitated the complicated transformation of their German and Jewish identities.

Not surprisingly, these communities were dominated by Conservative or Orthodox German Jews who lived and worked there and needed the facilities of an organized community more than their liberal brethren since they adhered to an observant lifestyle. Here they maintained their German-Jewish traditions; continued to speak German; published their own papers, such as the *Jewish Way*;[56] and re-created a microcosm with a strong Old World atmosphere and culinary traditions, although the word "German" was removed from the names of their favorite foods and replaced with local references or labeled as "homemade."[57]

Their congregations and synagogues followed the south German rites and prayer books and were typically organized around local traditions similar to landsmanshaftn (immigrant organizations defined by the traditions and regional origins of their members) that functioned as a tie between the past and present. Congregants and rabbis continued to speak and preach in German. Many rabbis completed their careers to retirement age in this environment. These institutions were not built to last for more than one or two generations, at which point the inevitable Americanization and integration into American Judaism would lead to their collapse. Such a community and its services would likely not appeal to the refugees' children, or the congregation failed to recruit a spiritual leader or members from this population.

Among the many small congregations in Washington Heights, Kahal Adass Jeshurun mastered the transition to the United States as an informed, proud, and forward-thinking group under the leadership of Joseph Breuer, who was almost sixty when he arrived in New York City. This congregation's success was likely due to the large number of former members who reassembled under its new roof, and Joseph Breuer, who expended an enormous amount of energy and ambition to rebuild not only a synagogue but a kahal, a community and governing body that provided services in a mikvah (ritual bathing place), a yeshiva, a public school, adult education, supervision in kashruth (dietary laws), and a school for women. Favoring the importance of education, knowledge, and the Torah over outward appearance and decorum, Breuer used the congregation's resources wisely to reestablish an attitude of self-awareness and knowledge for the next generation. He did this long before he invested in a synagogue edifice, which was not built until 1952 and was never particularly representative aesthetically as some American synagogues were.[58]

Nevertheless, by providing a full community and services to German-Jewish Orthodoxy, Kahal Adass Jeshurun became an important institution in Washington Heights. It attracted other German Orthodox groups and small congregations, who benefited from the Breuer congregation's services and features, such as educational institutions, social groups, hometown traditions, and a kosher delicatessen. A network-oriented study on the rescue and resettlement of the Breuer community to New York and its growth, prosperity, and effect on the Orthodox refugee community in that city might be revealing, even if that kahal was similar to (but not exactly the same as) a center for German Orthodoxy in that it provided a community network, a family lifestyle, and a cultural home even for those who did not share the same specific religious convictions and orientations.

Unlike in German Orthodoxy, formerly liberal refugee congregations found support and tolerance within the American Reform movement, which helped integrate them into their new environment over time. Typically, these refugees lived outside an ethnic neighborhood, and their congregation recruited a spiritual leader who had established himself in Germany.

One example is Congregation Habonim in Manhattan, led by Hugo Hahn, a rabbi from Essen who was forty-seven when he took on the pulpit of this refugee congregation. He remained its leader until 1965. The congregation—one of the few that still thrives today—found a very suitable successor in Bernhard Cohn, the son of Emil Moses Cohn, who was killed in a tragic car accident in Los Angeles in February 1948.

Bernhard Cohn finished high school in New York City in 1941 and then followed his parents to California, where he studied at the University of California, Berkeley, and served in the US Army from 1943 to 1946. After the Second World War, he followed his father in the rabbinate and studied from 1948 to 1953 at HUC-Jewish Institute of Religion (JIR) in New York. It was there that he started dating Hugo Hahn's daughter, whom he eventually married.

In 1965, Bernhard Cohn, quite familiar with New York City and the German families in the congregation, followed his father-in-law as the leader of Habonim. For the next generation, Cohn's presence secured the congregation's survival and continuity because he encouraged the members to change and adapt, such as learning the English language.

In 1995, the congregation switched to the Conservative movement in American Judaism and thereby uncovered a dilemma that many liberal German Jews were facing in the United States: while the Reform movement had its origins in Germany, liberal Judaism was far more conservative in practice than its American counterpart and felt perhaps even more at home in the American Conservative movement. Yet at the same time, German spiritual leaders struggled in the movement, which ethnically had a strong east European leaning.

However, Karl Rosenthal, who had officiated in Berlin's only Reform Temple, failed to integrate into American Reform Judaism for a variety of reasons that were linked to serious Holocaust and personal trauma as well as substantial cultural and religious discrepancies between the two Reform movements.

After *Kristallnacht*, Rosenthal fled from Berlin to Britain, where he stayed until after the Second World War ended. Like many of his colleagues, he had to leave Germany quickly and was therefore separated from his wife, Trudie, and his two sons, Georg and Klaus, who did not want to follow him because they did not speak English well enough. While his older son Klaus managed to leave Germany in time and get a job in the family business of relatives in Wisconsin, Trudie and Georg were arrested in Amsterdam during the German occupation. Georg was deported to Mauthausen camp in 1941, where he died by the end of the year; Trudie was arrested a little later and taken to Bergen-Belsen.

Limited in agency and movement as a refugee in Britain, Rosenthal tried everything to save his wife. After years of effort, he was able to purchase a South American passport for her with the assistance of aid organizations. She was liberated in 1944 and taken to Switzerland as part of an exchange for German prisoners of war. A few weeks later, she relocated to a UN camp in Algiers for the duration of the war.[59]

The trauma involved in the family's attempts to flee from Germany and the separation and tragic loss of their son Georg overwhelmed the parents. After seven years, in late 1945, Karl and Trudie reunited in Philadelphia, where Karl had found a position.

At this first meeting, Trudie reported that Karl looked ill and was psychologically scarred. Over the following years, he held several short-term positions, first in Fredericksburg, Maryland, then as the rabbi of Temple Brith Sholom in Springfield, Illinois, and finally a two-year employment in Wilmington, North Carolina. There, suffering from severe heart disease, Karl died in 1952, only a short time after the couple's surviving son Klaus met an untimely death caused by an infection.[60]

Oral histories by former congregants in Springfield, Illinois, reveal that this Reform rabbi from the metropolitan and progressive background of Berlin, who had gone through the painful experiences of flight, separation, displacement, loss, and the Holocaust, was a controversial figure to a petty Reform congregation in small-town America. Rosenthal and his wife stood out in many ways. For one, the couple raised serious doubts because they rode on the bus on Shabbat and did not own a car when they first arrived. The American middle-class status symbol was expected from a spiritual leader, and the congregation made sure that the couple purchased a car in their second year at Springfield.

Other problems arose: the Rosenthals were not "observant" in the exact same way their congregants expected. Karl did not object to a Christmas tree in a Jewish home, occasionally ate pork, and permitted the children of the congregation to eat doughnuts on Passover.

The congregation was almost torn apart by the conflicts triggered by the German Reform rabbi. His liberal lifestyle challenged Jewish conventions that he did not understand to be contrary to being a Reform Jew. This, unsurprisingly, affected the degree to which the Rosenthals were accepted and caused Karl great distress. Under continuing financial pressures after many years of flight, displacement, and temporary employment, Karl was unable to retire and take care of his health. His heart disease progressed, and he suffered a heart attack during Shabbat services in Springfield before the couple left for Wilmington, North Carolina.[61]

Financial pressures and the loss of status and social standing were major concerns of the refugees, as Rabbi Hans Enoch Kronheim's correspondence illustrates. The rabbi secured positions in the United States and even expanded his tenure in his first pulpit in Jamestown, New York, to seven years before he found a permanent place in the merger of Mayfield Temple and Congregation Shaarey Tikvah in Cleveland, Ohio, where he concluded his career. After arriving in America, one of Kronheim's former congregants wrote a letter of support to Rabbi Samuel Cohen of the United Synagogue of America, saying that it was quite difficult "to earn a living in the profession for which he was best fitted."

While we can only guess at Kronheim's initial salary range from the nonquota visa arrangements, which usually provided an annual salary of around

$2,000, the Kronheim collection details how these salaries developed. The contract for his position in Cleveland in 1952 lists an annual salary of $4,400.[62]

There is little documentation of other cases in which serious problems developed with congregations similar to that of the Rosenthals, the database German Refugee Rabbis in the United States after 1933 documents a number of rabbis who struggled in their early years to find a good fit with a congregation or religious movement. This is reflected by the multiple congregations they served, the changes in their religious affiliations, and the alternatives they found or the additional tasks they took on to make ends meet or reach out to a larger community of Jews.

Even prominent rabbis like Joachim Prinz, who left Germany before the pogrom of 9 November 1938, struggled to find a suitable position that would support him and his family. Originally hired by the United Palestine Appeal as a public lecturer, Prinz was quite irritated by the challenges of effective public speaking in the United States, the different expectations of the audiences, and the tendency of American Jews to cluster in their ethnic communities.

Perceiving American rabbis as intellectually mediocre and in their Jewishness unfit to lead a congregation appropriately, Prinz did not want to take on a pulpit. However, as financial pressures rose and his family grew, he was forced to compromise and accept a position as rabbi of the independent congregation at Temple B'nai Abraham in Newark, New Jersey, a town that experienced rapid social change after the Second World War, the consequences of which also resonated in the community.

With a beginning salary of $6,000, he felt he was well paid, even though he stressed that this position did not equal the situation that German rabbis had once enjoyed in which they were well compensated by the state, employed for life, and could count on a pension.

Prinz accepted the offer from this congregation, which previously had only had a cantor as its "rabbi," a person whose intellectual leadership Prinz questioned. B'nai Abraham acquainted him with a new type of congregant and the social reality of gang life in New Jersey, a completely new experience even for Prinz and quite distant from the middle-class life he had known in Berlin with scholarly and bourgeois Jewish elites.[63]

Data shows that the integration of refugee rabbis was the smoothest in the American Reform movement, even without a special training strategy to prepare German rabbis for American congregations. The movement, particularly strong in the American South and West, benefited from placing the newcomers in small congregations in more remote areas of the country. For example, Max Nussbaum's first congregation was in Muskogee, Oklahoma, before he became a substitute rabbi for Morton Bauman, who served in the army during the Second World War, at Temple Israel in Hollywood, California, a position Nussbaum never left. These congregations regarded the rescue of German rabbis not only as a special mitzvah (a religious duty) but also as a chance for them to recruit a rabbi at a time when American rabbis were difficult to find, partly because many of these spiritual leaders were joining the army.

The movement also placed refugees alongside a more experienced American rabbi in a larger congregation, where the former gained experience serving as an "assistant rabbi" and could explore the American rabbinate and congregation with an experienced partner, often someone he had known before his flight from Germany. One such pair was Emil Moses Cohn and Stephen Wise at the Free Synagogue in New York City.

The Conservative movement offered classes and sometimes additional funding to German refugees to help them pursue a doctorate at the JTS in preparation for an American career.[64] Nevertheless, there were still problems with congregations and the transition into the American rabbinate. As mentioned before, the refugees were prepared for a profession in which the rabbi was a scholar and spiritual leader of a Gemeinde, and his position therein was reflected by his status, job security, and scholarship, which underscored his leadership role. The Gemeinde and its staff provided services and an administration around the synagogue and assisted its leader, who focused largely on his intellectual and spiritual guidance within the Gemeinde, not within a specific synagogue. This American synagogue, however, functioned as a single congregation in a religious environment that challenged the rabbi in different ways. There was little job security and not enough staff to run the congregation, but it was controlled by a uniquely powerful lay leadership. The American rabbi depended on the lay leadership's approval and could easily be fired if he did not meet expectations. A rabbi's fit with the congregation depended on ethnicity, cultural background, and how the congregation felt it should be represented in society. Therefore, the role of the American rabbi was an obviously political one. In Germany, such a role was rejected until the Nazi years permitted that a younger generation of rabbis who had already developed political attitudes in the 1920s was able to officially step up and express them in the Gemeinde. Many of the tasks of managing a congregation fell to the rabbi himself, as the congregations were frequently understaffed. This included fundraising and other administrative challenges the refugees had never been prepared for. Altogether, they felt that their congregants had little or only superficial Jewish knowledge and that the rabbis' scholarship was not appreciated. As newcomers facing a language barrier, they immediately felt a loss of status and security and were challenged by having to accommodate the three religious movements by which American congregations defined themselves, unless they chose a refugee congregation outside the realm of American Judaism.

Ismar Schorsch, the son of Emil Schorsch, formerly the rabbi of Hannover, remembers when his father arrived in Pottstown, Pennsylvania, with his family as rabbi of a Conservative Hungarian congregation. Those early days were fraught with tension among the ethnically different congregation, and only his father's persistence solved the problems because he knew that he had to succeed in this position to make a living. Like other German refugees, Ismar noted that the professional profile and status of the German rabbi differed from his American counterpart.

With an excellent Jewish and secular education, Emil Schorsch was not intellectually satisfied with his rabbinate in Pottstown, for he had been well trained and had even studied psychology to fulfill his duties. Both as a chaplain and a rabbi, he showed a certain gravitas in his office that prompted respect. His choice to enter the rabbinate was the result of his experience with and active participation in the First World War, his confrontation with the collapse of society after the war, and his intellectual desire to find answers to the questions posed by these events in the postwar years. However, he simply could not find the same professional and intellectual identity among his American colleagues, and so he never attended the national conventions of the Rabbinical Assembly.[65]

According to historian Eli Faber, his father, Salamon Faber, one of the last graduates of the Jüdisch-Theologisches Seminar in Breslau, went through a number of congregations to find the right fit for his rabbinate in the Conservative movement of American Judaism.

Faber, who grew up in a small town near Nowy Sącz in Poland, did not struggle with the ethnic sensibilities of east European congregants and was very comfortable in a German environment, but he was challenged by the American congregation and what it expected of its rabbi.

Coming from a Hassidic background and extremely well trained in traditional Jewish texts and the Talmud from an early age, Faber obtained a secular education in Poland, then studied at the seminary in Breslau and later at the Friedrich-Wilhelms-Universität in Berlin, where he was trained for the modern "German" rabbinate, after having already received a *Smicha* in Dobra near Novy Sacz in 1934.

His ordination document from Breslau was dated 10 November 1938 and was likely dated after the students had taken their last exams in December of that year in their professors' homes. Some of the administrators must have rescued the exam forms and the seal of the seminary to make these emergency graduations possible for the students who were still in Breslau after the closing of the seminary following the pogrom. Many of them were foreigners, at the time, not as targeted as the German Jews, and were spared by the events of the pogrom, as Salamon was.

After he arrived in the United States, Salamon began a two-year contract at Congregation Shaarey Shamayim in Philadelphia, an ethnically mixed congregation where he met his wife. This was followed by another two years in Coatesville, Pennsylvania, with an American congregation. This was "not a happy marriage" because its members were not very well educated in matters of the Jewish faith, his son explained.

The third two-year contract took Salamon Faber to San Antonio in Texas, an environment where his new wife was unhappy. Ultimately, he returned to Philadelphia to his first congregation.

After an intermediate stay in Pittsburgh as the educational director of a Jewish day school, Faber found a pulpit in Warren, Ohio, in 1949, his first success in the American rabbinate. Here he was included in the social life of the town, joined the Rotary Club, found many friends and supporters among Christians and Jews, and got along very well with the Conservative congregation. Over time, however, he did miss a more Jewish environment and opportunities for his children, which prompted him to relocate to Anshe Shalom in Kew Gardens in Queens, New York, in 1954.

The Anshe Shalom congregation was composed of American-born Jews and German and European refugees. They represented an extremely well-educated, elegant, and intellectual crowd. Salamon Faber finally felt at home and held this position until he retired. Among the congregation, he was lovingly referred to as "our rabbi," and he enjoyed the beautiful organ music of the service, much of which was composed by the notable German-Jewish composer Louis Lewandowski.[66]

If rabbis could not find a place with an American congregation or rejected its doctrines, they found alternatives in the Hillel movement. This was true of Alfred Jospe, Frank Fisher, and Erwin Zimet, who joined Hillel campus ministries. They often found positions that allowed them to combine their academic skills and an interest in Jewish studies with an innovative ministry on campus.

Others found a home in a different community or additional income as military chaplains, civilian chaplains (such as Emil Schorsch, who found more intellectual stimulation in the Valley Forge Army Hospital environment), or social workers (the Orthodox Ralph Neuhaus) in a wide range of institutions that catered to American Jewish people.

There were two rabbis who left their positions and any affiliation with Jewish institutions after a few years in American congregations. Luitpold Wallach turned to a full-time academic career, specializing in medieval history, a profession that took him back to Germany many times after 1945. Harry May graduated from the Breslau seminary with a PhD from Charles University in Prague. The JTS had expended enormous amounts of time and energy to carry out his complicated rescue, yet later in his life, May ran a profitable junk business with his father-in-law.[67]

It was the German Orthodox rabbis who had the hardest time finding a place in the American Jewish religious environment. Data from the database German Refugee Rabbis in the United States after 1933 show a significant shift in their careers after emigration, and it is not known if Orthodox seminaries tried to retrain them or facilitate their integration into the American rabbinate. Unlike those who joined the Reform and Conservative movements, these rabbis did not seem to have a strong link to a specific American rabbinical college or institution that would support them in assimilating into American Judaism. This and their desire to be part of wider society led many of them to continue their careers either in the Conservative movement of American Judaism (like Felix Aber, Helmut Frank, and Hermann Dicker, who was a military chaplain) or the Reform movement (like Leo Trepp, Jakob Petuchowski, Arthur Bluhm, Joseph Asher, and Selig Auerbach).

They seem to have struggled specifically with leading Orthodox congregations in the United States because many of them ended up working long-term administrative positions in educational institutions, Jewish day schools, religious organizations, the kosher food industry, or publishing houses.

This was also true even for some young men representing the second generation, such as Ludwig Nadelman. He attended Yeshiva College at Yeshiva University to obtain his bachelor of arts but did not stay for rabbinical training, choosing instead to train at the JTS in New York and Columbia University. Although he was a rabbi at the Society for the Advancement of Judaism and served only briefly as a rabbi in a congregation, he turned to Reconstructionism, a new religious movement in American Judaism that combined historical Judaism with a strong commitment to Jewish cultural and ethnic identity. In this new movement, he made his mark as an intellectual leader and professor at the Reconstructionist Rabbinical College in Pennsylvania in the 1970s and 1980s.[68]

Among the German Orthodox rabbis who had officiated in Germany and sought integration into American Judaism, Samson Raphael Weiss had perhaps the biggest impact on American Orthodoxy. He taught for the obligatory visa-related two years at Ner Israel Rabbinical College in Baltimore. This did not seem to be a good permanent fit for him so he left to lead an Orthodox congregation in Detroit and taught at Yeshiva Beth Yehuda in that city. In 1944, the energetic and charismatic Orthodox leader and intellectual returned to a congregation in New York City until he found a position that allowed him to leave the American congregation and focus on larger educational and scholarly matters at the Young Israel Institute for Jewish Studies in New York. There he founded Torah U'mesorah, the umbrella organization of Orthodox Jewish day schools, served as the vice president of the Union of Orthodox Jewish Congregations, and dedicated his energies to advancing higher education and scholarship in the Orthodox world by founding Torah University in Los Angeles. Subsequently, he served as dean of Jewish studies at Touro College in New York. His influence at these two institutions enhanced Orthodoxy's exchange with secular knowledge in the post-Holocaust world.

Kurt Klappholz, retrained at the JTS in New York, ultimately turned to the Orthodox movement and served in an administrative position at the Central Yeshiva Beth Joseph in Brooklyn.

Ezekiel Landau worked for the Hebrew Immigrant Aid Society and ministered to several congregations in New York City.

Ralph Neuhaus took up social work in the Jewish Welfare Society, HIAS, and the National Refugee Service after leading a small congregation. These professional choices underscore his continued dedication to the refugee milieu.[69]

Rabbi Tuvia Lasdun found long-term employment with Feldheim Publishers, an Orthodox publishing company in New York.

Helmut Frank, who held positions at several small congregations in Philadelphia, supported himself for years by working as a typesetter for a publisher and as an army chaplain until he began leading the small German Orthodox congregation Agudath Achim, where he stayed until 1973.

Rabbi Michael (Yehiel) Munk was an Orthodox rabbi born to a prominent German-Jewish family in Berlin. He spent three years in Britain before he came to the United States on a nonquota visa in 1941. Munk deliberately turned away from the American congregation. In an interview with the Research Foundation for Jewish Immigration in 1972, he explained his motivation for this move as being "because I did not want to sell my soul." He pointed to the short-lived nature of an American rabbi's employment, the lack of respect congregants had for the office, the dependency of a rabbi on the congregation, and the lack of status and business-related responsibilities as issues that he did not want to deal with. As a result, Munk continued his career as an educator in the Orthodox education system: as a founder of the Beth Jacob School in Brooklyn, director of the Yeshiva Samson Raphael Hirsch, and founder of the Orthodox summer camp "Camp Munk." He also worked as a therapist, counselor, and shechita (ritual slaughter) supervisor in the wider American Orthodox community.[70]

Aaron Rabenstein of Cincinnati, who grew up in the United States and was ordained by Eliezer Silver in Cincinnati, maintained his strong ethnic and religious ties to New Hope, the German Orthodox congregation of that city, where his father was an important lay leader. He had never felt at home in American Orthodoxy but spent most of his life in the Orthodox education and day-school system of Cincinnati.[71]

It was the very same Orthodox German-Jewish Congregation New Hope, the one that never hired a rabbi as leader, that attracted members who played a promising and later essential role at the city's Reform seminary. Interestingly, one such person who was attracted by the Orthodox congregation New Hope in Cincinnati was Jakob Petuchowski, who, although professionally committed to Reform Judaism, chose to join this Orthodox German congregation with his family.

The Petuchowski family had been rooted for many generations in the German Orthodox tradition with a long lineage of Orthodox rabbis, all of whom perished during the Holocaust. Petuchowski found the spirit and style of this lost German Gemeinde in Congregation New Hope from 1965 to 1975. Despite his professional affiliation with the Reform movement, Petuchowski's membership was not only tolerated but highly valued by the congregation because of his family's reputation and academic achievement. It was ten years before dissent among the congregation over halachic law brought it to the brink of collapse, and Petuchowski was at the center of the conflict because he criticized the idea of absolute rabbinical authority that these congregants had embraced.

This was the moment when the bonds of ethnic religion revealed their limitations, and Petuchowski criticized that the congregation was committed to "a Judaism of a different time and different place," a Judaism of the past that separated him from the other congregants and was contrary to his commitment to a progressive Judaism. The episode ended with the Petuchowski family leaving the congregation.[72]

A New Beginning: From Statelessness to American Citizenship

Hand in hand with acculturation and integration went the legal process of "becoming American," a process that corrected a sensitive and painful problem in the lives of the refugees; namely, the restitution of their nationality and citizenship. Citizenship and nationality were two separate legal categories in German legislation, each anchored in the different speeds of the development of nationality and the German nation-state on the one hand, and the enfranchisement of Germans as citizens within this nation-state on the other.[73] From 1933 on, expatriation had been a common tool of the Nazi government to rid itself of both unwanted political opposition and its Jewish population.

In July 1933, the Law on the Revocation of Naturalizations and the Deprivations of German Citizenship (*Gesetz über den Widerruf von Einbürgerungen und die Aberkennung der deutschen Staatsangehörigkeit*) introduced into the German legal system a wicked tool for both denaturalization and forced expatriation and gave the Nazi Party a means with which to realize its racial visions of an ethnically homogeneous nation.[74] This legislation triggered the subsequent review of *all cases of naturalization* in Germany since 1918 and thus hurt many foreign-born citizens who had lived in Germany for decades before their actual naturalization.

But the real targets of this law were recently naturalized east European Jews, who suffered disproportionately from the loss of nationality, as that meant economic and social exclusion. The new legislation created widespread statelessness, which increased among "foreign" Jews, meaning those not born as Germans in Germany, from 10 percent in 1933 to over 50 percent in 1939 in Germany.[75] The law ultimately turned against all Germans who lived abroad, including émigrés who had fled the Hitler regime for political reasons and distanced themselves from Nazi Germany. Furthermore the law provided for their expatriation and for the seizure of their property in Germany.[76]

In 1935, the passage of the Nuremberg Laws and the removal of German citizenship stripped Jews of political rights and added to the fragility of their legal status. They were left solely with a category called "German nationality" (*Staatsangehörigkeit*) and thus were reduced to the minimum status of national belonging (without civil rights), according to the Nazis' racist thinking.[77] Once they left Germany, these Jews lost access to consular protection and administrative services, and their passports were not renewed.

Finally, in November 1941, German legislation expatriated *all former German citizens abroad*. This mass expatriation was meant to rid the country permanently of the stream of refugees from Nazism.[78] If German-Jewish refugees had not been officially stateless and vulnerable earlier, they certainly were so from this point on,[79] a circumstance that was reflected in the rabbis' biographies. Not only were many of them born outside of the contemporary German Reich; some did not have German citizenship or had only recently become naturalized citizens.

A close evaluation of their exact legal status and its changes between 1919 and 1941 would provide great insight into the question of the availability of Jewish agency during flight and expulsion for German rabbis. Such a study would also give a clearer picture of the practices of Nazi exclusion and its connection with German citizenship and immigration legislation.

We know that prominent rabbis like Jacob Hoffmann—who fled to the United States in 1938 and was a dual citizen of Hungary and Germany, naturalized in 1929—had their naturalization revoked in 1934 on the grounds of the abovementioned legislation. Left with only his Hungarian citizenship and as a prominent Orthodox Jew in Germany, he was in a vulnerable position. When Hoffmann was arrested by the Gestapo in March 1937, it was only due to the Hungarian government's intervention that he was released from prison, which gave him a chance to escape Germany. Officially, he was expelled from Germany and declared an "enemy of the state." This experience alarmed Hoffmann and kept him from accepting the position of chief rabbi of Vienna, which was his first destination upon fleeing. However, he foresaw Austria falling under the influence of Nazi Germany and quickly moved to the United States.[80]

Other well-documented cases reflecting the practice of expulsion include those of Joachim Prinz, Michael Munk, and Ira Sud. Prinz, although German-born, was expelled in 1937 for his political outspokenness and Jewish leadership.[81] Munk, also German-born, was refused a signature on his passport, which was the same as confiscating that passport. Thus he had to cross the border to Holland illegally and with no travel documents. There he received a "Nansen passport."[82] In November 1938, Sud was expelled from the Sudetenland, the German ethnic area in the Czech Republic, which Germany occupied in September 1938.[83]

In the United States, the growing fear concerning Axis spies and the advent of the Second World War meant that some refugees were faced with yet another problem, being considered "Germans" in the public eye. The passing of the Enemy Alien Act on 7 October 1941 in the United States heightened the suspicion toward all supposed "Germans," including German-Jewish refugees.[84]

With no regard to their background as refugees from Nazism or as victims of persecution and flight, Americans who considered them "German immigrants" first perceived them as "enemy aliens," especially in hot spots of pro-Nazi activity, like New York City, where Max Gruenewald reported strong anti-German sentiments during the war.[85] In this way, Jewish refugees were placed on the same shelf as Nazi-friendly immigrants of the interwar period and followers of the German-American Bund, an organization that actively spread Nazism and antisemitism in the German-speaking community in the United States during these years. These refugees had to register with the US government as potential agents of Nazi Germany, a grotesque situation that eased only after some time and created significant tension among ethnic Germans during the war years.[86]

The serious effects of such uninformed rejection by "old-stock" Americans were noticed by Rabbi Simon Schwab and his family in Baltimore. Their application for naturalization had been rejected in 1941 by a local judge under the pretext that their "German citizenship" made them subject to the legislation applicable to "enemy aliens." Schwab, who had raised over $1,000 for war bonds in his congregation, went to court to appeal this denial of citizenship, and a lengthy and humiliating legal case ensued. Not until 1944 was a final decision handed down in Schwab's favor, and the family were able to become American citizens.[87]

After these trials and tribulations, it was no surprise that the reestablishment of nationality and citizenship, of legally belonging to a society and nation-state was of vital importance in the lives of the refugee rabbis. It was a significant part of recovering from years of humiliation, reasserting their self-esteem, and healing their souls.

Some of them accelerated the naturalization process by taking advantage of the Second World War Powers Act of 1942,[88] which expedited the naturalization process to two years instead of five for those who served in the military of their newly adopted country.

The study of many records, autobiographies, and interviews revealed how intensely almost all of the rabbis remembered the date of their naturalization as that of a new beginning. Their conversion to a new citizenship opened up opportunities, put them back on track in life, renewed their dignity, and bestowed on them civil and political rights. Naturalization was far from just an administrative formality; it was an essential point in the process of gaining back agency, pride, and status.[89]

FIVE

Careers Lost and Found

Paths of Professional Success and Failure and the Making of the "Last Generation of the German Rabbinate"

Working toward their professional future and thinking ahead were essential for the refugee rabbis, but it was their history and the trauma of their experiences that crystallized as an important factor that drove the future of many of them. None could forget the persecution they had experienced; the loss of family, friends, and congregants; their physical and cultural home; and the destruction of European Jewry resulting from the Nazi war against the Jews. They were grappling with the fact that the Holocaust and their people's annihilation had started in Germany, the country and culture they had called home and had been so proud to embrace.

Modern Judaism was a product of Judaism's profound encounter with German culture, which deeply affected modern Judaism's and German culture's *Jewish* identities. Every effort to build new lives and careers reminded them of their cultural differences, what they had left behind, the former seminaries or the *Lehrhaus* movement as centers of a world lost to them, and of a collective identity as modern "German" rabbis that had been shattered.

Displacement, Trauma, and Exploring the Chances for a Future of the German-Jewish Past after the Holocaust

This sense of trauma and loss was especially apparent among students at the Hebrew Union College (HUC), where the refugees had a unique presence and place, yet it resonated in the Reform movement more than anywhere else. None of the other American Jewish religious movements was tied as closely to the German-Jewish tradition, which had its own past and identity. As the end of the Second World War and the Holocaust revealed the full extent of the destruction of European Jewry, it became even more apparent that these refugees were the last of a special group: those who were to write the final chapter of the German rabbinate, German Judaism, and *Wissenschaft,* and who would take a uniquely modern approach to Judaism.

Historian Ismar Elbogen was aware of the historicity and paradigm shift of the time and his students' role as standard-bearers of their tradition therein. Just before his untimely death on 1 August 1943, Elbogen had contributed an article titled "American Jewish Scholarship" to the *American Jewish Yearbook* on the centennial of Kaufmann Kohler's birth.[1] Elbogen did not live to see its publication. The article was a written legacy to his fellow refugees, American colleagues, and friends at HUC.

In the article, he stressed how modern Jewish scholarship in Germany and the United States had long been intertwined and how they had developed a unique transnational symbiotic relationship in which people such as the German-born Kaufmann Kohler, former president of HUC, played a critical, creative, and inspiring role. This fruitful relationship, he supposed, had been extinguished by recent history. The noted Jewish historian postulated that Nazism and the Shoah[2] had changed what was to be the center and periphery of modern Jewish scholarship. The relationship depended *solely* on regeneration from within American Jewry because its European counterpart had ceased to exist. His article reads like a testament to his colleagues and friends and especially to the younger refugees, whom he called on to serve as the last representatives of this European tradition:

> "Heinrich Heine aptly said that the Jew had a portable fatherland. Wherever the Jew migrated, he carried with him his spiritual heritage. Different countries at different periods of Jewish history have held the hegemony in Jewish studies. During the past fifty years, the mantle of Elijah has fallen on the United States. America was fast becoming a center of Jewish scholarship, and within the past decade it has become the sole center—with the exception of Palestine."[3]

He ended by writing:

> Soon Nazi brutality in Central and Western Europe compelled a goodly number of Jewish scholars to seek refuge in the United States. Their knowledge, expertness and scientific method will, given an opportunity, become real assets to American Jewish scholarship.... We are at the end. Our survey shows that from what small beginnings Jewish scholarship in America has developed. The growth has been rapid, even great.... For until recently

American Jewry has had a constant influx of intellectual forces from Europe. This reservoir is now destroyed. American Jewry will henceforth have to produce native scholars of its own.[4]

Leo Baeck's Global Leadership and the Remnants of His Students

Like Elbogen, Rabbi Leo Baeck, who survived years in the ghetto of Theresienstadt and was the intellectual and moral leader of the modern German rabbinate, worried about the future of modern Judaism and the German-Jewish tradition. Baeck settled in Great Britain, where a few of his former students and sectors of the refugee community reassembled around this iconic figure and the project to reestablish a liberal institution of higher learning in the form of the Jewish Theological College in London, the precursor of the Leo Baeck College.[5] However, Baeck knew that it was primarily the American rabbinical colleges, especially HUC, that could successfully preserve this tradition.[6] German Jewry had been destroyed, but Baeck hoped that the émigrés might uphold, develop, and even revive its spirit, dedication to humanity, and messianic hope.[7]

From 1948, Baeck worked from November to April at HUC in Cincinnati to complete *Dieses Volk* (This People), a manuscript he had begun before his deportation. He was also teaching a two-hour seminar. Most of the attendees were his former German students, but a few of them were Americans. The latter struggled to understand his English and references to Greek and Latin sources and histories as most of them were not as familiar with classical texts as the Europeans.

Among the students interested in attending Baeck's lectures was Albert Friedlander, with whom Baeck had developed a personal relationship and shared the hope that the German Jews who had found a new home in the United States might revive the spirit of German Jewry and bring their European traditions back to life in the dynamic American environment.[8]

Besides Friedlander, who translated Baeck's *Dieses Volk* into English and made his teacher's words available to a new audience, there were many former Germans on campus, such as Joseph Asher, Ernst Conrad, Wolfgang Hamburger, Robert Lehman, Jakob Petuchowski, Alexander Schindler, Nathan Peter Levinson, and Steven Schwarzschild.

The significance of these young men to the future of modern Judaism and their role in the work of Baeck and other leaders of progressive Judaism is apparent when one considers that three of them were selected to be among the first liberal Jews to return to Germany for the World Union for Progressive Judaism (WUPJ), starting with Joseph Asher's six-week trip in 1947.

CAREERS LOST AND FOUND 139

Leo Baeck with students on the Cincinnati campus of Hebrew Union College, ca. 1952: AJA, pc0212.07.

After Asher returned with a detailed report on the situation and needs of the communities, Steven Schwarzschild was sent to officiate as a liberal rabbi in Berlin from 1948 to 1950. At that time, Nathan Peter Levinson took over the liberal rabbinate there and focused on the situation of Jews and the prospects for liberal Judaism in Germany. In addition to Lily Montagu and Julian Morgenstern, Baeck, as president of the WUPJ, helped select this group of young men for these exploratory missions, which will be discussed in more detail in chapter 6.[9]

The influence of Leo Baeck and his connection to the refugees, the social fabric of their lives, and their communications defined these men as a special group inspired by a distinct memory and legacy. Even though Baeck's reunions with his former students were quiet, reserved, and even seemingly impersonal encounters at a glance, Baeck's survival and presence were enormously important to this group. Just how meaningful and emotional these encounters with their former teacher from Berlin were is illustrated in descriptions by former students and their biographers.

One example is a recollection from young Abraham Joshua Heschel, who called Baeck at his New York hotel during one of Baeck's annual visits to the United States. Yet even after all the years that he had heard his former teacher speak on the phone, this time, Heschel was speechless; he simply lost the ability to talk. He was overwhelmed to hear this voice from the past and to realize that Baeck's reappearance, his survival, and once again his availability to his former students built a bridge from that past to the present. The questions uppermost in Heschel's mind about Baeck's survival, his arrest in Theresienstadt, and the last days of the Hochschule in Berlin went unspoken but were keenly sensed by Baeck, who mastered the situation by complimenting Heschel on an article on the essence of prayer that Heschel had authored. Summarizing his plight in the ghetto with unexpected grace, Baeck stressed how important this work had been to him during his time in Theresienstadt.[10]

Nathan Peter Levinson described a similar scene that took place in 1947 at the Hotel Commodore next to Grand Central Station in New York. He and Wolfgang Hamburger had taken a long train ride from Cincinnati to New York to welcome their teacher on his first postliberation visit to the United States. At this reunion, the two former students felt incredibly moved to once again be in the presence of a man who had never lost his dignity, warmth, or genuine interest in those close to him and had never complained about his fate.[11]

Baeck returned to Berlin for his first postwar visit in 1951. Levinson, who at that time had a pulpit in the city, picked up the former leader of German Jewry at Tempelhof Airport. Welcoming Baeck back to Berlin, the city that had once been his home, the center of *Wissenschaft*, and the place from which he had been deported to Theresienstadt, Levinson struggled with intense emotions, as he described in his memoir:

> Words cannot describe the emotions that I felt, while I accompanied him [Baeck] for several days in Berlin—to the places of his former work, most of whom were in rabble and ashes, to the cemetery in Weissensee, where his wife was buried. He preached on Shabbat in the synagogue, talked to the delegates of the Central Council (of Jews), came to a reception that I had organized in my house ... I do not remember what Leo Baeck said on that

occasion. The press reported on it extensively. I am sure he encouraged the Jews of Berlin and did so without nostalgia and pathos, with theological and philosophical depth, with the understatement that was already typical for him, before he stayed in England. He always spoke without notes, in a style ready for print, and always he stood above things, *the cardinal*, how he was referred to in the past already so very appropriately. I remember lastingly the impression I had of Baeck on the pulpit in a Berlin synagogue. The patriarch of German Jewry, the formidable Jewish spirit of our century, proclaimed dead, who had taken back his position—he was a symbol of indestructible Jewish spirit, of the victory of Torah over destruction and death. Baeck embodied [the essence of his book] *Dieses Volk* [*This People*] that he started to write in Theresienstadt and had completed in freedom. A piece of eternity has become manifest by his life and work among us.[12]

Communitization and Transformation to "The Last Generation of the German Rabbinate"

These reflections and memories mirrored the deep collective trauma experienced by this group of refugees and ultimately forced them to recognize that, while the German-Jewish community as they knew it had not survived, the identity of the modern Jew that had grown from this community did have a chance to survive precisely because it was modern and portable. It had conquered the problem of a physical location and still had a functioning framework, especially in the United States. It was not necessarily tied to a physical place.

Rather than a physical place, the idea might replace the intellectual *Heimat* (home) that had been lost. Nathan Peter Levinson also expressed this idea in his autobiography *Ein Ort ist, mit wem du bist*, the title of which comes from a quote he attributed to John Steinbeck: "A place is not a place, a place is who you're with." He signaled that reconstruction was dynamic, did not depend on Germany as a physical center, and could thrive by way of the social and intellectual interaction and engagement of those who survived.[13]

The collective trauma of the refugees caused a deep crisis of meaning for that group. Not only were their chances for survival in question, their very identity was at risk, specifically German Jewry's path of assimilation and social inclusion since the emancipation period.

The process of questioning that path had already begun in the 1920s and was enforced by Nazism, but it required active intellectual deliberations in the post-Holocaust era if modern Judaism was to survive. Markus Krah has recently discussed how American Jews constructed a "usable east European past" in reaction to the serious identity crisis they experienced after the Shoah. This constructed past reflected the widely held perception that modern Judaism in general and its German heritage in particular—which had so intensely impacted American Jewry during the nineteenth century—had ended in a major failure.[14]

Therefore, the confrontation with their identity, history, and memory stood front and center in their efforts to survive. Their rabbinate had a strong social and political presence in society, and their engagement with a modern Judaism met the needs of modern Jews therein. This included a commitment to analyze the events of the Holocaust and how such a thing could have happened and to preserve the memory and history of German Jewry, all of which helped the refugee rabbis in their reconstruction.

They not only documented what happened to their collective but also provided creative ways to deal with their crisis and create a "usable past." Many of the refugees were trained historians and committed to a form of Judaism that they recognized was subject to history and change. Their sense of the role that history had played in Judaism must have spoken to them in this hour of need when their collective survival was threatened.

It is no surprise that liberal rabbis in particular took on an active role in society, representing the dynamic Jewish spirit assigned to liberal Judaism. They were instrumental in the communication of their history and the use of the past in the public sphere. The lessons they taught and the role models they presented resonated in this sphere because American Jews were in a state of insecurity, longing for solutions to current problems, and struggling with challenges and paradigm changes.

There was by no means an atmosphere of silence on matters related to the Holocaust, as claimed by historian Peter Novick.[15] A closer look at American Jewish communities and their rabbinical leadership proves that dealing with survival, coping with the loss of Europe as a center of Jewish knowledge and civilization, and making sense of the Holocaust were issues of vital importance to popular, scholarly, religious, and political discourses at the time.[16]

Ultimately, the threat the refugees experienced prompted a search for meaning and opened up ways to develop a transgenerational self-image that ensured the survival of the collective group and sparked intense discussions about its past and history, antisemitism, racism, the failure of German society and religious groups, memory, and the future of modern Judaism.[17]

Their search for new meaning, their drive to inform the present of their past, and the connection they generated among the past, present, and future were part of a generation-building process and their formation as "the last generation of the German rabbinate." This phrase was used repeatedly in their descriptions of their experiences as the last rabbi of a town, the last rabbi to leave Germany, the last students to be ordained in one of the seminaries, or the last witnesses of the destruction of a particular Jewish community. Their memoirs and autobiographies highlight their past and the new meaning they found in being part of the final chapter of their institutions and traditions and in accepting the resulting responsibilities.

The titles of their autobiographies and the Festschrifts published in their honor clearly show how they perceived themselves and were perceived over the course of history: Emil Fackenheim's *Epitaph for German Judaism*, Levinson's *Ein Ort ist, mit wem Du bist* (A place is not a place, but with whom you are), the memorial volume of former Berlin rabbis *Gegenwart im Rückblick* (The present in retrospect), W. Gunther Plaut's *Unfinished Business*, Herbert Strauss's *In the Eye of the Storm*, Joseph Asher's Festschrift *The Jewish Legacy and the German Conscience*, Norbert Weinberg's *Courage of the Spirit*, Walter Jacob's *The Seventeenth Generation*, Paul Lazarus's commemorative book titled *Beiträge zur Würdigung der letzten Rabbinergeneration in Deutschland* (Contributions to honor the last generation of rabbis in Germany), and Jakob Petuchowski's *Mein Judesein: Wege und Erfahrungen eines deutschen Rabbiners* (My Jewish being: Paths and experiences of a German rabbi), the latter two of which—like Levinson's autobiography—were notably *only* published in German!

Their messages were also echoed in the Festschrifts and histories of their former communities, congregants, and institutions, including commemorative volumes in their honor, such as *To Leave Your Mark*, a handbook for the college ministry, posthumously edited in honor of Alfred Jospe by his widow and son. This handbook provided meaningful instruction on how to involve the next generation of American college graduates in Judaism by using Jospe's texts and highlighting the example he set.[18]

These refugee scholars left behind a large number of materials: autobiographical writings, including unpublished ones like the memoir of Alfred Wolf, a member of the "band of five";[19] film material (Glatzer and Trepp);[20] and extremely well-designed websites, such as the perfectly groomed site commemorating Leo Trepp,[21] who passed away in 2010 but whose website keeps his memory and work alive with news to this day. All of these materials can be used to understand the history of the German rabbinate, document the refugee's life experiences, and bring a special legacy into the twenty-first century and beyond. They are excellent resources for further textual and literary analysis, a task that cannot be done justice in this book and that deserves closer attention by scholars in the fields of autobiographical literature and Holocaust memoirs.[22]

In the generation-building process, these publications and other societal, political, and religious platforms were essential elements in communicating the rabbis' depiction as "the last generation of the German rabbinate" and the guardians of a special legacy.

The collection of biographical data in MIRA states that one special age cohort, mainly men born after 1895–1900 and the so-called second generation, stood out in this generation-building process. The data also reveals that most had a background in liberal Judaism or the American Reform movement. This may have been because men of this age had a large part of their lives ahead of them and thus the time to be part of or even shape such a transformation. The very nature of the liberal Reform rabbinate encouraged rabbis to take an active role in aligning the past with the present and emboldened them to communicate their concepts for "a usable past" to society more than was the case among more traditional Jews, who rejected historical Judaism. Their emergence as a special group with a unique legacy was supported by objects, individuals, institutions, rituals, and political themes that linked them with the past.

American seminaries provided both the central organizational framework and vehicles advancing this process. The seminaries were the place where the refugees' past continued to have meaning and where these men received support in their professional transition. Even the hybrid identities of the second generation found a home on American seminary campuses.

The scholarly culture of the colleges, the German refugee professors who taught there, the interest in the curriculum and *Wissenschaft*, and the events that brought the group together time and again, such as commemorations and visits of survivors or those who pioneered returning to postwar Europe, resonated in the community. Most significant was the presence of Ismar Elbogen, former rector of the Hochschule in New York in 1943, whose funeral in August 1943 was attended by a large number of his students and colleagues. The same attention was given to Leo Baeck, who made regular visits and spent one semester each year in Cincinnati from 1947 on. Likewise, his portrait, painted by Eugene Spiro, reminded future generations of Reform rabbis and scholars of this icon of German-Jewish leadership in the rabbinate into the millennium.[23]

The founding and naming of B'nai B'rith lodges after role models, like the Leo Baeck Lodge in New York, helped define this group as the last of an otherwise extinct German rabbinate, as did memorials, support for the formation and research activity of the Leo Baeck Institute (LBI), the refugees' scholarship and teaching at the colleges, their publications, and the regular visits to

Nelson Glueck congratulating Hugo Hahn on his honorary doctor of divinity, HUC-JIR New York city, 1963: AJA, pchuc33ny.001.

their former German communities. These events, institutions, and exchanges enabled them as a group to present their collective memory and develop new meaning as the last of a special kind. The communication between the refugees and their new academic institutions was not a one-way street.

Throughout the 1960s and 1970s, the colleges recognized these men as the "last generation of the German rabbinate." They gave them honorary degrees—sometimes in groups—later in their lives, thereby illuminating and honoring the historical context that had brought them to the United States and the institution. They honored their service and lifetime achievements for the respective religious movements and confirmed that these men had found a new intellectual and professional home.[24]

This was an important recognition, far more significant than receiving a scholarly degree. It expressed that the respective rabbi had overcome a long, difficult, and sometimes painful transformation and had found a new personal and professional framework where he was at home. It was part of a professional metamorphosis and signaled that the recipient had completed a long journey to another culture.

This recognition was especially important to those refugees who had never been able to obtain a PhD in Germany due to the banning of Jews from German universities. They had thus felt that they were missing a crucial piece of their careers because this academic qualification had always been considered essential for German rabbis.

When Karl Richter gave a eulogy for his friend and colleague Ulrick Steuer on 21 October 1973, he emphasized that none of the rabbis who had received their education in Europe and were able to come to this blessed land during the years of the great upheaval had an easy road. "We had to begin anew. We had to learn to express our thoughts in a new language. We had to cross the barriers of custom and culture to become useful members of American communities. Ulrick Steuer felt that his tireless work was crowned with success when HUC-Jewish Institute of Religion acknowledged his contribution by awarding him the honorary degree of Doctor of Divinity, thereby making him an adopted son of the college. He told me that he considered this the greatest honor ever bestowed upon him."[25]

At the 2002 inaugural ceremony of David Ellenson as the new president of HUC in Cincinnati, a gesture by Wolli Kaelter likewise stressed that HUC had preserved a certain continuity for many of the refugees following the destruction of the Hochschule and their hometowns. The aged Kaelter handed the Torah scrolls of his hometown's synagogue in Danzig—where his father had served as rabbi—to Ellenson, who accepted this treasure, thereby symbolically taking on the Holocaust victim's legacy in the UAHC.[26]

Contemporary discourse, the zeitgeist, and the unexpected challenges American Jewry faced as the largest diaspora community helped to communicate the professional, theological, and cultural expertise these men gained before and during Nazism and publicly enhanced their image as "the last generation of the German rabbinate."

More specifically, these men were able to cultivate their role as the last generation and develop as the guardians of a special legacy in their new American environment, thanks to the opportunities that came with the emerging American civil rights movement, the Vietnam War, the growing alienation within the American congregation, the efforts to make sense of the Holocaust through educational or memorial projects, the survival of modern Judaism, and the confrontation of postwar Germany.

Toward a Revival of Judaism in American Society: Cultural Transfers, New Leadership, and Keeping It "Involved"

Their engagement generated significant activity in this cohort and opened up new ways for them, as modern Jews, to connect with both Jewish and non-Jewish Americans in the post-Holocaust years. Although their American colleagues had taken a stand on many of the topics the refugees addressed, the refugee rabbis had been present during the actual crisis, had stood side by side with their congregations in the darkest hour of Jewish history, and had confronted Nazism. Their experiences made them a living link between history and the present, and they impressed many Americans with their desire for renewal. Their history gave them unparalleled authenticity, charisma, and authority when they talked about the past and the present, the societal and religious problems that existed then and now, and their suggestions for Jewish solutions to the crisis of the modern Jew.

American Jews were open to their messages. Marked by a strong commitment to pluralism, American Jews took on the unexpected role of the largest Jewish community globally and as natural spokespersons for the survivors of the Shoah. In many ways, American Jews were challenged by confronting Germans in the postwar era on restitution and Holocaust-related issues in the wake of the catastrophe. Representing the largest Jewish community in the diaspora and committed to a distinctly modern and participatory role of Jews in society, these men felt it was essential to continue to build a supportive and respectful relationship with other religious and ethnic groups in American society as Americans and Jews. Not surprisingly, the lasting segregation and persecution of African Americans in the American South and the civil rights movement irritated American Jews and posed questions about their own "whiteness." Would America stand true to its promise of freedom for all? Had America learned the lessons of the Holocaust?[27]

Scattered among many differing political and theological groups, American Jews lacked cohesion and community and thus felt it necessary to secure growth and Jewish survival. Congregational affiliation, however, was in sharp decline, and members knew they must deal with the changing demographics caused by intermarriage and suburbanization. New models for a meaningful and timely Jewish identity were especially needed by the children of the most recent immigrant generation from eastern Europe. These young people could not be reached by classic Reform Judaism with its highly Protestantized forms or by the prevailing traditional Orthodoxy.

While Orthodoxy tried to accept a timely, competitive, and yet traditional Judaism, which appealed to its congregants and allowed them to play a role within modern American society, the American Reform movement embraced the idea of Jewish peoplehood, Zionism, and the newly founded state of Israel as the center of Jewish life, even if the reality of Judaism in the Yishuv (the Jewish settlement in Palestine) did not live up to its American pluralist ideals. Modern Judaism, with its strong emphasis on reason, progress, and social inclusion, seemed to have failed in light of the Shoah, a "fact" that seemed to crystallize over time in the very history of German Jewry.[28]

The annihilation of Jewish education and knowledge in Europe was a major concern of American Jews, and they felt the need to preserve, develop, and define models for modern Jewish education inside and outside the synagogue and to revive community, knowledge, and the synagogue as a center of their activity.

Many communities fought the process of alienation, a development German Jewry was very familiar with because of its similar experiences with the high degree of assimilation that occurred starting in the late nineteenth century. Almost all of the refugee rabbis noted the ignorance of the basics of Jewish knowledge and their students' and congregants' inability to study Judaism using the ancient texts. These rabbis felt that educating and encouraging their congregants to actively engage with their tradition and bringing Judaism in line with modern times would be important assets for the future of modern Judaism.[29]

The refugee rabbis—especially those who had officiated in Germany before their emigration, a younger cohort born after 1895 or 1900—provided meaningful and authentic answers to their American congregants in the synagogue or the religious movements of American Judaism. Unlike their American colleagues, these firsthand witnesses to Nazism had stood by their communities until they were forced to flee. This shaped their character, leadership, and professional experience and enabled them to speak to their American congregants with authenticity and authority, which was highly appreciated.

Their experience with alienation and the mission to reconnect their congregants to a meaningful and timely experience of Judaism helped them identify and address the problems in the American synagogue and on the minds of their congregants. In fact, it was precisely because they had been confronted with similar problems earlier in the German context that they felt a special call to act, to combat alienation, to instill the missing spirit of community, to fill the gaps in Jewish knowledge, to encourage study, and on the whole to promote a strong sense of how American Jews could make a uniquely *Jewish* contribution to American society.

These rabbis had been influenced by a Jewish revival during the First World War and the years of the Weimar Republic (1919–1933). Their rabbinates in

Europe had been innovative, had embraced eastern European culture and Zionism, and had defined new ways to reach out to congregants of all ages, according to their specific needs and interests in the community.

Their skills, experience, and knowledge appealed in a special way to American Jews, who found themselves after the Second World War and the Shoah confronted with new tasks related to their changing place on a new global map of the Jewish world. As the largest Jewish community globally, American Jewry was not only responsible for representing the interests of the Holocaust survivors in the United States; it had also become a hub for the survival of an explicitly modern and pluralistic Jewish diaspora.

At the forefront of these efforts stood the youth. Youth rabbis had emerged during the Weimar years to address the needs of the next generation of Jews in so-called youth services or congregations, which used customized educational materials such as youth bibles. The Jewish youth movement during the Weimar Republic had inspired the next generation. It had made Judaism attractive and provided ethnic cohesion and hope. Jewish history and identity had been communicated in an informal environment, which emphasized camaraderie, friendship, and belonging. It shaped a new, active, and conscious adolescent generation, which frequently also embraced Zionism.

Movements like the German Blau-Weiss, Wanderbund, Kadimah, the Kameraden, and even the Orthodox Ezra had pulled together an entire generation of German-Jewish youth in a revolutionary way. These movements helped them turn away from the highly assimilationist nineteenth-century lifestyle of their parents, which they felt did not provide solutions to their everyday challenges as young Jews in Germany in the 1910s and 1920s.

In many ways, the emerging Jewish youth movements embraced elements of the larger German youth movements (*Jugendbewegung*), which criticized some of the same societal issues and were very popular. However, these German movements often developed an attitude against young Jews. Jewish youth organizations became increasingly popular in the wake of growing antisemitism in German society and a general social crisis.

A growing understanding that the assimilationist model had failed and that most German Jews had lost their understanding of what it meant to be Jewish in their everyday life drove the successful recruitment of young German Jews in such innovative organizations. They tried to facilitate a discovery of the "subjective Jewish problem" of how to deal with two identities, German and Jewish, and to develop more "Jewish substance," meaning in-depth knowledge of Judaism and an inherently Jewish lifestyle in which they found satisfaction and answers to their questions.[30] At the center of their approach stood a new form of pedagogy, which encouraged the young to explore, research, and discuss original Jewish sources independently from the prevailing hierarchical model of predefined knowledge under the supervision of a schoolteacher.

The youth movements gave this age group new agency to actively explore Judaism, create a community of their own, and experiment with a Jewish lifestyle apart from existing conventions. Joint study and a new social fabric—sometimes with socialist or Zionist leanings—replaced the boring and detached participation in a service with standardized prayers and a sermon given by a rabbi whose age usually set him apart from the younger generation.

Hiking, camping, scouting, spending time outdoors, camaraderie: this new social experience stimulated an entire generation of German Jews to infuse their lives with "Jewish substance," meaning inner strength and resilience in life that grew from a strong and fulfilling identity as Jews. The new social interaction of boys and girls across the boundaries of class and gender spurred curiosity, group cohesion, and joint learning and allowed the youngsters to reinvent themselves as young Jews in an environment that provided creativity and responsibility.

Young and especially trained "youth rabbis" created at these camps an atmosphere of equality, friendship, discovery, a new spirituality, and deep inner connection to Judaism.[31] These new concepts did not end at camp; they affected this generation in their everyday lives and continued to create a lifelong bond with the value system of the respective movements once the members had outgrown adolescence.

Identifying themselves as part of a new Jewish leadership with a special mission to form a new "German-Jewish identity," many former members became leaders of their youth movements, found an intellectual home in the *Lehrhaus* movement inspired by Martin Buber and Franz Rosenzweig, or initiated new methods of Jewish learning at home and abroad.[32] Signposts of these movements were projects like the School of Jewish Youth, founded by Joachim Prinz in Berlin in 1928, which established a school that was organized and conducted exclusively by its young pupils.[33]

Like Prinz, the younger group of refugee rabbis were associated with these youth movements. They sought new ways to develop a German-Jewish identity because they were seeking new forms of community, study, and a meaningful reality as Jews or, as was the case for the so-called second generation of refugee rabbis, they grew up in these movements and were deeply affected by that experience. Some of these young rabbis were identified by their expressed values and Jewish substance on the HUC campus in Cincinnati, where they continued to participate in the Jewish camp experience and youth work. This group included Ernst Lorge, Herman Schaalman, Alfred Wolf, Wolli Kaelter, and Karl Weiner, who had been ordained at the Jüdisch-Theologisches Seminar in Breslau in 1938.

In the late 1940s, this group became the nucleus of a new type of Reform Jewish camp that incorporated its experiences from the German-Jewish youth movement. Schaalman, Weiner, and Lorge found employment as young rabbis in the Chicago area and had frequent and positive encounters with the American Protestant youth movements. This experience spoke to their own social experience and Jewish roots and underscored the great potential for youth work in American society, which had not yet been fully developed within the Reform movement.

Their careers in the rabbinate provided the necessary framework for this kind of youth work: Herman Schaalman was appointed as the new director of the Chicago Federation of UAHC and played a key role in recruiting resources and human capital for the purchase of Union Institute, which today is called the Olin Sang Ruby Union Institute (OSRUI).[34]

In March 1951, the Chicago Federation of UAHC officially voted to purchase a camp in the vicinity of the city that would give the next generation of Reform Jews a place to gather regularly. At this meeting, German-born Ernst Lorge and his two American-born colleagues Joseph Buchler and Arnold Wolf enthusiastically supported the idea and found a suitable campsite called Briar Lodge in Oconomowoc, Wisconsin. Thanks to the involvement and successful fundraising of the local temple sisterhoods, the project was launched in late 1951. Efficient organization, an inspiring vision, and cooperation between lay and rabbinical leadership enabled the group to secure the deed for the camp in February 1952.

The property was officially incorporated in May of that year. The newly founded Union Institute worked closely with the National Foundation of Temple Youth (NFTY), a group within the UAHC that formally organized and rented campsites for the Reform Jewish youth. The establishment of Union Institute under the directorship of Schaalman was the first youth camp actually owned by the UAHC.

The institute introduced youth rabbis and designed daily schedules featuring baseball, storytelling, studying, group singing, and a high level of creativity. Group singing in particular played a special role in developing community and grassroots involvement and emotionally binding the adolescents to Judaism. This was recently stressed by Judah Cohen and cannot be underestimated in this context. Like in the German synagogue, music was essential to worship, community building, and the aesthetics of modern Jewish identity.

At camp, the repertoire included more than liturgical music; campers sang German folk songs from the emancipation era, like "Die Gedanken sind frei" (Thoughts are free), a song sung by the liberal movement before the German revolution in 1848 that idealized freedom of thought in the absence of freedom of speech.[35]

In 1958, OSRUI opened up a Teacher Training Institute, reaching out to teachers at religious schools in the Reform movement. The facility flourished with the steady involvement of many German refugee rabbis in the region. Besides Schaalman, Lorge, and Weiner, Karl Richter, who officiated in Michigan, was also involved in the project. Its success was so compelling that it encouraged other regions to set up permanent camps and scouting activities for their adolescents and adults.[36]

It is no wonder that this pilot project soon inspired the opportunity to establish a Reform Jewish camp, Camp Saratoga, in Southern California, where Rabbi Phineas Smoller was serving as regional director of the UAHC in Los Angeles. Smoller had once served in Chicago in the same position that Herman Schaalman held in the past. Following his departure, Smoller had been involved in the NFTY Institutes, the precursor to established Reform Jewish camps. In 1951, Smoller contacted Ben Swig, a layman and San Francisco philanthropist who offered to donate between $5,000 and $50,000 to establish a Reform Jewish camp in California.

In the summer of 1952, the first camp opened in Oconomowoc, Wisconsin. Herman Schaalman orchestrated a "happy marriage" when he invited his friend from the Hochschule and HUC Wolli Kaelter to visit the newly founded camp with his wife Sarah for a few weeks. At the time, Kaelter was seeking alternatives to his current employment as a community rabbi in McKeesport, Pennsylvania. Both Sarah and Wolli were active in the German-Jewish youth movement and jumped at the chance to participate.

In the summer of 1953, Swig invested $25,000 in the Union Institute's purchase of the 208-acre property in Saratoga, which enabled the Union Institute to launch its next project there and hire Wolli Kaelter, who was enthusiastic about its prospects.[37] Besides directing the new camp in Saratoga, Wolli Kaelter was also to become director of the Union Institute's Pacific Northern California and Northern Pacific Northwest Region and director of the West Coast NFTY. He was expected to infuse this position with energy and enthusiasm. He owed his appointment not only to Schaalman's recommendation but also to his own commitment and expertise and the strong connections between the Union Institute and the German camp leadership in Oconomowoc.[38]

Once in California, Kaelter contacted Alfred Wolf, who had been part of the "band of five," the group sent as refugee students from Berlin to HUC. Wolf held a pulpit as rabbi at Wilshire Boulevard Temple in Los Angeles, where he gained experience with new camps Camp Hess Kramer and Gindling Hilltop Camp in Malibu. Kaelter benefited from his organizational experience locally and in 1953 launched Saratoga—The Camp for Living Judaism, which was named "Camp Swig" after the man who continued to be involved in the growth and prosperity of the enterprise.[39]

Aside from the Reform movement, German Orthodox rabbis also were part of a transfer of elements of the German-Jewish youth movement into the American Orthodox education system. Data shows that ethnic refugee community congregations like Gates of Hope in Washington Heights reinstituted a youth rabbi among their ranks, a position for which they could recruit Rabbi Leo Adler, a former student of the ILBA in Würzburg. Adler had transferred from Würzburg to the Yeshiva Mir in 1935 to study there but had fled with the whole Yeshiva Mir to Vilna in 1939. He did not reach the United States via Shanghai until after the end of the war.[40]

One of the most active Orthodox rabbis in this faction of Judaism was Michael Munk, a champion of Jewish education who left the American congregational rabbinate in the United States. Besides his work at the Beth Jacob School of Boro Park, New York, he launched a private Jewish summer camp called Camp Munk in Ferndale, New York, in 1955.

In an interview with the Research Foundation for Jewish Immigration, Munk stressed that the camp functioned as well as it did because he and his wife could draw from their German experience. Munk had been active in the Orthodox Ezra youth movement in Germany and was inspired by this experience when he and his wife set up Camp Munk in the United States. The campsite attracted students from all over the country and offered a wide range of education in Jewish and general studies, athletics, and outdoor activities. These opportunities were offered to boys of all ages, but not to girls. Like its liberal counterparts, the camp advocated self-administration and encouraged the older and better-educated boys among the campers, such as yeshiva boys, by making them camp counselors and even substitutes for young rabbis.[41]

It is unclear if Samson Raphael Weiss, director of the National Council of Young Israel from 1947 to 1956 and founder and dean of the Young Israel Institute for Jewish Studies from 1945 to 1956, was involved with the scouting programs of the new American Orthodox movement, however, further research in mid-twentieth-century Jewish pedagogy might expand on this topic and the involvement of refugee rabbis in plans to set up Orthodox education for girls.

Weiss was dedicated to the renewal of Jewish education. He headed Torah U'mesorah, the first Orthodox Jewish day-school movement in the United States and Canada. This movement offered compelling Jewish education to young Orthodox Jews who might otherwise have lost their connection to Judaism and Yiddishkeit ("Jewishness," especially in a traditional east European Ashkenazi- and Yiddish-speaking context) in a solely secular environment that enforced assimilation. At the time, most young Jewish students created a nexus between Jewish and secular education by attending both public school and additional afternoon classes in a Jewish school, but this denied them a more integrated education that could merge secular and religious study. Instead, the Torah U'mesorah model combined a curriculum with Jewish and secular education in one school. The schools, which were only for boys, were directed by an ordained Orthodox rabbi who worked with an associate principal responsible for secular academic study. Together, they designed a curriculum that would meet both the religious and secular educational requirements.[42]

Data indicates that as early as 1943, rabbis were among the founders of the Manhattan Jewish Day School, the first of its kind in Manhattan. One of these rabbis was Jacob Hoffmann, the former Orthodox rabbi of the Jewish community of Frankfurt and after 1938, the rabbi of the Hungarian congregation Ohav Zedek in Manhattan.[43]

Finally, several refugees found meaningful employment at the Hillel Campus Organization of the Independent Order of B'nai B'rith. Here, too, the desire to create future generations of college-educated, conscious Jews was at the center of their work. The Hillel Foundation had been founded in 1923 so as not to lose those talented young Jews who were getting a secular education at American universities to a secular and purely American world. As a campus organization connected to and founded by the B'nai B'rith, Hillel successfully created a presence on American campuses that equaled that of both Christian campus ministries and the typical American fraternities.

Organized by one or several rabbis, the "Hillel house" became a meeting place not only for students and faculty on campus—where the Shabbat and other holidays could be observed in a Jewish setting and according to Jewish law—but also for the diverse young community. The Hillel centers provided services for Reform, Conservative, and Orthodox students and organized Oneg Shabbat, the Friday-night meal after Shabbat services, in the setting of the respective academic community. In addition, the group offered the young students a family away from home, counseling, trips, lectures, and discussion and study groups on Jewish and secular topics to stimulate intellectually well-considered Jewish positions on contemporary issues. In short, Hillel provided common ground for the plurality of Jews at college to develop a universal Jewish bond, to bridge the Jewish diversity they experienced away from home, and to stimulate creative Jewish intellectual leadership among young American Jews.[44]

Like the youth organizations of the religious movements in American Judaism, Hillel offered a number of German refugees a place to develop their enthusiasm and skills for youth work.

The fact that Leo Lichtenberg, the fifth student of the "band of five," started his career in 1943 as the rabbi of Temple Israel and Hillel director at Florida State University in Tallahassee supports the idea that the Union Institute may have encouraged the five students from the Hochschule to engage in youth work. W. Gunther Plaut was the only one who did not pursue a career in that field.

Besides Lichtenberg, Rabbi Erwin Zimet served as a Hillel adviser at Vassar College from 1950 to 1970, and Rabbi Frank Fisher directed the Hillel organization at both Duke University and the University of North Carolina from 1980 to 1993.[45]

The man who brought the Hillel organization to the national leadership level during the 1950s and 1960s was Alfred Jospe, a young Berlin rabbi who directed a number of local Hillel houses and led a local congregation after he immigrated to the United States. In 1939, he accepted the position as rabbi of the Tree of Life Congregation in Morgantown, Virginia, and served as Hillel director on the University of West Virginia campus from 1940 on.

His tenure in Morgantown as Hillel director must have been successful because he was promoted to Hillel director at Indiana University in Bloomington in 1944.[46] In 1949, he served as national director of the Hillel Campus Organization in Washington, DC, until he retired in 1971. His many publications demonstrate that he approached his work as a personal mission and did so in a systematic fashion by discussing the methods and purposes of Hillel programs on campus.

A sample reader of his writings published in his honor by his wife and son, Eva and Raphael Jospe, highlights his background, approach, and mission. His primary goals were to fight alienation from Judaism and provide an understanding of Jewish heritage and meaning, and help adapt these to a rapidly changing secular world and ever-emerging new challenges for every Jew.[47]

As a Jewish leader in the 1950s and 1960s, Jospe was in the middle of an explosive transformation of American society. He noticed that in the postwar era, young Jews did not polarize religion and rationalism; they perceived the dichotomy as being between the "conventional faith of their parents" and a "highly individualized quest for salvation." They wanted to rediscover the religion of their parents but on their own terms. Likewise, other young Jews were experimenting with new "quasi-religious lifestyles and communes and *havurot*" with a great interest in transcendentalism, subjects on which mainstream religions had little to offer.[48]

Jospe's children emphasized that the young rabbi's mission was deeply affected by his close relationship with Leo Baeck. This connection and Jospe's dedication to *Wissenschaft des Judentums*, his children claimed, were the foundation for his work providing the next generation with Jewish knowledge and a tool kit to incorporate Jewish meaning into their lives.[49]

It was the personal approach, intellectual aura, and deep level of self-awareness that set apart the leadership, knowledge, religious perspectives, and social activism of these men of the last generation and created a sense of ethnic Jewish pride. They demonstrated that modern Judaism could connect to its traditions, that it contained eternal messages that would never lose their appeal, and that it was an important resource for providing answers to contemporary problems facing modern Jews. Patterns to create Jewish resilience they had experimented with or developed during the crisis in Germany made them outstanding leaders in American synagogues, communities, and secular organizations.

The rabbis who had officiated in Germany rarely rose to leadership positions in their respective religious movements; however, they gained status in congregations and Jewish organizations. Besides knowledge and training, their history, experience, and tenacity in standing with their communities and demonstrating unusual skill, credibility, and authenticity made these men role models in their synagogues and organizations in which they worked. They used their past experiences and the knowledge they acquired in Germany as a sort of social (or religious) capital with which to generate new meaning of life and enhance their Americanization and leadership in American society. Their concepts, approaches, and teachings of Judaism spoke to American Jewry, especially the youth, and enhanced the significance of their work and voices. More importantly, their experience was valued by American Jews who increasingly viewed it as paradigmatic of their own diaspora experience in a post-emancipatory age.

The sermons of Max Nussbaum, some of which have been collected in a commemorative volume published in his honor, illuminate how important the experiences and personal histories of the refugees were to services, the part they played in their spiritual messages to congregants, and how politics were woven into their ministry against the backdrop of the past and present.

In his sermon "Chosenness and Forgiveness" on Yom Kippur 1953, Nussbaum described to his congregants what the concept of "chosenness" meant for the modern Jew in light of the covenant. It was not a social privilege but a moral obligation: service to others in the spirit of God, even if personal suffering resulted from upholding these ideals. To illustrate the power of living up to these spiritual values, he presented the story of Werner Theshow (Tessier), one of the murderers of Walther Rathenau, the German secretary of state who was killed in 1922 by a group of antisemites. Twenty years after the murder, in 1941, Theshow happened to meet Rathenau's nephew in the French Foreign Legion in North Africa. Nussbaum described how the encounter took an unexpected turn. Instead of feeling hostility and hatred, Theshow was so touched to meet the young man that he confessed that he had killed his uncle. He then pulled out a slip of paper that he had carried in his pocket for the past twenty years and presented it to the young legionnaire.

It was a letter written by Walthers Rathenau's mother, Mathilde, to the mother of his murderer, stating that she "in the name and spirit of him he has murdered, forgive[s], even as God may forgive." Theshow told the nephew that this letter had changed his life and converted him from an active antisemite to an admirer and student of Jewish history and Hebrew who was profoundly dedicated to saving Jewish people by word and deed. Nussbaum concluded by saying that "this is the meaning of Israel's election, our purpose and the very meaning of Jewish life."[50]

On Rosh Hashanah 1961, Nussbaum spoke about how the Eichmann trial and the Bar Mitzvah of the Israeli state were not coincidental but were an expression of the connection between memory and identity.[51]

At the height of the 1961 Berlin crisis, Nussbaum expressed his concern over American Cold War politics and the desire to protect Berlin and safeguard a potential reunification of Germany. He called this "a nightmare" for the Jewish refugee from Germany who had become an American citizen and concluded that "Germany could not possibly be divided into too many parts as far as the destiny of our people is concerned, as far as the peace of the world is concerned."[52]

Nussbaum's first pulpit in the United States was in Muskogee, Oklahoma, but his rabbinate did not end there. He advanced to Temple Israel of Hollywood, where he stayed for the rest of his life. Temple Israel provided the perfect setting for young Nussbaum, who represented modernity and tradition, used the bimah like a stage, and had an illustrious history and reputation as a rabbi who had stood up to the Nazis, something he often referred to from the pulpit.

The handsome couple Max and Ruth Nussbaum were custom-made for Hollywood, and Nussbaum's ministry reached many Jews and non-Jews, both locally and internationally. His presence affected and influenced those far beyond the synagogue. It extended to the vast secular public sphere and a wide array of typically secular Jewish organizations in America, such as the United Jewish Appeal, the Zionist Organization of America, the American Jewish Congress, and the World Jewish Congress. He was actively engaged in all of these organizations and even served as president of the American Jewish Congress in 1946, a remarkable position for a recent immigrant.

Joachim Prinz participated more actively in the US political arena than he had in Germany. In his autobiography, he explained how the US State Department suppressed the first reports on the mass extermination of European Jews, which were submitted by Rabbi Stephen Wise. This experience triggered survivor guilt and ignited in Prinz the growing conviction that "organized religion would go under unless it became a potent force in society . . ., that meant in political life. Unless religion became the guardian of decency and morality in the community and in the country, it had no right to exist."[53]

He continued to assert that both the synagogue and the rabbi had a responsibility to sharpen the political conscience of the congregation and society and engage actively in both. Some aspects of American society, especially the prevailing racism in the still-segregated American South, motivated Prinz and Nussbaum and many others to take action. The refugees' experience of racial and social exclusion, degradation, and the denial of civil rights was still alive in their memory. They could not tolerate the discrepancy between the American ideal of freedom—promoted front and center in American politics during the cold war years—and the reality of racial and social inequality they witnessed in American society, especially in the South.

From the beginning, the American civil rights movement spoke to the refugee rabbis in a special way. The growing number of American-born rabbis involved in this movement as it gained momentum in the 1950s and 1960s, however, could not speak up for the civil rights cause with the same authority as Holocaust survivors or refugees from Nazism. Both of these groups had suffered racial persecution by a government that was officially acknowledged as inhumane and against the American ideal of freedom for all.

Their involvement not only served the civil rights movement and the public but also the refugees themselves. This was especially true of Joseph Asher. Asher felt uprooted after an almost global journey as a refugee and had considered going back to Melbourne, Australia, where he felt "at home."[54] However, as he worked pulpits in the South—Tuscaloosa, Florida, and Greensboro, North Carolina—he found new meaning in his work and a new home in the engagement for the American civil rights movement. This movement provided an opportunity for meaningful involvement as a refugee rabbi with such a distinctive past.

In May 1963, Asher was invited to participate in the local Ministers' Forum on behalf of Greensboro's civil rights activists. After the event, he said to his friend and director of the UAHC Social Action Committee, Albert Vorspan, that the matter spoke to his heart in a special way and explained that this engagement had benefited him: "As for myself, I slept well last night. It [the meeting] may not have done anything for the Negro, but it did a great deal for myself... I have a feeling that subsequent to last night's events, there will be other local white ministers who will want to participate in future mass meetings of this kind. I feel rather pleased that I should have been a pioneer."

While we do not know if Asher suffered from survivor guilt like Prinz did, he clearly saw it as his duty and a special privilege as a refugee from Nazism to mediate between the African American cause and the white religious elites. Among these elites, he, a Jew and the rabbi of Temple Emanu-El, was respected as a "white" element of their community but could point with authority to the injustices of American society like no one else could.[55]

Joachim Prinz also became active in the American civil rights movement, although in a different way from Asher. The rabbi stressed the interconnectedness of the historical experience of Jews and African Americans in the Western world. At the famous March on Washington on 28 August 1963, he warned all Americans, particularly American Jews, against standing silently by while their African American fellow citizens experienced racially motivated exclusion similar to what Germany's Jews had faced at the onset of the Nazi regime.[56] Then he proceeded to introduce the most important speaker at the march: Martin Luther King Jr.

Prinz, however, saw the alliance between Blacks and Jews as more than just a contribution to racial and social justice in America. He also viewed it as a way to alert American Jews to the crisis of modern Judaism in the diaspora of the post-Holocaust years. According to Prinz's biographer David Jünger, the former Berlin rabbi perceived the crisis as a matter of survival for a [modern, meaningful, and socially dynamic][57] Judaism in the diaspora, which had failed in Germany and was threatened with extinction. In Prinz's eyes, American Jewry was the last standard-bearer of modern Judaism within a pluralistic diaspora, but it was standing at the edge of an abyss.

The Berlin rabbi considered the biggest threats to a dynamic, cohesive, and pluralistic American Judaism to be the loss of the intellectually inspiring influences of European Jewry, the broad acceptance of American Jews in society, and an Israeli-American relationship that curtailed American Jewry's right to speak out for world Jewry. Prinz argued that these limitations would destroy the creative forces of a modern Judaism that could only survive, develop, and prosper in a modern and pluralistic society such as existed in the United States. Jünger believes that this was why Prinz turned to the civil rights issue.

While the rabbis' political and social engagement on behalf of the American civil rights movement was itself a just cause, its main purpose was to mobilize millions of American Jews and enforce the impact of a living religion, a religion that put ethical values at the center of true humanity and had the potential to breathe new life into the idea of "religion." Prinz hoped this experience would ignite an intense intellectual exchange among American Jews and secure the future of Judaism.[58] Jünger states that Prinz's vision of a modern and dynamic Judaism linked to tradition, history, and Zionism grew out of the idea of a full-fledged Jewish civilization similar to Reconstructionism in modern Judaism.[59]

Prinz and Nussbaum entered the political arena not only as rabbis and religious leaders but also as presidents of a number of Jewish organizations, including the American Jewish Congress, the Zionist Organization of America, and the Conference on Jewish Material Claims against Germany. Abraham Joshua Heschel, however, stepped into the political arena as a theologian who emphasized that religion did not end in the spiritual realm but called for intense societal and political engagement based on the Hebrew Bible.

While Heschel is often characterized as representing an east European Jewish tradition because of his Hassidic family background[60]—which undoubtedly is an important part of his theology—his scholarship must also be understood as a result of his encounter with modern rationalism and modern Judaism.

Like other young Jews raised in a traditional Jewish environment in countries east of Germany who studied and began a career in Germany, Heschel's understanding of religion and the role it should play in the life of modern Jews was influenced by his training at the Hochschule and the intense intellectual contact with modern Jewish thought and scholarship in Germany. His background in traditional Hasidic Judaism and spirituality and a systematic philosophy of religion spoke to modern Jews precisely because of its unusual blend of tradition and modernity. Heschel, who rejected Prinz's path of turning to Reconstructionism and Judaism as a "civilization," wanted to maintain faith in modern religion, which he considered essential to reintroducing the reality of God to modern-day life.

Heschel criticized those who tried to substitute religion with rationalism and who gave up faith as a spiritual element. He tried to reawaken and nourish a deep inner piety as a leitmotif in people's lives, arguing that there was a lasting relationship between humanity and God. The adoption of this concept was a pathway to developing a new or long-forgotten dimension of faith to solve contemporary problems and engage in worldly matters.

The study of religious texts and an ongoing conversation with God were to give people a new perspective on life and to reestablish a long-lost, dynamic personal relationship with the divine. In this theological model, God not only spoke to a person; that person would also be in close communication with God and would find guidance, answers to problems, and encouragement to political and social action.[61] Putting the Hebrew prophets at the center of his theology, as he did in his dissertation in Berlin, Heschel claimed that their texts reminded all people to speak out for the voiceless, the poor, and the oppressed and encouraged social justice and political agitation as the result of the conversation between God and humankind.[62]

While in Germany, Heschel found a home in the *Lehrhaus* movement aside from his studies at the Hochschule. There, new methods of learning, progressive pedagogy, and a desire to obtain innovative firsthand Jewish knowledge from original sources challenged antiquated methods of lecturing and preaching and was a means to reconnect assimilated Jews to their Jewish identity. First started by Franz Rosenzweig and Martin Buber in Frankfurt, the *Lehrhaus* movement launched a revival of Jewish identity and experience in Germany that peaked during the Nazi years.[63]

Heschel's faith-based theology introduced a new spirituality, religious feeling, direct communication with God, and a new sense of Jewishness that spoke to modern American Jews, many of whom were overwhelmed by alienation and a Judaism eroded by criticism of its strong assimilationist orientation. Heschel's theology allowed American Jews to connect with a lost tradition, reconstruct their identities as Jews within the modern world, and find ways to display a specifically Jewish standpoint in politics and society. For Martin Luther King Jr. and the civil rights movement, Heschel was an ideal match among Jews.

The Exodus was a theme of King's theology and movement as well as in the Hebrew Bible. His Christian faith was linked with politics, as was Heschel's concept of Judaism, by his perspective on the prophets in the Bible. For many African American followers of King, Heschel represented a Jew who had experienced actual "enslavement" [and the onset of the Holocaust] in Germany in a war against Jews, but it was also evident that he could build a close theological, political, and personal relationship with King.[64]

Heschel inspired American Jews to a spiritual renewal in the post-Holocaust era, fulfilling a need in many people. Heschel's vita, theology, Hasidic background, and friendship with Martin Luther King prompted these two men and many Christians and Jews to fight America's participation in the Vietnam War in the name of the civil rights movement. Besides his theological arguments, Heschel's experiences as a refugee from Nazism and a Jew who had lost his family to Europe's antisemitism, racism, and fascism resonated in his political activism.

Speaking out for universal freedom and equality and against America's unethical war in Vietnam, Heschel enabled other American Jews to respond not only to the current crises but also to historical ones and thus to demonstrate that Americans—Jewish and non-Jewish alike—would act with more agency *this time*. After all, in the highly ideological conflict over Vietnam, the United States exhibited political tendencies and practices widely perceived as "fascist" by many within the political left and created a situation whereby those who had experienced and survived Nazism in Germany felt obligated to raise their voices with authority and authenticity.[65]

In addition to Asher, Prinz, and Heschel, other refugee rabbis inspired American Jews with ideas that evolved from the transfer of Jewish thought from Europe to the United States and from the blending of such knowledge with their new American environment, where many people were unable to read the original German texts.

Besides the abovementioned Albert Friedlander, who translated Leo Baeck's *Dieses Volk* (This People) into English, there was Orthodox scholar Alexander Altmann, who joined the Jewish studies faculty of Brandeis University in 1954, first as visiting professor, then as a full faculty member. In 1973, Altmann presented the first comprehensive English-language study on Moses Mendelssohn, which not only crowned Altmann's career but also made Mendelssohn's complex personality and scholarship accessible to an English-speaking audience. Altmann's vision and ambition helped launch a number of projects that resulted in unique microfilm collections at Brandeis University, which provided the basis for future scholarship.[66]

Stephen Whitfield impressively highlights how Simon Rawidowicz and Nahum N. Glatzer, both born in eastern Europe but trained in Germany, influenced the first decades of the Judaic Studies Department at Brandeis, a flagship Jewish institution. Glatzer, a student of Gershom Scholem, Franz Rosenzweig, and Martin Buber, had received his doctorate from the University of Frankfurt and later taught there, replacing Martin Buber. Even though Glatzer was never ordained, he was closely associated with the *Lehrhaus* movement that emerged around his former teachers in that city and continued his career in the United States, where he taught in the Near Eastern Studies and Judaic Studies Departments of Brandeis University from 1950 until 1973.

He continued his career in the Religion Department at Boston University. Extremely productive as a scholar in his field, Glatzer introduced Americans to the life and work of Franz Rosenzweig with his translation of *Star of Redemption* and to Martin Buber with his translation of Buber's letters and by deliberating Buber's dialogical exploration of Jewish thought.[67]

Glatzer impacted modern Jewish thought not only as a university teacher but also as the editor-in-chief of the Schocken Publishing Company, which he cofounded and worked for after the company moved to the United States. He also was a contributing editor to *Judaism: A Quarterly Journal*, whose editor in chief from 1961 to 1969 was his fellow refugee rabbi Steven Schwarzschild. The journal, published by the American Jewish Committee, provided an important platform for discussion of modern Jewish scholarship and the zeitgeist in the 1960s and 1970s.

Schwarzschild belonged to the so-called second generation of refugee rabbis and had studied at HUC in Cincinnati, where he received a doctorate in 1955 with a dissertation on Nachman Krochmal and Herman Cohen.[68] Schwarzschild's neo-Kantian approach to Judaism—which he acquired as a student of Samuel Atlas at HUC—brought an ethical perspective on Jewish thought and identity to the forefront of his encounter with contemporary reality and introduced the American public to key elements of German-Jewish thought by publishing the works of Herman Cohen, Franz Rosenzweig, and other European Jewish thinkers.[69]

Unlike the cohort born around 1900, the youngest refugees, those trained and ordained in the United States, had a significant impact on the Reform movement in American Judaism. Their knowledge of Jewish history and tradition acquired first in Europe and later in the United States gave them with a unique self-awareness that allowed them to bridge the dichotomy between tradition and modernity in a special way. They were driven by the experiences of their survival and aware of the legacy they sought to secure; namely, the timely appeal and survival endurance of a modern Judaism for future generations.

W. Gunther Plaut, Alexander Schindler, Herman Schaalman, Ismar Schorsch, Walter Gottschalk, Jakob Petuchowski, Walter Jacob, Walter Würzburger, and Leon Feldman were among those who drew from their cultural hybridity when defining their leadership in their respective religious movements. They had a lasting impact on American Judaism because they combined traditional knowledge with a progressive outlook and turned Judaism into more than just a religion. In their hands, modern Judaism developed into a rich, meaningful, contemporary, and dynamic experience of community that spoke to American Jews—even Orthodox Jews—in a new and appealing way.

Walter Würzburger, the Harvard-trained rabbi, scholar, and president of the Rabbinical Council of America, raised questions about the relationship between American Orthodoxy and modernity, modern philosophy, pluralism, politics, and the ethics of halacha (the body of Jewish laws), which opened up avenues for the participation and new positioning of Orthodox Jews within American society. As a rabbi and scholar, he demonstrated an ability and openness to discuss controversial contemporary and religious positions with Reform and Conservative Jews.[70]

Like Würzburger, Leon Feldman had been educated at the Rabbi Isaac Elchanan Theological Seminary (RIETS) and the New School for Social Research. He was ordained in 1947 and obtained in 1957 a Doctor of Hebrew Letters from the Bernard Revel Graduate School at Yeshiva University, the same university where he taught as professor of Jewish education from 1954 to 1962. After completing his training as an Orthodox Jewish theologian, he branched out to earn a PhD in Jewish History from Columbia University and started a very successful academic career at Rutgers University in 1962, where he taught Jewish studies until he retired thirty years later.

It is interesting that, although Feldman was trained at the RIETS of Yeshiva University, this Orthodox leader pursued a career as a scholar in Jewish studies and education at secular universities. In 1963, he successfully founded the Hebraic Studies Department at Rutgers University, making Jewish studies as a field broadly available to many students.[71]

Another refugee in the Reform movement, W. Gunther Plaut, was originally trained in German law before he joined the Hochschule in order to pursue rabbinical studies, which he had to do because he could not obtain a doctorate in law as he had originally planned. It is not surprising that, as a scholar, he had a uniquely broad perspective on Judaism and *Wissenschaft* and submitted the American Reform movement's first non-Orthodox Torah commentary, in which he anchored modern Reform thought in the scholarly work of biblical exegesis.[72]

Walter Jacob, one of the youngest refugee rabbis, became that movement's first expert on halacha with a timely perspective on Jewish law and the challenges modern times posed for modern Judaism. He followed in the footsteps of Solomon Freehof as rabbi of Congregation Rodef Shalom in Pittsburgh and also became the Reform movement's expert on responsa, defining the legal and theological development of that movement's perspective on Judaism for several decades, supported by traditional knowledge that could hardly be found among American-born Reform Jews.[73]

Alexander Schindler, born in Munich, headed the UAHC as its president for twenty-three years, from 1973 to 1996. He led the UAHC in responding to

Ordination of Walter Jacob at HUC in Cincinnati, 1955: AJA, pc2005.01.

many issues that made Reform Jewish congregations fit for a new era. Among the issues the Reform movement faced were the rising number of interfaith marriages and, as a result of these unions, the religious future of their offspring. Schindler argued that such a development did not have to dilute and weaken Reform congregations.

He claimed that if people had a clearly defined and informed concept of their identity as modern Jews, then they had the support and strength to reach out to those in intermarriage, their children, and also the unaffiliated. This effort might ignite a new and dedicated interest in Judaism among these people rather than losing them forever. Schindler encouraged the Reform movement's decision to discuss and adopt patrilineal descent and the inclusion of non-Jewish partners. He supported the ordination of female rabbis and continued to bring up other pressing contemporary issues within the Reform movement because he felt it should have a defined position on issues like nuclear weapons, the arms race, rearmament, and the emerging AIDS crisis. He was not alone in supporting such bold moves.

Herman Schaalman, president of the Central Conference of American Rabbis (CCAR) from 1981 to 1983; W. Gunther Plaut, who served in the same organization as vice president and as Schaalman's successor as president of the CCAR until 1985; and Walter Jacob, who headed that organization from 1992 to 1994, also supported the bold moves being made within the movement. These tactics were backed not only by their leadership in the Reform Jewish rabbinical organization but also by the work being done in the movement's ethics, responsa, and interfaith committees, which laid the groundwork for the massive shift the movement was making at the time.

The *New York Times* obituary of Alexander Schindler in November 2000 emphasized that Schindler had not only been dedicated to Reform Judaism as the modern face of Judaism but had also shared a deep sense of Yiddishkeit and felt at home in his father's Hasidic world. That part of his empathetic and engaging personality and his political talent allowed him to build bridges within American Jewry and speak with authority for all American Jews, a fact that helped him find support as president of the Conference of Presidents of Major American Jewish Organizations.[74]

Finally, the academic centers of the Reform movement and the Conservative movement—HUC and the JTS, respectively—were headed in the late twentieth century by two refugees of the second generation. These men, Alfred Gottschalk and Ismar Schorsch, played a central role in preparing both movements for the twenty-first century.

Alfred Gottschalk served as president (1971-1996) and chancellor (1996-2000) of HUC and was one of the German-born leaders of the Reform movement in the 1970s and 1980s. HUC stood at the heart of the movement and connected the rabbinical organization of its graduates (CCAR) to the UAHC, where the college placed its graduates and thus shaped the movement's growth and prosperity in an essential way.

Gottschalk's leadership was important for the academic growth and orientation of the movement as well as for the practical implementation of changes within it. As a graduate of HUC, he headed the expansion of the college in the postwar era, a time when HUC was globally the *only* seminary training modern Reform rabbis.

After HUC merged with the Jewish Institute of Religion (JIR) in New York in 1950 to create its second campus, Gottschalk was actively involved in the expansion of the institution to Los Angeles in 1954, where he served first as director, then as dean from 1957 to 1971. He also strongly advocated for a fourth campus of HUC in Jerusalem. Establishing a Jerusalem campus was a historical accomplishment for two reasons.

Herman Schaalman: AJA, pc3966.05.

Alexander Schindler: AJA, pc4002.03.

Alfred Gottschalk: AJA, pc5001.

Leon Feldman: Yeshiva University, Gottesman Library, Special Collections, PR People Photo Box 61001.

First, it connected the movement with the newly founded state of Israel and created new avenues for the modern movement to use this campus for archaeological research in the Holy Land and thus link the movement to ancient Jewish history in a new way.

Second, it established a vanguard of the distinctly modern, timely, and pluralistic Reform movement in the Jewish homeland, where modern Judaism was rejected by an established traditional Orthodox state religion, a concept American Jews have always struggled with in their general support for the Zionist state.

Belonging to the youngest group of the refugee rabbis, Gottschalk spoke publicly about a special legacy and commitment to the development, growth, and prosperity of modern Judaism after the Shoah. He saw his position and profession as tools that allowed him to shape the training and ordination of a future modern Jewish rabbinate in a special way.

As the head of HUC for almost thirty years, he oversaw the ordination of the first female rabbi, Sally Priesand in 1972 at HUC in Cincinnati, the opening of the college's doors to more female students, and also the ordination of the first female Reform rabbi officiating in Israel. In 1995, HUC accepted openly gay and lesbian students for the rabbinate.[75]

In the 1990s, the end of the Cold War and Germany's reunification created an unexpected historical opportunity for Gottschalk and his peers. This opportunity might have been missed if key Reform Jewish leaders with a special relationship to Germany—Schaalman, Plaut, Jacob, Schindler, and Gottschalk—had not been in positions to make an idea come alive; namely, the founding of a modern rabbinical seminary just outside of Berlin that would revive an ultimately German tradition.

The founding of the Abraham-Geiger-Kolleg in 1999 at the University of Potsdam was a significant achievement, for it provided a new perspective on modern Judaism in its historic center on the European continent and proved that "the last generation of the German rabbinate" had fulfilled its mission to secure the survival, if not the symbolic undoing, of Hitler's destruction, an accomplishment that is discussed in more detail in chapter 6.[76]

Ismar Schorsch, an ordained rabbi and secularly trained historian, headed the JTS as chancellor from 1986 to 2006. During his twenty-year tenure, he steered the JTS through a process of innovation. Schorsch supported the Schechter Institute of Jewish Studies in Jerusalem in 1984, an institution linked to Conservative Judaism, to establish a broader perspective on Judaism in Jerusalem. He also helped create Project Judaica, an initiative that strengthened the education and resources of a new Jewish elite in Russia after the collapse of the former Soviet Union.

He expanded Ramah (youth) camps and established a Conservative Jewish high school system across the country known as "Schechter Schools." He was politically active during his tenure, speaking out and developing a distinctly Conservative point of view on issues like the separation of church and state, universal health care, welfare, and environmental concerns. He was actively engaged in the Arab-Israeli peace process as part of President Bill Clinton's delegation in 1994.

While his official vita on the JTS website mentions his many academic credentials and achievements,[77] it overlooks his presidency of the New York–based LBI, part of a global research facility dedicated to researching German-Jewish history since 1955, with branches in New York, London, and Jerusalem. In this position and as part of his lifelong scholarship, Schorsch exhibited a special dedication to his German-Jewish heritage and the LBI.[78] This highlights Schorsch's deep commitment to *Wissenschaft*, historical Judaism, and the role of history as a scholarly discipline in the interpretation and understanding of modern Judaism. This was particularly valuable for the Conservative movement in Judaism, which was committed simultaneously to a historical Judaism and to tradition. By its very nature, it continued to pressure Judaism to make difficult choices between tradition and modernity. Unlike its cousin movements, which leaned from the beginning toward Reform or Orthodoxy, the Conservative path was continuously challenged to fulfill both perspectives and remain authentic and true to its doctrines and traditions.

Ever since its founding, the LBI has been devoted to the memory and legacy of German Jewry and its history and has provided a central location for refugee rabbis to express their dedication to the refugee community.

For this special German-Jewish intellectual elite, the institute and its collections and publications provided a platform to uphold and study the German-Jewish legacy, address the role of the German rabbi posthumously, and explore the reasons why the once-promising German-Jewish experiment failed.

From the beginning, the refugee rabbis were deeply involved in setting up and supporting the institution as members (Leo Baerwald, Nahum Glatzer, Max Gruenewald, Alfred Jospe, and Dagobert D. Nellhaus) and leaders (Rabbi Max Gruenewald, the institute's international president from 1974 to 1992).

Because many of the refugee rabbis had been trained as historians as part of their secular education, they incorporated their experiences, role models, and professional profiles into their work during the institute's early years. Among them were contributors to the first volume of the *Leo Baeck Institute Year Book*, published in 1956: Max Gruenewald, with an article on the Reichsvertretung in 1956; Nahum Glatzer, with a piece on the Frankfurt *Lehrhaus* in the same year; and Alexander Altmann, with a piece on Jewish theology in the twentieth century.

In the second issue of the journal, Wolfgang Hamburger published an article on Leo Baeck, with whom he had developed an especially close relationship; Kurt Wilhelm, a rabbi who had fled to Palestine, presented a piece on the Jewish community in the post-emancipation period; Max Gruenewald discussed the professional profile of the "modern rabbi"; and Alfred Kober explored the history of religious instruction in Germany.

In the 1960 volume, Fritz Bamberger, a scholar of modern Jewish studies who graduated from the nonrabbinical track of the Hochschule, contributed an article on Julius Guttmann, Nahum Glatzer presented his thoughts on Leopold Zunz, Leo Adler elaborated on Jewish community organization in Württemberg, and Alexander Carlebach shared his autobiographical experiences in eastern Europe in 1961.[79]

The rabbis' commitment to memorializing their experiences and backgrounds remained strong long after the journal was first published. In the 1974 issue, which dealt with "typologies," the authors once again discussed—after Gruenewald's initial attempt in 1957—the professional profile of the "German rabbi." Alexander Altmann wrote an explanation of this special "type," and Alfred Jospe detailed the changes and challenges the profession experienced between 1910 and 1933. Both contributed to preserving the memory of their peers and themselves, a professional group that had ceased to exist decades earlier and whose traditions they upheld and shared until late in their lives. In the same issue, Max Gruenewald analyzed the professional profile of the modern Jewish teacher, Ismar Schorsch discussed German antisemitism after the Second World War, and Emil Schorsch, Ismar's father, described the rural Jewish experience in Germany.[80]

The list of examples of their participation in writing their history and shaping their legacy is long and continues to this day.

In this context, their record underscores once again that these refugee rabbis were the last of a group who sought to pass on its traditions to future generations. Because their understanding of Judaism and its history was dynamic and scholarly, their study and research of German-Jewish history was more than a chronicle of an extinct community from a lost time and place.

This research and documentation became part of larger historical contexts, such as German history, European history, and to a degree, American history, and serve as a model for the perception and history of Jews and other minorities in modern societies. German-Jewish history, the history of a minority with fewer than six hundred thousand members, has attracted researchers of diverse backgrounds who increasingly view German-Jewish history as a paradigmatic model for finding answers to questions of inclusion and exclusion posed in the context of other ethnic and religious groups in modern societies.

Aside from strengthening American Judaism and making the achievements of German Jewry available to a broader public in the United States, the Reform movement's refugee rabbis dealt with questions about their experiences under Nazism. Even though they had become American citizens, were proud of their new citizenship, and wanted to leave their past behind, they realized that they were marked by a lasting cultural difference and therefore stayed connected with central Europe, if only to understand what had *really* happened to them and their former communities.

They publicly contemplated how their exclusion and persecution, which stood at the beginning of the Shoah, had been possible and to what extent, if any, they had been part of German society. They especially tried to understand why such a large portion of German society remained silent when Jews and others were ostracized, excluded, and persecuted in German society, and why the Christian churches showed so little solidarity with German Jewry, even those Jews who were baptized and members of their organizations.[81]

How could any religion ignore the common moral values, humanity, and respect of its members and, worse, contribute to the racialization of German society, which ultimately turned it into nothing less than a *racial community*?

Religiously motivated antisemitism, long present and established in European Christian churches, and the role of the state in the European religious landscape encouraged the Christian religious group's complicity with Nazism and its racist goals.

While the practices of religious freedom and the separation of state and church in the American Constitution have hardly eliminated antisemitic stereotypes among Christian groups in the United States, their connection to a government or political party and their official establishment as a state religion was always legally impossible. American pluralism and the strength of an overarching "civil religion," a concept that defined the commitment of the diverse nation to basic moral values, were responsible for mutual concern among religions for societal cooperation, and they helped American religions to stress shared values. Therefore, in the United States, interfaith cooperation had already been established in society when the National Conference of Christians and Jews (NCCJ) was founded in 1928 in the wake of WWI atrocities. Among the movement's leaders were Rev. Samuel Cavert, NCCJ president Rev. Everett Clinchy, Rabbi Stephen Wise, Jonah Wise, and Felix Warburg.[82]

The Holocaust, the war, and other events in Europe alerted American religious leaders to the status of humanity and the failure of religion in modernity[83] and prompted a hence-unknown effort toward interfaith cooperation among Christians and Jews. The refugee rabbis were intensely involved in these efforts at both the local and wider public levels. After all, they could speak not only as theologians but also as authorities who had experienced firsthand the events around the Holocaust and the collapse of German society.

As theologians as well as representatives of secular Jewish institutions, the rabbis' analysis mattered. They engaged deeply in interfaith dialogue, stressing that no one should forfeit their identity or demand that of another, but people should respect each other's distinction and values.[84] The civil rights movement, its theology and rightful claim to civil equality, and its alliance with Christian churches provided a way for rabbis and their Christian counterparts to communicate with each other based on their shared commonalities.

This inspired the growth of the American interfaith movement. Abraham Joshua Heschel was appointed by the American Jewish Committee to join a commission of Jewish theologians and experts in groundbreaking negotiations with the Vatican in Rome in 1961. One year earlier, Pope John XXIII had approached the German-born Augustin Cardinal Bea, one of his closest advisers, about contacting the American Jewish Committee to discuss accusations against the Catholic doctrine of "teaching contempt" against Jews.

This was the beginning of a long and difficult process of negotiations throughout the early 1960s, which finally resulted in 1965 in the successful adoption and publication of a groundbreaking position paper by the Catholic Church toward non-Christian religions, called *Nostra Aetate* (In our time). The document encouraged the growth of ecumenical relations between Catholics and Jews mainly because it refrained from labeling Jews as "Christ-killers" and Judaism as a religion supposedly inferior to Christianity.

The events of the Holocaust resonated among those conducting the negotiations in Rome not only because the talks were mostly held in German, a lingua franca among the participants, but also because most of those willing to launch the project between Catholics and Jews had a historical connection to and a special concern for the country of the perpetrators.[85]

The degree to which the Holocaust and the participants' personal histories mattered in the negotiations is illustrated by Edward Kaplan in his book on Heschel. In September 1964, Heschel had a difficult and officially "failed" audience with the pope. He could not make the pope understand why Jews were unable to agree to a recent draft by the Church that expressed hope that Jews would ultimately convert to Christianity.[86]

At one point in the conversation, Heschel could not hold back and departed from protocol by mentioning the history of Jewish suffering under Christianity. The pope then felt threatened and indicated that the discussed agreement was at stake. Heschel, hit in his most sensitive spot, "urged the Pope to condemn antisemitism... and to remove it once and for all from the church teachings."[87]

After the meeting, which had taken place amid the Jewish High Holy Days, Heschel did not hide his dissatisfaction and emotional involvement in the matter. He said publicly that he would rather go to Auschwitz than consider conversion—a message that was played up in the press and considered to be inappropriate pressure on the Vatican and a threat to the success of the historical dialogue.

Surprisingly, however, Heschel's emotional outburst and powerful words contributed to the Vatican's acceptance of the Jewish declaration in October 1965. The contested blame for "deicide" and the expressed desire for conversion to Catholicism had been removed. Thus the historic *Nostra Aetate* agreement with the Catholic Church broke the ground for a new and promising relationship between Judaism and Catholicism.[88] The episode highlighted the importance of Heschel's involvement in the negotiations, of including a Jew who was not just a religious scholar but also a witness to and survivor of the Holocaust. Even though his behavior initially seemed inappropriate and offensive—even to the Jewish establishment—Heschel could not help but express his feelings with a clear voice and great pain in light of a history that the Catholic Church could not ignore after it had signaled it was prepared to depart from historical patterns.

While not quite as dramatic as these negotiations, interreligious councils sprung up during the postwar era in almost every American city and institutionalized the communication of religious leaders within a community. These councils not only enabled new exchanges on local matters, congregational cooperation, and communal collaboration among Christians and Jews; it also produced surprising friendships across religious boundaries, which in turn permitted religious leaders on both sides to develop new avenues for further cooperation.

Among the refugee rabbis who were particularly successful in this area was Rabbi Alfred Wolf of Wilshire Boulevard Temple in Los Angeles, the third-largest Reform synagogue in the country. Wolf belonged to the "band of five," the group of students from the Hochschule in Berlin who had continued their training in Cincinnati from 1935 on. Wolf's first pulpit was in Dothan, Alabama, starting in 1941. In the years that followed, he officiated in Olympia in Washington State and at the liberal Hyde Park Congregation of Chicago. Then he served in the US Army until 1946, after which he continued his career in California as regional director of the UAHC and the Reform Jewish congregations, and served as a guest preacher at Wilshire Boulevard Temple, where he joined Senior Rabbi Edgar Magnin as an associate in 1949 before he succeeded him as senior rabbi in 1984.

In this position, Wolf, a hands-on leader who was deeply committed to a "Judaism in the total context of humanity," launched and oversaw two youth camps of the Reform movement: Camp Hess Kramer in Malibu (1952) and Gindling Hilltop Camp (1968). In the 1960s, he found a friend and companion in his fight for civil rights and interfaith dialogue in Monsignore Royale Vadakin, a Catholic priest of the Archdiocese of Los Angeles. With Vadakin, whom he had met during the Watts Riots, Wolf founded an Interreligious Council for the Los Angeles area, and both men embarked on a life dedicated to interfaith dialogue. Wolf authored *Journey of Discovery: A Resource Manual for Catholic-Jewish Dialogue* in 1989 and organized the first National Interreligious Conference for Seminaries in 1993. He also met with Pope John Paul II during his 1987 visit to Los Angeles.[89]

In a similar fashion, Herman Schaalman began a deep personal friendship with Cardinal Joseph Bernardin, who had been appointed archbishop of Chicago in 1982 and soon after reached out to the communal leaders of other faiths by introducing himself as "their brother Joseph." He founded a Council of Religious Leaders, which became the Council of Religious Leaders of Metropolitan Chicago in 1984.[90] In 1995, Schaalman traveled with Bernardin to Jerusalem, and the two leaders walked down the Via Dolorosa before entering the Church of the Holy Sepulchre.

On this trip, Bernardin presented his groundbreaking lecture "Anti-Semitism: The Historical Legacy and the Continuing Challenge for Christians" at Hebrew University. The friendship between the two religious leaders was so close that Schaalman was part of the mass in honor of Cardinal Bernardin at his Catholic house of worship.[91]

The friendship between Schaalman and Bernardin was extraordinarily close, but it was not unique; other refugee rabbis followed similar paths. Rabbi Manfred Swarsensky, who held the Reform Jewish pulpit in Madison, Wisconsin, for thirty-six years, was a beloved leader in the community and highly esteemed among his colleagues during his tenure, a fact emphasized by Marvin Zolot in Swarsensky's biography.[92]

Driven by the conviction that the Holocaust could have been prevented if religious leaders in Germany before 1933 had been able to create solidarity with Jews and Judaism that would have strengthened the value system of German society and precluded the persecution of its Jews, refugee rabbis looked to the American religious landscape for opportunities to build a new relationship between Christians and Jews, and the religious institutions educating the rabbinate supported this activity.

In 1981, HUC in Cincinnati established a professorship for Judeo-Christian studies for the first time in its history and appointed Jakob Petuchowski as the Sol and Arlene Bronstein Professor of Judeo-Christian Studies. Petuchowski started his career as Professor of Jewish Theology and Liturgy at HUC, and his scholarship connected him with the larger world of the Abrahamic religions and especially the relationship between Christianity and Judaism, a research area he explored from the mid-1970s on.

Midlife, Petuchowski was motivated to expand his engagement with Christian colleagues in Germany, although he had previously avoided any contact with his homeland. He wrote a number of works in German, including a short autobiography (published exclusively in his native tongue) in which he described his Jewish identity as being rooted in Germany: *Mein Judesein: Wege und Erfahrungen eines deutschen Rabbiners* (My Jewish being: Paths and experiences of a German rabbi).[93]

It is interesting that Petuchowski referred to himself as a "German" rabbi on the cover of his autobiography after having lived over thirty years in other countries such as England, Scotland, and the United States. Geared toward a German audience, the book framed his scholarly work there with the story of his life, flight, and legacy as a rabbi. This put his engagement with religious dialogue in Germany in a special Holocaust context. It allowed him to highlight the historical significance of the German-Jewish tradition in Jewish history and thought, explain that current Jewish life in Germany had nothing to do with a past that was lost, and make a strong statement about why learning about Judaism was worthwhile, particularly for Germans.

Finally, the experience of the Holocaust in politics and collective memory enabled this last generation of German rabbis to present themselves as such and communicate their role and special mission. Even while the Second World War was still underway, the rabbis stayed in touch with their dispersed former congregants and cultivated the deep relationship they had created, supporting them by making sure of their whereabouts and experiences during their flight and under Nazism.

In 2007, Walter Jacob, the son of Rabbi Ernest Jacob, published with Gernot Römer a 472-page edited collection of the many letters his father had written to his former community members during and after the Shoah. In these letters, Ernest Jacob assured them that he continued to be their rabbi, their chaplain, the "last rabbi of Augsburg," and the cohesive center of a community in dispersion. The publication not only underscores the strong personal bond Ernest Jacob maintained with his congregants long after his position in Saint Joseph, Missouri; it also demonstrates his self-awareness as a rabbi and spiritual leader who would not abandon them. After all, who else could effectively minister to them in their tradition, especially after their joint experiences under Nazism and the end of German-Jewish life in that city?

In the immediate postwar era, German refugee rabbis who spoke the language, who understood the consequences of Nazism, who witnessed the atrocities inflicted on Jews by the Nazis, and who knew the social and political problems Germany was facing in the 1920s and 1930s were wanted as experts and representatives of survivor interests in an American Jewish community that was challenged by the responsibility of representing the rights and concerns of Diaspora Jewry vis-à-vis postwar Germany. The moral qualities attributed to the German refugee rabbis, their firsthand experiences during the Nazi period, and speaking the language of the perpetrators made them effective and trustworthy negotiators on behalf of the refugees and survivors.

Therefore, it was no accident that the Conference on Material Claims against Germany appointed Joachim Prinz to be its spokesperson or that both Prinz and Nussbaum held major leadership positions in the American Jewish Congress, an organization that was involved in postwar negotiations with West Germany.

Emil Fackenheim, a Jewish philosopher and rabbi at the University of Toronto, claimed that after the Shoah, there was to be a "614th" commandment, or mitzvah, added to the 613 existing mitzvot. The new supplementary commandment was to instruct all Jews to maintain the moral imperative to secure Jewish survival. Through this commandment, all Jews, secular or religious, were called on to make it their duty to do everything they possibly could to work against the historic efforts like those made during the Holocaust to annihilate Judaism and Jews as a people. Jews were to stand loyal to their faith and people and fill their lives with new Jewish meaning.[94]

Like Fackenheim, the refugee rabbis felt obliged to lead discussions on the legacy of the Holocaust for Jews, Judaism, and humanity. These activities spread from the local synagogue, where the pogrom of 9 November 1938 was commemorated; to the communities, where Yom HaShoah (Holocaust

Remembrance Day) was observed; and finally to national and international institutions, where Holocaust studies and Jewish studies programs were established and the memories of survivors were collected and archived.

Alfred Gottschalk and Joseph Asher were invited in 1980 to serve on the US Holocaust Memorial Council, the commission appointed by President Jimmy Carter to plan a national American Holocaust museum in Washington, DC. The commission contributed for over a decade to the design and establishment of this groundbreaking institution, which highlighted the legacies of the Holocaust for all Americans and reassured its Jewish community that their unique past and concerns about their future as Americans were being recognized.

To this day, the US Holocaust Memorial Museum in the nation's capital, which opened to the public in April 1993, is a central research body for the emerging field of Holocaust studies, raising funds and promoting the field's growth and encouraging a previously unknown degree of international cooperation among archives and universities. Focusing on more than scholarly research, the institution has stimulated an intense social and political dialogue on the lessons of the Holocaust far beyond its historical framework in central Europe and has given the Holocaust a universal structure that has shaped the moral fabric for the definition of "human relations" in Western societies ever since.

For many of the refugees, the professional and intellectual engagement with their persecution during Nazism and their loss of home, family, friends, wealth, and cultural context was an attempt to come to grips with a difficult and painful rupture in their lives. Once they had dealt with the immediate consequences of flight and displacement and had established themselves in American society, many of them wanted to fill in the gaps of their memories and come to terms with their shattered identities, whereby a difficult past continued to shadow the present.

These feelings and the passing of time facilitated their return to their birthplace and a culture they still faintly remembered. They knew that there, and only there, they could finally find answers to the many questions about their lives and those of their families. They came to understand their identities and their past.[95] They also knew that the most powerful and sustainable statements and actions regarding their past could and should be made in the place where the persecution happened.

Chapter 6 examines the many facets of refugee returns to Germany, a process that began even before the Second World War ended and continues to this day. The refugee returns were an essential part of their generation's identity as the "last generation of the German rabbinate" for themselves, American

Jews, Germans, and even the postwar Jewish communities in Germany, which largely consisted of displaced persons and Holocaust survivors from eastern Europe who deliberately referred to themselves as "Jews in Germany" to underscore that German Jewry had ended with the flight and dispersion of that community and its annihilation in the Holocaust.[96] The journeys of these refugee rabbis back to Germany also constitute a hence-unknown element of transnational engagement, one that played an essential role in German-Jewish post-Holocaust relations.

SIX

Refugee Returns
Transatlantic Encounters and the Legacy of the "Last Generation of the German Rabbinate"

Refugee returns to the country of their birth, to the country of their persecution, and ultimately to the places of their expulsion have been studied by historians and sociologists. For many refugees, the journey to return was a milestone in their life cycle,[1] typically taking place in middle to later life at a time when they sought explanations for their experiences and trying to heal from the ruptures caused by persecution and flight.[2] These later-in-life encounters led to a new and important phase in their lives. The passage of time facilitated satisfying conversations with the perpetrators or their children and helped mend the painful biographical fractures, if not the general pain, associated with the missing pieces in a history that has caused enormous suffering due to the actions of Nazism and the events of the Holocaust. However, this was only possible if the injustices that led to their persecution and expulsion were recognized by Germans and an effort was made from that side to initiate indemnification and reconciliation and to learn from the past.

Refugee Returns—Completing the Life Cycle

Holocaust memory studies have addressed questions of memory, transnationalism, and the hybrid identities that flight, survival, and relocation have generated.[3] Since the 1990s and the end of the Cold War, there has even been discussion of "Holocaust tourism," which would allow access to the largely Polish sites of German atrocities during the Holocaust.[4]

Few studies, however, have focused on the return of refugee rabbis to (West) Germany in the postwar years.[5] Although this area of research has been largely neglected by scholars of American Jewish history and German history, its study provides insight into the attempts to explore the chances for continuity and change within a framework of larger cultural and diplomatic changes in the postwar world order. The lack of data on this subject might be because there were a few surviving German-Jewish refugees or that the interpretation of their culture and identity required knowledge of German history *and* Jewish history. The many German historians who have researched postwar German-American relations may not have recognized the soft skills and the morally and religiously motivated concerns and the significance they had for postwar German-American relations, because they lacked experience with Jewish history and focused only on classical diplomatic history.

Furthermore, for American Jews, the idea of Jews returning to Germany may have been highly controversial, if not unthinkable in the post-Holocaust Jewish world. Nevertheless, research indicates that many refugees had an ongoing interest in Germany, for better or worse, and continued their relationship with the country of their birth. Starting from the Second World War, their journeys back to Germany, even if short visits, were a part of their personal and professional experiences, involving them once again in a direct encounter with their past. Their returns were an essential element in the generation-building process as the "last generation of the German rabbinate" and highlighted the massive changes that had occurred in the Jewish communities of Germany.

Refugee Rabbis in the American Army

The first group of refugees who returned to Germany were active participants in the American war effort. Several of the second-generation refugee rabbis enlisted in the US Army with the expressed desire to fight Nazism in person. Their motivation, cultural background, familiarity with the situation in Germany, and proficiency in German were useful to the army during the invasion and later, during the administration of Germany. Among the young refugee rabbis who enlisted and served as chaplains were W. Gunther Plaut, Alexander Schindler, Herman Dicker, Sol Landau, and Ernst Lorge.

While they came as Americans, they brought with them their unique experience and special understanding of the situation. They knew they could have been among the survivors or victims of the concentration camps if they had not been able to leave Germany a few years earlier. Their presence as Jewish chaplains flagging the Magen David (Star of David) amid American forces liberating concentration camp survivors demonstrated that the Jewish people had withstood the Nazis' efforts to eliminate them in Europe and signaled hope and spiritual support to the most fragile of the survivors. While the liberated concentration camp survivors suffered from malnutrition and other symptoms of horrific physical abuse, the returning rabbis pointed out that their spiritual needs were just as urgent. Meeting a rabbi for the first time in six years, saying a prayer together, attending services, and mourning the dead—these were among the first spiritual services provided by the rabbis. In addition, the rabbi as military chaplain was the first Jew in uniform the survivors had seen—a Jew with secular authority who could inspire pride in a new Jewish identity among these downtrodden souls who had suffered years of physical mistreatment, mental torture, humiliation, and loss. This spiritual guidance was far more essential for the survivors than any material goods. In addition, military chaplains helped the Jewish survivors to re-create a sense of identity, establish a functioning community, provide protection, and assist them in a number of areas.

The chaplains assisted the survivors in a number of ways: searching for surviving family members, helping with the emigration process, and supporting them through the challenges faced by displaced persons (DPs). These were refugees who had been relocated to Germany as a result of the war and the Holocaust during the years immediately after the Second World War in the three Western-occupied zones of Germany. They received help with medical issues, getting an education or vocational training, communicating with surviving family members, and finding a place to live and work.[6]

Their experience with Germany as the epicenter of the Second World War, the Holocaust, and the crimes committed by Germans across Europe was extremely emotional for all the Jewish returnees. It often triggered a personal evaluation of the antisemitism that their families had encountered there and raised questions about the state of humanity in general. Alexander Schindler, born in 1925 in Munich, visited his former hometown while serving in the Alpine division of the US Army when he was stationed in the area. The shocking destruction he witnessed in the Jewish community and among his family in Munich moved the young man to abandon his engineering studies to enter the rabbinate instead.[7]

Postwar Encounters: New Communities, but No Continuity

At the time, few of the returning refugees considered permanently relocating to central Europe, even though the number of Jews in the larger postwar setting of the Western zones of Germany was growing and their presence and services were urgently needed. Jewish life in the Western occupation zones had transformed dramatically under the shadow of Nazism, the Holocaust, and the Second World War. German Jewry, with its identity, modernity, and special place in German society, had either been destroyed by the Holocaust or had fled Nazism and relocated elsewhere before 1941.

Only about ten thousand former German Jews had managed to survive in what became the territory of West Germany after the Second World War. They were mostly intermarried Jews, or so-called half-Jews, who had not been deported because their family supported them, they were used as wartime forced labor, or they went into hiding with the help of non-Jewish family members. The majority of these German Jews lived in the north and west of West Germany and in Berlin, while the southern and central part of Germany, overlapping with the American occupation zone, was dominated by a growing number of Jewish DPs of east European background, a community that continued to grow in the aftermath of the war.

Most of German Jewry's communities and institutions had been destroyed. What was left was largely in the hands of a new and growing Jewish community, one with an entirely different ethnic composition and religious background: wartime slave laborers and the survivors of concentration camp death marches during the final days of the war were responsible for the influx of largely eastern European Jews into Germany. Liberation from the camps made these eastern European Jews resurface into German public life as Jewish DPs because they could not and did not want to return to their former home countries after the war. They had lost not only their communities but also their families.

They also refused to return because of the strict policies of the Soviet army regarding supposed "collaboration" with Nazism, an accusation often made against those who had been captured by the Germans and were forced into labor.[8] These circumstances and newly rising antisemitism triggered additional Jewish emigration from east Europe in the immediate postwar years. There were approximately three hundred thousand Jewish DPs in the Western occupation zones of Germany, part of the even larger group of non-Jewish DPs, which totaled around nine million people.

This migration reestablished an unexpected Jewish presence, one that differed culturally and religiously from German Jewry and completely altered the identity and culture of the resident Jewish community in Germany. In areas with a strong DP presence, like in the American zone, the people's east European Jewish identities rapidly transformed Jewish life in Germany and changed the manner of observance to that of traditional east European Orthodox communities, which had little in common with German Jewish life as it was before 1941. Unlike their German-born brethren who were still culturally connected with Germany, the liberated east European survivors of German extermination camps despised Germany and the Germans for their cruel and dehumanizing treatment during the Shoah. Finally, their legal status under the postwar Allied administration differed. As a result of Allied policies,[9] Jewish Germans were classified as German citizens, and non-German Jews were classified as Jewish DPs. The former group was subject to the same administration as non-Jewish Germans, and the latter was given an exclusive status.[10]

Except for several rabbis who were involved with the DPs and served them as rabbis after liberation and remigration, there was little overlap and continuity between these two Jewish groups and their religious traditions. Among the first rabbis to return to the pulpits in Germany was a small group of students and rabbis who had survived the Holocaust by hiding in Germany, had been held in concentration camps, or had survived behind the German lines in eastern Europe and returned shortly after liberation.

One of the first to return was Wolfgang Hamburger, who had continued studying with Baeck until 1942. As the son of a Jewish father and a Christian mother, he was forced to perform slave labor in Berlin from 1941 on and survived only because he escaped and hid outside the capital in the Stettin area on the Baltic Sea, with the help of his mother. By 1946, he was back in Berlin and enrolled as a student at the reopened Humboldt University, where he also started to work as a "preacher" in the Berlin Jewish community. By 1947, he left Germany and continued his education and professional plans as a student for the rabbinate in Cincinnati, where he was formally ordained in 1952 before beginning his rabbinic career in the United States.[11]

Like Hamburger, Rabbi Ralph Neuhaus returned to his former pulpit after liberation in the Theresienstadt ghetto. Neuhaus had been rabbi of Mühlheim (Ruhr) until 1933, then moved to Frankfurt am Main, where he served the Jewish community as rabbi, preacher, and director of the local Philanthropin, an elementary Jewish school. In August 1942, he and his wife were deported to the Theresienstadt ghetto, where he worked side by side with Leo Baeck as rabbi of the Magdeburger Kaserne (Magdeburg Barracks, a quarter in Theresienstadt) and as a member of the Jewish Council.

Right after liberation, he returned to his former pulpit in Frankfurt, where he was assigned by the American military government in charge of civil and religious affairs to reestablish the Jewish community with the surviving five hundred German Jews living in the city at the time. Neuhaus quickly became a central figure in the re-emergence of Jewish life there, starting in late 1945, when he was elected chairman of the provisional executive board of that community, launched a paper that communicated the concerns and needs of the Jewish communities within the American occupation zone, and reorganized the Jewish elder care home in that city. He officially headed an interest group of Jewish communities working with the American military government. After the emergence of a Hessian state government, he continued to serve as commissioner of Jewish affairs to that government, a position that overlapped with the newly established Hessian Chief Rabbinate, a prestigious office hence unknown to German Jewry. In mid-1946, Neuhaus, who was already sixty-seven, joined his son Ralph in the United States. There he continued his rabbinate at Congregation Gemiluth Chassodim in Detroit until his death in 1954.[12]

Rabbi Neuhaus was succeeded by Rabbi William Weinberg, a former student of the Hochschule in Berlin, whose difficult flight from Nazism had taken him eastward, far behind the Soviet lines, where he was rescued under challenging circumstances. After the war ended, he traveled to Austria and then to the American occupation zone of Germany. He first officiated in a DP camp in Hallein near Salzburg, where he also helped launch a DP university[13] to help young survivors receive an education and professional training. From there Weinberg moved to Frankfurt, where he became chief rabbi of Hesse from 1948 until his eventual immigration to the United States in 1951. His activities in the postwar setting as chief rabbi included the rededication of the synagogues still standing as Jewish houses of worship, including the Salzburg synagogue and, in 1950, Frankfurt's main synagogue, which became the first permanently established synagogue operating in Hesse after the war. It had been destroyed in 1938, but after its restoration, it once again provided space for one thousand congregants. Despite these positive achievements, Weinberg's recollections, as shared by his son Norbert, make clear that antisemitism continued to prevail among the majority of the German population[14] and the survivors did not see a future for themselves in central Europe. Weinberg hung a plaque in the Salzburg synagogue in honor of its rededication right after the war that admonished future generations of Jews in Hebrew and German to "Remember what Amalek did to you / Jew do not forget the concentration camp!"[15]

To remember and to bring to justice the perpetrators of the crimes against Jews during Nazism motivated the refugee rabbis to get involved in postwar German and Allied legal proceedings, even though they could not travel there. In their efforts to testify, they may have been supported by the Allied occupation forces. Rabbi Felix Aber and Rabbi Siegmund Hanover, two men who had suffered greatly with their communities under the Nazis before they emigrated from Germany, served as witnesses—Aber in Bremen and Hanover in Würzburg—in several legal cases between 1945 and 1949 regarding Nazi crimes and the restitution of Jewish property.[16]

Other refugee rabbis may have contributed similarly to attempts to bring the perpetrators to justice. These efforts were taken very seriously and deserve more systematic exploration than can be done within the framework of this book. A study on these activities would provide a better understanding of the agency the refugees gained as witnesses in postwar trials. The fractured and inconsistent nature of the legal system in Germany at the time prevents a thorough examination of this topic, but a database of related legal cases in the archives of the Institut für Zeitgeschichte in Munich provides information related to these issues.[17]

During the immediate postwar years, refugee rabbis coming back on visits from the United States also tried to help the survivors of their former communities and come to grips with the reality of the remaining civilization they had left behind in their hasty flight. International Jewish aid organizations such as the Joint Distribution Committee (JDC), which traditionally catered to the needs of Jewish refugees globally, were instrumental in facilitating the return of former German rabbis to assist their brethren in Germany. The JDC worked hand in hand with the Central British Fund for German Jewry in London and, in late 1944, set up the Council for Jewish Relief and Rehabilitation, which organized the task of providing for the religious and spiritual needs of the liberated and growing Jewish community in Germany.

However, soon after the council was established, competing ideological views of the nature of the Orthodox representation created serious tensions among Mizrachi (religious Zionists), Zionists, non-Zionists, and Agudists (members of the Agudah Israel, a political movement of Orthodox Jewry founded in 1912 in Kattowitz). This ultimately led to the withdrawal of Rabbi Elie Munk, who had struggled with having "only" been nominated as the *alternate* representative to H. A. Goodman.[18] Nevertheless, his younger brother, Michael Munk, who arrived in New York after finding temporary refuge in England, returned to Berlin's Jewish community for a year in 1947 with the assistance of the JDC and was among the first of several refugee rabbis who were sent there.

Although Munk claimed that he was the first rabbi in the city, he actually followed Conservative rabbi Moritz Freier, who had been exiled to Great Britain in 1938 and returned to Berlin nine years later, where he remained into the early 1950s.[19] Munk's arrival in Berlin marked his return to the city, where he had officiated as rabbi of the Adass Jisroel community. His return indicated a deep emotional attachment to his former community. In an interview with the Research Foundation for Jewish Immigration, Munk stated that he would have liked to stay longer but had to return to New York to be with his family, who could not join him in Germany because of the difficult circumstances there.

While in Berlin, he served as a rabbi for the whole community and explained how he tried to smooth over the differences among the factions of that newly assembled community, including those in the DP camps, and to reduce the tensions between the old and new members of that group.[20] This involved collecting information on the numbers and needs of surviving German Jews and their communities and institutions and determining whether some sort of religious revival in central Europe was possible, even if only temporary.

These same issues also concerned the liberal German refugee rabbinate. The World Union for Progressive Judaism (WUPJ), centered in Britain, represented liberal Judaism worldwide and believed itself to be the leader in protecting the remnants of the Jewish community in Germany. Its administrators tried to find information on the state of Jewish life in the country, asking questions similar to those of Munk. Leo Baeck, liberated from the Theresienstadt ghetto, had reunited with his family in England in 1945 and resumed his presidency of the WUPJ, a natural center of the dispersed global community. Under his guidance and in concert with Lily Montagu, the WUPJ decided to send a capable representative to occupied postwar Germany to explore the possibilities for religious revival there.[21]

The person chosen for this difficult and delicate mission was the young Orthodox-trained rabbi Joseph Asher. He had just returned to England from Australia—where he had served as a chaplain in the Australian army—to reunite with his parents. Once in London, he met Leo Baeck and other liberal German Jews who must have stimulated his interest in liberal Judaism. The milieu of refugee rabbis there and the guidance of Leo Baeck set the stage for him to develop an interest in liberal Judaism and to continue his studies at the Hebrew Union College (HUC) in Cincinnati, starting in the fall of 1947. However, before Asher left for Cincinnati, he was picked as the ideal representative for the WUPJ in Germany. He spent two months there in the summer of 1947.

Young, healthy, motivated, a native German speaker, and a military man, Asher spent most of his time in the British-occupied zone. Upon his return to England, he described with great frustration the complete destruction of Judaism as a culture and the loss of Jewish civilization in Germany. He complained about the emergence of a mere *"Paket-Judentum"* or "parcel Judaism," meaning a Judaism lacking inner motivation and dedication, committed only to material interest in the contents of parcels or care packages from brethren abroad, which became a currency on the black market. In this context, he also addressed the problem of "corruption" in the newly emerging Jewish community of postwar Europe led by DPs. Facing a community that had lost its values, self-respect, and religious commitment in the concentration camps, Asher made a strong point to develop a long-term program for their moral and spiritual restitution so they might become "normal citizens in whatever country they may eventually settle." He asked, "What are we doing to re-establish these [Jewish] values so that we can be assured of normal citizens to emerge from the ruins of Europe?"[22]

The WUPJ decided to follow Asher's advice. In 1948, in the first elections of the Berlin Jewish community, 80 percent of the vote was in favor of liberal Judaism, which encouraged the WUPJ to send the very first liberal rabbi to Berlin on its behalf. The organization chose Rabbi Steven Schwarzschild, born in 1924 in Frankfurt am Main and a recent and promising graduate from HUC in Cincinnati. His first pulpit had been in Berlin's postwar Jewish community with a membership of ten thousand Jews under challenging circumstances. After one year there, his reports on the situation in Berlin underscored that—unlike earlier arrivals in Germany—he saw a future for a small yet permanent Jewish community in Germany. He felt that a community like this could evolve from the large number of migrant Jews in the country who were prepared to leave as soon as they were permitted to do so. He estimated that about twenty-five thousand Jews might stay permanently in Germany and would need and deserve the support of liberal Jews in Britain, the United States, and Israel to survive and lead a Jewish life again. Under these circumstances, this Jewry might take on a significant and productive role in central Europe, which, if successful, would prove that Adolf Hitler's goal of exterminating European Jews had failed.[23]

During his mission, Schwarzschild had to deal with the complete absence of any Jewish infrastructure, educational materials, and institutions in a highly diverse community. He also had to handle conflicts over illegal black-market trading, antisemitic stereotyping, and policing that created tension between the German civilian authorities and the military police, which was exclusively responsible for handling any legal infractions by DPs.

Schwarzschild was also confronted with a significant demand for questionable conversions. Those applying for a religious transformation were usually the children or spouses of Jews who had been persecuted as Jews during the Nazi era and wanted to undo an earlier conversion to Christianity that had failed to protect them. Others who wanted to convert had opportunistic motives, such as finding a way to emigrate quickly or better food rations or administrative treatment. With almost three thousand individuals asking to be converted in Berlin alone, Schwarzschild was quite challenged as a young liberal rabbi. He had to work under the critical eyes of his Orthodox colleagues, where he had established new and revolutionary standards to permit conversion, a ritual that was more the exception than the rule in Judaism and raised the suspicion of his colleagues. Schwarzschild's success and reports were evaluated at the meeting of the WUPJ's governing body in London in July 1949. Although the community frequently referred to him as "chief rabbi" in Berlin—a title that was foreign to German Jews and may have been introduced by British or Orthodox elements—Schwarzschild rejected it, and the WUPJ urged the disuse of it. At the same time, the WUPJ wanted to send a second emissary permanently to West Germany and urged its leadership to raise the necessary funds.[24]

Steven Schwarzschild returned to the United States in 1950 to take on a pulpit in Fargo, North Dakota. His liberal rabbinate in Berlin continued after he left and after Germany's difficult and insecure postwar situation had created two separate German states with Berlin under Allied administration. Emigration to the newly founded state of Israel and North America caused a rapid reduction in the number of Jews living in Germany, which continued to have only *one* Jewish community. This community needed to define its role and place in the new political order as embodied by the two newly founded German states: the Federal Republic of Germany (West Germany) and the German Democratic Republic (East Germany).

This was a difficult task for many reasons: the ongoing rivalry among the various branches of Judaism, the condemnation faced by Jews in Germany from Jews in other countries who disapproved of their decision to stay in Germany, and the lack of funds to rebuild an infrastructure to facilitate Jewish life in Germany, such as synagogues, hospitals, elder care homes, and schools. The lack of means was due to the small number of community members but also to the restitution of Jewish property as stipulated by the Luxembourg Agreement in 1952 among West Germany, the Conference on Jewish Material Claims against Germany (hereinafter Claims Conference), and the state of Israel. The agreement did not support the rebuilding of Jewish life in West Germany.[25]

These circumstances were considered by the WUPJ during the meeting of its governing body in February 1950. Participants emphasized that the organization's perspective on Jewish life in Germany differed from that of the larger Jewish community and that it intended to explore the expansion of a Jewish presence and to facilitate Jewish life there. In light of the criticism it faced internationally, the organization made its stance clear: "The World Union for Progressive Judaism, as the organization of liberal Jews all over the world, strongly believes that Jews have the right to live and work as Jews in all places and at all times."[26]

Financial considerations weighed heavily on the communities, as is reflected in the discussion accompanying the selection of Schwarzschild's successor in Berlin. This position was given to another refugee rabbi and graduate from HUC in Cincinnati, Nathan Peter Levinson. Levinson, born and raised in Berlin, was twenty-nine and an officer of the US Army Reserve. He had officiated as a rabbi in Selma, Alabama, before the WUPJ sent him to Berlin after challenging negotiations with the Central British Fund for German Jewry to sponsor a liberal rabbi in addition to the Orthodox colleague who was already there.[27]

In his memoirs, Levinson explains in detail the difficult state faced by the community. His description of the challenges confronting the rabbinate in the form of black marketeers, military police, old and new antisemitism, and reestablished German authorities are reminiscent of Joachim Prinz's descriptions of a Jewish milieu in New Jersey, one that was not free of corruption. However, Levinson also explained that he enjoyed the vibrant cultural and political life of Berlin as a city that was at the center of global attention. Levinson and his family felt at home in Berlin and believed that Jewish life had a future there, even though few Jews lived there at the time.

Returning as American Army Chaplain: Nathan Peter Levinson

Nathan Peter Levinson's wife, Helga, began studying medicine there while her husband explored the possibility of using his status as a reserve officer at the American Army Headquarters in Wiesbaden to stay in the country. This plan met with mixed success because the advice he received took him back to the United States in 1953 to enter a program for military chaplains. However, after completing his education, he was deployed not to Germany in 1955 but to Japan.[28]

Levinson returned from Japan with a new deployment from the Jewish Welfare Board to the US air base in Ramstein, West Germany, in 1958. The Levinsons used their time in the Palatinate region of Germany in multiple ways. Helga completed her preliminary exams in medicine, and Nathan continued his chaplaincy in the US Army, awaiting his next deployment. Their uncertainty about how long they would remain in Germany posed a serious challenge to the completion of Helga's studies and became the reason, Levinson claimed in his autobiography, why he tried to find ways to stay in Germany more permanently by seeking employment outside the army.[29] In 1961, Levinson was appointed as rabbi of Mannheim, and then became Landesrabbiner (chief rabbi) of the state of Baden in 1963, at which time the family moved to the larger university town of Heidelberg.[30]

While Levinson did not describe anything like normality in his memoirs, the reality of Jewish life in Germany in the late 1940s clearly differed from that of the late 1950s. While the processes of political cleansing, restitution, and reflection on German crimes against Jews during the Nazi era were far from being completed, the new West German government took significant steps toward acknowledging German guilt (if not collective guilt), securing restitution and indemnification of Holocaust victims, and legally persecuting the perpetrators of Nazi crimes.[31] German postwar democracy was not perfect and must be criticized for many reasons, including the continuity of political and legal elites; still, the majority of political leaders wanted to demonstrate that the "new" Germany had clearly departed from the patterns of Nazi Germany.

During the early 1950s, the framework and fabric of German-Jewish relations gradually started to change. Even though no official relations between Germany and the state of Israel existed before 1965, a successful working relationship emerged from the settlement and practical application of indemnification and restitution agreements. American Jews also participated in this relationship in conjunction with the Claims Conference. The diasporic German-Jewish refugee community and its organizations were not benefiting from the restitution payments Germany made on "heirless property," such as the real estate property of the former German-Jewish community. Therefore, refugees appealed directly to the German government—specifically, the German diplomatic representatives abroad—for compensation and assistance, a move that created a new relationship between the German refugee community and West Germany.[32]

The correspondence between the German consulates in the United States and the Political Department of the German Foreign Office in Bonn reveals how such close relationships developed and were used to strengthen ties with the refugees.

The Federal Republic of Germany and German Refugee Rabbis: Launching Personal Dialogues and Exchanges

As early as April 1956, the consulate of the Federal Republic of Germany in Atlanta, Georgia, reported to the Foreign Office in Bonn on a visit by a German consular representative to Rabbi Dr. Max Landman, a refugee rabbi in Florida who had obviously contacted the German consulate in his area with questions about restitution and other matters in preparation for a trip to Germany. During the conversation, the rabbi introduced the German diplomat to the board members of his temple, and they openly discussed the events of the Third Reich as well as the efforts of the Federal Republic to deal with the Nazi inheritance. Rabbi Landman, who planned to visit Germany in June, asked for assistance in learning more about the two siblings he had left behind in Germany before the war and who perished in the Shoah.

The German report emphasized the positive tone of the conversation, which was conducted in a friendly atmosphere, even though, or perhaps because, everyone was aware of the historical burdens in this relationship. At the end of the conversation, the rabbi invited the German diplomat to address West German postwar development before his congregation sometime in the future. In return, the Atlanta-based diplomat offered to inform the Foreign Office in Bonn of Rabbi Landman's trip, request assistance for his research on the fate of his relatives, and put the rabbi in touch with officials who were involved in the restitution agreement with Israel. The friendly offer encouraged the rabbi to ask for a recommendation as to where he could address a German audience about American Jewry's attitudes toward and concerns about postwar Germany. The German Foreign Office happily agreed to support this request, recognizing the potential for a productive exchange that might contribute to a valuable dialogue.

By the time Landman arrived in Germany, the Foreign Office had helped arrange for him to give a talk at the Society for Christian-Jewish Cooperation in Bonn and to meet a number of West German parliamentarians, including Professor Dr. Franz Böhm, who headed the society in Frankfurt and was a chief negotiator of the reparations agreement.[33]

How far-reaching and broad these contacts were was apparent in the correspondence of German-Jewish congregations in the United States who asked German consulates for financial aid to build new synagogues because they had not received sufficient funds from the restitution agreement. Among these congregations were the Orthodox German-Jewish congregation New Hope in Cincinnati and Congregation Shaarey Tikvah in Cleveland, which asked the German consulate in Cleveland for a contribution to the Enoch Kronheim Memorial Fund. The West German government's decision to make a contribution was motivated by its desire to seize the opportunity to restore Germany's public image among Jews in the United States and open up a dialogue with them. It seemed best to start with those American Jews who were native German speakers.[34]

The conversation between the West German government and the refugee rabbis about the refugees' experiences and Germany's future in the democratic West was rewarding for both parties, and the publicity it generated had great potential for multiplication in both the German and the American Jewish press.

By 1960, if not earlier, the government of the Federal Republic of Germany was dealing with an increasing number of neo-Nazi voters and concerns for the survival of the young democracy. Under pressure to promote a better image of the republic and antisemitism, the West German government sought the cooperation and ongoing dialogue with those who would and could judge the progress of the country and who would be above any criticism of moral weakness because they had been in Germany until 1938 or later, had suffered from the Nazis themselves, now represented an articulate Jewish elite in the United States, yet still demonstrated a critical but constructive willingness to work with the Germans to address the joint past and the long history of antisemitic and racist attitudes in Germany's history.

The Federal Republic's government began to support the refugee rabbis' trips to Germany for guest lectures, joint commemorations, dedication or rededication ceremonies for renovated synagogues, and other purposes through a program that was publicized in the United States by the Jewish Chautauqua Society in New York. For many rabbis, including Cuno Lehrman, Kurt Metzger, and Max Nussbaum, this program facilitated their first return to their former synagogues and communities, starting in the late 1950s and continuing throughout the 1980s.

Based on the success of these programs, German cities began developing plans to bring back refugees and Jewish community leaders. These invitations demonstrated that West Germany had not forgotten the injustices or expulsions and that the presence and voices of these refugees were appreciated and welcomed in the "new" Germany. In return, they provided guidance as to what American Jews felt was needed to progress in this difficult relationship. This was part of a larger German-American alliance in the Cold War that also offered a unique opportunity for personal contacts, ongoing exchanges, and the moral recognition of West Germany's activities on behalf of reconciliation.[35]

The refugee rabbis were often extremely emotional on these visits, and they sometimes criticized what they saw and expressed serious concerns. However, the personal encounters and exchanges allowed both sides to learn from each other's perspectives and experiences. In addition, the rabbis relayed their experiences with the "new" Germany back to their congregations, religious organizations, and the American public, a mechanism the Political Department of the German Foreign Office was very interested in and recorded in their files. The engagement of these returning rabbis in West German politics and society sometimes caused difficulties, exposed a lack of understanding, or was driven by a concern that West Germany was falling back into old antidemocratic and antisemitic patterns, even as the economy was recovering and the country was regaining political influence. The way to reconciliation could not be found solely by overplaying the dark chapters of Germany's history or by granting financial restitution to the victims of the Holocaust. Rather, the key to the success of this process would be an active discourse and the acknowledgment of the harsh facts in Germany's recent history.[36] The rabbis' visits became a platform they used to communicate the past to the future from the perspective of the last generation of the German rabbinate. Many of the refugee rabbis visited their former communities and hometowns, and it was there that they were particularly identified in the press, their explanations, and the perception of the German public as the "last rabbi" of their former town or community. In no other context was the fact of their past lives and traditions more striking in terms of what had happened to them and how they resurfaced as American rabbis. In this environment, their intense exchanges explored ways to remember, overcome, and prevent situations similar to what they had experienced and to work with the Germans to keep these events from ever happening again.

These efforts were most evident in the well-recorded and publicized appearances of more prominent refugee rabbis, such as Joachim Prinz. In July 1959, Prinz returned many times to Germany as president of the American Jewish Congress and the director of the Claims Conference. Before this trip, Prinz strategically announced via the German Embassy in Washington, DC, that he sought a personal face-to-face exchange with West Germany's president and asked him to send an official message to the Jewish World Congress, an event that Prinz would attend in Stockholm following his visit to Germany.[37]

Prinz felt that the Germans were still unable to fully grasp the recent past and their complicity, and he detected a lack of democratic practice in their political attitudes and perceptions. His opinions were printed in the American press and surfaced in a World Jewish Congress (WJC) report on antisemitism in Germany, which not only surprised the German Central Council of Jews, which felt they should be the only judges of Germany and the Germans; it may also have shocked some German diplomats.[38]

These comments by Prinz and other returnees were detrimental to the self-righteous postwar self-perception of West Germany, a prodigy of a country that had risen to become America's closest ally during the Cold War and felt that the problems of the past had already been overcome. However, Prinz and others, including Max Nussbaum, visited West Germany regularly and encouraged the country to address its past rather than belittle it in the country's quest to successfully and sustainably embrace democracy.

In January 1963, Prinz shared his thoughts with journalist and historian Joachim Fest after a meeting with the conservative American Council for

Germany, a centrally positioned group of business and political leaders in the transatlantic relationship:

> The discussions, particularly those conducted by the American delegates, were very disturbing. It was an attempt to say that everything in Germany is marvelous, that Hitler was after all only one of the many totalitarian leaders, that all Nazi remnants have been eliminated and that Germany is now a shining example of a wonderful democracy. The Germans who participated were much better, but the whole thing was a distinct attempt to disregard the moral issue which calls for a brave and decent, honest confrontation with the facts, and with an effort to deal with these problems of the past in terms of education for the present... I would have very much liked to discuss all these matters with you because I am looking for a group of people in Germany who would be willing to participate in an honest give-and-take which would refrain from any kind of cliché and propaganda, but which would try to understand the problem. I hope that if I find such a group some of us could come to Germany and discuss these matters seriously.[39]

The difficulty of assembling a group like this is reflected in Prinz's correspondence with Werner Steltzer, director of the Information Center of the City of Berlin. In July 1966, he wrote with great frustration about the failed attempt to gather the necessary people for a discussion of the abovementioned issues. In general, all who were invited applauded the idea and its intention but reacted not as individuals (as had been expected and desired) but as functionaries of the groups they represented. In the end, each invitee declined by claiming that they did not think they were the best choice to participate in such a dialogue—a reaction that completely undermined the project.[40]

While the envisioned group had perhaps never been imagined as a standing group, the American Jewish Congress was becoming increasingly impatient with the lack of progress. So, too, was Prinz, who, as president at the time, was the driving force behind the involvement in West Germany. In February 1966, Will Maslow, executive director of the American Jewish Congress, wrote to Prinz: "We simply must begin to move on the Dialogue."[41]

Eager to make progress, especially in light of the rising public support in West Germany in the mid-1960s for the Nationaldemokratische Partei (National Democratic Party), Prinz addressed the appropriate people on a one-to-one basis. Among them were Kurt Eberhardt, managing director of the Ecumenical Council of the City of Berlin in 1966; Chancellor Konrad Adenauer; Christian Democratic Union politician Rainer Barzel, whom he had met during Barzel's trip to the United States; and Pater Dr. Stephan Schaller of the

Benedictine Monastery in Ettal, Bavaria, who had asked Prinz for advice when revising the text of the Passion Play to the satisfaction of both Catholics and Jews. Prinz also tried to hold an early exhibit in New York City on Auschwitz and Birkenau, but he struggled to raise the funds for that endeavor, even though the WJC supported the project.[42]

He also introduced a dialogue to educational institutions with the support of Abraham Sachar, president of Brandeis University, who invited him to meet with Axel Springer, a highly influential German publisher who was visiting the university. Unfortunately, Prinz could not accept the invitation because of other obligations. However, in February 1966, the German ambassador in Washington, DC, Heinrich Knappstein, met with Prinz for a public discussion titled "Germans and Jews—Is There a Bridge?" The event, which pioneered public discourse between Germans and Jews in the United States, was evaluated as a great success by historian Abraham Sachar, who turned to Prinz after the meeting and said, "I am gratified, Joachim, that the healing process we hope to see has begun here. Now we must carry it forward in action as well as in words, among the young, on whom all depends."[43]

Berlin played a special role in this process, thanks to its large and mostly liberal Jewish community, its Allied status, and the presence of many former rabbis who had survived the Nazi regime. Almost all of the former Berlin rabbis visited the city to support the Jewish community in Berlin and to honor their own histories. Therefore, in 1970, during the commemoration of the twenty-fifth anniversary of the reinstitution of Berlin's Jewish community, the refugees were invited to publish their memories in the memorial volume *Gegenwart im Rückblick* (The present in retrospect). Most did indeed contribute, telling their story as the last witnesses to a period of destruction and renewal.[44]

Besides Prinz, many other refugee rabbis participated in these exchanges and gave West Germany helpful feedback on its progress and shortcomings in becoming a democratic nation. As early as 1953, Max Nussbaum went to Berlin on a trip organized by the United Jewish Appeal. He revisited Berlin in 1958 and 1965, this last time at the invitation of the Federal Republic's government after West Germany had established diplomatic relations with Israel, which he considered to be promising for the future. All of his visits were covered in the press and Jewish publications, where he explained his impressions and thoughts on Germany. In October 1959, Nussbaum wrote an article titled "Ist Versöhnung möglich?" [Is reconciliation possible?] and published a sermon on the occasion of Yom Kippur in the refugee paper *Aufbau*.

He called on West Germany to follow Berlin's progressivism and launch an open and honest dialogue between Germans and Jews. He presented the issue on the Los Angeles radio station KNX and the Voice of America on RIAS Berlin and explained the situation in West Germany to the American Jewish Congress during its biennial convention in 1960, saying that American Jews should think twice about rejecting the idea of Jews living in Germany because this attitude would only support Hitler's goals. Nussbaum argued that Jews today had the right to live in Germany, and their treatment there would have to be seen as a criterion of the sincerity of that effort.[45]

An example of how intensely some of the rabbis were moved and then inspired by their travels is Rabbi Joseph Asher's trip to Wiesbaden, where he was born and educated. In 1964, he returned to his former Gymnasium, a German academic high school in Wiesbaden, where he had been humiliated and mistreated by classmates over twenty years ago. He spent eight weeks there, met former classmates, joined classes, tried to understand how the Holocaust was being taught, and talked with students, teachers, and former classmates.

The school had prepared for Asher's visit—which had been negotiated by the German ambassador in Washington and the Foreign Office—and tried to demonstrate that German students were indeed studying the Holocaust. However, Asher discovered through several conversations that the school had just started to deal with the Shoah when his trip was announced.

He encountered many stereotypes about Jews among the students, most of whom had never met a Jew. In several relaxed but frank discussions with Ernst, the classmate who had tormented Asher the most as a child, Asher learned that only nine of his forty-eight classmates had survived the war—most of them had died on the Eastern Front. The conversations with Ernst and the students emphasized that the Germans needed help in dealing with their past; they needed to learn about Jews, Judaism, and the Jewish experience; and they needed a way to understand a different perspective and move forward in the process of confronting their past. The younger generation in particular needed these experiences to avoid making the same mistakes their parents had made.

The trip benefited Asher as well, as he tried to understand the anatomy of prejudice, faced some of his own misguided convictions as a Jew, and ultimately learned how important the individual encounter with the Germans had been to move forward. Asher discussed the trip with Rabbi Balfour Brickner, head of the interfaith committee of the Union of American Hebrew Congregations (UAHC), then published his thoughts in the April 1965 edition of *Look* magazine under the bold title "A Rabbi Asks: Isn't It Time We Forgave the Germans?" The article concluded with these thoughts: "The spiritual victory I feel that I have won lies in the reducing of bitterness and converting it into the stuff of which civilized human relations are made. 'God desires not the death

Joseph Asher with his son Raphael Asher at Raphael's ordination from HUC in Cincinnati in 1977: AJA, pc0170.001.

of the wicked, but that he return from his evil ways and live.' That is the Jewish concept of God. Since Man is created in His image, it behooves him to desire likewise. As wickedness springs from small and individual acts, thus does compassion begin in an individual's heart."[46]

In the following months, Asher shared his thoughts and plans in several publications and public talks, discussing his strong feelings and informative experiences in American Jewish circles. He argued in favor of taking a "New Look at Germany,"[47] a bold and controversial stance that got a lot of attention in the United States. For Asher, it was the beginning of a special type of engagement with the Germans. In conjunction with the Evangelical Lutheran Church, he tried to launch an exchange between rabbinical students from HUC and German Christian theology students to support more understanding and knowledge about Jews and enhance personal relations. Many visits to West Germany, specifically to Berlin, followed. Asher was among the driving forces for establishing the memorial House of the Wannsee Conference (Haus der Wannsee-Konferenz), an educational memorial site in Berlin founded in 1992 to commemorate the destruction of European Jewry, which had been decided in this place.[48]

Returning Rabbis, B'nai B'rith, A Center for the Study of Antisemitism and a New Hochschule in Heidelberg

Reinforcing the right of Jews to live in Germany, the WUPJ made a bold decision to invite its youth to West Berlin on 4–11 April 1965 for the first WUPJ Youth Section conference in the city, the former center of liberal Judaism in Europe. The Berlin Jewish community had requested that this first youth meeting take place in their city, and the committee accepted the suggestion to underscore that Jewish life in Berlin was a fact that had been ignored and even condemned for far too long. Their decision acknowledged that "a new generation of Jew and Gentile is growing up in Germany and both need the education and contact of such a conference to help them understand their situation and create a new future."[49]

The youth delegates came primarily from England, the Netherlands, and, not surprisingly, from Mannheim, Germany, where Nathan Peter Levinson had established a progressive Jewish community. They also came from the United States and included Nathan Peter Levinson, Kuno Lehrmann (the rabbi of Berlin), and Ignatz Maybaum. They were received by the Jewish community of Berlin, the B'nai B'rith lodge, the Progressive Jewish Youth Group, and the Berlin Senate. At the conference, unexpectedly open discussions centered around the reasons why Jews returned to Germany and if it was legitimate to live in Germany as a Jew.

One of the most important outcomes of the meeting was the consensus that the identity of this neglected and controversial community might change if its members had their own rabbis, rabbis who were educated and familiar with the particular circumstances and concerns of their congregants, rather than "imported rabbis" from abroad, who typically stayed for only a short time and never became more than a "sympathetic outsider." This conclusion motivated four German conference participants to begin studying for the rabbinate at the

Leo Baeck College in London,[50] the only European school with a distinctly liberal German-Jewish climate that existed after the Shoah.[51]

The German-born rabbis who officiated in Germany at the time were prominent as rabbis and scholars, but their placement by and connection with American, British, or Swiss Jewish organizations was seriously criticized by the German Central Council of Jews. The organization for the German-Jewish community felt that they were being "colonized" in a way by spiritual leaders from other Jewries.[52] The degree to which religious jealousies and rivalries between Orthodoxy and liberal Judaism may have played a role in these concerns is hinted at in Nathan P. Levinson's recollection of his efforts to become a member of the German Rabbinical Conference under the leadership of the Orthodox rabbi Isaak Emil Lichtigfeld of Frankfurt.

Lichtigfeld not only had trouble accepting the rabbinic authority of Levinson as a member of the Central Conference of American Rabbis (CCAR, the American Reform movement's rabbinical organization); he also prevented Levinson from joining the rabbis' festive parade into the Worms synagogue on the occasion of its rededication in December 1961, seating him instead with the Christian theologians and professors of secular universities, not with the rabbinate. Levinson was only accepted as a member of the Rabbinical Conference after he officially protested against such treatment to Werner Nachmann, the president of the Jewish Council of Baden.[53]

Later in the 1960s, the Levinson family relocated to Heidelberg, an old, vibrant, culturally rich, and in its own way very "American" university town that had been shaped by the continued postwar presence of the US Army. The Levinsons all appreciated the qualities of this city, and Helga especially approved of its proximity to the university where she lectured. This atmosphere also seemed to have spurred Nathan Peter Levinson's rabbinate and work. Acknowledged as the chief rabbi of Baden and part of the city's public life, Levinson rose to become the Jewish chairman of the Coordinating Council for Jewish-Christian Cooperation and the editor of the journal *Emuna* (faith), which became a pioneering platform for interfaith dialogue in Germany featuring many refugee rabbis as contributors. *Emuna* also gave them a forum to share their life stories and experiences, which further motivated them to dedicate their time and energies to Christian-Jewish dialogue. In the fall of 1971, an entire issue of *Emuna* was dedicated to the rabbis and their new careers abroad. Among others, Rabbi Levinson published a contribution by Max Nussbaum.

While Levinson had long refrained from participating in interfaith dialogue after his first disastrous experiences in Berlin, where Protestant Christians had made little effort to acknowledge Jews, the situation was different in Heidelberg.

Fifteen years later and in an inclusive civic culture, Levinson finally saw this dialogue with his Christian counterparts as an essential tool to prevent future acts of genocide and religious stereotyping.[54]

More importantly, Heidelberg offered Levinson the intellectual climate and infrastructure to launch a visionary project fully in line with the long-term goals of the WUPJ and the sensibilities of many of the refugee rabbis. This project would acknowledge that there was a permanent Jewish community in Germany and its members would be supported and protected by rabbis, cantors, and teachers from Germany. Unlike the "imported" rabbis, these scholars would be familiar with the local circumstances, habits, and sensitivities of their communities.

A rabbinical seminary, or Hochschule für Jüdische Studien (HJS, Higher Institute for Jewish Studies)—a central institution of higher education for training Jewish teachers, rabbis, and cantors in Germany—was sponsored by the Central Council of Jews in Germany and the West German government. In Heidelberg, a town with a strong academic culture, the oldest German university, and Christian faculties of theology, Levinson found an environment where this idea resonated and could be realized.

It only took a year from the time the first official suggestion of the project was made, and the plan was ultimately accepted by both the key West German educational body (the Kultusministerkonferenz [Conference of German Ministers of Education]) and the Central Council. The dedication of the HJS in Heidelberg took place in 1979. Its founding for the first time reintroduced a Jewish institution of higher learning to Germany after the closing of the Hochschule für die Wissenschaft des Judentums in Berlin in 1941.

Jakob Petuchowski was asked to be the founding director, but he declined. The second candidate was Herbert Strauss, a former student of the Hochschule in Berlin who had relocated to New York City. He taught history at the City University of New York and directed the Research Foundation for Jewish Immigration. This organization's vast collection of research materials is preserved in the archives of the Leo Baeck Institute in New York and constitutes a valuable resource for research on German-Jewish flight and relocation in the United States. Strauss turned down the job to take care of his aging mother in New York.

The third candidate, whom Levinson approached, was Leon Aryeh Feldman, an Orthodox professor of Judaic studies at Rutgers University who had attended the Adass Jisroel School in Berlin with Levinson and was willing to relocate to Germany. Soon after he signed his contracts, Feldman settled in Heidelberg and moved energetically forward on a project that was for him a matter of the heart: the founding of the HJS as a separate institute of higher learning that maintained a loose relationship with the University of Heidelberg.

By the time the HJS opened its doors to its first students in 1979, it had recruited a number of scholars who rotated as professors rather than holding a permanent chair, which added to the variety of Jewish perspectives taught there. Levinson's recollections stress a competitive relationship between the project and the Leo Baeck College in London, whose president then was Albert Friedlander. Friedlander, who had also been trained in Cincinnati, belittled the project and claimed that there were not enough students or faculty to teach *Wissenschaft des Judentums* again in Germany.[55]

Indeed, the HJS attracted more Christians interested in Jewish studies than Jews from Germany. The reason that so few Jewish students wanted to prepare for a role in the synagogue was the small size of the community, which never exceeded thirty thousand Jews. However, the founding of the HJS proved that the German government wanted and supported the school and thus an ongoing presence of Jews in Germany.[56]

When Leon Aryeh Feldman compiled a schedule of courses for the first semester starting in the fall of 1979, he approached colleagues he considered capable of teaching at the Hochschule to a German-speaking audience, ideally in German. Among them were refugee scholars and rabbis, including Alexander Guttmann, who taught in Heidelberg in the fall of 1980 and in the spring of 1981 and 1982.

Guttmann had been saved as a young scholar by HUC in Cincinnati and had been teaching as the college's Talmudist since 1940. Guttmann and the other well-compensated professors who taught for a year in the appealing city of Heidelberg felt great pride accompanied by memories of how their previous careers in Germany had ended. In Heidelberg, they were invited, reinstituted, and welcomed by a newly founded institution funded by the West German government to teach *Wissenschaft des Judentums* for the first time in Germany since their expulsion and the forced closing of the seminaries in Berlin and Breslau.

Under these circumstances, the scholars' return created hope for the future of modern Jewish studies in a country that had so radically abandoned that academic asset and its people. This country was celebrating the return of those once persecuted. Inspired by the reopening of a new Hochschule for Jewish studies in Germany early on, Guttmann enthusiastically offered his services for the first ordination of a new generation of rabbis in Germany, which never took place there. The West German and American press published articles stating that the endeavor would retrieve and rejuvenate knowledge that had long been buried—a euphemism for the persecution and expulsion these scholars had experienced but used to play up the special occasion.

Hebrew Union College in Cincinnati and the school's press were eager to hear from Alexander Guttmann about his experience teaching in this special and sensitive environment. They sent Guttmann a list of questions about why he went back, if he had been back previously, how many students studied at the Hochschule and how many of them were Jewish, who else was on the faculty and why he accepted the particular position. In his report, among other details, Guttmann stressed that he came to contribute to the revival of Judaism in Europe.[57]

Germany's Reunification: A Changing Jewish Community as a Working Ground for American Rabbinical Seminaries

Unfortunately, the Hochschule in Heidelberg did not fulfill German Jewry's hopes of becoming an institute of higher learning of *Wissenschaft des Judentums*; however, there was a great interest in the scholarly study of Judaism in Germany due to the Holocaust. The main reason so few Jewish students joined the rabbinate was that, among the small Jewish community in Germany, the young people did not necessarily envision a future in West Germany, or they spent several years abroad in larger Jewish communities to establish themselves and find a Jewish spouse.

The situation changed radically and unexpectedly in 1989 with the collapse of the Cold War order, the fall of the Berlin Wall, and the German reunification in October 1990. During the year before German reunification, a new East German government, under the lens of a global public, tried to make amends for ignoring Jewish victimhood during the Second World War and the Holocaust in that state and for never considering or discussing restitution to survivors of the Holocaust. Instead, during this short phase of renewal, the East German government passed legislation that invited Jewish refugees from the former Soviet Union to immigrate to East Germany under special conditions.

After reunification, the Federal Republic of Germany maintained this commitment to Jewish refugees from the former Soviet Union, many of whom also sought refuge in Israel and the United States. The country considered this migration, which brought approximately two hundred thousand Jews to a united Germany between 1990 and 2010, as an opportunity to stabilize Jewish life in Germany. The Jewishness of these immigrants was debated among Germany's largely Orthodox communities because the newcomers did not always meet halachic expectations and few of them had hardly any religious Jewish identity.

Nevertheless, about one hundred thousand of these immigrants joined Jewish religious communities in Germany, which caused these communities to quadruple in membership. Since the refugees were evenly distributed throughout Germany, new Jewish communities emerged even in small towns. Consequently, more than ever before, Jewish life in Germany was challenged by the overwhelming number of community members who needed instruction in Judaism, enhanced social services, and spiritual leadership. The integration of this diverse majority of Jews from the former Soviet Union also created other issues. For example, since these people had not been raised in traditional Orthodoxy, many of them preferred a liberal affiliation.

This bothered the large German Orthodox Gemeinde, where religious pluralism had hardly existed after 1945. They witnessed independent liberal communities emerging *outside* the Gemeinde, attracting a mix of former Russian Jews and Jews who came to Germany as a result of the globalization. They saw this development as a threat to their survival and domination of the Gemeinde. The Gemeinde had to adapt not only to the growing number of members but also to the task of integrating and educating them and making possible a future with religious pluralism in Germany. The independent communities outside the Gemeinde, most of which were connected to the American Reform movement or the Leo Baeck College in London, were demanding permanent and unified Jewish spiritual leadership from Germany to claim their rights as part of an integrated community. Rabbis, cantors, and teachers educated in Germany were urgently needed, for without them, "integration" into the Gemeinde and long-term peace among the Jewish factions would never be possible.[58]

In this climate, fifty years after the Shoah, the WUPJ sensed a unique opportunity to reinitiate a new and more organized presence of modern Judaism in Germany. How such a historical change could be realized was unclear at the beginning. In 1994, Nathan Peter Levinson proposed closing the Hochschule in Heidelberg and moving it to Berlin, where German reunification had made available the property of the Hochschule für die Wissenschaft des Judentums in the former Artilleriestrasse (today Tucholskystrasse). In Levinson's opinion, this move would reclaim that space for Jewish Wissenschaft. However, he and his second wife, Pnina Navè Levinson, were planning their retirement in Mallorca, Spain.[59]

In November 1995, the WUPJ invited one of the youngest refugee rabbis of the second generation, Rabbi Walter Jacob of Congregation Rodef Shalom in Pittsburgh, to a seminar with lay leaders in Vienna, where the situation and potential of the rising number of small liberal congregations in Germany and their neglect outside the state-funded Gemeinde were passionately discussed among German-speaking grassroots sympathizers. Jacob, who had risen to a prominent leadership position in the American Reform movement, took up the issue. He promised to send short-term visiting rabbis, but he emphasized that in the long term, they needed "Torah," or the instruction of the law, synonymous with rabbinical training in Germany.[60]

Rabbi Jacob had left Germany as an eight-year-old when his father, the rabbi of Augsburg, fled Germany and relocated first to England and then to the United States. He did not return to Germany until the mid-1970s, even though a cultural bond with Germany continued to exist. He never lost his proficiency in German and married a German-born woman, Irene Lowenthal, who had come to the United States as a refugee. They passed on the German language to their children, who studied it. Returning to the country of his birth, however, seemed impossible for a long time, and Jacob asserted that a revival of Judaism in Germany would have been bluntly rejected by his father.[61]

However, in his rabbinate and personal encounters with Holocaust survivors like Elie Wiesel, Jacob claimed that he started to understand that confronting the past allowed a person to make individual choices about how to deal with tragedy. A person could be eternally caught in tragedy, or he could understand that tragedy offered lessons for the future. Jacob started to take the latter path. From the mid-1970s on, he and his wife visited Augsburg and his father's former synagogue several times. Eric Lidji, Jacob's biographer, explained that the visits to Germany deeply engaged Jacob both personally and as a rabbi and convinced him that Jews should not turn exclusively to the Holocaust as the single leading motif of their Jewishness. Instead, he believed, they should remember that flight and emigration of ancient Jews had enabled their forefathers to leave their anger and bitterness behind in Egypt and gave them the freedom to start over with new empathy and energy. Only such an attitude would allow them to embark on new paths and build something new, something good.[62]

During his travels, Jacob learned about the realities of communities, met young Germans, got involved with German officials on behalf of the communities and in organizing joint commemorations, and increasingly became a mediator in the complex mélange of Jews and Germans, history and memory, Jewish survival and a potential Jewish future in Germany.

As a rabbi, he interpreted what he saw as being not unlike the Jews' forty years of wandering through the wilderness and the enormous difficulties they encountered before finding the Promised Land. He drew parallels to the biblical example: the Holocaust had left an entire generation of Jews in Germany in a spiritual desert, forced to leave the realization of their goals to the next generation. In the mid-1990s, at the height of his career in the Reform movement and the end of his CCAR presidency and WUPJ vice presidency, Jacob felt that American Jewry had failed to provide the support it should have given long ago and took the matter into his own hands.

Jacob encouraged young and retired rabbis to officiate at the small liberal congregations that were beginning to emerge in German-speaking Europe. He became chief rabbi of Munich's Beth Shalom Congregation after his retirement in 1996. Part of his decision to volunteer and support this development of liberal Judaism was an unusually rich friendship with Walter Homolka, a young Bavarian convert to Judaism who had trained for the rabbinate at Leo Baeck College in London. Homolka was gay and unwilling to hide that fact, and at the time, neither HUC nor Leo Baeck College ordained openly gay rabbis. This might have stood in the way of Homolka's career path and desire to serve a congregation, but Jacob resolved the conflict. He conducted a private ordination ceremony at Beth Shalom in Munich, which gave Homolka his *Smicha* and permitted him to continue his career. Fully aware of the symbolism, Jacob included the academic robes of his parents from Drury College in Missouri in the ceremony: he wore his mother's robe, and Walter Homolka donned his father's robe.

The ordination was accompanied by the Swiss, Austrian, and German lay participants of the Vienna seminar in 1995, who, as a result of the festive gathering, formed a unit of the newly founded Union of Progressive Jews in Germany, Austria, and Switzerland. This paved the way for the WUPJ to take root organizationally in central Europe after the Holocaust and develop a network to send rabbis to orphaned congregations.[63]

With an organizational framework and the membership of the WUPJ in place and approximately forty liberal (proto-) congregations with no trained rabbis, Rabbis Jacob and Homolka turned to the UAHC for assistance in raising the practical standards among this largely lay-led group. As a result, an ad hoc four-week training program was established in 1998 for laypeople in the United States, where they were acquainted with liturgical music, social activities, and leadership skills.

At the same time, Rabbi Walter Homolka explored the options for instituting a program for modern rabbinical training within the large and tuition-free German state university system, which already offered a number of Jewish studies centers. Ultimately, the decision was made to establish a rabbinical seminary in partnership with the University of Potsdam, where the Moses Mendelssohn Center had been founded after German unification. Not only did this new seminary constitute the largest Jewish studies center of the country; it also stressed the historical impact that Moses Mendelssohn, the Haskala, and

Alfred Gottschalk ordaining the first German-trained liberal rabbis at the first ordination ceremony of the Abraham-Geiger-Kolleg, Potsdam, with Walter Homolka and Walter Jacob in the upper right: Abraham-Geiger-Kolleg, © Margrit Schmidt.

German Jewry had had on the region and provided a pillar to support this project within the University of Potsdam, right next to Berlin, its historical center.

Substantial financial backing for the project was raised by the newly founded American Friends of the Union of Progressive Jews in Germany, Austria, and Switzerland, whose members, many of them former refugees, included Chancellor Alfred Gottschalk (HUC), Alexander Schindler (former president of the UAHC) W. Gunther Plaut (head of the responsa committee), historian Michael A. Meyer (HUC), Joshua Haberman, Lore Metzger (wife of Kurt Metzger), Ruth Nussbaum (wife of Max Nussbaum), Elizabeth Petuchowski (wife of Jakob Petuchowski), Karl Richter, Herman Schaalman, and Alfred Wolf.[64]

Abraham Geiger, the nineteenth-century father of liberal, historical Judaism, became a role model and standard-bearer of the training program. This new institution satisfied Geiger's demand to have Jewish theology for the first time stand on equal footing with Christian theological faculties at German state universities. Incorporated in 1999, opened in 2000, and graduating its first class of German-educated liberal rabbis in 2006, it heralded a new beginning in post-Holocaust Jewish history in Germany and paved the way for the other two

American Jewish movements, the Conservative movement and the Orthodox movement in Judaism, to follow suit.

In 2009, the Orthodox Rabbinerseminar reestablished a rabbinical school in Berlin with the assistance of the Lauder Foundation and the remaining members of the dispersed Orthodox community. The school was led by Heinrich Chanoch Ehrentreu, son of Jonah Ernst Ehrentreu, as rector and supported by Prof. Meir Hildesheimer, great-grandson of the founder of the original seminary who taught Jewish history at Bar-Ilan University outside of Tel Aviv. The Orthodox seminary established academic cooperation with secular universities such as Berlin's Humboldt University (law faculty) and the University of Applied Science in Erfurt (social work/social sciences).[65]

In 2013, the Conservative movement in American Judaism established the Zacharias Frankel College[66] in Potsdam, which, together with the Abraham-Geiger-Kolleg, has been educating and graduating new generations of a modern European Jewish rabbinate in the University of Potsdam's recently founded Jewish School of Theology since then. Rabbi Walter Homolka was not only professor and managing director of the Abraham-Geiger-Kolleg and the Zacharias Frankel College, guiding the intellectual and organizational growth of the Jewish School of Theology in a unique and energetic fashion; he also became the prototype and role model for a new generation of modern rabbis from Germany until the Geiger-Kolleg was recently confronted with severe accusations of abuse of power that are challenging the seminary's future.[67]

For those who supported the reestablishment of these rabbinical schools, the ordination of the first modern, German-trained rabbis in 2006 at the Abraham-Geiger-Kolleg was one of the last steps in finding closure and meaning in their personal lives and professional careers. The return of these former refugee rabbis to Germany not only benefited them in their personal quest for resolution; they also seized the opportunity to pass on a tradition that they thought had been completely lost. They embraced the chance to demonstrate to the world that, after their flight and renewal, they had never lost agency. They were able to—at least symbolically—undo a process that had started with Nazism.[68]

CONCLUSION

The history of the "last generation of the German rabbinate" provides a perspective that is absent from the multifaceted narrative of this leadership at the heart of German-Jewish history. It emphasizes how the unique leadership of the "German" rabbis was dedicated to putting a *Jewish* solution to Nazism front and center, before, during, and after the Nazi era.

In this effort, they succeeded in upholding and strengthening what Nazism targeted namely, the German model of a modern Judaism that saw itself and the modern Jew as an integral part of modern society. This model continued to be their guiding principle even though it faced criticism for its assimilationist attitudes and was suspected—as German Judaism was thought to have done—of facilitating a similar catastrophe in the future in the United States.

The long-term analysis of this group proves the opposite, namely, that they actively confronted history and the supposed shortcomings of their tradition in a unique effort to provide answers to essential questions that modern Judaism had to deal with in the postwar era. In fact, they were essential in answering many questions American Jews had at the time and were architects of a postwar revival of modern Judaism that made the United States its new center.[1]

A close look at what happened in German-Jewish communities in the 1920s, however, reveals an enormous transformation by the impact of Zionism and the reemergence of a Jewish ethnic identity was already taking place that would help German Jews find answers during a similar crisis triggered by Nazism. For them, finding inner strength, if not pride, in a distinct Jewish identity was essential and created resilience. In this process, a dynamic young generation stood out, one that rebounded to a large degree in the American rabbinate after being rescued by their colleagues in the United States.

Dedicated to a modern and hence authentic Judaism from their own life experience, German Jews felt responsible for finding answers to the questions facing modern Judaism in post-Holocaust America and for writing the last chapter of the modern German-Jewish rabbi. Their systematic expulsion from Germany from the mid-1930s on and especially after the pogrom of 9 November 1938 seemed to have destroyed a proud German-Jewish religious elite that understood itself as a communal leadership dedicated to a timely Jewish identity in modern society, to the zeitgeist, and to modern Jewish *Wissenschaft*. Persecution, flight, and subsequently the Holocaust seemed to have destroyed their scholarship, identity, cohesion, communication, and professional networks. Displacement in new and sometimes completely foreign cultural contexts as well as the loss of those who perished in the Shoah threatened the continuity of a distinctly modern Jewish identity, which had had its historic center in German-speaking Europe.

While the refugee experience meant survival, it came at a high price: dislocation, uprootedness, cultural estrangement and adaptation, and the loss of home, family, security, community, and a sense of belonging. The trauma of being expelled or forced to flee remained with the refugees, shaping their lives forever. While their flight technically ended upon arrival in the United States, their experience of flight, displacement, destruction, and relocation did not.

This fact is often neglected, as the methodology, practicability, and lack of in-depth knowledge about the receiving communities prohibited long-term studies, group biographies based on extensive data, and the thorough evaluation of data that tracked more than flight or survival. For practical reasons, few studies can invest enough time and resources to look at the larger picture. Therefore, most biographical studies focus on individuals and neglect to reveal the deep intellectual encounter of this postwar community with the Holocaust. That is why this book focuses on the individual rabbis' personal thoughts and recollections of their roles, trauma, memories, and attempts at building a legacy, especially as they gained a new agency as Jewish leaders in the process.[2]

The analysis of the refugees' careers; their lives from cradle to grave and across political epochs, global migrations, and transnational networks; their late-life returns to Germany; and their exchange of knowledge and scholarship shows that it was the very nature of their Judaism, one dedicated to societal engagement, that made it portable and adaptable and that helped most of the refugees not only to survive in their professions but to develop promising careers. This ultimately led to the creation of a legacy and a future for the movement, one that continued to thrive, created a new center in the United States, and experienced a postwar renewal in which these rabbis played a central role.[3]

Approaching this project via the digital humanities allowed a more nuanced analysis of the approximately 250 biographies of refugee rabbis and revealed who these people were, where they came from, what guided them, and how they concluded their lives after their sometimes global migrations. Many of them had been born shortly before or after 1900 and were affected by societal trends and movements that developed around the First World War: reflections on the loss of an original Jewish identity by assimilation, exposure to eastern European Jewish role models and lifestyles, the experience of the war, the rise of Zionism, and the growing encounter with antisemitism.

Fifty percent of the students for the German rabbinate were from parts of Europe east of post-1918 Germany. These central or east European regions had either belonged to Germany before the war or maintained an intense cultural relationship with Germany or Austria that drew young men westward to attend German universities and rabbinical schools. They usually arrived in Berlin and Breslau with an excellent knowledge of traditional Jewish scholarship as well as a great curiosity for modernity and secular studies.

These factors created a new and distinct youth culture that was revolutionary, curious, innovative, and rooted in Jewish knowledge.[4] These students challenged the Jewish establishment by popularizing new role models and searching for a lively and deep-seated inner Jewish identity that they passed on to their congregants. As rabbis and youth leaders, these men exhibited a fervor for Judaism and inner renewal. Jewish knowledge drove their social and political roles in society and the community, especially after the Nazi rise to power in 1933. Their leadership shaped the men who later became known as the second generation of refugee rabbis, those who emigrated as children and studied in the United States but whose Jewish ideals remained rooted in the difficult but dynamic years spent in their Jewish communities in Germany.

During these difficult years and more than ever before, such ideals, practices, and religious teachings were not only in high demand in a community facing humiliation, persecution, mass flight, and ultimately destruction, but turned into a form of capital that transformed synagogues into centers of Jewish resilience and mutual support—the only support this minority could hope for at the time. For many congregants, this meant more than just practical assistance in their difficult lives.

Their Jewish being came alive, and they found a home in the synagogue. The experience with community, learning new skills and practices, political structures, and the ability to connect the present with Jewish history and identity remained with them in their new surroundings. Their knowledge and methods were implemented in their new communities in a cultural transfer that has rarely been seen in a refugee group. Their political messages fit well into the American synagogue and sometimes exceeded the expectations of their new congregants. While American Jewry was not on the brink of outward collapse, some refugees felt that the lack of Jewish knowledge, indifference, and the weakness of the Jewish identity among American Jews had led them to the edge of an abyss that might endanger the survival of modern (Diaspora) Judaism. They felt that it was their responsibility to act against that threat.[5]

This was particularly true for the liberal and Reform groups among the refugees, who found a new home in and around the Hebrew Union College. The college facilitated their integration into the American Reform movement more than any other movement in American Judaism. Because this religious movement of American Judaism shared their German heritage, it is far from surprising that their careers benefited from their efforts to come to grips with their past, to communicate intensely with society on political and religious issues, and to facilitate transfers of knowledge not only from Europe to the United States but eventually also from the United States back to Europe.[6]

Some of the formerly liberal refugee rabbis and students were integrated into the Conservative movement in American Judaism, but that movement embraced far fewer of the German refugees than the Reform movement. This was mainly due to the ethnic composition of its congregations, a reluctance to burden the Jewish Theological Seminary (JTS) with too many German refugee students in a short period, and the fact that German students needed an American BA degree to join the JTS. The students and rabbis who found a home at the JTS influenced the institution with their presence and leadership; however, their visibility as "Germans" was less obvious, and the institution hastened their Americanization with additional training and strict guidance from the beginning.

While many modern Orthodox Jews fled from Germany to the United States, very few found a home in the congregations of the American Orthodox movement or in the rabbinical department of Yeshiva University, the Rabbi Isaac Elchanan Theological Seminary. Very few found a place in an American Orthodox congregation and managed to satisfy the ethnic and religious expectations of their congregants and fit into their cultural backgrounds. The majority of the refugees who were part of the Yeshiva University system were either second-generation refugee rabbis who graduated from that institution or found a place for themselves in education, in publishing, in scholarship, in the youth movement, in the administration of American Orthodoxy, or at secular universities.

Nevertheless, the experience of Ner Israel Rabbinical College in Baltimore and Herman Naftali Neuberger's dedication to rescuing many students from the Israelitische Lehrerbildungsanstalt of Würzburg proves that a closer look at smaller schools and Orthodox networks can reveal surprising insights.

Although the history of German Orthodox refugee rabbis in the United States is an important part of this study, it is not complete, for it depends on the large number of small independent refugee communities whose records are in private hands. Such a study would focus on the educational institutions and a number of independent yeshivot in the United States, where the presence of these refugee rabbis was felt. Their history is hard to trace due to the absence of a cohesive archive, a record of the multiple facets of their new lives outside Germany, and the dispersed transnational nature of their individual groupings after they lost their centers in Germany.

As we have learned from this research, a more detailed analysis of this community has to bring together the rescue effort of the *Vaad Hatzalah* and that of the modern German rabbinate, as several of the "German" rabbis started their flight from Nazi Germany with a stay in eastern Europe in the prominent yeshivot of traditional Orthodoxy. Here they were confronted with the Nazi's aggressive invasion that drove them farther east, via Shanghai to the United States.

Not only does the global dispersion of this community deserve scholarly attention but so, too, do the Breuer family and the legendary Kahal Adass Jeshurun of Washington Heights in New York City, where Rav Joseph Breuer reassembled a part of his former Frankfurt Orthodox separatist community to continue his teachings and those of Samson Raphael Hirsch. By establishing the Rabbi Joseph Breuer Foundation, his family launched a transfer of knowledge from the Hirschian legacy by ensuring the translation of the most important works of their intellectual leaders into English and other languages and by disseminating these books.[7]

Based on the data collected and processed in the digital humanities database MIRA, it was possible to trace the individual paths of flight and resettlement, career development and academic recognition, and professional affiliations and placements of this large and diverse group of rabbis and scholars. The evaluation of this data revealed the role that old and new professional networks have played in the rebuilding of their careers.

The refugees who thrived in the United States were not only the young English-speaking rabbis but also those who found a professional network that valued their history and cultural differences and assisted them professionally and personally in transitioning to the American rabbinate, thus enabling these rabbis to contribute their unique intellectual and personal perspectives. Here the American rabbinical schools played a unique role in the assimilation of the German rabbis, the transfer of knowledge and scholarship, and the societal and congregational resonance of their messages to the public and respective movements in American Judaism. The schools became a framework for communicating concerns and positions in a generation-building process of these men as "the last of a special kind," a generation with a special legacy. This process was most significant in the American Reform movement, whose history was so deeply rooted in a German-Jewish past.[8]

More importantly, the refugees' public negotiations of their past and legacy paved the way for new careers in the political arena, either locally or as national leaders of American Jewry. In their effort to explain who they were and where they derived their special motivation to contribute to major post-Holocaust discourse, they communicated their past and personal experiences with Nazism, antisemitism, and racism, and continued to build a bridge between the past and the present.

In this way, the refugees not only presented themselves as "the last generation of the German rabbinate"; they also created a special legacy, one that would ensure the survival of their Jewish tradition and knowledge, that adapted it to new societal challenges, and that was determined to provide Jewish leadership, knowledge, and inner strength to the next generation of modern Jews globally. Their contribution to shifting the center of modern Judaism from central Europe to the United States in the postwar era, where their messages were heard in both the Jewish community and scholarly institutions, was remarkable and inspiring and made the United States the center of modern Judaism and Jewish scholarship after the Holocaust.

The knowledge transfer embraced modern Jewish scholarship, which became a special blend of modern and traditional Jewish knowledge with new forms to ignite people's interest in Judaism and provide new paths to finding and incorporating the personal God in their everyday lives. This was an important achievement for many modern Jews who had lost that connection not only through assimilation but also because of the Holocaust. The refugees from Nazism had unique messages and experiences to share and were heard far beyond the synagogues. Their words reached other religious movements and the larger American public. Beyond their scholarship—teaching at prominent academic institutions, publishing scholarly works that were translated into English—their personal experience of racism, antisemitism, and Nazism drove their commitment into the political arena and society at large.

The refugees' support of the American civil rights movement had a religious but also biographical background. They considered the commemoration, research, and education of the Holocaust to be important not only for Jews but also for society at large because they feared that a similar societal and political collapse would result in a second Holocaust.[9] Interfaith dialogue played a crucial role in the efforts to prevent this. Such a dialogue had been absent in Germany, where the churches had failed to support the country's Jewish community in times of crisis and had not questioned Christianity's historical positions toward Jews or their own historical antisemitism.

Finally, the reflections of the refugee rabbis on their fractured pasts and hybrid identities resulted in return journeys to postwar Germany late in their lives. These trips frequently helped them come to grips with their past and find answers to questions that had preoccupied them since their hurried and difficult flight. Their visits also helped the Germans participate in essential postwar exchanges about their history, the shortcomings of German society, and its history of antisemitism. Their presence buttressed and defended the existence of a small but visible community of liberal Judaism in postwar Germany amid the many newly formed or restructured Jewish communities under the authority of traditionally Orthodox east European Holocaust survivors who in no way felt fully at home in the country of the perpetrators.

Globally dispersed, while a new and culturally different community of Jews slowly grew from the survivors of the death marches at the end of the Second World War in Germany, they continued to negotiate their values, pasts, and futures in Germany.

Just as the refugee rabbis found unique opportunities in a demographically expanding and increasingly diverse united Germany with a growing and increasingly pluralistic Jewish community, the second generation of the refugee rabbinate also saw the chance to reinstitute modern Jewish training in central Europe, starting with the Abraham-Geiger-Kolleg at the University of Potsdam in 1999.[10] They thereby secured the reinstitutionalization and survival of modern Judaism for the next generation of European Jews. Ultimately, "the last generation of the German rabbinate" was not the last liberal rabbis to be ordained in Germany. Neither did Jewish life in Germany end, as had been expected only several years earlier. Both of these facts deeply satisfied those who had returned to Germany, for they felt they had not only met the expectations their teachers had instilled in them but had also concluded this last chapter of the German rabbinate. They set up new centers for modern rabbinical training just outside of Berlin, the city where the Haskala and their history had originated in the nineteenth century, and they were supported in this endeavor by their new American Jewish home institutions, which helped them survive, readjust, and "rekindle the flame."[11]

While the return of the diverse modern rabbinical seminaries could not (and will not) bring back a Jewish culture like the one destroyed by Nazism and the Shoah, the efforts led by the refugee rabbis to train modern rabbis in German-speaking central Europe helped to fill the leadership void there. These new leaders were dedicated to defining their role as Jews in post-Holocaust Europe within European societies, especially at a time when a newly united Europe provided the space where modern Judaism was once at home, long-lost *central* Europe.

Using the digital humanities to analyze the history of this relatively large group of refugees helped structure their biographies and compare the collected data on their lives and careers. The digital humanities also made it possible to analyze their migrations in more detail, to explore the transnational nature of this dispersed community in a more cohesive fashion, and to draw conclusions about the survival of modern Judaism within a globally mobile cohort, whose global interactions in the post-Holocaust period, aside from the focus on the United States, is a desideratum.

The results of this study provided new insights into the group as a whole and ensured that the details that characterized their biographies and illuminated their experiences as refugees from Nazism were not overlooked. Being able to systematically collect and compare these details allows us to better comprehend the Jewish experience in Nazi Germany and the role played by the synagogues, the rabbinate, and the *Gemeinde* and to understand why the rabbinate and community were targeted by the Nazis. Both the leadership demonstrated by German rabbis in Nazi Germany and the rescue of the German rabbinate, students, and scholars by the rabbinical schools in Germany and the United States illuminate the agency and solidarity they demonstrated during the crisis.

The details of their biographies highlight the rabbis' battles against everyday problems resulting from persecution and social exclusion, their level of self-organization, and the remarkable agency they gave their communities. Even if they could not prevent Nazi persecution, the rabbinical seminaries (and communities) managed to rescue a number of their leaders through emigration. This mainly included young scholars, students, and former graduates who were either willing to leave or were so intimidated by the Nazis that they could no longer work in their profession. When discussing the leadership of the German-Jewish rabbinate during this time, we must also remember those rabbis who did not emigrate but stayed with their communities and ultimately perished with them in German concentration or extermination camps. Although they cannot tell their stories, they lived up to the ideals that inspired them, and their experiences also deserve further research.

Among those who were able to flee Nazism, it was those who relocated to the United States who had the best options to continue their careers in American

Judaism. Their close relationship with the American rabbinical seminaries and especially the connection between the American Reform movement and liberal Judaism in Germany enhanced their agency after displacement and gave them the institutional support to re-create a certain continuity, build a legacy, and reach out to American Jews with the messages they drew from their experiences. Their communications were part of a discourse on Judaism, Germany, the Holocaust, Nazism and racism, and interfaith dialogue that not only resurfaced in American society after the Second World War but also addressed existing concerns.[12]

Their messages spoke to non-Jewish and Jewish Americans alike and were underscored by Hasia Diner's criticism of Peter Novick's conclusions on the prevailing "silence" over the Holocaust in American culture in general and American Jewish culture in particular after the Second World War.[13] The MIRA database houses archival and digital materials on this refugee group and their endeavors to educate people about the past and transform society and religion to prevent in the United States what they had experienced in Germany. This resonated strongly in American society and allowed modern Judaism to flourish in the United States, turning that country into the new center of modern Judaism in the post-Holocaust world, which was not only the result of a renewal of east European traditions alone.[14]

I hope that this book, in conjunction with the digital humanities database MIRA, will enhance scholarly interest in this group of refugees and ignite more in-depth research on individual rabbis and their experiences, Judaism, social activism, and scholarship. The development of a global perspective would also be important, one that can examine the other major destinations of the German refugees, such as Palestine and Great Britain. Research like this will allow us an even more nuanced interpretation of the migrations and post-Holocaust activities of the refugee rabbis.

NOTES

Introduction

1. Michael A. Meyer, *Response to Modernity: A History of the Reform Movement in Judaism* (New York: Oxford University Press, 1988), 225–295; Christian Wiese, "Translating Wissenschaft: The Emergence and Self-Emancipation of American Jewish Scholarship, 1860–1920," in *American Jewry: Transcending the European Experience?*, ed. Christian Wiese and Cornelia Wilhelm (London: Bloomsbury Academic, 2016); Wiese, "The Philadelphia Conference 1869 and German Reform: A Historical Moment in a Transnational Story of Proximity and Alienation," in Wiese and Wilhelm, *American Jewry*, 136–158; Wiese, "Auf Deutsch nach Amerika: Über den Transfer der Wissenschaft des Judentums im 19. und 20. Jahrhundert," in *Sprache, Erkenntnis und Bedeutung—Deutsch in der jüdischen Wissenskultur*, ed. Arndt Engelhardt and Susanne Zepp (Leipzig: Leipziger Uni-Verlag, 2015), 57–86.

2. Meyer, *Response*, 264–289.

3. Wiese, "Auf Deutsch nach Amerika," 57–86.

4. Michael Brocke and Julius Carlebach, eds., *Biographisches Handbuch der Rabbiner*, 2 vols. (Munich: De Gruyter, 2004–2009); Michael A. Meyer, ed., *Joachim Prinz, Rebellious Rabbi: An Autobiography—The German and Early American Years* (Bloomington: Indiana University Press, 2008), or Edward K. Kaplan and Samuel Dresner, *Abraham Joshua Heschel: Prophetic Witness* (New Haven, CT: Yale University Press, 1998). See, for example, Alan Steinweis, *Kristallnacht 1938* (Stuttgart: Reclam, 2011).

5. Michael A. Meyer et al., eds., *German-Jewish History in Modern Times: Renewal and Destruction, 1918–1945*, vol. 4 (New York: Columbia University Press, 1998), 391–402.

6. Ian Tyrell, "What Is Transnational History?," https:/iantyrelol.wordpress.com/what-is-transnational-history; David Thelen, "The Nation and Beyond: Transnational Perspectives on United States History," *Journal of American History* 86 (1993): 1045–1077; Heinz Gerhard Haupt and Jürgen Kocka, eds., *Comparative and Transnational History: Central European Approaches and New Perspectives* (New York: Berghahn Books, 2009). For American Jewish history specifically, see, for example, Ava F. Kahn and Adam Mendelsohn, eds., *Transnational Traditions: New Perspectives on American Jewish History* (Detroit: Wayne State University Press, 2014).

7. Steven Lowenstein, *Frankfurt on the Hudson: The German-Jewish Community of Washington Heights, 1933–1983, Its Structure and Culture* (Detroit: Wayne State University Press, 1989).

8. See, for example, Timothy L. Smith, "Religion and Ethnicity in America," *American Historical Review* 83:1155–1185.

9. Schenderlein stressed this circumstance in her recent work, Anne Clara Schenderlein, *Germany on Their Minds* (New York: Berghahn Books, 2020).

10. Leo Baeck, "Israel und das Deutsche Volk," *Merkur* 10 (October 1952): 911; Michael A. Meyer, "Denken und Wirken Leo Baecks nach 1945," in *Leo Baeck 1873–1956: Aus dem Stamme von Rabbinen*, ed. Georg Heuberger and Fritz Backhaus (Frankfurt am Main: Jüdischer Verlag, 2001), 144.

11. Kaja Kaźmierska, *Biography and Memory: The Generational Experience of the Shoah Survivors* (Boston: Academic Studies, 2012).

12. Baeck, "Israel," 911; Meyer, "Denken und Wirken," 144.

13. The exchange took place mainly in West Germany and Berlin. Only West Germany acknowledged the existence of a unique *Jewish victimhood* in the Holocaust and addressed its responsibilities toward the Jewish people in World War II and the Shoah in the postwar era. East Germany never enforced restitution or indemnification for Jewish victims of Nazism until after the fall of the Berlin Wall in 1989. Nevertheless, since the Jewish community of Berlin functioned as one united Jewish Gemeinde until 1961, for a while, there was some overlap, and a few rabbis, like Ernst Lorge, even visited East Berlin when returning to Germany. Since displaced persons had avoided East Germany for ideological reasons after 1945, few German-Jewish survivors remained. Moreover, Jewish life among the survivors suffered antisemitic Stalinist purges in the early 1950s, which triggered another wave of emigration, leaving Jewish life in East Germany very weak outside of Berlin. See Jay Howard Geller, *Jews in Post-Holocaust Germany, 1945–1953* (Cambridge: Cambridge University Press, 2005).

14. Baeck, "Israel," 911; Meyer, "Denken und Wirken," 144.

15. This is a uniquely neglected topic that deserves more attention. Some work has been done by Shlomo Shafir. Shlomo Shafir, *Ambiguous Relations: The American Jewish Community and Germany since 1945* (Detroit: Wayne State

University Press, 1999). Shafir, however, mainly discusses this topic from the perspective of diplomatic history.

16. Abraham-Geiger-Kolleg, https://www.abraham-geiger-kolleg.de/; Zacharias Frankel College, http://zacharias-frankel-college.de/; Rabbinerseminar zu Berlin, https://rabbinerseminar.de/.

17. Cornelia Wilhelm, "Saved by the Seminary: German Refugee Rabbis' Careers during and after the Holocaust: A Transnational Perspective," in *Academics in a Century of Displacement: The Global History and Politics of Protecting Endangered Scholars*, ed. Leyla Dakhli, Pascale Laborier, and Frank Wolff (Wiesbaden: Springer, 2024), 73–99.

18. Michael A. Meyer, "A Centennial History," in *Hebrew Union College—Jewish Institute of Religion at One Hundred Years*, ed. Samuel Karpf (Cincinnati: HUC Press, 1976); Meyer, "The Refugee Scholars Project of the Hebrew Union College," in *A Bicentennial Festschrift for Jacob R. Marcus*, ed. Bertram Wallace Korn (New York: HUC Press, 1976), 359–375; with new findings about their returns to postwar Germany, see Wilhelm, "Saved by the Seminary"; see also Richard Damashek, *A Brand Plucked from the Fire: The Life of Rabbi Herman E. Schaalman* (Brooklyn: KTAV, 2013); Meyer, "The Refugee Rabbis: Trials and Transmissions," *LBIY* 57 (2012): 87–103; and Marsha Rozenblit, "The Seminary during the Holocaust Years," in *Tradition Renewed: A History of the Jewish Theological Seminary of America*, vol. 2, ed. Jack Wertheimer (New York: Jewish Theological Seminary, 1997), 274. See also Roger Daniels, *Guarding the Golden Door: American Immigration Policy and Immigrants since 1882* (New York: Hill and Wang, 2004), 74, 49–58, 84–97.

19. For the practice of naturalization in Germany, particularly in Prussia, at the time, see Dieter Gosewinkel, *Einbürgern und Ausschließen: Die Nationalisierung der Staatsangehörigkeit vom Deutschen Bund bis zur Bundesrepublik* (Göttingen: Vandenhoek & Ruprecht, 2001), 328–368.

20. See James Turner and Paul Bernard, "The 'German Model' and the Graduate School: The University of Michigan and the Origin Myth of the American University," *History of Higher Education Annual* 13 (1993): 69–98.

21. Andreas Daum, Hartmut Lehmann, and James Sheehan, eds., *The Second Generation: Émigrés from Nazi Germany as Historians* (New York: Berghahn Books, 2016).

22. Ulrike Jureit, *Generationenforschung* (Göttingen: V&R, 2006), 86–92.

23. An excellent example is Joachim Prinz's introduction to Martin Luther King's speech during the March on Washington, 28 August 1963. See also David Jünger, "Prinz and King," *Frankfurter Allgemeine Zeitung*, 25 August 2013, https://www.faz.net/aktuell/politik/die-gegenwart/vor-50-jahren-prinz-und-king-12546288.html.

24. Jureit, *Generationenforschung*, 86–92.

25. Ibid., 91.

26. This large database could not be made accessible to the public due to privacy laws and data protection: it just provides the analysis for this book. However, a smaller set of data that can be researched independently in an online database named MIRA is accessible through the Ludwig-Maximilians-Universität München at http://mira.geschichte.lmu.de/. The database also provides updated information on the location of research papers and biographical literature and links its information to the online version of *Biographisches Handbuch der Rabbiner*, ed. Michael Brocke and Julius Carlebach, parts 1 and 2 (Munich: K. G. Saur, Imprint of Walter de Gruyter, 2004–2009). For an electronic version, see http://www.steinheim-institut.de/wiki/index.php/Biographisches_Handbuch_der_Rabbiner_(BHR).

27. See C. Wilhelm, ed., "German Refugee Rabbis in the United States after 1933," http://mira.geschichte.lmu.de/.

28. Jureit, *Generationengeschichte*, 92–93, 114–123.

1. German Jewry under Nazism

1. Simone Lässig, "How German Jewry Turned Bourgeois: Religion, Culture, and Social Mobility in the Age of Emancipation," *Bulletin of the GHI* 37 (2005): 59–73.

2. Michael A. Meyer et al., eds., *German-Jewish History in Modern Times: Renewal and Destruction, 1918–1945*, vol. 4 (New York: Columbia University Press, 1998), 198.

3. For the Law against the Overcrowding of German Schools and High Schools of 25 April 1933, see Richard Fuchs, "The 'Hochschule für die Wissenschaft des Judentums' in the Period of Nazi Rule," *LBIY* 12 (1967): 9.

4. The law was enacted on 15 April 1937, ibid., 9.

5. For the Decree of the Reich Secretary of Education, enacted on 8 December 1938, ibid., 9.

6. Germany's Jewish communities were—unlike the American congregation—tied to the superstructure of the Gemeinde, a kehillah-like organization that coordinated and financed Jewish life locally. It also embraced the religious life of the local communities, usually with several synagogues of different religious backgrounds. Unlike in the United States, where the congregational structure of religious life secured complete freedom of conscience for one congregation, the Gemeinde blocked such individualism and enforced religious compromise instead to cooperate successfully. Only a few congregations quit the Gemeinde because they did not feel represented by their religious and social setup. Such congregations were the modern orthodox "Breuer Gemeinde" in Frankfurt, the Orthodox Adass Jisroel, and the radical Reform Congregation in Berlin.

7. Alfred Jospe, "A Profession in Transition: The German Rabbinate, 1910–1939," *LBIY* 19 (1974): 55. See also Astrid Zajdband, *German Rabbis in*

British Exile: From 'Heimat' into the Unknown (Boston: De Gruyter, 2016), 50ff. Zajdband argues that the changes started during the Nazi era.

8. This ordination was carried out by a single rabbi in accordance with the liberal wing of the Allgemeiner Rabbinerverband Deutschlands. The ordination was not granted by the Hochschule für die Wissenschaft des Judentums.

9. Liz Elsby, "I Shall Be What I Shall Be—The Story of Rabbiner Regina Jonas," *Yad Vashem*, https://www.yadvashem.org/articles/general/rabbiner-regina-jonas.html.

10. Bernard Drachman, "Activities, Contacts, and Experiences in Breslau," in *Das Breslauer Seminar: Jüdisch-Theologisches Seminar (Fraenkelscher Stiftung) in Breslau 1854–1938*, ed. Guido Kisch (Tübingen: Gedächtnisschrift, 1963), 319.

11. The term "Jewishness" is in quotation marks here because it refers to a racial construction of Jewishness by the Nazis and does not match the halachic definition of Jewishness.

12. Fuchs, "Hochschule," 7, 29.

13. Ibid., 8; Fuchs refers here to the American Jewish Joint Distribution Committee and the Central British Fund.

14. Max Nussbaum was still a Romanian citizen, and for that reason, he was not always affected by legal measures targeting *German* Jews. The same claim is made by the biographers of Abraham Joshua Heschel. Kaplan and Dresner claim that even Polish Jews had a better status than German Jews in Germany before the forced expulsion in October 1938. Edward K. Kaplan and Samuel Dresner, *Abraham Joshua Heschel: Prophetic Witness* (New Haven, CT: Yale University Press, 1998), 220.

15. Ibid., 274.

16. Esriel Hildesheimer, "Die Studenten des Rabbinerseminars zu Berlin," in *Das Berliner Rabbinerseminar 1873–1938*, ed. Chana Schütz and Hermann Simon (Berlin: Hentrich & Hentrich, 2008), 44.

17. Kisch, *Das Breslauer Seminar*, 384–388.

18. For recent and innovative scholarship on the relationship between Germans and Jews in Eastern Europe, see Tobias Grill, "Preface," in *Jews and Germans in Eastern Europe: Shared and Comparative Histories* (New Perspective on Modern Jewish History 8), ed. Tobias Grill (Berlin: De Gruyter, 2018), vii–xxii. See also the other contributions in this volume, which explore this relationship with great historical depth. See also Hillel Kieval, "The Lands Between: The Jews of Bohemia, Moravia and Slovakia to 1918," in *Where Cultures Meet: The Story of the Jews of Czechoslovakia*, ed. Natalia Berger (Tel Aviv: Beth Hatefutsoth/Ministry of Defence, 1990), 23–51.

19. See C. Wilhelm, ed., "German Refugee Rabbis in the United States, 1933–1990," http://mira.geschichte.lmu.de/.

20. Isi Jacob Eisner, "Reminiscences of the Berlin Rabbinical Seminary," *LBIY* 12 (1967): 37f.

21. Michael Brenner, *The Renaissance of Jewish Culture in Weimar Germany* (New Haven, CT: Yale University Press, 1996), 22–35, 36–65; Donald L. Niewyk, *The Jews in Weimar Germany* (New Brunswick, NJ: Transaction, 2001).

22. Eisner, "Reminiscences," 41ff.

23. Fuchs, "Hochschule," 7.

24. As a young rabbi in the Berlin Jewish community, Cohn was dismissed from his post of religious teacher at the Berlin Jewish high school run by the Jewish community, for he was liberally expressing his Zionist thoughts on (national) Jewish identity. As a result, he was banned from the Jewish community, which did not want to be identified with Zionism and underscored that it vehemently rejected an outspokenly Zionist and political rabbi. Consequently, Cohn turned to a second career, started studying jurisprudence, and successfully developed his talents as a playwright and poet. In 1925, he returned to Berlin as a rabbi in a "private" synagogue outside the Berlin Jewish community. Deborah Horner, *Emil Bernhard Cohn: Rabbi, Playwright and Poet* (Berlin: Hentrich & Hentrich, 2009), 23–42.

25. Irene Kaufmann, *Die Hochschule für die Wissenschaft des Judentums (1872–1942)* (Berlin: Hentrich & Hentrich, 2006), 22.

26. Upper Silesia was annexed by Prussia from the Austrian Habsburgs in 1742 and became Polish territory following Germany's defeat in the Second World War. The multiethnic region, with cities like Wrocław (Breslau) and Opole (Oppeln) featuring large Jewish communities, had already been massively affected by territorial disputes and changes after the Treaty of Versailles.

27. Lewis M. Barth and Ruth Nussbaum, eds., *Max Nussbaum: From Berlin to Hollywood. A Midcentury Vision of Jewish Life* (Malibu: Pangloss, 1994), 8.

28. Latin, French, and English.

29. Barth and Nussbaum, *Max Nussbaum*, 8ff.

30. Max Nussbaum, "Kantianismus und Marxismus in der Socialphilosophie Max Adlers" (PhD diss., University of Würzburg, 1931).

31. Michael A. Meyer, ed., *Joachim Prinz, Rebellious Rabbi: An Autobiography—The German and Early American Years* (Bloomington: Indiana University Press, 2008), xiv.

32. Joachim Prinz, "Zum Begriff der religiösen Erfahrung: Ein Beitrag zur Theorie der Religion" (PhD diss., University of Giessen, 1927).

33. Meyer, *Joachim Prinz*, xv–xix, xxii.

34. Prinz, "Zum Begriff der religiösen Erfahrung"; Joachim Prinz, *Der Freitagabend* (Berlin: Brandus, 1935).

35. Many of them were popular histories: Joachim Prinz, *Helden und Abenteuer* (Berlin: P. Baumann, 1930); Prinz, *Jüdische Geschichte* (Berlin: Verlag für Kulturpolitik, 1931); Prinz, *Die Geschichten der Bibel* (Berlin: Erich Reiss, 1934).

36. Such as a chessboard game called Durch Wüstensand ins Heilige Land (Through Desert Sand to the Holy Land), in Emil Cohn, ed., *Jüdischer*

Kinderkalender (Berlin: Jüdischer Verlag, Jg. 1 and 2, 1927, 1928): Leo Baeck Institute New York (LBI), r 162.

37. Ibid., xix-xxi.
38. Meyer, *Joachim Prinz*, xx.
39. Joachim Prinz, *Wir Juden* (Berlin: Erich Reiss, 1934).
40. Emil Cohn, *Judentum, ein Aufruf an die Zeit* (Munich: Georg Müller, 1923).
41. Ibid., 185ff, 201ff, 217ff.
42. Simon Schwab, *Heimkehr ins Judentum* (Frankfurt am Main: Hermon, 1934), 16–26.
43. Moses Auerbach, "Die Bildungsfrage in Der Thora-Treuen Judenheit Deutschlands," in *Vom Sinn des Judentums: Ein Sammelbuch zu Ehren Nathan Birnbaums*, ed. Abraham Elijah Kaplan and Max Landau (Frankfurt am Main: Hermon, 1925), 225–232; Isaac Breuer, "Die Deutsche Orthodoxie im Jahre des Weltkrieges," *Jüdische Monatsschrift* 2, no. 2 (1915): 60–64; Breuer, *Ein Kampf Um Gott* (Frankfurt am Main: Verlag von Sander and Friedberg, 1920); Breuer, "Rabbiner Hirsch als Wegweiser in die Jüdische Geschichte," *Nachlaß Z'wi: Eine Monatsschrift für Judentum in Lehre und Tat* 5, no. 4 (February 1935): 69–84; Maximilian Landau, "Samson Raphael Hirsch und Unsere Zeit," *Nachlaß Z'wi: Eine Monatsschrift für Judentum in Lehre und Tat* 7, no. 1 (October 1936): 27–35.
44. Hans Steidle, *Jakob Stoll und die Israelitische Lehrerbildungsanstalt: eine Spurensuche* (Würzburg: Israelitische Kultusgemeinde, 2002), 57.
45. Ibid., 28–59.
46. For a good description of the changes and challenges Nazism introduced to the communities, see Meyer, *Joachim Prinz*, 98ff.
47. Ibid., 105.
48. Ibid., 100.
49. Among them were, for example, Max Gruenewald (Prinz's brother-in-law), Manfred Swarsensky, Heinrich Lemle, Siegfried Ucko, Selig Sigmund Auerbach, Ulrich Steuer, Robert Raphael Geis, and Emil Schorsch. Walter Homolka and Heinz-Günther Schöttler, *Rabbi—Pastor—Priest: Their Roles and Profiles through the Ages* (Berlin: De Gruyter, 2013), 341.
50. See Meyer, "Refugee Rabbis," 90n13.
51. Nussbaum, "Kantianismus und Marxismus."
52. Sermon "Das Fest der Erstlinge und das Fest des Buches" [The festival of the newcomers and the festival of the Book], Dr. Max Nussbaum, Berlin: Courtesy of the Jacob Rader Marcus Center of the American Jewish Archives, Cincinnati, Ohio, at americanjewisharchives.org (AJA), MS-705, box 3, folder 2.
53. Sermon "Das Fest der Erstlinge."
54. Sermon "First day of Rosh Hashanna," Friedenstempel, 6 September 1937: AJA, MS-705, A, box 3, folder 3, p. 1; here he explains at length the deep-seated value of the Jewish tradition and its historical consciousness; the sermon

carries the handwritten subtitle "Wohl Dir, dass Du ein Enkel bist," pointing at the benefits of being part of a lineage of Jewish generations.

55. "Purim—Los, Lösung, Erlösung im Judentum," presentation given on 17 March 1938 at the Jewish Cultural League: AJA, MS-705, A, box 3, folder 4, p. 10. Here Nussbaum claims: "Man muss eine neue jüdische Generation erziehen. Deswegen sind Vorträge über Purim, wenn sie nicht antiquiert anmuten sollen, wichtig.... Der Sinn der großen Kräfte-Konzentration, die wir in diesen Jahren betreiben, besteht darin, dass in jedem Schritt vorwärts zum Aufbau ein Stück Erlösung sichtbar werden muss." [One has to educate a new generation of Jews. That is why lectures on Purim are important, if they are not to sound antiquated.... It is the higher meaning of our joining forces during these years that we move forward to building up visible salvation (for our congregants)...] Translated by the author.

56. "Glück! (Ursachen unseres Unglücks)" [...], sermon presented for Kol Nidre, 14 September 1938 in the Neue Synagoge Oranienburgerstr: AJA, MS-705, A, box 3, folder 3, p. 4.

57. "Welt ohne Frieden, Welt ohne Recht," sermon, 1. Tag Rosh Hashanna 5699 (1938), Friedenstempel, 26 September 1938 [handmarked]: AJA, MS-705, A, box 3, folder 4.

58. *Galut* = Jewish exile.

59. Michael A. Meyer, *Response to Modernity: A History of the Reform Movement in Judaism* (New York: Oxford University Press, 1988), 61–99.

60. "Judentum als Erlebnis einer großen Liebe," *Jüdische Rundschau*, no. 18, 5 March 1937, 2: AJA, MS-705, A, box 3, folder 3.

61. "Vierzig Jahre Zionismus," sermon given on 4 August 1937 in Friedenstempel, Berlin: AJA, MS-705, A, box 3, folder 3. The concluding sentence reads: "Jüdisches Volk, tritt Dein Erbe an!" ("Jewish people, embrace your heritage!")

62. Under extreme pressure to complete his degree as a Jew at a university increasingly controlled by Nazis, Heschel prolonged his stay in Germany and published his dissertation in 1936 with the Polish Academy of Science and the financial support of the German-Jewish publisher Erich Reiss. See Kaplan and Dresner, *Abraham Joshua Heschel*, 180–233.

63. *Rav* is the Hebrew term for rabbi, typically used in a religiously traditional setting for an eminent rabbinical scholar.

64. Alexander Altmann, "The German Rabbi, 1910–1939," *LBIY* 19 (1974): 19; Jospe, "Profession in Transition," 51–61; Max Gruenewald, "The Modern Rabbi," *LBIY* 2 (1957): 85–97.

65. Max Gruenewald, "The Beginning of the Reichsvertretung," *LBIY* 1 (1956): 57–67.

66. This change of status of the Hochschule was ordered on 24 June 1933; see Kaufmann, *Die Hochschule*, 45. The Hochschule had already been degraded once before to a *Lehranstalt* from 1883 to 1918, ibid., 33. See also Fuchs, "Hochschule," 4.

67. Fuchs, "Hochschule," 13.
68. Ibid., 15–16.
69. "Memorandum betreffend einige Punkte der Ausbildung der Rabbiner in der Lehranstalt für die Wissenschaft des Judentums," by Professor Dr. Otto Toeplitz, undated (approximately 1937): AJA, MS-663, box 1/18.
70. "Memorandum betreffend einige."
71. See Eisner, "Reminiscences," 32–52. The history of the orthodox rabbinical seminary is not very informative concerning the Nazi years: Mordechai Eliav and Esriel Hildesheimer, *Das Berliner Rabbinerseminar, 1873–1938: Seine Gründungsgeschichte, seine Studenten* (Berlin: Hentrich & Hentrich, 2008), Marc B. Shapiro, *Between the Yeshiva World and Modern Orthodoxy: The Life and Works of Rabbi Jehiel Jacob Weinberg, 1884–1966* (Oxford: Littman Library of Jewish Civilization, 1999), 110–164, and Kisch, *Das Breslauer Seminar*.
72. Kisch, *Das Breslauer Seminar*, 159. Many students gave up their studies to seek vocational training, which they considered more useful for a potential immigration to Palestine. Only courses in modern Hebrew grew significantly at the seminary to facilitate immigration.
73. Kisch, *Das Breslauer Seminar*, 160; see also Fuchs, "Hochschule," 20–21.
74. Leo Baeck to Ismar Elbogen, 25 April 1939: LBI, AR66, III, Elbogen.
75. Eisner, "Reminiscences," 49, and Christhard Hoffmann, "Early, but Opposed—Supported, but Late: Two Berlin Seminaries Which Attempted to Move Abroad," *LBIY* 36 (1991): 267–304.
76. Hoffmann, "Early, but Opposed," 279–282. See also Robert Jütte, "Not Welcomed with Open Arms: German Rabbis in Eretz Israel, 1938–1948," *LBIY* 57 (2012): 105–117.
77. Hoffmann, "Early, but Opposed," 282.
78. Michael A. Meyer, "The Refugee Scholars Project of the Hebrew Union College," in *A Bicentennial Festschrift for Jacob R. Marcus*, ed. Bertram Wallace Korn (New York: Hebrew Union College Press, 1976), 362–363, and Hoffmann, "Early but Opposed," 283–296.
79. Ruth Nattermann, *Deutsch-Jüdische Geschichtsschreibung nach der Shoah: Die Gründungs- und Frühgeschichte des Leo Baeck Institute* (Essen: Klartext, 2004), 31.
80. Ibid., 35, and Hoffmann, "Early but Opposed," 283–295.
81. Kaufmann, *Die Hochschule*, 46–47; see also Fuchs, "Hochschule," 26ff.
82. Wolfgang Hamburger, "Teacher in Berlin and Cincinnati," *LBIY* 2 (1957): 30. See also Fuchs, "Hochschule," 30. See also the autobiographies of Nathan Peter Levinson and Herbert Strauss for the last days of the Hochschule: Nathan Peter Levinson, *Ein Ort ist, mit wem Du bist: Lebensstationen eines Rabbiners* (Berlin: Edition Hentrich, 1996), 48ff, and Herbert Strauss, *In the Eye of the Storm: Growing Up Jewish in Germany, 1918–1943* (New York: Fordham University Press,

1999), 83ff. See also Hartmut Bomhoff, *Ernst Ludwig Ehrlich—Prägende Jahre: Eine Biographie* (Berlin: De Gruyter, 2015), 28–32.

83. Michael A. Meyer, "A Centennial History," in *Hebrew Union College— Jewish Institute of Religion at One Hundred Years*, ed. Samuel Karpf (Cincinnati: Hebrew Union College Press, 1976), 1–284, and Jeffrey Gurock, *The Men and Women of Yeshiva: Higher Education, Orthodoxy, and American Judaism* (New York: Columbia University Press, 1988). See also Jack Wertheimer, ed., *Tradition Renewed: A History of the Jewish Theological Seminary* (New York: Jewish Theological Seminary Press, 1997).

84. Roger Daniels, *Guarding the Golden Door: American Immigration Policy and Immigrants since 1882* (New York: Hill and Wang, 2004), 74, 49–58, 84–97, and Meyer et al., *German-Jewish History in Modern Times*, 196–197.

2. Rescue and Flight

1. Samuel H. Goldenson to William Rosenau, 28 November 1932, Wm. Rosenau to Samuel H. Goldenson, 23 November 1932, and circular letter by Wm. Rosenau, 21 February 1933: AJA, MS-34, box 15, folder 13.

2. Circular letter by Wm. Rosenau, 21 February 1933: AJA, MS-34, box 15, folder 13.

3. Henry M. Rosenthal to Wm. Rosenau, 1 March 1933, Wm. Rosenau to Samuel Goldenson, 8 March 1933: AJA, MS-34, box 15, folder 13.

4. Minutes of the Admin. Council Meetings, 20 March and 30 March 1933, UOJCA: American Jewish Historical Society (AJHS), I-66, box 3, folder 7. The UOJCA also rejected the proposed Zionist World Jewish Congress.

5. Circular letter by Wm. Rosenau with results of the query to American Jewish organizations, 19 May 1933 and letter of CCAR to members, 5 June 1933: AJA, MS-34, box 15, folder 13.

6. On the ideological background of the movement for a World Jewish Congress and on Stephen Wise as a leading Reform rabbi and visionary, see Zohar Segev, *The World Jewish Congress during the Holocaust: Between Activism and Restraint* (Berlin: De Gruyter, 2014), 1–22. The WJC was founded in 1936. William Rosenau was a member of the anti-Zionist American Council of Judaism, and the correspondence of the two Reform rabbis highlights the different worlds they came from: Stephen Wise to Wm. Rosenau, 10 April 1933, Stephen Wise to Wm. Rosenau, 19 April 1933 and Wm. Rosenau to S. Wise, 15 April 1933, Wm. Rosenau to S. Wise, 21 April 1933: AJA, MS-34, box 15, folder 13.

7. Since the Nazis persecuted a variety of people as "Jews" who were neither halachically nor religiously Jewish but were subject to the exclusionary policies and their racial thinking, I use quotation marks here for the term "Jewish."

8. Post Conference Executive Board Meeting, CCAR, Milwaukee, Wisconsin, 26 June 1933: AJA, MS-34, box 15, folder 11.

9. Michael A. Meyer, "The Refugee Scholars Project of the Hebrew Union College," in *A Bicentennial Festschrift for Jacob R. Marcus*, ed. Bertram Wallace Korn (New York: Hebrew Union College Press, 1976), 359.

10. Marsha Rozenblit, "The Seminary during the Holocaust Years," in *Tradition Renewed: A History of the Jewish Theological Seminary of America*, vol. 2, ed. Jack Wertheimer (New York: Jewish Theological Seminary, 1997), 274.

11. Cyrus Adler to Louis Finkelstein, 29 May 1933: JTS, Archives and Special Collections (JTS), Ratner Center (RC), Finkelstein Archive, Corr. 1920–1939.

12. Stephen Duggan and Betty Drury, *The Rescue of Science and Learning: The Story of the Emergency Committee in Aid of Displaced Foreign Scholars* (New York: Macmillan, 1948), 173–175.

13. Ibid., 7.

14. Ibid., 177, 180–181.

15. Ibid., 180ff. Roger Daniels, *Guarding the Golden Door: American Immigration Policy and Immigrants since 1882* (New York: Hill and Wang, 2004), 74, 49–58, 84–97.

16. The *Encyclopedia of the Social Sciences* is an American encyclopedia project on social sciences that was meant to highlight the relevance of the study of human affairs. The project benefited enormously from the involvement of German refugee scientists at the New School for Social Research in New York City. Edwin R. A. Seligman and Alvin Johnson, eds., *Encyclopedia of the Social Sciences*, 8 vols. (New York: Macmillan, 1934).

17. Daniels, *Guarding the Golden Door*, 80.

18. Cyrus Adler to Edwin Seligman, 3 May 1933: JTS, RC, Finkelstein Archive, Corr. 1920–1939, folder ECAGS, and circular letter of Edwin A. Seligman to Anonymous, 26 April 1933: JTS, RC, Finkelstein Archive, Corr. 1920–1939, folder ECAGS. The envisioned project urgently needed funding, and Johnson turned to Seligman to support his fundraising initiative: Alvin Johnson to E. A. Seligman, 24 April 1933: RC, Finkelstein Archive, Corr. 1920–1939, folder ECAGS, and Seligman to Adler, 29 April 1933: RC, Finkelstein Archive, Corr. 1920–1939, folder ECAGS.

19. Cyrus Adler to Stephen Duggan, 31 January 1934: JTS, RC, Finkelstein Archive, Corr. 1920–1939, folder ECAGS.

20. See also Cyrus Adler to Stephen Duggan, 31 January 1934: The New York Public Library. Astor, Lenox, and Tilden Foundations (NYPL), Emergency Committee in Aid of Displaced Foreign Scholars records (ECAFS), box 139, folder 35.

21. See Rozenblit, "Seminary," 274. For a younger scholar, the salary was considered adequate, especially since the college also provided room and board to Sperber in the JTS dormitory for many years.

22. Ibid. The hiring of Leo Rosenzweig was rejected by Cyrus Adler for this reason.

23. Ibid., 275.

24. Isaac Landman and Israel Goldstein to Samuel Goldenson, 15 March 1934: AJA, MS-34, box 16, folder 2.

25. Everett R. Clinchy to Henry J. Cadbury, 9 May 1934, and Samuel Goldenson to Felix A. Levy, 10 May 1934: AJA, MS-1834, box 15, folder 18.

26. Cadbury was a lifelong Quaker who had been forced out of his teaching position at Haverford College in 1918 due to a letter he wrote criticizing the American war effort that appeared in the *Philadelphia Public Ledger*.

27. Pre-Conference Meeting of the Executive Board CCAR, Wernersville, PA, 13 June 1934: AJA, MS-34, box 16, folder 6.

28. The Rabbinical Council of America was the rabbinical organization of the Union of Orthodox Congregations of America.

29. Meyer, "Refugee Scholars Project," 362–363.

30. The effort was financially supported by HUC, the JTS, Dropsie College, and the JIR; the invitation was extended by HUC, where this project was organized; Jacob Rader Marcus offered to provide the affidavit.

31. Ismar Elbogen to JTS, 25 May 1937: JTS, RC, RG 3, B, box 1.

32. Julius Lewy to Cyrus Adler, 17 September 1937: JTS RC, RG 3, B, box 1.

33. HUC offered him a teaching position in Cincinnati, but he declined.

34. Meyer, "Refugee Scholars Project," 3623–3663. It took until early May 1938 for the four colleges to raise the funds for Elbogen's fellowship: Julian Morgenstern, "To Whom It May Concern," 2 May 1938: JTS, RC, JTSGF, A box 18/Julian Morgenstern. On Elbogen's arrival, see Cyrus Adler to J. Morgenstern, 2 November 1938: JTS, RC, RG 3, B, box 1.

35. Meyer, "Refugee Scholars Project," 363.

36. Ibid., 362. Nestor is a character from the *Iliad* and the eldest of the Greek leaders in the Trojan War. A great warrior as a young man, at advanced age he was noted for his wisdom and for sharing his knowledge.

37. For example, he helped Max Landau to make contact with Yeshiva University; see Christhard Hoffmann, "Early, but Opposed—Supported, but Late: Two Berlin Seminaries Which Attempted to Move Abroad," *LBIY* 36 (1991): 282.

38. Meyer, "Refugee Scholars Project," 127. Here it is stated that at some point, the number of new German faculty members equaled the existing faculty positions.

39. JTS Press Release, 29 June 1934: JTS, RC, Finkelstein Archive (unprocessed), Corr. 1920–1939, ECAGS. The funds for the positions of Lewy and Sperber were retrieved from the Rockefeller Foundation.

40. At about the time that Wilensky's permitted stay was to end, his wife, Mary, a medical doctor who had stayed in Lithuania, convinced Julian Morgenstern in a dramatic correspondence that her husband's return to Lithuania would mean his death; eventually, HUC allowed him to stay, and his wife joined him.

See the correspondence of Julian Morgenstern with Michael and Mary Wilensky in the Julian Morgenstern manuscript collection of the American Jewish Archives: AJA, MS-30, box 12, folder 25.

41. Meyer, "Refugee Scholars Project," 360.
42. Ibid., 361.
43. J. Morgenstern to A. Guttmann, 6 April 1939 (invitation letter), and Guttmann asking for the support of Chief Rabbi of Great Britain J. Hertz to get a temporary permit for Great Britain, as visa problems for the United States were developing: A. Guttmann to J. Hertz, 10 August 1939; Anderson Dana Hodgdon, American Consul in Germany to Secretary of State, 12 January 1940; Israel Schapiro to J. Morgenstern, 12 March 1940 on having turned to Senator Taft's office for assistance on behalf of Alexander Guttmann and the other refugee scholars: AJA, MS-30, box 3, folder 2.
44. Julian Morgenstern to Franz Landsberger, 6 April 1939: AJA, MS-30, box 7, folder 5; Julian Morgenstern to Franz Landsberger (already residing in Oxford, England), 5 July 1939, in which Morgenstern mentions difficulties with the State Department, and J. Morgenstern to American Consul, London, 10 July 1939: AJA, MS-30, box 7, folder 5.
45. Meyer, "Refugee Scholars Project," 363.
46. Ibid.
47. Ibid., 364.
48. Ibid., 365.
49. Ibid., 366.
50. Taft was the US House representative for Cincinnati, Ohio, the city in which HUC had its historical campus.
51. For Morgenstern's correspondence on Sonne's behalf, see his file in the Morgenstern papers: AJA, MS-30, box 10, folder 27.
52. A. Heschel to J. Morgenstern, 1 June 1939: AJA, MS-30, box 5, folder 23.
53. William H. Cordell, American Vice Consul, Warsaw to A. Heschel, 18 April 1939: AJA, MS-30, box 5, folder 23.
54. A. Heschel to J. Morgenstern, 28 July 1939: AJA, MS-30, box 5, folder 23.
55. J. Morgenstern to A. Heschel, 21 September 1939: AJA, MS-30, box 5, folder 23.
56. Ibid.
57. J. Morgenstern to the American Consul in Dublin, 25 September 1939: AJA, MS-30, box 5, folder 23.
58. A. Heschel to J. Morgenstern, 25 March 1940: AJA, MS-30, box 5, folder 23.
59. Meyer, "Refugee Scholars Project," 370; see also correspondence of Julian Morgenstern with E. Taeubler: AJA, MS-30, box 11, folder 7. For the reasons for Taeubler's delayed departure, see Ruth Nattermann, *Deutsch-jüdische Geschichtsschreibung nach der Shoah: Die Gründungs- und Frühgeschichte des Leo Baeck*

Institute (Koblenz: Klartext, 2004), 37–65. Nattermann claims that Taeubler was involved in making plans for the transfer of Jewish scholars to a Jewish Academy with bases in New York, Jerusalem, and Cambridge.

60. Meyer, "Refugee Scholars Project," 372.
61. Rozenblit, "Seminary," 274.
62. Ibid., 275; Meyer, "Refugee Scholars Project," 360. It took until early May 1938 for the four colleges to raise the funds for Elbogen's fellowship: Morgenstern, "To Whom It May Concern." On Elbogen's arrival, see Cyrus Adler to J. Morgenstern, 2 November 1938: JTS, RC, RG 3, B, box 1.
63. Interview Jack Wertheimer and Herbert Strauss for the Research Foundation for Jewish Immigration with Max Gruenewald, 14 and 21 June 1971: LBI, AR 25385, 21.
64. Robert Jütte, *Die Emigration der deutschsprachigen "Wissenschaft des Judentums": Die Auswanderung Jüdischer Historiker nach Palästina* (Stuttgart: Steiner, 1991). Interview Jack Wertheimer and Herbert Strauss for the Research Foundation for Jewish Immigration with Max Gruenewald, 14 and 21 June 1971: LBI, AR 25385, 21–22.
65. Robert Jütte, "Not Welcomed with Open Arms: German Rabbis in Eretz Israel, 1938–1948," *LBIY* 57 (2012). See also Oral History Interview Simon Schwab, July 1971: LBI, AR 25385, 4.
66. Heinrich Kronstein to Cyrus Adler, 13 December 1937: JTS, RC, JTSGF, A, box 10, MG.
67. Cyrus Adler to H. Kronstein, 23 December 1937: JTS, RC, JTSGF, A, box 10, MG.
68. Finkelstein to US Consul, Tel Aviv, 13 January 1939: JTS, RC, JTSGF, A, box 10, MG.
69. Obviously, the JTS tried to obtain funding for Gruenewald's family, but without success: L. Finkelstein to Frederick Borchardt, 25 October 1939: JTS, RC, JTSGF, A, box 10, MG.
70. L. Finkelstein to City Clerk, NYC, 13 February 1940: JTS, RC, JTSGF, A, box 10, MG, and M. Gruenewald to L. Finkelstein, 2 November 1939: JTS, RC, JTSGF, A, box 10, MG.
71. Morgenstern, "To Whom It May Concern," L. Finkelstein: JTS, RC, JTSGF, A, box 10, MG.
72. Louis P. Spicer to Ernest Gruenewald, 2 July 1940: JTS, RC, JTSGF, A, box 10, MG. See also Interview Jack Wertheimer and Herbert Strauss for the Research Foundation for Jewish Immigration with Max Gruenewald, 14 and 21 June 1971: LBI, AR 25385, 22.
73. M. Gruenewald to L. Finkelstein, 9 March 1941 and Affidavit of Support for Dr. Max Gruenewald by L. Finkelstein, dated 1941: JTS, RC, JTSGF, A, box 10, MG. Interview Jack Wertheimer and Herbert Strauss for the Research

Foundation for Jewish Immigration with Max Gruenewald, 14 and 21 June 1971: LBI, AR 25385, 25.

74. Gruenewald to Finkelstein, 30 November 1943; Finkelstein to Gruenewald, 19 June 1944, M. Gruenewald to Finkelstein, 5 January 1944: JTS, RC, JTSGF, A, box 10, MG. Marian Meisner, *A History of Milburn Township* (Millburn, NY: Millburn Short Hills Historical Society, 2002), 19, https://millburnlibrary.org/wp-content/uploads/2021/05/HistoryMillburnTownshipEbook.pdf.

75. B. Revel to S. Duggan, 26 November 1933: NYPL, ECADFS, box 19.

76. Cecilia Raskovsky-Davidson to E. R. Murrow, 26 June 1934: NYPL, ECADFS, box 19.

77. E. R. Murrow to B. Revel, 10 August 1934: NYPL, ECADFS, box 19. Yeshiva University is the superstructure for a college for general studies with some graduate schools, such as the rabbinical school.

78. Revel to Duggan, 26 November 1933 with attachments (short bios of suggested scholars): NYPL, ECADFS, box 19. See also Office Memo, Betty Drury to E. R. Murrow, 8 December 1933: NYPL, ECADFS, box 19.

79. Hartstein to Roger Howson, 6 June 1936, Hartstein to Gutkind, 15 March 1938, and Erich Gutkind to Hartstein, 3 April 1938: Special Collections, Gottesman Library, Yeshiva University (YU), Hartstein, box 14, Gutkind, Erich, 1936–39, 9/2-35.

80. List of Yeshiva College Faculty, Spring Term 1936: YU, Faculty, Hartstein, box 31, 1937–44, 17/3-68; Gutkind to Hartstein, 21 September 1936: YU, Hartstein, box 14, Gutkind, Erich, 1936–39, 9/2-35.

81. Reprint of Announcement in *School and Society*, 13 January 1934, and Ida Landau to E. R. Murrow, 1 March 1934: NYPL, ECAFS, box 19. See also "Dr. Keyser Invited Here," *New York Times*, 24 December 1933: NYPL, ECAFS, box 19.

82. Landau to B. Revel, 14 May 1939: YU, Hartstein, 13/3/40, Foreign Faculty. See also Marc Shapiro, "Torah im Derekh Eretz in the Shadow of Hitler," *Torah u-Maddah Journal* 14 (2006–2007): 87–88, and Hoffmann, "Early but Opposed," 282.

83. Shapiro, "Torah," 88. M. Landau to H. Friedenwald, 26 June 1939: YU, Hartstein, 13/3/40, Foreign Faculty.

84. Hoffmann, "Early but Opposed," 282.

85. Ibid.

86. Mordechai Eliav and Esriel Hildesheimer, *Das Berliner Rabbinerseminar, 1873–1938: Seine Gründungsgeschichte, Seine Studenten* (Berlin: Hentrich & Hentrich, 2008), 167.

87. David Kranzler and Dovid Landesman, *Rav Breuer: His Life and Legacy* (New York: Feldheim, 1998), 115–116.

88. Ephraim Zuroff, *Response of Orthodox Jewry in the United States: The Activities of the Vaad Ha-Hatzala Rescue Committee, 1939–1945* (Philadelphia: KTAV, 2000).

89. See also David Kranzler, *Holocaust Hero: The Untold Story and Vignettes of Solomon Schonfeld* (Jersey City, NJ: KTAV, 2004).

90. *Bildung* refers to character formation by self-improvement, including the improvement of heart and mind, following the nineteenth-century German ideal of "Bildung."

91. Jonathan Sarna, *American Judaism* (New Haven, CT: Yale University Press, 2004), 280.

92. Rubinstein, a dedicated Zionist (Mizrachi), was the chief rabbi of Vilnius. He attended the World Zionist Congress in Geneva in 1939 and returned to Vilnius at the outbreak of WWII to assist his community. When the city was back under Soviet control, he fled to the Soviet Union. He arrived in the United States in 1941 and started teaching at Yeshiva University in New York City.

93. Shatzkes did not accept this offer at the time, but he stayed in Poland, then fled to Vilnius after Poland was divided between Nazi Germany and Russia. After Vilnius fell back under Soviet control, Shatzkes managed to flee to Japan via the Soviet Union with the assistance of Chiune Sugihara. He arrived in the United States in 1941, where he was appointed as senior Rosh Yeshiva at RIETS. Once in the United States, he continued to support the flight of over five thousand refugees from Vilna, many of whom were rabbis, including those from the evacuated Yeshiva Mir.

94. "Faculty Promotions Honor Yeshiva College Scholars," *Yeshiva College Quarterly* 4, no. 5 (December 1941): 1, 4. See also Scholarship Fund Dinner for Refugee Students at Yeshiva College, 2 April 1939, Hotel Astor: YU Press Releases, box 163.

95. Minutes of the Admin. Council Meetings, 15 May, 19 August, UOJCA: AJHS, I-66, box 3, folder 8; Minutes of the Admin. Council Meetings, 26 October 1941, UOJCA: AJHS, I-66, box 3, folder 13.

96. Among them were, for example, Henry Siegman, Eli Chaim Carlebach, Walter Würzburger, and Shlomo Carlebach.

97. He contributed to the founding of Mesivta Chaim Berlin, Telshe Cleveland, and Beis Medrash Gehova.

98. Apparently, there were problems in obtaining a state license for the schools because Joseph Breuer mentions troubles with the Education Association in a letter to Leo Jung, whom he asks for assistance in obtaining some subventions. Joseph Breuer to Leo Jung, 30 November 1939: Archives of Agudath Israel of America.

99. *Mitteilungen—Organ der K'hall Adass Jeshurun und der K'hall Agudath Jeshorim* 1 (September 1939): 1.

100. Jacob Breuer, "Die Beth-Jacob-Schule unserer Gemeinde," *Mitteilungen* 2 (9 August 1940): 1–2.

101. Joseph Breuer, "Samson Raphael Hirsch Jeshiva," *Mitteilungen* 6 (June/July 1944): 1. The yeshiva was to have the characteristics of an American public school; the model of a parochial school was rejected.

102. "Teachers Seminary for Girls," *Mitteilungen* 24 (June/July 1963): 1.

103. Jacob Breuer, "Probleme der Jüdischen Schule in Amerika," *Mitteilungen* 3 (January 1942): 2–3; Breuer, "American Yeshiva Problems," *Mitteilungen* 17 (December 1955): 1–2.

104. Breuer, "Probleme," 2–3; Breuer, "American Yeshiva," 1–2.

105. B. Drury to B. Revel, 29 November 1940: YU, Emergency Committee in Aid of Displaced Foreign Scholars (ECADFS), 5/4/26. Since the records of the Emergency Committee did not show any further communication, this grant application may have been turned down. It may have been hard to prove that the mesivta was equal to other institutions, such as colleges and universities of higher learning in the United States.

106. Ruderman had emigrated two years earlier from Daŭhinava in Belarus and was in contact with American colleagues who had studied with him at the Yeshiva Knesses Yisroel at Slabodka.

107. Hans Steidle, *Jakob Stoll und die Israelitische Lehrerbildungsanstalt: Eine Spurensuche* (Würzburg: Israelitische Kultusgemeinde, 2002), 57.

108. Namely, Siegfried Bendheim.

109. A. M. Warren to H. Neuberger, 6 June 1939: YU, Vaad Hatzalah Papers, box 3.

110. Ibid.

111. Steidle, *Jakob Stoll*, 59, and Herman N. Neuberger, *Treasuring His Legacy: Perpetuating the Mission* (Baltimore: Ner Israel Rabbinical College, 2006), 22.

112. Steidle, *Jakob Stoll*, 60, and Biographical Questionnaire Samson R. Weiss, Biographische Dokumentation der deutschsprachigen Emigration 1933–1945 in Kooperation mit der Research Foundation for Jewish Immigration (Biographische Dokumentation): IfZ, MA 1500/63B.

113. "Rav Shimon Schwab, zt"l, Recollections of His Years in Baltimore on the Occasion of This 13th yahrzeit," adapted by Yitzchok Levine, *Hamodia Magazine* 14 Adar 5768 (20 February 2008), http://personal.stevens.edu/~llevine/recollections_r_schwab.pdf.

114. Andreas Daum, Hartmut Lehmann, and James Sheehan, *The Second Generation: Émigrés from Nazi Germany as Historians* (New York: Berghahn Books), 2016.

115. Wolli Kaelter and Gordon Cohn, *From Danzig: An American Rabbi's Journey* (Malibu, CA: Pangloss, 1997); W. Gunther Plaut, *Unfinished Business: An Autobiography* (Toronto: Lester & Orpen Dennys, 1981); and Plaut, *More Unfinished Business* (Toronto: University of Toronto Press, 1997); see also the unpublished interviews with Alfred Wolf by his son Dan Wolf made available to the author for research purposes; see also Michael A. Meyer, "A Centennial History," in *Hebrew Union College—Jewish Institute of Religion at One Hundred Years*, ed. Samuel Karpf (Cincinnati: Hebrew Union College Press, 1976), 123–124; see Meyer, "Refugee Scholars Project," 312, 359–75; Richard Damashek, "The Gang of Five: The Impact of Five German Rabbinic Students on Twentieth-Century

Reform Judaism: From Berlin to Cincinnati," *CCAR Journal* 63 (Fall 2016): 5–21; and Damashek, *A Brand Plucked from the Fire: The Life of Rabbi Herman E. Schaalman* (Jersey City, NJ: KTAV, 2013).

116. Julian Morgenstern to Louis Finkelstein, 15 June 1938: JTS, RC, JTSGF, A, box 18, J. Morgenstern.

117. Kaelter and Cohn, *From Danzig*, 44.

118. Plaut, *Unfinished Business*, 47.

119. Damashek, *Brand*, 52–53.

120. Kaelter and Cohn, *From Danzig*, 44–45.

121. See unpublished interview # 385 with Alfred Wolf by his son Dan Wolf made available to the author for research purposes.

122. Damashek, "Gang of Five," 7.

123. The term was coined by Richard Damashek.

124. Herman Schaalman met his girlfriend and soon-to-be fiancée Lotte Strauss in 1938. She died tragically in Palestine shortly before their planned wedding. Damashek, *Brand*, 86–103; Plaut, *Unfinished Business*, 72–78.

125. Kaelter and Cohn, *From Danzig*, 15–16, 21–22, 58.

126. The secretary of the Emergency Committee.

127. Joseph Abrahams to Cecilia Razovsky, 27 November 1935: JTS, RG 1, A, box 19/19.

128. See AJA, MS-672, Ernst Lorge Collection.

129. Julian Morgenstern to Louis Finkelstein, 15 June 1938: JTS, RC, JTSGF, A, box 18, J. Morgenstern.

130. Ibid.

131. See correspondence Joe Weber (AJA) with Cornelia Wilhelm, 4 and 9 May 2017: private correspondence Cornelia Wilhelm.

132. Julian Morgenstern to Louis Finkelstein, 15 June 1938: JTS, RC, JTSGF, A, box 18, J. Morgenstern.

133. Nathan Peter Levinson, *Ein Ort ist, mit wem Du bist: Lebensstationen eines Rabbiners* (Berlin: Edition Hentrich, 1996), 87.

134. Ibid., 66.

135. Ibid., 69.

136. Plaut, *Unfinished Business*, 85.

137. "Biographical Note," Stephen Schwarzschild Papers, AR 25376, Leo Baeck Institute, New York, http://digifindingaids.cjh.org/?pID=475354.

138. Hartmut Bomhof, *Ernst Ludwig Ehrlich: Prägende Jahre, Eine Biographie* (Berlin: De Gruyter, 2015), 32. See also *Rabbinic Ordinations* at HUC, 188: AJA.

139. The HMT *Dunera* was a British steamer that transported German and Austrian refugees to their internment as enemy aliens in Australia.

140. Moses Rischin, "The German Imperative and the Jewish Response," in *The Jewish Legacy and German Conscience*, ed. Moses Rischin and Raphael Asher (Berkeley, CA: Judah L. Magnes Museum, 1991), 3.

141. Faculty Minutes, 17 November 1937 and 19 January 1938: JTS, RC, RG 3, Faculty Minutes, A, box 1, 1937–38.

142. Kaelter and Cohn, *From Danzig*, 35, 62.

143. Information on Lewkowitz taken from the Bericht des Jüdisch-Theologischen Seminars (Fraenkelscher Stiftung), Hochschule für Jüdische Theologie, für das Jahr 1937 (Breslau: Kuratorium der Fraenkelschen Stiftungen, 1938), 5.

144. The BA degree was only introduced in Germany in the context of the European Bologna process in 1998.

145. Faculty Minutes, 24 September 1937: JTS, RC, RG 3, Faculty Minutes, A, box 1, 1937–38.

146. Faculty Minutes, 24 September 1937 and 17 November 1937: JTS, RC, RG 3, Faculty Minutes, A, box 1, 1937–38.

147. Faculty Minutes, 17 November 1937: JTS, RC, RG 3, Faculty Minutes, A, box 1, 1937–38.

148. Faculty Minutes, 19 January 1938: JTS, RC, RG 3, Faculty Minutes, A, box 1, 1937–38.

149. Ibid.

150. Alexander Marx was born in Elberfeld, Germany, in 1878, and trained at the Orthodox Rabbinerseminar and continued to have lasting relationships with German colleagues.

151. Faculty Minutes, 19 January 1938: JTS, RC, RG 3, Faculty Minutes, A, box 1, 1937–38; see also Edward K. Kaplan, *Spiritual Radical: Abraham Joshua Heschel in America* (New Haven, CT: Yale University Press, 2007), 347n18.

152. Katrin Hopstock, "Bis zum Ende-Die letzen 50 Jahre der jüdischen Gemeinde," *Vierteljahresheft des Verkehrsvereins Speyer in Zusammenarbeit mit der Stadtverwaltung* (Winter 1988), 10, https://www.speyer.de/de/bildung/kulturelles-erbe-stadtarchiv/benutzung/digitale-praesentationen/vierteljahreshefte-speyer/vierteljahrshefte-pdfs/1961-1991/247-1988-4.pdf?cid=zq4.

153. Faculty Minutes, 19 January 1938: JTS, RC, RG 3, Faculty Minutes, A, box 1, 1937–38.

154. Ibid.

155. Faculty Minutes, 28 February 1938: JTS, RC, RG 3, Faculty Minutes, A, box 1, 1937–38.

156. Ibid.

157. Faculty Minutes, 13 April 1938: JTS, RC, RG 3, Faculty Minutes, A, box 1, 1937–38; see also Eva Goldschmidt Wyman, *Escaping Hitler: A Jewish Haven in Chile* (Tuscaloosa: University of Alabama Press, 2013), 127.

158. Faculty Minutes, 31 May 1938: JTS, RC, RG 3, Faculty Minutes, A, box 1, 1937–38.

159. Adler was a young rabbi, ordained at the Hochschule in Berlin in November, 1938. He officiated at the private synagogue in Schulstrasse in Berlin. He obviously waited until he had completed his doctorate to emigrate. See Michael

Brocke and Julius Carlebach, eds., *Biographisches Handbuch der Rabbiner*, part 2, vol. 1 (Munich: De Gruyter, 2009), 4.

160. He had joined the JTS in Breslau in 1936; see *Bericht des Jüdisch-Theologischen Seminars*, 5.

161. Susanne Heim, ed., *Verfolgung und Ermordung der Juden*, vol. 2: *Deutsches Reich 1938-August 1939* (Munich: Oldenburg, 2009), 394.

162. Faculty Minutes, 26 October 1938: JTS, RC, RG 3, Faculty Minutes, A, box 1, 1937–38.

163. Ibid.

164. Faculty Minutes, 26 October 1938: JTS, RC, RG 3, Faculty Minutes, A, box 1, 1937–38.

165. Curt Arndt to L. Finkelstein, 24 October 1938; Finkelstein to Arndt, 8 December 1938; Arndt to Finkelstein, 15 January 1940; Finkelstein to Arndt, 7 February 1940; Arndt to Burnstein, 29 November 1940; Finkelstein to Arndt, 20 January 1941; Burnstein to Finkelstein, 7 February 1941; Finkelstein to Burnstein, 7 May 1942: JTS, RC, RG 1, A, box 2/17.

166. Werner Lampel was the son of the cantor at the Leipzig liberal synagogue and managed to immigrate to England in March 1939, where he served in the Auxiliary Military Pioneer Corps, then in the Royal Navy. He changed his name to Herbert Werner Langford at the end of the war, married a Christian woman, converted to Christianity, and became a minister of the Anglican Church. See "Rev. Herbert Walter Langford (1919–1992)," Winthorpe, http://www.winthorpe.org.uk/Rev.-Herbert-Walter-Langford-1919-1992.

167. Faculty Minutes, 23 November 1938: JTS RC, RG 3, A, Faculty Meetings, box 1, 1938–39.

168. Brocke and Carlebach, *Biographisches Handbuch*, 329. Here the first name of Kempner is referred to as "Herbert" and "Fritz," and in the JTS faculty minutes, he is mentioned as "Kempner, Fritz W." See Faculty Minutes, 18 January 1939: JTS, RC, RG 3, Faculty Minutes, A, box 1, 1937–38.

169. Faculty Minutes, 27 February 1940: JTS, RC, RG 3, Faculty Minutes, A, box 1, 1939–40.

170. C. Wilhelm, ed., "German Refugee Rabbis in the United States, 1933–1990," http://mira.geschichte.lmu.de/159.

171. Faculty Minutes, 15 May 1940: JTS, RC, RG 3, A, Faculty Meetings, box 1, 1939–40.

172. Vita Harry May, undated (presumably 1938): JTS, RC, RG 1, A, box 19/17.

173. HICEM: Jewish emigration organization formed in 1927 as a merger of three organizations: the Hebrew Immigrant Aid Society, the Jewish Colonization Association, and Emigdirect. The organization provided an important international emigration network to European Jews before and throughout the Nazi era.

174. Noam Penkower, *The Holocaust and Israel Reborn: From Catastrophe to Sovereignty* (Urbana: University of Illinois Press, 1994), 268n66.

175. Harry May to JTS, 2 August 1938, Harry May to ZOA, 3 August 1938, and HICEM to JTS, 3 August 1938: JTS, RC, RG 1, A, box 19/17. Dora Magnus to C. Adler, 23 July 1938, and Elisha Friedman to C. Adler, 23 August 1938: JTS, RC, RG 1, A, box 19/17.

176. The NCC was founded in 1934 as an umbrella organization for about twenty Jewish and non-Jewish aid organizations for German refugees. The committee was the precursor of the National Refugee Service, established in 1939. See Lyman Cromwell White, *300,000 New Americans: The Epic of a Modern Immigrant Aid-Service* (New York: Harper, 1957).

177. C. Adler to E. Friedman, 26 August 1938: JTS, RC, RG 1, A, box 19/17.

178. Joseph B. Abrahams to H. May, 14 September 1938: JTS, RC, RG 1, A, box 19/17. See Vivien Enoch, "A Holocaust Story Searching for Family Roots in a Photo on PBS," *My Jewish Detroit*, http://myjewishdetroit.org/2015/03/in-search-of-family-roots/.

179. H. Galliner to L. Finkelstein, 29 October 1937: JTS, RC, RG 1, A, box 8, Galliner.

180. H. Galliner to L. Finkelstein, 29 October 1937, H. Galliner to L. Finkelstein, 3 November 1937, Memorandum by L. Finkelstein, 9 November 1937, L. Finkelstein to H. Galliner, 19 November 1937: JTS, RC, RG 1, A, box 8, Galliner.

181. H. Galliner to L. Finkelstein, 5 December 1937: JTS, RC, RG 1, A, box 8, Galliner.

182. H. Galliner to L. Finkelstein, 15 December 1937: JTS, RC, RG 1, A, box 8, Galliner.

183. L. Finkelstein to US Consul, Berlin, Germany, 29 December 1937: JTS, RC, RG 1, A, box 8, Galliner.

184. Telegram by I. Elbogen and E. Mittwoch to L. Finkelstein, 24 January 1938: JTS, RC, RG 1, A, box 8, Galliner.

185. H. Vogelstein to J. Bloch, 7 January 1938: JTS, RC, RG 1, A, box 8, Galliner.

186. Certificate "To Whom It May Concern" by Joseph Abrahams, 4 March 1938: JTS, RC, RG 1, A, box 8, Galliner.

187. L. Finkelstein to Mrs. Frieda Schiff Warburg, 2 May 1941: JTS, RC, RG 1, A, box 8/Galliner.

188. L. Finkelstein to C. Adler, 21 February 1939: JTS, RC, RG 1, A, box 8/Galliner.

189. Memorandum by A. Marx, 28 February 1939: JTS, RC, RG 1, A, box 8/Galliner.

190. Note of H. Galliner to L. Finkelstein, 6 April 1939 and response on same sheet: JTS, RC, RG 1, A, box 8/Galliner.

191. A. Marx to L. Finkelstein, 2 February 1940: JTS, RC, RG 1, A, box 8/Galliner.

192. L. Finkelstein to Mrs. Frieda Schiff Warburg, 2 May 1941: JTS, RC, RG 1, A, box 8/Galliner.

193. L. Finkelstein to H. Galliner, 11 March 1940, and L. Finkelstein to Mrs. Frieda Schiff Warburg, 2 May 1941: JTS, RC, RG 1, A, box 8/Galliner.

194. L. Finkelstein to Mrs. Frieda Schiff Warburg, 2 May 1941: JTS, RC, RG 1, A, box 8/Galliner. It is important to note that Finkelstein does not ask for support of Helmut Galliner; he just explains his case at length to Frieda Schiff Warburg. See also L. Finkelstein to H. Galliner, 16 May 1941: JTS, RC, RG 1, A, box 8/Galliner.

195. L. Finkelstein to H. Galliner, 19 September 1941: JTS, RC, RG 1, A, box 8/Galliner.

196. H. Galliner to L. Finkelstein, 1 September 1942: JTS, RC, RG 1, A, box 8/Galliner.

197. Hoffmann, "Early but Opposed," 282.

198. Jeffrey Gurock, *The Men and Women of Yeshiva: Higher Education, Orthodoxy, and American Judaism* (New York: Columbia University Press, 1988), 82–120.

199. Questionnaire Henry Siegman, Biographische Dokumentation: IfZ, MA 1500/55B.

200. The ILBA was an Orthodox institution founded by Rav Seligman Baer Bamberger in 1864, and it had a serious impact on the professionalization of Jewish teacher training in Germany.

201. Steidle, *Jakob Stoll*, 91. Steidle refers to the students Fritz Veit, Kurt Perlmutter, and Heinz Roberg. While the first two students managed to immigrate to the United States, Heinz Roberg stayed with his family and ultimately perished in the Shoah. See Max Ottensoser and Alex Roberg, *ILBA: Israelitische Lehrerbildungsanstalt Würzburg, 1864–1938* (Detroit: Harlo, 1982), 240–253. See also Oral History Interview with Ib Nathan Bamberger, 7 July 2013: UHMM, RG-50.677.0006, Accession Number: 2011.177.6, https://collections.ushmm.org/search/catalog/irn90194. See also "״א. גרופע דייטשע ישיבה בחורים אין דער באלטימארער ישיבת, גר ישראל׳." *Jewish American, Family Magazine and Gazette* 37, no. 36 (7 July 1939): 1–3.

3. Flight and Rescue

1. Oral history interview Simon Schwab, July 1971, Research Foundation for Jewish Immigration: LBI, AR 25385, 4.

2. Leo Jung was born in 1890 in Moravia and grew up in a German-speaking environment. His father, Dr. Meir Tzvi Jung, followed the philosophy of Samson Raphael Hirsch and had held a pulpit in Mannheim. Leo was educated

in Talmudic and secular studies at Cambridge University, the University of London, the yeshiva of Galanta and Eperies, and the Rabbinerseminar in Berlin, where he was ordained by Rabbi David Zvi Hoffmann of Berlin. He also received semicha from Rabbi Mordechai Zevi Schwartz and Rabbi Abraham Isaac Kook. In 1920 he arrived in the United States and first officiated in Cleveland; in 1922 he was offered the rabbinate of the Jewish Center Synagogue in New York City, which he accepted.

3. "Rav Shimon Schwab, zt"l, Recollections of His Years in Baltimore on the Occasion of This 13th Yahrzeit," adapted by Yitzchok Levine, *Hamodia Magazine* 14 Adar 5768 (20 February 2008), 13–14, http://personal.stevens.edu/~llevine/recolletions_r_schwab.pdf.

4. Michael A. Meyer, ed., *Joachim Prinz, Rebellious Rabbi: An Autobiography—The German and Early American Years* (Bloomington: Indiana University Press, 2008), 162.

5. Ibid., 141, 163.

6. Max Koppel earned a doctorate from the University of Breslau in 1931 and was ordained in 1933.

7. Max Koppel's paternal grandfather settled in Albany, Georgia, before the First World War, Oral History Interview with Emmie Vida: United States Holocaust Memorial Museum (USHMM), RG-50.184.0001, Accession no.: 1995.A.0658.1.

8. Oral History Interview Max Koppel, Research Foundation of Jewish Immigration: LBI, AR 25385, Max Koppel, 2.

9. Deborah Horner, *Emil Bernhard Cohn: Rabbi, Playwright and Poet* (Berlin: Hentrich & Hentrich, 2009), 47–57. See also Interview with Emil Bernhard Cohn, 1 June 1971, Research Foundation for Jewish Immigration: LBI, AR 25385, 5. Cohn's wife and daughter joined him in Holland in 1937 and followed him to New York, with a short stay in Southampton to meet their son and brother Emil Bernhard, who had gone to a boarding school in Brighton directly from Berlin in 1937. After a short reunion in Southampton on the way to the United States, they joined Rabbi Emil Moses Cohn in New York City. Stephen Wise also assisted Cohn's family in obtaining a visa and communicated directly with Cordell Hull about their visas.

10. Martha Appel Memoirs, dated 1940/1941: LBI Berlin, ME1168; published in Monika Richarz, ed., *Jüdisches Leben in Deutschland: Selbstzeugnisse zur Sozialgeschichte, 1918–1945*, vol. 3 (Stuttgart: DVA, 1982), 231–243.

11. Ibid.

12. Wolf Gruner, "Die Radikalisierung der NS-Verfolgung und die Berliner Jüdinnen und Juden," in *Ausgewiesen! Berlin, 28.10.1938: Die Geschichte der "Polenaktion,"* ed. Alina Bothe and Gertrud Pickhan (Berlin: Metropol, 2018), 117.

13. Ibid., 118–121.

14. See also Alan Steinweis, *Kristallnacht 1938* (Stuttgart: Reclam, 2011), 13–14.

15. Gesetz über die Neugestaltung deutscher Städte of 4 October 1937, in Reichsgesetzesblatt I, 1054–1055, https://www.stadtgrenze.de/s/p3r/gnds/gnds.htm.

16. *Festpredigt zum 50jährigen Jubiläum der Synagoge in München, gehalten in der Synagoge zu München am 5. Sept. 1937, Erew Rosch-Haschonoh 5698* (Munich: Vorstand der Israelitischen Kultusgemeinde, 1937).

17. "Die erste Synagoge, die den Nazis zum Opfer fiel," *Süddeutsche Zeitung (SZ)*, 8 June 2018, https://www.sueddeutsche.de/muenchen/juedische-geschichte-wie-muenchen-vor-80-jahren-seine-synagoge-verlor-1.4004815-2.

18. Ibid.

19. Document no. 336 in Otto Dov Kulka and Eberhard Jäckel, *Die Juden in den geheimen Stimmungsberichten 1933–1945* (Düsseldorf: Droste, 2004).

20. Jens Ostrowski and Oliver Volmerich, "'Reisst ab den Judentempel'—Dortmunds NSDAP-Chef vor Gericht," *Ruhr Nachrichten*, 28 October 2018, https://www.ruhrnachrichten.de/dortmund/dortmunds-nsdap-chef-vor-gericht-als-friedrich-hesseldieck-die-synagoge-verschwinden-liess-plus-1341012.html.

21. Hannelore Künzl, *Islamische Stilelemente im Synagogenbau des 19. und frühen 20. Jahrhunderts* (Frankfurt: Peter Lang, 1984), 99ff.

22. Dieter Gosewinkel, *Einbürgern und Ausschließen: Die Nationalisierung der Staatsangehörigkeit vom Deutschen Bund bis zur Bundesrepublik* (Göttingen: Vandenhoek & Ruprecht, 2001), 356–368.

23. Edward K. Kaplan, *Spiritual Radical: Abraham Joshua Heschel in America* (New Haven, CT: Yale University Press, 2007), 274, and Erwin Zimet, "1933: The Beginning of the End of German Jewry," *Jewish Museum Berlin*, https://www.jmberlin.de/1933/en/05_18_student-identification-card-issued-to-erwin-zimet-by-the-friedrich-wilhelm-university-of-berlin.php; for Moses Sister, see Emil Fackenheim, *An Epitaph for German Judaism: From Halle to Jerusalem* (Madison: University of Wisconsin Press, 2007), 53–54.

24. Cyrus Adler to Dr. Greenberg, 29 July 1938: JTS, RC, RG1, A, box 19/17.

25. Abraham Klein to Cyrus Adler, 17 August 1938: JTS, RC, RG1, A, box 19/17, and a second letter in German from A. Klein and Joseph Horovitz to Cyrus Adler, 17 August 1938: JTS, RC, RG1, A, box 19/17.

26. That was the case with Fritz Plotke, who left his Schneidemühl pulpit for Berlin in October 1938 before *Kristallnacht*, and with Max Gruenewald, who left his position in Mannheim for Berlin in April 1938. Karl Richter of Mannheim went into hiding after *Kristallnacht*. See C. Wilhelm, ed., "German Refugee Rabbis in the United States, 1933–1990," http://mira.geschichte.lmu.de/4.

27. Leo Trepp, *Die Oldenburger Judenschaft* (Oldenburg: Heinz Holzberg, 1973), 308–366. See also Meyer, *Joachim Prinz*, 98–186, and Marvin Zolot, *Mensch: Biography and Writings of Manfred Eric Swarsensky* (Madison, WI: Edgewood College Press, 2009), 18–31.

28. Cyrus Adler to Dr. Greenberg, 29 July 1938: JTS, RC, RG1, A, box 19/17. Adler called his colleagues to action and reminded them to lose as little time as possible, even during the Jewish High Holidays, C. Adler to H. Parzen, 1 September 1938: JTS, RC, RG1, A, box 19/17.

29. Cyrus Adler to William Rosenwald, 2 November 1938: JTS, RC, RG1, A, box 19/17; Adler explains here that since August, the number of people willing to leave Germany for the United States was rapidly growing.

30. See Lyman Cromwell White, *300,000 New Americans: The Epic of a Modern Immigrant Aid-Service* (New York: Harper, 1957), 34–50.

31. After the Nazis revoked Hoffmann's German citizenship in 1934, he still had his original Hungarian citizenship. This may have saved his life in 1937 when he was arrested by the Gestapo. The Hungarian government intervened on his behalf. Although Hoffmann was freed from prison, the German government demonstrated its desire to banish this well-known Zionist and leader of the Mizrachi organization by marking him as an "enemy of the state" in 1937, which amounted to expulsion from Germany.

32. For more information on Cecilia Razovsky, see White, *300,000 New Americans*, 37–38.

33. "Problem of Refugee Jewish Religious Functionaries," Meeting, 13 October 1938: JTS, RC, RG1, A, box 19/17.

34. Resume Special Committee Meeting to Consider Problems of Refugee Jewish Religious Functionaries, 24 October 1938: JTSRC, RG1, A, box 19/17.

35. Parzen was born in Ozorkow, a Polish town in Prussian Poland, the area occupied by Prussia from 1793 to 1919. He came to the United States in 1906, earned a BA from the University of Michigan, and received his graduate education at the JTS in New York. He thus fulfilled the committee's requirements for the future chairman since he also spoke English, German, and Yiddish.

36. Resume Special Committee Meeting to Consider Problems of Refugee Jewish Religious Functionaries, 24 Oct. 1938: JTSRC, RG1, A, Box 19/17.

37. Cyrus Adler to S. C. Kohs, 10 November 1938: JTS, RC, RG1, A, box 19/17, and Cyrus Adler to Rabbi Schwab, 28 March 1939: JTS, RC, RG 1, A, box 19/17.

38. Steinweis, *Kristallnacht*, 9–16, 103–122. See also Nancy Rupprecht and Wendy Koenig, eds., *Holocaust Persecution: Responses and Consequences* (Newcastle: Cambridge Scholars, 2010), 12. The main synagogue in Mannheim and its Jewish cemetery were blasted away during that night, Forchheim experienced the same brutality, and the synagogue in Braunschweig was destroyed after the pogrom; Institut für Zeitgeschichte München, NSG-Datenbank "Die Verfolgung von NS-Verbrechen durch deutsche Justizbehörden nach 1945," https://www.ifz-muenchen.de/das-archiv/benutzung-und-service/nsg-datenbank/.

39. On the situation of the communities, see Interview with Jacob Breuer, 12 June 1972, Research Foundation for Jewish Immigration: LBI, AR 25385, 14.

40. Contract between Congregation Agudass Achim, Zurich, and Dr. Erich Löwenthal, Berlin, 16 November 1938: Private collection, Dr. Abraham Lowenthal.

41. Letter Dr. Abraham Lowenthal to Cornelia Wilhelm, 5 August 2015: Private archives of the author.

42. The Fires on the Rhine, An Eyewitness Account of the Burning of the Synagogues of Cologne, 10 November 1938, by Alfred Kober: JTS, RC, RG 1, A, box 19/17.

43. Manfred Swarsensky to Liebenau family, 16 December 1939: AJA, SC-15217.

44. An Autobiographical Sketch, by Leo Trepp: AJA, SC-12426.

45. Eric Lidji, *The Seventeenth Generation: The Lifework of Rabbi Walter Jacob* (Pittsburgh: Rodef Shalom Press, 2018), 34–43.

46. Booklet listing the passengers who sailed on the SS *Manhattan* on 13 June 1939, including Senta, Gabriele, and Susanne Kronheim: LBI, Hans Kronheim Collection, AR 3156, box 3.

47. Questionnaire Hans Harris Hirschberg, Biographische Dokumentation: IFZ, MA 1500/90.

48. Interview with Ismar Schorsch by Cornelia Wilhelm, 13 November 2013: Private archives of the author and LBI (unprocessed).

49. David Kranzler and Dovid Landesmann, *Rav Breuer: His Life and Legacy* (New York: Feldheim, 1998), 106–111; see also Interview with Jacob Breuer, 12 June 1972, Research Foundation for Jewish Immigration: LBI, AR 25385, 14–15.

50. Kranzler and Landesman, *Rav Breuer*, 110–111.

51. Fackenheim, *Epitaph for German Judaism*, 62–75.

52. Questionnaire Research Foundation for Jewish Immigration, Naphtali Hartwig Carlebach: IfZ MA 1500/76B.

53. Norbert Weinberg, *Courage of the Spirit* (Pensacola, FL: Indigo, 2014).

54. Excerpts from an unpublished autobiography contributed to the Berlin Festschrift of the Jubilee Volume on the occasion of the twenty-fifth anniversary of the reestablished postwar Jewish community in Berlin: AJA, MS-705, Series A, box 1/9.

55. Interview with Eli Faber by Cornelia Wilhelm, 17 April 2019, part 1: Private archives of the author and LBI (unprocessed).

56. Leo Baeck to Ismar Elbogen, 25 April 1939: LBI, AR66, III, Elbogen. Max Dienemann returned to his congregation after he was released from a concentration camp; Manfred Swarsensky had promised Leo Baeck that he would stay in Berlin to help those Jews still living in the city after he was discharged from Sachsenhausen in March 1939; however, the Gestapo pressured him to leave as promised; see Manfred Swarsensky Oral History Transcript, p. 180: Wisconsin Historical Society, Wisconsin Survivors of the Holocaust, https://www.wisconsinhistory.org/HolocaustSurvivors/Swarsensky.asp.

57. Alexander Burnstein to Cyrus Adler, 13 December 1938: JTS, RC, RG 1, A, box 19/17.
58. Ibid.
59. Circular letter by Alexander Burnstein, 21 December 1938: JTS, RC, RG 1, A, box 19/17.
60. Henry Pels, Secretary of Chief Rabbi's Religious Emergency Fund, to A. Burnstein, 22 December 1938: JTS, RC, RG 1, A, box 19/17. That letter was circulated to approximately six hundred rabbis; see Report of Meeting of Executive Board, Committee on Refugee Jewish Ministers, 16 January 1939: JTS, RC, RG 1, A, box 19/18.
61. Report of Meeting of Executive Board, Committee on Refugee Jewish Ministers, 16 January 1939: JTS, RC, RG 1, A, box 19/18.
62. White, *300,000 New Americans*, 35–36. For the growing list of Jewish and non-Jewish members of the NCC, see p. 39. Almost all of the larger American Jewish organizations joined the effort, including the American Friends Service Committee and the American Committee for Christian-German Refugees.
63. While Burnstein talks about "rabbis," this number might refer instead to "Jewish religious functionaries," including cantors, mohels, shohetim, religious teachers, and so on. Report of Meeting of Executive Board, Committee on Refugee Jewish Ministers, 16 January 1939: JTS, RC, RG 1, A, box 19/18.
64. A. Burnstein to C. Adler, 20 February 1939: JTS, RC, RG 1, A, box 19/18.
65. Report of Meeting of Executive Board, Committee on Refugee Jewish Ministers, 16 January 1939: JTS, RC, RG 1, A, box 19/18.
66. Cyrus Adler to A. Burnstein, 19 January 1939: JTS, RC, RG 1, A, box 19/18, and A. Burnstein to C. Adler, 22 January 1939: JTS, RC, RG 1, A, box 19/18.
67. Burnstein to [first name unreadable] Cohen, 20 February 1939 (found in Adler's correspondence): JTS, RC, RG 1, A, box 19/18; see also Burnstein to Adler, 1 May 1939: JTS, RC, RG 1, A, box 19/18.
68. Report "The United Synagogue as a Functioning System, 1937": JTS, RC, RG 1, A, box 27/6; see also "Extension Activities, From July to September 1940": JTS, RC, RG 1, A, box 27/6.
69. Cyrus Adler to A. Burnstein, 22 February 1939: JTS, RC, RG 1, A, box 19/18, and Cyrus Adler to Mr. A. Shual, 2 May 1939: JTS, RC, RG 1, A, box 19/18.
70. A. Burnstein to C. Adler, 17 March 1939: JTS, RC, RG 1, A, box 19/18.
71. Edward S. Maney to Eugene Horovitz, 19 February 1940: JTS, RC, RG 1, A, box 19/18.
72. Supplement to Report to Board of Directors of the Jewish Theological Seminary of America, 5 June 1940: JTS, RC, RG 2, box 2/3.
73. White, *300,000 New Americans*, 34–59.

4. The Refugees' First Years in the United States

1. W. Gunther Plaut, *Unfinished Business: An Autobiography* (Toronto: Lester & Orpen Dennys, 1981), 59.
2. Ibid., 51–54.
3. Wolli Kaelter and Gordon Cohn, *From Danzig: An American Rabbi's Journey* (Malibu, CA: Pangloss, 1997), 52.
4. Interview with Ismar Schorsch by Cornelia Wilhelm, 15 November 2013 at LBI, New York: Private archives of Cornelia Wilhelm and LBI New York (unprocessed).
5. Plaut, *Unfinished Business*, 54.
6. Kaelter and Cohn, *From Danzig*, 48.
7. Plaut, *Unfinished Business*, 76.
8. Ibid., 66–67.
9. Ibid., 143.
10. Kaelter and Cohn, *From Danzig*, 48.
11. Plaut traveled with Herman Schaalman: Plaut, *Unfinished Business*, 77.
12. Ibid., 76–78.
13. Edward K. Kaplan, *Spiritual Radical: Abraham Joshua Heschel in America* (New Haven, CT: Yale University Press, 2007), 7, 47.
14. On anti-German feeling at the New York versus Cincinnati campuses, see Interview of Jack Wertheimer and Herbert Strauss with Max Gruenewald, 14 and 21 June 1971 (Research Foundation for Jewish Immigration): LBI, AR 25385, 25.
15. C. Wilhelm, ed., "German Refugee Rabbis in the United States, 1933–1990," http://mira.geschichte.lmu.de/.
16. Steven Schwarzschild, "Two Modern Jewish Philosophies of History: Nachman Krochmal and Hermann Cohen" (DHL diss., HUC, 1955); Walter Jacob, "The Contemporary Jew in the German Novel and Short History, 1800–1914" (DHL diss., HUC, 1961); W. Gunther Plaut, "Contributions to the History of German Jewry in the Eighteenth Century, from Hebrew and Missionary Sources" (rabbinic thesis, HUC, 1939); Wolfgang Hamburger, "Abraham Geiger as Reformer and Theologian: First Phase, as Presented in Wissenschaftliche Zeitschrift fuer Juedische Theologie" (rabbinic thesis, HUC Cincinnati, 1952); Robert Lehman, "Herzl's Zionist Ideology" (rabbinic thesis, HUC Cincinnati, 1954); Ismar Schorsch, "Jewish Reactions to German Anti-Semitism, 1870–1914" (PhD diss., Columbia University Press, 1972); Walter Würzburger, "Brentano's Theory of a Priori Judgments" (PhD diss., Harvard University, 1951); Joshua Haberman, "The Validation of Revelation" (DHL diss., HUC Cincinnati, 1966).
17. Wilhelm, "German Refugee Rabbis," http://mira.geschichte.lmu.de/57. He considered going back to London early in the 1950s; see Joseph Asher to

Herman Saenger, 16 January 1950: Bancroft Library, University of California at Berkeley (BANC), Mss. 2010/783, box 1.
18. Kaplan, *Spiritual Radical*, 14.
19. Ibid., 29.
20. Ibid., 20.
21. Ibid., 20.
22. Ibid., 39.
23. Kaelter and Cohn, *From Danzig*, 56.
24. Guido Kisch, ed., *Das Breslauer Seminar: Jüdisch-Theologisches Seminar (Fraenkelscher Stiftung) in Breslau 1854–1938* (Tübingen: Gedächtnisschrift, 1963), 125, 138–141.
25. Kaplan, *Spiritual Radical*, 49.
26. Ibid., 36–37.
27. Ibid., 36.
28. See Abraham J. Heschel, *Das prophetische Bewusstsein* (Kraków: Verlag der Polnische Akademie der Wissenschaft, 1935) (PhD diss., Berlin, 1935) and Samuel Atlas, "Man and the Ethical Idea of God," *CCAR Journal* 15 (1968): 40–53.
29. Alexander Guttmann to Julian Morgenstern, 1 October 1942: AJA, MS-663, box 6/32.
30. Ibid.
31. Mirzinker? [unreadable] to Alexander Guttmann, 22 October 1942: AJA, MS-663, box 6/32.
32. See Franz Landsberger to Julian Morgenstern, 10 January 1943: AJA, MS-30, box 7/5.
33. Eugen Taeubler to Julian Morgenstern, 31 March 1947, and Memorandum for the Board of Governors of HUC, c/o President Dr. Morgenstern, 31 March 1947: AJA, MS-30, box 11/7.
34. Prussian landed aristocracy, which is considered to have been the backbone of Germany's political conservatism and antidemocratic spirit as well as Prussian militarism.
35. Eugen Taeubler to Julian Morgenstern, 31 March 1947.
36. Ranke, the director of the Egyptian Institute at the University of Heidelberg, was a member of the Heidelberg Academy of Sciences, as was Taeubler. He lost this membership and his academic credentials in 1937, among other things, because his wife was considered a "half-Jew."
37. Hajo Holborn was a history professor at the University of Heidelberg who lost his position in 1933 because he was married to a Jewish woman. From 1936 to 1942, he taught at Tufts University; during the Second World War, he worked for the Office of Strategic Services. After the war, he taught at Yale University.
38. An advanced *Privatdozent*, without tenure track.

39. *Privatdozent* is the status of an untenured faculty member who has completed a second book, which is the qualification for full professorship.

40. Eugen Taeubler to Julian Morgenstern, 31 March 1947, and Memorandum for the Board of Governors of HUC, c/o President Dr. Morgenstern, 31 March 1947: AJA, MS-30, Box 11/7.

41. Ibid.

42. Eugen Taeubler to Julian Morgenstern, 2 May 1947: AJA, MS-30, box 30/7.

43. Julius Lewy to Julian Morgenstern, 22 April 1947: AJA, MS-30, box 11/7.

44. Eugen Taeubler to Julian Morgenstern, 2 May 1947: AJA, MS-30, box 30/7.

45. Eugen Taeubler to Jacob R. Marcus, 8 October 1950: AJA, MS-210, box 11/4, courtesy of Gary Zola, director of the American Jewish Archives.

46. "Problem of Refugee Jewish Religious Functionaries," Meeting, 13 October 1938: JTS, RC, RG1, A, box 19/17.

47. Interview of Jean Lessing with Max Gruenewald, 16 March 1971, Research Foundation for Jewish Immigration: LBI, AR 25385, 8.

48. Max Gruenewald to Louis Finkelstein, 12 June 1944: JTS, RC, RG 1, box 34/19.

49. Interview of Jack Wertheimer and Herbert Strauss with Max Gruenewald, 14 and 21 June 1971, Research Foundation for Jewish Immigration): LBI, AR 25385, 28.

50. Wilhelm, "German Refugee Rabbis," http://mira.geschichte.lmu.de/143.

51. David Kranzler and Dovid Landesman, *Rav Breuer: His Life and Legacy* (New York: Feldheim, 1998), 110.

52. Jeffrey Gurock, *The Men and Women of Yeshiva: Higher Education, Orthodoxy, and American Judaism* (New York: Columbia University Press, 1988). While Gurock hints that refugees were among faculty and students, he does not elaborate on this.

53. Wilhelm, "German Refugee Rabbis," http://mira.geschichte.lmu.de/91.

54. Michael A. Meyer, *Response to Modernity: A History of the Reform Movement in Judaism* (New York: Oxford University Press, 1988), 77–84.

55. Steven Lowenstein, *Frankfurt on the Hudson: The German-Jewish Community of Washington Heights, 1933–1983, Its Structure and Culture* (Detroit: Wayne State University Press, 1989).

56. Certainly the *Aufbau* was also read in this community, but unlike the *Jewish Way*, it represented a much larger, cosmopolitan group of refugees, few of whom were clustering in an ethnic neighborhood.

57. See the advertisement for "Rosens Bake Shop" in Washington Heights: Yeshiva University Archives, 2001.001 Congregation Beth Hillel and Beth Israel, box 1.

58. Kranzler and Landesman, *Rav Breuer*, 151–176.

59. Oral History Interview with Trudie Rosenthal, June 1976: USHMM, Oral History Collection, RG 50. 174. 0001, Accession Number: 1995.A.0872,

https://collections.ushmm.org/search/catalog/irn512258, and Martin M. Weitz, ed., *Interview with Mrs. Karl (Trudie) Rosenthal: Concentration Camp Survivor, Given in 1976* (Greenville, NC: Pambrit, 1993).

60. Ibid.

61. Oral History Interview, Cecile Meiers and Syma Mendelsohn, 1973: University of Illinois at Springfield, Norris L Brookens Library, Archives/Special Collections, The Jewish Experience Project, 34–40.

62. N. N. to Samuel Cohen, 2 October 1938 [difficult to read]: USHMM, Hans Enoch Kronheim Papers, box 3. Agreement between Congregation Gates of Hope and Hans Enoch Kronheim, no date [date of tenure in contract 1 January 1952 to 31 December 1953]: USHMM, Hans Enoch Kronheim Papers, box 3.

63. Michael A. Meyer, *Joachim Prinz, Rebellious Rabbi: An Autobiography— The German and Early American Years* (Bloomington: Indiana University Press, 2008), 205–223.

64. "Problem of Refugee Jewish Religious Functionaries," Meeting, 13 October 1938: JTS, RC, RG1, A, Box 19/17.

65. Interview of Cornelia Wilhelm with Ismar Schorsch, 15 November 2013, at LBI, New York: Private archives of Cornelia Wilhelm and LBI New York (unprocessed).

66. Interview with Eli Faber by Cornelia Wilhelm, 19 April 2019, part 1: Private archives of author and LBI New York (unprocessed).

67. Joseph Asher to Herman Saenger, 15 January 1952: BANC, Mss. 2010/783, box 1.

68. Wilhelm, "German Refugee Rabbis," http://mira.geschichte.lmu.de/58.

69. See the database German Refugee Rabbis in the US after 1933 for their short bios; Wilhelm, "German Refugee Rabbis," http://mira.geschichte.lmu.de/57.

70. Interview with Michael Munk by Jack Wertheimer and Michael Schwarzschild, part 1 (19) and part 2 (9, 20), 11 July 1972 (Research Foundation for Jewish Immigration): LBI, AR 25385.

71. Wilhelm, "German Refugee Rabbis," http://mira.geschichte.lmu.de/133.

72. Benny Kraut, *German-Jewish Orthodoxy in an Immigrant Synagogue: Cincinnati's New Hope Congregation and the Ambiguities of Ethnic Religion* (New York: Markus Wiener, 1988), 55ff.

73. An excellent and comprehensive analysis of the development of German nationality and citizenship can be found in Dieter Gosewinkel, *Einbürgern und Ausschließen: Die Nationalisierung der Staatsangehörigkeit vom Deutschen Bund bis zur Bundesrepublik* (Göttingen: Vandenhoek & Ruprecht, 2001).

74. Expatriation of politically or "racially" unwanted individuals was facilitated by the Law on the Revocation of Naturalizations and the Deprivations of German Citizenship (Gesetz über den Widerruf von Einbürgerungen und die Aberkennung der deutschen Staatsangehörigkeit) of 14 July 1933.

See Klaus Pfeiffer and Joachim Rott, eds., *Die erste Ausbürgerungsliste vom 25. August 1933* (Berlin: Hentrich & Hentrich, 2016). See also the post-1945 restoration of citizenship for those affected by this legislation: "Restoration of German Citizenship," Consular Services, German Missions in the United States, https://www.germany.info/us-en/service/03-Citizenship/restoration-of-german-citizenship/925120.

75. Gosewinkel, *Einbürgern und Ausschließen*, 373.

76. Ibid., 379–383.

77. Ibid., 383–393.

78. "11. Verordnung zum Reichsbürgergesetzt vom 25," November 1941, http://www.ns-quellen.at/gesetz_anzeigen_detail.php?gesetz_id=4410&action=B_Read.

79. Miriam Rürup and Doerte Bischoff, eds., *Ausgeschlossen: Staatsbürgerschaft, Staatenlosigkeit und Exil* (Exilforschung; 36) (Munich: Edition text + kritik, 2018), 9–20.

80. Michael Brocke and Julius Carlebach, eds., *Biographisches Handbuch der Rabbiner*, part 2, vol. 2 (Munich: K. G. Saur, 2009), 287.

81. Meyer, *Joachim Prinz*, 140–141, 160–161.

82. In the wake of the Russian Revolution, the League of Nations introduced this travel document for refugees. This was not a "passport" in the legal sense and was issued by the nation that received a refugee. It allowed the refugee to continue to travel legally and to return to the country that issued the document within its one-year validity, if necessary.

83. Wilhelm, "German Refugee Rabbis," http://mira.geschichte.lmu.de/62.

84. Cornelia Wilhelm, *Bewegung oder Verein? Nationalsozialistische Volkstumspolitik in den USA* (Stuttgart: Franz Steiner, 1998), 266.

85. Interview of Jack Wertheimer and Herbert Strauss with Max Gruenewald, 14 and 21 June 1971 (Research Foundation for Jewish Immigration): LBI, AR 25385, 25.

86. Wilhelm, *Bewegung*, 265–277.

87. Interview of Jack Wertheimer with Simon Schwab, July 1971 (Research Foundation for Jewish Immigration): LBI, AR 25385, 15–16, and 145 F.2d 672 (1944) SCHWAB et al. v. COLEMAN, US District Judge, No. 5293. Circuit Court of Appeals, Fourth Circuit, 10 November 1944, https://law.justia.com/cases/federal/appellate-courts/F2/145/672/1476121/.

88. *Second War Powers Act*, 56 Stat. 176, Senate Bill 2208, 27 March 1942.

89. Interview with Ismar Schorsch by Cornelia Wilhelm, 15 November 2013 at LBI, New York: Private archives of Cornelia Wilhelm and LBI New York (unprocessed). On the process of "taking out first papers" and the pride of becoming an American citizen, see Interview with Eli Faber by Cornelia Wilhelm, 19 April 2019, parts 1 and 2: Private archives of author and LBI New York (unprocessed).

5. Careers Lost and Found

1. Kaufmann Kohler was born in 1843 in Fürth and died in 1926 in Cincinnati. He came from a traditional Jewish background and education before studying at the universities of Munich, Berlin, and Erlangen, where he earned a PhD and became a follower of Samuel Holdheim. In 1869, he immigrated to the United States where he officiated first at Temple Beth-El in Detroit; then, after 1871, at Sinai Temple in Chicago; followed by Congregation Beth-El in New York. In 1870, he married Johanna Einhorn, the daughter of Rabbi David Einhorn, and in 1903, he was appointed president of HUC in Cincinnati. He was the founder of a systematic theology of historical Judaism and had a significant influence on the development of the American Reform movement, including on the Pittsburgh Platform. See Jakob Petuchowski, "Abraham Geiger and Samuel Holdheim: Their Differences in Germany and Repercussions in America," *LBIY* 22 (1977): 139–159.

2. In 1943, Elbogen was probably not fully aware of the extent of the Holocaust; in his publication, he refers to Nazi persecution as the driving force behind the developments.

3. Ismar Elbogen, "American Jewish Scholarship: A Survey. In Honor of the Centenary of Kaufmann Kohler," *American Jewish Yearbook* 45 (1943/44): 47.

4. Ibid., 64–65.

5. Astrid Zajdband, *German Rabbis in British Exile: From "Heimat" into the Unknown* (Boston: De Gruyter, 2016), 263–264.

6. Leonard Baker, *Hirt der Verfolgten* (Stuttgart: Klett-Cotta, 1982), 431.

7. Ibid., 432.

8. Ibid., 438.

9. Julian Morgenstern served as vice president of the WUPJ at the time. Lily Montagu was the woman leader of the movement for liberal Judaism in England and cofounder of the WUPJ founded in London in 1926. She also served as president of the WUPJ from 1955 to 1959. See the entries of the individuals in Cornelia Wilhelm, ed., "German Refugee Rabbis in the United States, 1933–1990," http://mira.geschichte.lmu.de. For the first in a series of publications, see Atina Grossman, "Rabbi Steven Schwarzschild's Reports from Berlin, 1948–1950," *LBIY* 60 (2015): 237–242.

10. Edward K. Kaplan, *Spiritual Radical: Abraham Joshua Heschel in America* (New Haven, CT: Yale University Press, 2007), 95–96.

11. Nathan Peter Levinson, *Ein Ort ist, mit wem Du bist: Lebensstationen eines Rabbiners* (Berlin: Edition Hentrich, 1996), 120.

12. Ibid., 121–123. Translated from the German by the author.

13. Ibid., 104.

14. Markus Krah, *American Jewry and the Re-Invention of the East European Jewish Past*, New Perspectives on Modern Jewish History 9, ed. Cornelia Wilhelm (Berlin: De Gruyter, 2018), 3–7.

15. Peter Novick, *The Holocaust in American Life* (Boston: Houghton Mifflin, 1999).

16. See also Hasia Diner, *We Remember with Reverence and Love: American Jews and the Myth of Silence after the Holocaust, 1945–1962* (New York: New York University Press, 2009).

17. Gilad Hirschberger, "Collective Trauma and the Social Construction of Meaning," *Frontiers in Psychology* 9 (2018): 1–14.

18. Eva Jospe and Raphael Jospe, eds., *To Leave Your Mark: Selections from the Writings of Alfred Jospe* (Hoboken, NJ: KTAV, 2000).

19. The first five students sent to HUC by the Hochschule in 1935.

20. "Der letzte Rabbiner: Die Geschichte des Leo Trepp," dir. Christian Walther, RBB Fernsehen, Rundfunk Berlin Brandenburg, DVD, Germany: 2010 (courtesy of Christian Walther) and "Nahum N. Glatzer and the German-Jewish Tradition," dir. Judith Wechsler, USA: 2011.

21. Leo Trepp, leotrepp.org/en/.

22. See, for example, Jan Taubitz, *Holocaust Oral History und das lange Ende der Zeitzeugenschaft* (Göttingen: Wallstein, 2016), Christopher Bigsby, *Remembering and Imagining the Holocaust: The Chain of Memory* (Cambridge: Cambridge University Press, 2006), and Martin Sabrow and Norbert Frei, eds., *Die Geburt des Zeitzeugen nach 1945* (Göttingen: Wallstein, 2012). See also Kaja Kaźmierska, *Biography and Memory: The Generational Experience of the Shoah Survivors* (Boston: Academic Studies, 2012).

23. Baker, *Hirt*, 444.

24. The following honorary degrees were bestowed (by institution and, if known, year): Yeshiva University: Jacob Hoffmann (1951); JTS: Ezekiel Landau (1977), Bert Woythaler, Erwin Zimet (1975), Norbert Weinberg, Max Gruenewald; HUC: Ulrick Steuer, Leo Lichtenberg (1965), W. Gunther Plaut (1964), Hugo Hahn (1963), Alfred Jospe (1972), Leo Trepp, Walter Jacob (1975), Max Nussbaum (1959), Steven Schwarzschild (1973), Nahum Glatzer, Gustav Buchdahl (1996), Alfred Wolf (1966), Iwan Grün (1962), Wolfgang Hamburger, Guido Kisch (1963), Frank Rosenthal (1964), Herman Vogelstein (1940). See Wilhelm, "German Refugee Rabbis."

25. Address at Funeral Services of Rabbi Ulrick Steuer, Milwaukee, Wisconsin, 21 October 1973 by Rabbi Karl Richter: AJA, SC-12008.

26. "Leader Looks to the Future," *Cincinnati Enquirer*, 14 October 2002, B 3.

27. Eric Goldstein, *The Price of Whiteness: Jews, Race, and American Identity* (Princeton, NJ: Princeton University Press, 2006), 209–239.

28. Jonathan Sarna, *American Judaism* (New Haven, CT: Yale University Press, 2004), 289–293.

29. For example, Kaplan, *Spiritual Radical*, 20 and Michael A. Meyer, *Joachim Prinz, Rebellious Rabbi: An Autobiography—The German and Early American Years* (Bloomington: Indiana University Press, 2008), 187–256.

30. Werner Rosenstock, "The Jewish Youth Movement," *LBIY* 19 (1974): 98–99.
31. Chanoch Rinott, "Major Trends in Jewish Youth Movements in Germany," *LBIY* 19 (1974): 80–83.
32. Walter Laqueur, *Geboren in Deutschland* (Berlin: Propyläen, 2000). For a recent evaluation, see Yotam Hotam, ed., *Deutsch-Jüdische Jugendliche im "Zeitalter der Jugend"* (Göttingen: Vandenhoek & Ruprecht, 2009).
33. Rinott, "Major Trends," 86.
34. "Our History," OSRUI, https://osrui.org/about/history/.
35. Judah Cohen, "Singing Out for Judaism: A History of Song Leaders and Song Leading at Olin Sang Ruby Union Institute," in *A Place of Our Own: The Rise of Reform Jewish Camping*, ed. Michael M. Lorge and Gary P. Zola (Tuscaloosa: University of Alabama Press, 2006), 173–208.
36. Michael Lorge and Gary Zola, "The Beginning of Union Institute in Oconomowoc, Wisconsin, 1952–1970: Creation and Coalescence of the First UAHC Camp," in *A Place of Our Own: The Rise of Reform Jewish Camping*, ed. Michael M. Lorge and Gary P. Zola (Tuscaloosa: University of Alabama Press, 2006), 52–71.
37. Lorge and Zola, "The Beginning," 57, 64.
38. Wolli Kaelter and Gordon Cohn, *From Danzig: An American Rabbi's Journey* (Malibu, CA: Pangloss, 1997), 116–138.
39. Ibid., 132.
40. See Questionnaire of Leo Adler, Biographische Dokumentation der deutschsprachigen Emigration 1933–1945 in Kooperation mit der Research Foundation for Jewish Immigration, Microfilm Series A and B: IfZ, MA 1500.
41. Interview Jack Wertheimer and Steven Schwarzschild with Michael Munk, 11 July 1972, Research Foundation for Jewish Immigration: LBI, AR 25385. While there were boys participating from the Breuer community in Washington Heights, the camp attracted a variety of American Jewish participants. For today's Camp Munk, see https://www.munkmemories.com/.
42. Questionnaire of Samson Raphael Weiss, Biographische Dokumentation der deutschsprachigen Emigration 1933–1945 in Kooperation mit der Research Foundation for Jewish Immigration, Microfilm Series A and B: IFZ, MA 1500. Alfonso Narvaez, "79-Year-Old Leader of Orthodox Jewry," *New York Times*, 8 February 1990, https://www.nytimes.com/1990/02/08/obituaries/rabbi-s-r-weiss-79-year-old-leader-of-orthodox-jewry.html.
43. Also Ralph Kingsley launched a day school in Boca Raton, Florida, as did Gunther Hirschberg in the 1970s in New York. See Wilhelm, "German Refugee Rabbis," ed. C. Wilhelm, http.//mira.geschichte.lmu.de/107.
44. Cornelia Wilhelm, *The Independent Orders of B'nai B'rith and True Sisters: Pioneers of a New Jewish Identity, 1843–1914* (Detroit: Wayne State University Press, 2011), 260.

45. Wilhelm, "German Refugee Rabbis," ed. C. Wilhelm, http://mira.geschichte.lmu.de/171,201and125.

46. Alfred Jospe to Harry Kaplan, 8 August 1944: AJA, BB Hillel Foundation, SC-1184.

47. Jospe and Jospe, *To Leave your Mark*, passim.

48. Ibid., 9.

49. Ibid., xxi.

50. Lewis M. Barth and Ruth Nussbaum, eds., *Max Nussbaum: From Berlin to Hollywood. A Midcentury Vision of Jewish Life* (Malibu: Pangloss, 1994), 82–90.

51. Ibid., 92–98.

52. Ibid., 101.

53. Meyer, *Joachim Prinz*, 224–225.

54. Joseph Asher to Herman Sanger, 22 September 1950: BANC, Mss. 2010/783, box 1.

55. Joseph Asher to Albert Vorspan, 27 May 1963: BANC, Mss. 2010/783, box 1. See also Goldstein, *The Price of Whiteness*, 212–216.

56. Speech given by Joachim Prinz during the March on Washington on 28 August 1963, "Civil Rights," Joachim Prinz, http://www.joachimprinz.com/civilrights.htm.

57. This is an addendum by the author, as Jünger speaks only about "Judaism," but the author thinks it is essential to highlight Prinz's strong commitment to defining a modern Jewish identity for Jews that was not purely assimilationist but that gave them a way to be part of modern society as Jews. He had great hopes that American society would provide a platform for this, but he became increasingly concerned that American Jewry could live up to that promise.

58. David Jünger, "In the Presence of the Past: Rabbi Joachim Prinz, Holocaust Memory, and the Fight for Jewish Survival in Postwar America," in *Reconstructing the Old Country: American Jewry in the Post-Holocaust Decades*, ed. Eliyana Adler and Sheila Jelen (Detroit: Wayne State University Press, 2017), 306–313. David Jünger uses the term "Judaism" throughout his arguments, but he does not differentiate between a modern historical Judaism that Prinz most probably had in mind and traditional forms of Judaism, such as the Israeli state religion.

59. Ibid.

60. Krah, *American Jewry*, 103–109.

61. Abraham Joshua Heschel, *Man Is Not Alone: A Philosophy of Religion* (New York: JPS of America, 1951); see also Heschel, *God in Search of Man: A Philosophy of Judaism* (New York: Farrar, Strauss and Cudahy, 1955).

62. Susannah Heschel, "Theological Affinities in the Writings of Abraham Joshua Heschel and Martin Luther King, Jr.," in *Black Zion*, ed. Yvonne Chireau and Nathaniel Deutsch (New York: Oxford University Press, 2000), 168–186.

Abraham Joshua Heschel, *Das prophetische Bewusstsein* (Kraków: Verlag der Polnische Akademie der Wissenschaft, 1935; PhD diss., Berlin, 1935); his dissertation was published in English only in 1962: Abraham Joshua Heschel, *The Prophets* (New York: Harper and Row, 1962).

63. Kaplan, *Abraham Joshua Heschel*, 164, 208–243.

64. Susannah Heschel, "God Talk, Friendship and Activism: The Theological Affinity and the Relationship between Abraham Joshua Heschel and Martin Luther King, Jr.," The Jewish Federations of America, https://www.jewishfederations.org/page.aspx?id=13296&print=1.

65. Wilfried Mausbach, "Auschwitz and Vietnam: West German Protests against America's War during the 1960s," in *Coping with the Nazi Past: West German Debates on Nazism and Generational Conflict, 1955–1975*, ed. Philipp Gassert (New York: Berghahn Books, 2006), 279–298; Robert D. Schulzinger, *A Time for War: The United States and Vietnam, 1945–1975* (New York: Oxford University Press, 1997), Brian Van De Mark, *Into the Quagmire: Lyndon Johnson and the Escalation of the Vietnam War* (New York: Oxford University Press, 1991).

66. Alexander Altmann, *Moses Mendelssohn: A Biographical Study* (London: Routledge & Kegan Paul, 1973); see also Allan Arkush, "The Contribution of Alexander Altmann to the Study of Moses Mendelssohn," *LBIY* 34 (1989): 415–420. Stephen Whitfield, "Brandeis University at the Beginning: Judaic Studies," *European Judaism* 45 (2012): 117–119.

67. Eugene Sheppard, "'I Am a Memory Come Alive': Nahum Glatzer and the Legacy of German Jewish Thought in America," *Jewish Quarterly Review* 94 (2004): 123–148, and Paul Mendes-Flohr, "Knowledge as Service: An Appreciation of Nahum N. Glatzer," *Jewish Studies* 31 (1991): 25–46.

68. Steven Schwarzschild, "Two Modern Jewish Philosophies of History: Nachman Krochmal and Hermann Cohen," (DHL diss., HUC, 1955). See also Nahum N. Glatzer, *Franz Rosenzweig, His Life and Thought* (New York: Schocken Books, 1961); Martin Buber, *On Judaism*, ed. Nahum Glatzer (New York: Schocken Books, 1967); and Franz Rosenzweig, *On Jewish Learning*, ed. Nahum Glatzer (New York: Schocken Books, 1955).

69. Steven Schwarzschild, "Franz Rosenzweig's Anecdotes about Hermann Cohen," in *Gegenwart im Rückblick: Festgabe für die Jüdische Gemeinde zu Berlin 25 Jahre nach dem Neubeginn*, ed. Herbert A. Strauss and Kurt R. Grossman (Heidelberg: Lothar Stiehm, 1970), 209–218; Schwarzschild, "Germanism and Judaism—Hermann Cohen's Normative Paradigm of the German-Jewish Symbiosis," in *Jews and Germans from 1860 to 1933*, ed. David Bronsen (Heidelberg: Universitätsverlag C. Winter, 1979), 129–172. See also Schwarzschild, *The Tragedy of Optimism: The Writings of Herman Cohen*, ed. George Y. Kohler (Albany: SUNY Press, 2018).

70. Alan Brill, "A Tiny, but Articulate Minority," *Tradition* 41 (2008): 13–15.

71. Daily News Bulletin, Jewish Telegraphic Agency XXX, 28 February 1963, 4 and CV of Leon Feldman, Sam Hartstein Papers, YU Archives.

72. W. Gunther Plaut, *The Torah: The Five Books of Moses* (Philadelphia: Jewish Publication Society of America, 1963); Plaut, *The Torah: A Modern Commentary* (New York: CCAR, 2005). See also Plaut, *Exodus: Commentary* (New York: Union of American Hebrew Congregations, 1983), and Plaut, *Deuteronomy: Commentary* (New York: Union of American Hebrew Congregations, 1983).

73. Walter Jacob, *Contemporary American Responsa* (New York: CCAR, 1998); Jacob, *Questions and Reform Jewish Answers: New American Reform Responsa* (New York: CCAR, 1992), and Eric Lidji, *The Seventeenth Generation: The Lifework of Rabbi Walter Jacob* (Pittsburgh: Rodef Shalom, 2018), 143–175.

74. Jacques Steinberg, "Rabbi Alexander Schindler, Reform Leader and Major Jewish Voice, Dies at 75," *New York Times*, 16 November 2000, https://www.nytimes.com/2000/11/16/nyregion/rabbi-alexander-schindler-reform-leader-and-major-jewish-voice-dies-at-75.html.

75. In 2021, the so-called Morgan Lewis Report commissioned by HUC to investigate allegations of sexual misconduct of HUC faculty also charged Alfred Gottschalk with misbehavior toward female students. See Morgan Lewis, "Report of Investigation into Allegations of Misconduct at the HUC-Jewish Institute of Religion, Cincinnati 2021," https://huc.edu/wp-content/uploads/HUC-REPORT-OF-INVESTIGATION-11.04.21.pdf.

76. Douglas Martin, "Alfred Gottschalk, Reform Rabbi, Dies at 79," *New York Times*, 15 September 2009, https://www.nytimes.com/2009/09/16/us/16gottschalk.html; Elaine Woo, "Alfred Gottschalk Dies at 79; a Leader of Reform Judaism," *Los Angeles Times*, 13 September 2009, https://www.latimes.com/local/obituaries/la-me-alfred-gottschalk13-2009sep13-story.html; "Dr. Alfred Gottschalk, z"l, Former President and Chancellor Emeritus of HUC-JIR," Hebrew Union College-Jewish Institute of Religion, 14 September 2009, http://huc.edu/news/article/2009/dr-alfred-gottschalk-zl-former-president-and-chancellor-emeritus-huc-jir.

77. "Ismar Schorsch," Jewish Theological Seminary, http://www.jtsa.edu/ismar-schorsch.

78. See also Ismar Schorsch, "The Leo Baeck Institute: Continuity amid Desolation," *LBIY* 25 (1980): ix–xii.

79. Max Gruenewald, "The Beginning of the 'Reichsvertretung,'" *LBIY* 1 (1956): 57–67; Nahum N. Glatzer, "The Frankfurt Lehrhaus," *LBIY* 1 (1956): 105–122; Alexander Altmann, "Jewish Theology in 20th Century Germany," *LBIY* 1 (1956): 193–216; Wolfgang Hamburger, "Teacher in Berlin and Cincinnati," *LBIY* 2 (1957): 27–34; Kurt Wilhelm, "The Jewish Community in the Post-Emancipation Period," *LBIY* 2 (1957): 47–75; Max Gruenewald, "The Modern Rabbi," *LBIY* 2 (1957): 85–97; Adolf Kober, "150 Years of Religious Instruction," *LBIY* 2 (1957): 98–118;

Fritz Bamberger, "Julius Guttmann: Philosopher of Judaism," *LBIY* 5 (1960): 3–34; Nahum N. Glatzer, "Leopold Zunz and the Revolution of 1948: With Four Letters by Leopold Zunz," *LBIY* 5 (1960): 122–139; Leo Adler, "Israelitische Religionsgemeinschaft of Wurttemberg: Development and Changes," *LBIY* 5 (1960): 251–261; Alexander Carlebach, "A German Rabbi Goes East," *LBIY* 6 (1961): 60–121.

80. Alexander Altmann, "The German Rabbi, 1910–1939," *LBIY* 19 (1974): 31–49; Alfred Jospe, "A Profession in Transition: The German Rabbinate, 1910–1939," *LBIY* 19 (1974): 51–61; Max Gruenewald, "The Jewish Teacher in Germany," *LBIY* 19 (1974): 71–76; Ismar Schorsch, "German Anti-Semitism in the Light of Post-War Historiography," *LBIY* 19 (1974): 257–271; Emil Schorsch, "The Rural Jew: Observations on the Paper of Werner J. Cahnman," *LBIY* 19 (1974): 131–135. Fritz Bamberger, who joined the faculty of HUC in New York in 1962 also contributed to this volume: Fritz Bamberger, "The Arden House Conference: 'Exploring a Typology of German Jewry,'" *LBIY* 19 (1974): 3–10.

81. Ursula Büttner and Martin Geschrat, *Die verlassenen Kinder der Kirche: Der Umgang mit Christen jüdischer Herkunft im "Dritten Reich"* (Göttingen: Vandenhoek & Ruprecht, 1998).

82. Joseph Foschepoth, *Im Schatten der Vergangenheit: Die Anfänge der Gesellschaften für Christlich-Jüdische Zusammenarbeit* (Göttingen: Vandenhoek & Ruprecht, 1993), 11; Benny Kraut, "Towards the Establishment of the National Conference of Christians and Jews: The Tenuous Road to Religious Goodwill in the 1920s," *American Jewish History* 77 (1988): 388–412.

83. One of the major initiatives on the tension between modernity and religion was the Conference on Science, Philosophy, and Religion, introduced by the JTS; see Cara Rock-Singer, "A Prophetic Guide for a Perplexed World: Louis Finkelstein and the 1940 Conference on Science, Philosophy, and Religion," *Religion & American Culture* 29 (2019): 179–215.

84. Joachim Prinz, "The Right to Be Different," in *Best Jewish Sermons of 5714*, ed. Rabbi Saul I. Teplitz, 125–133 (New York: Jonathan David, 1954).

85. Kaplan, *Spiritual Radical*, 239.

86. Ibid.

87. Ibid., 263.

88. Ibid., 239–276.

89. Myrna Oliver, "Alfred Wolf, 88; Noted Rabbi Started Jewish Youth Camps," *Los Angeles Times*, 2 August 2004, https://www.latimes.com/archives/la-xpm-2004-aug-02-me-wolf2-story.html.

90. Richard Damashek, *A Brand Plucked from the Fire: The Life of Rabbi Herman E. Schaalman* (Brooklyn: KTAV, 2013), 344.

91. Manya Brachear Pashman, "Rabbi Herman Schaalman, an Interfaith Pioneer, Dies at 100," *Chicago Tribune*, 1 February 2017, https://www.chicagotribune.com/news/obituaries/ct-herman-schaalman-obit-met-20170201-story.html.

92. Marvin Zolot, *Mensch: Biography and Writings of Manfred Eric Swarsensky* (Madison, WI: Edgewood College Press, 2009), 99–107.

93. Jakob J. Petuchowski, *Mein Judesein: Wege und Erfahrungen eines deutschen Rabbiners* (Freiburg: Herder, 1992). See also Jakob Petuchowski, ed., *When Jews and Christians Meet* (Albany: SUNY Press, 1988); Hans Küng and Walter Kasper, eds., *Jews and Christians* (New York: Seabury, 1975); Jakob J. Petuchowski, *Ferner lehrten unsere Meister . . . : rabbinische Geschichten* (Freiburg: Herder, 1983); Jakob J. Petuchowski, *Das Buch vom Volk des Buches: Jüdische Gedanken zur Buch- und Lesekultur* (Freiburg: Herder, 1982); Peter Eicher, Jakob Petuchowski, and Walter Strolz, eds., *Offenbarung im christlichen und jüdischen Glaubensverständnis* (Freiburg: Herder, 1982); Jakob Petuchowski and Clemens Thoma, eds., *Lexikon der christlich-jüdischen Begegnung* (Freiburg: Herder 1997). See also Michael A. Meyer, "Jakob J. Petuchowski (1925–1991)," *Proceedings of the American Academy of Religion* 58 (1992): 27–31.

94. Emil Fackenheim, *To Mend the World: Foundations of Future Jewish Thought* (New York: Schocken Books, 1994). See also Emil Fackenheim, *The Jewish Return into History: Reflections in the Age of Auschwitz and a New Jerusalem* (New York: Schocken Books, 1978).

95. Kaja Kaźmierska, *Biography and Memory: The Generational Experience of the Shoah Survivors* (Boston: Academic Studies, 2012), 14, 33–52.

96. For details on the difficult relationship between the two communities in postwar Germany, see Jay Howard Geller, *Jews in Post-Holocaust Germany, 1945–1953* (Cambridge: Cambridge University Press, 2005); Jeffrey Peck, *Being Jewish in the New Germany* (New Brunswick, NJ: Rutgers University Press, 2006).

6. Refugee Returns

1. Eric H. Erikson, *Identity and the Life Cycle* (New York: Norton, 1980).
2. Kaja Kaźmierska, *Biography and Memory: The Generational Experience of the Shoah Survivors* (Boston: Academic Studies, 2012), 37–52.
3. Judith M. Gerson and Diane L. Wolf, eds., *Sociology Confronts the Holocaust: Memories and Identities in Jewish Diasporas* (Durham, NC: Duke University Press, 2007).
4. See, for example, Erica Lehrer, *Jewish Poland Revisited: Heritage Tourism in Unquiet Places* (Bloomington: Indiana University Press, 2013).
5. Andreas Brämer, "'. . . die Rückkehr eines Rabbiners nach Deutschland ist keine Selbstverständlichkeit': Zur Remigration jüdischer Geistlicher nach Westdeutschland (1945–1965)," in *"Auch in Deutschland waren wir nicht wirklich zu Hause": Jüdische Remigration nach 1945*, ed. Irmela von der Lühe, Axel Schildt, and Stefanie Schüler-Springorum (Göttingen: Wallstein, 2008), 169–189; Andrea

Sinn, "The Return of Robert Raphael Geis to Germany: One of the Last Witnesses of German Jewry?," *European Judaism* 45 (2012): 123–138.

6. Jay Howard Geller, *Jews in Post-Holocaust Germany, 1945–1953* (Cambridge: Cambridge University Press, 2005), 17–52. See also Oral History Interview with Ernst Lorge, 27 April 1984: USHMM, Accession Number: 1989.346.43, RG-50.031.0043, https://collections.ushmm.org/search/catalog/irn507473, and Interview with Hermann Dicker, 29 November 1974: Hebrew University, Avraham Harman Institute of Contemporary Jewry, Oral History Division, Nr. 119, 18 A and B, https://www.youtube.com/watch?v=1_snbQzYLmc&list=PLZEGL2eD5gA1tO02gEP-Al-yMaM_XdiVF&index=36; see also W. Gunther Plaut, *Unfinished Business: An Autobiography* (Toronto: Lester & Orpen Dennys, 1981), 141–146.

7. Geller, *Jews*, 29–31, 34, 37, 46, 48–49, 50–51.

8. Ibid.

9. The report on the circumstances and special needs of Jewish DPs in Germany was commissioned by Harry Truman and prepared by Earl G. Harrison in the summer of 1945.

10. Ibid., 23–28. See also: Harrison Report, http://www.ushmm.org/exhibition/displaced-persons/politic6.htm.

11. Wolfgang Hamburger, Abraham Geiger as reformer and theologian, first phase, as presented in Wissenschaftliche Zeitschrift fuer Juedische Theologie, Rabbinic thesis: HUC Cincinnati, 1952. See also Hartmut Bomhoff, *Ernst Ludwig Ehrlich: Prägende Jahre, Eine Biographie* (Berlin: De Gruyter, 2015), 32. Hamburger served as rabbi in Lincoln, Nebraska; Duluth, Minnesota; Longview and Houston, Texas; and St. Joseph, Missouri.

12. Neue Deutsche Biographie, Leopold Neuhaus, https://www.deutsche-biographie.de/sfz71416.html.

13. Most likely an undertaking similar to the UNRRA DP-university in Munich; see Anna Holian, "Displacement and the Post-War Reconstruction of Education: Displaced Persons at the UNRRA University of Munich, 1945–1948," *Contemporary European History* 17 (2008): 167–195.

14. Weinberg, *Courage*, 212–213. See also Constantin Goschler, "The Attitude towards Jews in Bavaria after the Second World War," *LBIY* 36 (1991): 443–458.

15. Norbert Weinberg, *Courage of the Spirit* (Pensacola, FL: Indigo, 2014).

16. Edith Raim, *Nazi Crimes against Jews in German Post-War Justice* (Berlin: De Gruyter, 2015), 64; and courtesy of Edith Raim, who pointed at further records on these cases in the National Archives: Office of Military Government, Bremen (OMGBR) 6/62-2/33 re. Bremen and Office of Military Government in Bavaria (OMGBY) 17/183-3/12 re. Würzburg.

17. "NSG Datenbank," Institut für Zeitgeschichte, https://www.ifz-muenchen.de/das-archiv/benutzung-und-service/nsg-datenbank/.

18. Elie Munk to Anthony Rothschild, 12 November 1944; Joint Secretary of A. Rothschild to Elie Munk, 14 November 1944; B. Mindel to A. Rothschild, 18 December 1944; Joint Secretary to H. A. Goodman, 13 December 1944; P. Steinberg to A. Rothschild, 3 December 1944; E. Munk to M. Stephany, 21 December 1944; B. Mindel to M. Stephany, 3 January 1945; Joint Secretary to E. Munk, 18 January 1945, in *The Jewish People from the Holocaust to Nationhood: 1933–1960*, 74 microfilm reels (Woodbridge, CT: Research Publication, 1989), Reel 1, file 3.

19. Secretary CBF to H. Galinsky and J. Meyer, 11 October 1951, in *Jewish People from the Holocaust to Nationhood*, Reel 62, file 283.

20. Interview Jack Wertheimer and Michael Schwarzschild with Michael Munk, 11 July 1972, Research Foundation for Jewish Immigration: LBI, AR 25385.

21. Lily Montagu was the woman leader of the movement for liberal Judaism in England and cofounder of the World Union for Progressive Judaism (WUPJ) founded in London in 1926. She also served as president of the WUPJ from 1955 to 1959.

22. Joseph Asher to Editor of *Commentary* Magazine, 17 November 1947: BANC, Mss. 2010/783.

23. Steven Schwarzschild, "Report on Berlin on World Union for Progressive Judaism Conference in London, July 14–19, 1949," *LBIY* 60 (2015): 249–256, and Maimon Schwarzschild, "A Note from Steven Schwarzschild and the Letters from Berlin," *LBIY* 60 (2015): 243–247.

24. Schwarzschild, "Report on Berlin," 249–256; Report on Meeting of the Governing Body of the World Union for Progressive Judaism, 14 July 1949, London: AJA, MS-34, box 18.

25. Geller, *Jews*, 202–208, 219–272; "The Luxembourg Agreement between Israel and the Federal Republic of Germany, 10 September 1952," Treaties, United Nations, https://treaties.un.org/doc/Publication/UNTS/Volume%20162/volume-162-I-2137-English.pdf.

26. Report on Meeting of the Governing Body of the World Union for Progressive Judaism, 26 February 1950, London: AJA, MS-34, box 18.

27. Lily Montagu to Mr. Stephany, 11 July 1950, in *The Jewish People from the Holocaust to Nationhood*, Reel 21, file 114.

28. Nathan Peter Levinson, *Ein Ort ist, mit wem Du bist: Lebensstationen eines Rabbiners* (Berlin: Edition Hentrich, 1996), 104–136.

29. Ibid., 188–194. It is quite possible that Levinson tried to downplay how much the family enjoyed living in Germany because of the negative perception internationally.

30. Ibid., 194–216.

31. Michael Wolffsohn, *Eternal Guilt? Forty Years of German-Jewish-Israeli Relations* (New York: Columbia University Press, 1993), 1–67, 108–113, 138–150, 191–204.

32. See Anne Clara Schenderlein, *Germany on Their Minds* (New York: Berghahn Books, 2020), 143.

33. German Consulate General, Atlanta to Foreign Office, Bonn, 9 April 1956: Politisches Archiv (PA), Auswärtiges Amt (AA), B92, no. 128; Dr. König, Foreign Office, Bonn to German Consulate General, Atlanta, 8 May 1956: PA, AA, B92, no. 128.

34. German Consulate General, Cleveland to German Foreign Office, Bonn, 22 October 1958 and German Consulate General, Cleveland to German Foreign Office, 31 December 1958: PA, AA, B 92, no. 128.

35. Israelitische Kultusgemeinde Nürnberg to Cultural Department of the Federal Government, 16 December 1960 and German Foreign Office, Berlin, to German Foreign Office, Bonn, 1 March 1961: PA, AA, B92, no. 152; Embassy of the German Embassy in Luxembourg to German Foreign Office, Bonn, 24 September 1958: PA, AA, B92, no. 128. See also Lina Nikou, *Besuche in der alten Heimat: Einladungsprogramme für ehemals Verfolgte des Nationalsozialismus in München* (Frankfurt: Neofelis, 2020) and Nikou, *Zwischen Imagepflege und moralischer Verpflichtung und Erinnerungen: Das Besucherprogramm für jüdische ehemalige Hamburger Bürgerinnen und Bürger* (Hamburg: Dölling und Galitz, 2011). See also Schenderlein, *Germany on Their Minds*, 81–211.

36. Joachim Prinz, Special Debate "Germans and Jews," WJC 5th Plenary Assembly, Brussels 1966: AJA, MS-673, box 4/7. See also Tobias Winstel, "'Healed Biographies?' Jewish Remigration and Indemnification for National Socialist Injustice," *LBIY* 49 (2004): 137–152.

37. Telegram of the German Embassy to German Foreign Office, Bonn, 19 June 1959: PA, AA, B 92, no. 128.

38. A. L. Easterman to Joachim Prinz, WJC, 17 November 1959: AJA, MS-673, box 4/5. "Heuss Finds Anti-Semitism in West Germany Minor," *Int. Herald Tribune*, 24 July 1959: AJA, MS-673, box 1. "German Jew Scores A U.S. Jewish Group," *New York Times*, 11 November 1959: AJA, MS-673, nearprint-bio.

39. Joachim Prinz to Joachim Fest, 23 January 1963: AJA, MS-673, box 3/2.

40. Werner Steltzer to Joachim Prinz, 27 July 1966: AJA, MS-673, box 4/7. In his answer, Prinz expressed his hopes for a political change in Germany with the rise of the Social Democratic Party, which might ultimately bring change to society and politics. Joachim Prinz to Werner Steltzer, 30 August 1966: AJA, MS-673, box 4/7.

41. Memorandum from Will Maslow, AJC, to Joachim Prinz, AJC, 4 February 1966: AJA, MS-673, box 1/3.

42. Stephan Schaller to Joachim Prinz, 6 February 1968: AJA, MS-673, box 1/7; Joachim Prinz to Nachum Goldman, 4 May 1966: AJA, MS-673, box 1/5; A. L. Sachar to Joachim Prinz, 11 April 1968: AJA, MS-673, box 4/1; Joachim Prinz to Kurt Eberhardt, 27 January 1966: AJA, MS-673, box 1/3. C. Tesch to J. Prinz, 4 January 1967: AJA, MS-673, box 1/6.

43. Abraham Sachar to Joachim Prinz, 24 February 1966: AJA, MS-673, box 4/1; and Joachim Prinz, "Germans and Jews—Is There a Bridge?," manuscript: AJA, MS-673, box 7/5.

44. Herbert A. Strauss and Kurt R. Grossmann, eds., *Gegenwart im Rückblick: Festgabe für die Jüdische Gemeinde zu Berlin 25 Jahre nach dem Neubeginn* (Heidelberg: Lothar Stiehm, 1970).

45. Schenderlein, *Germany on Their Minds*, 145–153. Max Nussbaum, "Ist Versöhnung Möglich?," *Aufbau*, 9 October 1959. Voice of America, German Sermonette, 11 October 1959, and Church of the AIR, KNX, 11 October 1959, "Is Atonement with Germany Possible?": AJA, MS-705, box 5/6.

46. Joseph Asher, "A Rabbi Asks: Isn't It Time We Forgave the Germans?," *Look* magazine, 20 April 1965.

47. Simcha Kling, "A New Look at Germany . . .," *The Messenger Congregation Adath Jeshurun, Louisville, KY*, April 1967.

48. Niemeier, EKD (Evangelische Kirche Deutschlands), to J. Asher, 6 October 1971, and J. Asher to Niemeier, EKD, 14 February 1969: BANC, Mss. Coll. 2010/783, box 1. "Olive Branch or Grave—Which One?" *Daily News*, 2 November 1965; "He'll Reintroduce Germans to Jews: Greensboro Rabbi Will Teach at Berlin University," *Charlotte Observer*, 16 October 1966; Kling, "A New Look at Germany." Ekkehard Klausa to the participants of a conference discussing the memorial site Haus der Wannsee-Konferenz, 30 October 1987: BANC, Mss. Coll. 2010/783, box 4.

49. World Union for Progressive Judaism, Berlin Week, Program, 4–11 April 1965: courtesy of Gaby Müller-Oehlrichs (chief librarian), Haus der Wannsee-Konferenz, library.

50. See Levinson, *Ein Ort*, 231–232; among the young people who went to London were Uri Themal, Adi Asabi, and Daniela Tau.

51. Ibid.

52. Joachim Prinz to Balfour Brickner (UAHC Commission on Interfaith Activities), 16 March 1966: AJA, MS-673, box 1/3.

53. Levinson, *Ein Ort*, 199.

54. Ibid., 221–222. N. P. Levinson to Max Nussbaum, 21 June 1971; Max Nussbaum to N. P. Levinson, 13 September 1971, with the manuscript "Mein Leben in Amerika" by Max Nussbaum: AJA, MS-705, box 8/2.

55. Levinson, *Ein Ort*, 245–252.

56. Paul Martin, "Planting New Jewish Roots," *Newsweek*, 7 April 1980, 52. Alexander Guttmann to Leon Feldman, 18 February 1980: AJA, MS-663, box 4/15; and Alexander Guttmann to Robert S. Schine, 9 May 1980: AJA, MS-663, box 4/15.

57. Alexander Guttman to Leon Feldman, 28 September 1979: AJA, MS-663, box 4/15. See also the contract between the HJS and Alexander Guttmann, 27

August 1980: AJA, MS-663, box 4/15; Michael Hierholzer, "Verschüttetes Wissen bergen und wiederbeleben," *Frankfurter Allgemeine Zeitung*, 16 July 1981, 23: AJA, MS-663, box 4/15; Memorandum, HUC, from Adrienne Polster to A. Guttmann, 28 September 1981 and A. Guttmann to Harold Epstein, HUC-JIR, 4 October 1981: AJA, MS-663, box 4/15.

58. Jeffrey Peck, *Being Jewish in the New Germany* (New Brunswick, NJ: Rutgers University Press, 2006), 40–59.

59. Levinson, *Ein Ort*, 252.

60. Eric Lidji, *The Seventeenth Generation: The Lifework of Rabbi Walter Jacob* (Pittsburgh: Rodef Shalom, 2018), 195.

61. Ibid., 177.

62. Ibid., 182–184.

63. Ibid., 185–204.

64. Walter Jacob to Fae R. Asher, 28 February 2000: BANC, Mss. Coll. 2010/783, box 4.

65. Rabbinerseminar zu Berlin, https://rabbinerseminar.de.

66. Zacharias Frankel College, http://zacharias-frankel-college.de.

67. "Zentralrat der Juden empört über neuen Träger von Rabbinerschule," *Der Spiegel*, 13 January 2023, https://www.spiegel.de/panorama/bildung/abraham-geiger-kolleg-in-potsdam-streit-ueber-liberale-rabbinerschule-in-potsdam-hoert-nicht-auf-a-eea89ec6-4e38-477c-a783-19607569ef9e.

68. Walter Jacob, "Keepers of the Flame," *Reform Judaism* 35, no. 4 (2007): 61–63.

Conclusion

1. See, for example, Amos Elon, *The Pity of It All: A Portrait of the German-Jewish Epoch, 1743–1933* (London: Penguin, 2004).

2. See David Jünger and Anna Ulrich, "German-Jewish Agency in Times of Crisis, 1914–1938," *LBIY* 66 (2021): 3–5 and a collection of articles addressing this question in the *Leo Baeck Institute Yearbook*.

3. A number of works discuss refugee returns to Germany, but few explore this topic within the framework of the life cycle. Kaja Kaźmierska's stimulating work on Poland and Holocaust survivors takes this approach; see Kaja Kaźmierska, *Biography and Memory: The Generational Experience of the Shoah Survivors* (Boston: Academic Studies, 2012).

4. Yotam Hotam, ed., *Deutsch-Jüdische Jugendliche im "Zeitalter der Jugend"* (Göttingen: V & R Unipress, 2009).

5. David Jünger, "In the Presence of the Past: Rabbi Joachim Prinz, Holocaust Memory, and the Fight for Jewish Survival in Postwar America," in *Reconstructing the Old Country: American Jewry in the Post-Holocaust Decades*,

ed. Eliyana Adler and Sheila Jelen (Detroit: Wayne State University Press, 2017), 306–313.

6. See Stephanie Zloch, Lars Müller, and Simone Lässig, *Wissen in Bewegung: Migration und Globale Verflechtungen in der Zeitgeschichte seit 1945* (Berlin: De Gruyter, 2018), 1–35.

7. The Rabbi Dr. Joseph Breuer Foundation, https://www.rabbibreuerfoundation.org/; see also Zev Eleff, "Between Bennett and Amsterdam Avenues: The Complex American Legacy of Samson Raphael Hirsch, 1939–2013," *Tradition* 46 (2013): 8–27.

8. In fact, the history of this last generation is missing from the existing literature on the American Reform Movement, which has so far only focused on the knowledge transfer from Germany to America in the nineteenth century, not the twentieth century, and the return of the movement to central Europe after the reunification of Germany.

9. This is made clear in Prinz's speech during the March on Washington; see Joachim Prinz, "Civil Rights," http://www.joachimprinz.com/civilrights.htm.

10. See Eric Lidji, *The Seventeenth Generation: The Lifework of Rabbi Walter Jacob* (Pittsburgh: Rodef Shalom, 2018).

11. Walter Jacob, "Keepers of the Flame," *Reform Judaism* 35, no. 4 (2007): 61–63.

12. Jonathan Sarna, *American Judaism* (New Haven, CT: Yale University Press, 2004), 274–355.

13. Hasia Diner, *We Remember with Reverence and Love: American Jews and the Myth of Silence after the Holocaust, 1945–1962* (New York: New York University Press, 2009), 365–390.

14. Markus Krah, *American Jewry and the Re-Invention of the East European Jewish Past*, New Perspectives on Modern Jewish History 9, ed. Cornelia Wilhelm (Berlin: De Gruyter, 2018), 241–258.

BIBLIOGRAPHY

"א. גרופע דייטשע ישיבה בחורים אין דער באלטימארער ישיבת, נר ישראל." *Jewish American Family Magazine and Gazette* 37, no. 36 (7 July 1939): 1-3.
Adler, Leo. "Israelitische Religionsgemeinschaft of Wurttemberg: Development and Changes." *LBIY* 5 (1960): 251–261.
Altmann, Alexander. "The German Rabbi, 1910–1939." *LBIY* 19 (1974): 31-49.
———. "Jewish Theology in 20th Century Germany." *LBIY* 1 (1956): 193-216.
———. *Moses Mendelssohn: A Biographical Study*. London: Routledge & Kegan Paul, 1973.
Amann, William F. "The Displaced Scholar in America." *Journal of Higher Education* 21 (1950): 276-277.
Arkush, Allan. "The Contribution of Alexander Altmann to the Study of Moses Mendelssohn." *LBIY* 34 (1989): 415-420.
Asher, Joseph. "A Rabbi Asks: Isn't It Time We Forgave the Germans?" *Look Magazine*, 20 April 1965.
Atlas, Samuel. "Man and the Ethical Idea of God." *CCAR Journal* 15 (1968): 40–53.
Auerbach, Moses. "Die Bildungsfrage in Der Thora-Treuen Judenheit Deutschlands." In *Vom Sinn des Judentums: Ein Sammelbuch zu Ehren Nathan Birnbaums*, edited by Abraham Elijah Kaplan and Max Landau, 225-232. Frankfurt: Hermon, 1925.
Baeck, Leo. "Israel und das Deutsche Volk." *Merkur* 10 (October 1952): 911.
Baker, Leonard. *Hirt der Verfolgten*. Stuttgart: Klett-Cotta, 1982.
Bamberger, Fritz. "The Arden House Conference: 'Exploring a Typology of German Jewry.'" *LBIY* 19 (1974): 3–10.
———. "Julius Guttmann: Philosophers of Judaism." *LBIY* 5 (1960): 3-34.
Barth, Lewis M., and Ruth Nussbaum, eds. *Max Nussbaum: From Berlin to Hollywood. A Midcentury Vision of Jewish Life*. Malibu: Pangloss, 1994.

Bauer, Richard, and Michael Brenner, eds. *Jüdisches München: Vom Mittelalter bis zur Gegenwart*. Munich: C. H. Beck, 2004.

Bauman, Mark, and Berkley Kalin, eds. *Quiet Voices: Southern Rabbis and Black Civil Rights 1880s to 1990s*. Tuscaloosa: University of Alabama Press, 1997.

Benz, Wolfgang. "Rückkehr auf Zeit: Erfahrungen deutsch-jüdischer Emigranten mit Einladungen in Heimatstädte." *Exilforschung* 9 (1991): 196-207.

Berichte des Jüdisch-Theologischen Seminars (Fraenkelscher Stiftung) Hochschule für Jüdische Theologie, für das Jahr 1930-1937. Breslau: Breslau, 1930-1937.

Berkovits, Eliezer. "Final Solution—Universal?" *Confronting Omnicide* (1991): 259-267.

Bigsby, Christopher. *Remembering and Imagining the Holocaust: The Chain of Memory*. Cambridge: Cambridge University Press, 2006.

Bomhoff, Hartmut. *Ernst Ludwig Ehrlich—Prägende Jahre: Eine Biographie*. Berlin: De Gruyter, 2015.

Brämer, Andreas. "'... die Rückkehr eines Rabbiners nach Deutschland ist keine Selbstverständlichkeit': Zur Remigration jüdischer Geistlicher nach Westdeutschland (1945-1965)." In *"Auch in Deutschland waren wir nicht wirklich zu Hause": Jüdische Remigration nach 1945*, edited by Irmela von der Lühe, Axel Schildt, and Stefanie Schüler-Springorum, 169-189. Göttingen: Wallstein, 2008.

Braunwarth, Esther. *Interkulturelle Kooperation in Deutschland am Beispiel der Gesellschaften für christlich-jüdische Zusammenarbeit*. Munich: Utz, 2011.

Brenner, Michael. *The Renaissance of Jewish Culture in Weimar Germany*. New Haven, CT: Yale University Press, 2009.

Brenner, Michael, and Stefan Rohrbacher, eds. *Wissenschaft vom Judentum*. Göttingen: Vandenhoek & Ruprecht, 2000.

Breuer, Isaac. "Die Deutsche Orthodoxie im Jahre des Weltkrieges." *Jüdische Monatsschrift* 2, no. 2 (1915): 60-64.

———. *Ein Kampf Um Gott*. Frankfurt: Verlag von Sander and Friedberg, 1920.

———. "Rabbiner Hirsch als Wegweiser in die Jüdische Geschichte." *Nachlaß Z'wi: Eine Monatsschrift für Judentum in Lehre und Tat* 5, no. 4 (February 1935): 69-84.

Breuer, Jacob. "American Yeshiva Problems." *Mitteilungen* 17 (December 1955): 1-2.

———. "Die Beth-Jacob-Schule unserer Gemeinde." *Mitteilungen* 2 (9 August 1940): 1-2.

———. "Probleme der Jüdischen Schule in Amerika." *Mitteilungen* 3 (January 1942): 2-3.

Breuer, Joseph. "Samson Raphael Hirsch Jeshiva." *Mitteilungen* 6 (June/July 1944): 1.

Breuer, Mordecai. *Jüdische Orthodoxie im Deutschen Reich, 1871-1918*. Frankfurt: Jüdischer Verlag bei Athenäum, 1986.

Brill, Alan. "A Tiny, but Articulate Minority." *Tradition* 41 (2008): 1-35.
Brocke, Michael, and Julius Carlebach, eds. *Biographisches Handbuch der Rabbiner*. 2 vols. Munich: K. G. Saur, 2004-2009.
Buber, Martin. *On Judaism*. Edited by Nahum Glatzer. New York: Schocken Books, 1967.
Buchdahl, Max. *Return of the Exiled*. Baltimore: Buchdahl, 2014.
Büttner, Ursula, and Martin Geschrat. *Die verlassenen Kinder der Kirche: Der Umgang mit Christen jüdischer Herkunft im "Dritten Reich."* Göttingen: Vandenhoeck & Ruprecht, 1998.
Carlebach, Alexander. "The German-Jewish Immigration and Its Influence on Synagogue Life in the USA (1933-1942)." *LBIY* 9 (1964): 351-372.
―――. "A German Rabbi Goes East." *LBIY* 6 (1961): 60-121.
Carmilly-Weinberger, Moshe. *The Rabbinical Seminary of Budapest, 1877-1977: A Centennial Volume*. New York: Sefer-Hermon, 1986.
Cohen, Judah. "Singing Out for Judaism: A History of Song Leaders and Song Leading at Olin Sang Ruby Union Institute." In *A Place of Our Own: The Rise of Reform Jewish Camping*, edited by Michael M. Lorge and Gary P. Zola, 173-208. Tuscaloosa: University of Alabama Press, 2006.
Cohn, Emil. *Judentum, ein Aufruf an die Zeit*. Munich: Georg Müller, 1923.
Damashek, Richard. *A Brand Plucked from the Fire: The Life of Rabbi Herman E. Schaalman*. Jersey City, NJ: KTAV, 2013.
―――. "The Gang of Five: The Impact of Five German Rabbinic Students on Twentieth-Century Reform Judaism: From Berlin to Cincinnati." *CCAR Journal* 63 (Fall 2016): 5-21.
Daniels, Roger. *Guarding the Golden Door: American Immigration Policy and Immigrants since 1882*. New York: Hill and Wang, 2004.
Daum, Andreas, Hartmut Lehmann, and James Sheehan, eds. *The Second Generation: Émigrés from Nazi Germany as Historians*. New York: Berghahn Books, 2016.
Diner, Hasia. *We Remember with Reverence and Love: American Jews and the Myth of Silence after the Holocaust, 1945-1962*. New York: New York University Press, 2009.
Dobkowski, Michael N. "'The Fourth Reich': German-Jewish Religious Life in America Today." *Judaism* 27, no. 1 (1978): 80-95.
―――. *Jewish American Voluntary Organizations*. Westport, CT: Greenwood, 1986.
Duggan, Stephen, and Betty Drury. *The Rescue of Science and Learning: The Story of the Emergency Committee in Aid of Displaced Foreign Scholars*. New York: Macmillan, 1948.
Eicher, Peter, Jakob Petuchowski, and Walter Strolz, eds. *Offenbarung im christlichen und jüdischen Glaubensverständnis*. Freiburg: Herder, 1982.

Eisner, Isi Jacob. "Reminiscences of the Berlin Rabbinical Seminary." *LBIY* 12 (1967): 32-52.

Elazar, Daniel J., and Rela Mintz Geffen. *The Conservative Movement in Judaism: Dilemma and Opportunities.* Albany: SUNY Press, 2000.

Elbogen, Ismar. "American Jewish Scholarship: A Survey. In Honor of the Centenary of Kaufmann Kohler." *American Jewish Yearbook* 45 (1943/44): 47-65.

Eleff, Zev. *Modern Orthodox Judaism: A Documentary History.* Anthologies of Jewish Thought. Lincoln: University of Nebraska Press, 2016.

Eliav, Mordechai, and Esriel Hildesheimer. *Das Berliner Rabbinerseminar, 1873-1938: Seine Gründungsgeschichte, Seine Studenten.* Berlin: Hentrich & Hentrich, 2008.

Ellenson, David. "A Testimony to the World of German Orthodox Judaism: A Translation of Rabbi Jehiel Jacob Weinberg's Introduction to His Seridei Eish." In *The Individual in History: Essays in Honor of Jehuda Reinharz*, edited by ChaeRan Y. Freeze, Sylvia Fuks Fried, and Eugene R. Sheppard, 419-431. Waltham, MA: Brandeis University Press, 2015.

Erikson, Eric H. *Identity and the Life Cycle.* New York: Norton, 1980.

———. *The Life Cycle Completed.* New York: Norton, 1998.

Fackenheim, Emil. *An Epitaph for German Judaism: From Halle to Jerusalem.* Madison: University of Wisconsin Press, 2007.

———. *The Jewish Return into History: Reflections in the Age of Auschwitz and a New Jerusalem.* New York: Schocken Books, 1978.

———. *To Mend the World: Foundations of Post-Holocaust Jewish Thought.* Bloomington: Indiana University Press, 1994.

"Faculty Promotions Honor Yeshiva College Scholars." *Yeshiva College Quarterly* 4, no. 5 (December. 1941): 1, 4.

Festpredigt zum 50jährigen Jubiläum der Synagoge in München, gehalten in der Synagoge zu München am 5. Sept. 1937, Erew Rosch-Haschonoh 5698. Munich: Vorstand der Israelitischen Kultusgemeinde, 1937.

Fierman, Floyd S. "The Effort to Rescue Jewish Scholars from Nazi Germany." *El Paso Jewish Historical Review* 4 (1987): 1-30.

Foschepoth, Joseph. *Im Schatten der Vergangenheit: Die Anfänge der Gesellschaften für Christlich-Jüdische Zusammenarbeit.* Göttingen: Vandenhoek & Ruprecht, 1993.

Fuchs, Richard. "The 'Hochschule für die Wissenschaft des Judentums' in the Period of Nazi Rule." *LBIY* 12 (1967): 3-31.

Fuchs, Werner, Martin Kohli, and Fritz Schütze. "Vorwort der Herausgeber." In *Biographie und Gesellschaft*, edited by Werner Fuchs, Martin Kohli, and Fritz Schütze, vol. 1, 3–4 (= *Methoden der Biographie und Lebenslaufforschung*, edited by Wolfgang Voges). Opladen: VS Verlag für Sozialforschung, 1987.

Gabler, Neal. *An Empire of Their Own: How the Jews Invented Hollywood.* New York: Anchor Books, 1988.

Geller, Jay Howard. *Jews in Post-Holocaust Germany, 1945-1953*. Cambridge: Cambridge University Press, 2005.
Gerson, Judith M., and Diane L. Wolf, eds. *Sociology Confronts the Holocaust: Memories and Identities in Jewish Diasporas*. Durham, NC: Duke University Press, 2007.
Gillman, Neil. *Conservative Judaism: The New Century*. West Orange, NJ: Behrman House, 1993.
Gilmore, Glenda Elizabeth. *Defying Dixie: The Radical Roots of Civil Rights, 1919-1950*. New York: Norton, 2008.
Ginat, Jochanan. "The Jewish Teacher in Germany." *LBIY* 19 (1974): 71-95.
Glatzer, Nahum N. "The Frankfurt Lehrhaus." *LBIY* 1 (1956): 105-122.
———. *Franz Rosenzweig, His Life and Thought*. New York: Schocken Books, 1961.
———. "Leopold Zunz and the Revolution of 1848: With Four Letters by Leopold Zunz." *LBIY* 5 (1960): 122-139.
Goldstein, Eric. *The Price of Whiteness: Jews, Race, and American Identity*. Princeton, NJ: Princeton University Press, 2006.
Goodwin, James. *Autobiography: The Self Made Text*. New York: Twayne, 1993.
Goschler, Constantin. "The Attitude towards Jews in Bavaria after the Second World War." *LBIY* 36 (1991): 443-458.
Gosewinkel, Dieter. *Einbürgern und Ausschließen: Die Nationalisierung der Staatsangehörigkeit vom Deutschen Bund bis zur Bundesrepublik*. Göttingen: Vandenhoek & Ruprecht, 2001.
Greenberg, Cheryl Lynn. *Troubling the Waters: Black Jewish Relations in the American Century*. Princeton, NJ: Princeton University Press, 2006.
Grill, Tobias. "Preface." In *Jews and Germans in Eastern Europe: Shared and Comparative Histories*, vii–xxii. New Perspective on Modern Jewish History 8, edited by Tobias Grill. Berlin: De Gruyter, 2018.
Grobman, Alex. *Rekindling the Flame: American Jewish Chaplains and the Survivors of European Jewry, 1944-1948*. Detroit: Wayne State University Press, 1993.
Grossmann, Atina. "Rabbi Steven Schwarzschild's Reports from Berlin, 1948–1950." *LBIY* 60 (2015): 237–242.
Gruenewald, Max. "The Beginning of the 'Reichsvertretung.'" *LBIY* 1 (1956): 57-67.
———. *Here, There & Above*. New York: KTAV, 1979.
———. "The Jewish Teacher." *LBIY* 19 (1974): 63-69.
———. "The Modern Rabbi." *LBIY* 2 (1957): 85-97.
Gruner, Wolf. "Die Radikalisierung der NS-Verfolgung und die Berliner Jüdinnen und Juden." In *Ausgewiesen! Berlin, 28.10.1938: Die Geschichte der "Polenaktion,"* edited by Alina Bothe and Gertrud Pickhan, 71–90. Berlin: Metropol, 2018.

Gurock, Jeffrey. *The Men and Women of Yeshiva: Higher Education, Orthodoxy, and American Judaism.* New York: Columbia University Press, 1988.

Guttmann, Alexander. *Hochschule Retrospective : Reminiscences on the Occasion of the One Hundredth Anniversary of the Opening of the Hochschule Für Die Wissenschaft Des Judentums.* New York: Central Conference of American Rabbis, 1972.

———. "Humane Insights of the Rabbis Particularly with Respect to the Holocaust." *HUC Annual* XLVI (1975): 433-455.

Haberman, Joshua O. "The Revelation in Modern Jewish Theology." DHL diss., HUC Cincinnati, 1966.

Haberman, Joshua. "The Validation of Revelation." DHL diss., HUC Cincinnati, 1966.

———. *Three Cities in the Making of a Rabbi: Vienna, Washington, and Jerusalem.* Washington, DC: New Publishing Partners, 2012.

Hamburger, Wolfgang. "Abraham Geiger as Reformer and Theologian: First Phase, as Presented in Wissenschaftliche Zeitschrift fuer Juedische Theologie." Rabbinic thesis, HUC Cincinnati, 1952.

———. "Teacher in Berlin and Cincinnati." *LBIY* 2 (1957): 27-34.

Harris, Bonnie Mae. "From German Jews to Polish Refugees: Germany's Polenaktion and the Zbaszyn Deportations of October 1938." *Kwartalnik Historii Żydów* 230 (2009): 175-205.

———. "The Polenaktion of October 28, 1938: Prelude to Kristallnacht and Pattern for Deportation." In *Holocaust Persecution: Responses and Consequences*, edited by Nancy Rupprecht and Wendy Koenig, 56-76. Newcastle upon Tyne: Cambridge Scholars, 2010.

Haupt, Heinz Gerhard, and Jürgen Kocka, eds. *Comparative and Transnational History: Central European Approaches and New Perspectives.* New York: Berghahn Books, 2009.

Heim, Susanne, ed. *Verfolgung und Ermordung der Juden.* Vol. 2: *Deutsches Reich 1938–August 1939.* Munich: Oldenburg, 2009.

Henrix, Hans Hermann. "Jakob J. Petuchowski (1925-1991): Rabbi, Scholar, Ecumenist." In *Jewish and Christian Liturgy and Worship: New Insights into Its History and Interaction*, edited by Albert Gerhards and Clemens Leonhard, 7-28. Leiden: Brill, 2007.

Heschel, Abraham Joshua. *God in Search of Man: A Philosophy of Judaism.* Philadelphia: Jewish Publication Society, 1955.

———. *Man Is Not Alone: A Philosophy of Religion.* New York: Octagon Books, 1951.

———. *Das prophetische Bewusstsein.* Kraków: Verlag der Polnische Akademie der Wissenschaft, 1935. PhD diss., Berlin, 1935.

———. *The Prophets.* New York: Harper and Row, 1962.

Heschel, Susannah. "Theological Affinities in the Writings of Abraham Joshua Heschel and Martin Luther King, Jr." In *Black Zion*, edited by Yvonne Chireau and Nathaniel Deutsch, 168-186. New York: Oxford University Press, 2000.

Heusler, Andreas. *Das Braune Haus: Wie München zur "Hauptstadt der Bewegung" wurde*. Stuttgart: DVA, 2008.

Heusler, Andreas, and Angelika Baumann, eds. *München arisiert: Entrechtung und Enteignung der Juden in der NS-Zeit*. Munich: C. H. Beck, 2004.

Hildesheimer, Esriel. "Die Studenten des Rabbinerseminars zu Berlin." In *Das Berliner Rabbinerseminar 1873-1938*, edited by Chana Schütz and Hermann Simon, 49-271. Berlin: Hentrich & Hentrich, 2006.

Hirsch, Richard G., and World Union for Progressive Judaism. *A Letter from Jerusalem to the Leadership of Our Movement*. Jerusalem: World Union for Progressive Judaism, 1984.

Hirschberger, Gilad. "Collective Trauma and the Social Construction of Meaning." *Frontiers in Psychology* 9 (2018): 1-14.

Hoffmann, Christhard. "Deutsch-jüdische Geschichtswissenschaft in der Emigration, das Leo Baeck Institut." In *Die Emigration der Wissenschaften nach 1933*, edited by Herbert Strauss, 257-279. Munich: Saur, 1991.

———. "Early, but Opposed—Supported, but Late: Two Berlin Seminaries Which Attempted to Move Abroad." *LBIY* 36 (1991): 267-304.

Holian, Anna. "Displacement and the Post-War Reconstruction of Education: Displaced Persons at the UNRRA University of Munich, 1945-1948." *Contemporary European History* 17 (2008): 167-195.

Holton, Gerald, and Gerhard Sonnert. *What Happened to the Children Who Fled Nazi Persecution*. New York: Palgrave Macmillan, 2006.

Homolka, Walter, and Heinz-Günther Schöttler. *Rabbi—Pastor—Priest: Their Roles and Profiles through the Ages*. Berlin: De Gruyter, 2013.

Hopstock, Katrin. "Bis zum Ende: Die letzen 50 Jahre der jüdischen Gemeinde." *Vierteljahresheft des Verkehrsvereins Speyer in Zusammenarbeit mit der Stadtverwaltung* 1 (1988): 2-18.

Horner, Deborah. *Emil Bernhard Cohn: Rabbi, Playwright and Poet*. Berlin: Hentrich & Hentrich, 2009.

Hotam, Yotam, ed. *Deutsch-Jüdische Jugendliche im "Zeitalter der Jugend."* Göttingen: V & R Unipress, 2009.

———. *Populäre Konstruktionen von Erinnerung im deutschen Judentum und nach der Emigration*. Göttingen: Vandenhoeck & Ruprecht, 2004.

Jacob, Walter. *Contemporary American Responsa*. New York: CCAR, 1998.

———. "The Contemporary Jew in the German Novel and Short History, 1800-1914." DHL diss., HUC, 1961.

———. "Keepers of the Flame." *Reform Judaism* 35, no. 4 (2007): 61-63.

---. *Questions and Reform Jewish Answers: New American Reform Responsa.* New York: CCAR, 1992.

The Jewish People from Holocaust to Nationhood. Series 1, Archives of the Central British Fund for World Jewish Relief: 1933–1960; A Listing and Guide to the Research Publications, microfilm collection. Reading: Research Publications, 1989.

The Jewish People from the Holocaust to Nationhood: 1933-1960, seventy-four microfilm reels, Woodbridge, CT: Research Publication, 1989.

Joselit, Jenna Weissman. *New York's Jewish Jews.* Bloomington: Indiana University Press, 1990.

Jospe, Alfred. "A Profession in Transition: The German Rabbinate, 1910-1939." *LBIY* 19 (1974): 51-61.

Jospe, Eva, and Raphael Jospe, eds. *To Leave Your Mark: Selections from the Writings of Alfred Jospe.* Hoboken, NJ: KTAV, 2000.

Jünger, David. "In the Presence of the Past: Rabbi Joachim Prinz, Holocaust Memory, and the Fight for Jewish Survival in Postwar America." In *Reconstructing the Old Country: American Jewry in the Post-Holocaust Decades*, edited by Eliyana Adler and Sheila Jelen, 306-313. Detroit: Wayne State University Press, 2017.

Jünger, David, and Anna Ulrich, "German-Jewish Agency in Times of Crisis, 1914–1938." *LBIY* 66 (2021): 3–5.

Jureit, Ulrike. *Erinnerungsmuster: Zur Methodik lebensgeschichtlicher Interviews mit Überlebenden der Konzentrations- und Vernichtungslager.* Hamburg: Ergebnisse, 1999.

---. *Generationenforschung.* Göttingen: V&R, 2006.

Jureit, Ulrike, and Michael Wildt, eds. *Generationen: Zur Relevanz eines wissenschaftlichen Grundbegriffs.* Hamburg: UTB, 2005.

Jütte, Robert. *Die Emigration der deutschsprachigen "Wissenschaft des Judentums": Die Auswanderung Jüdischer Historiker nach Palästina.* Stuttgart: Steiner, 1991.

---. "Not Welcomed with Open Arms: German Rabbis in Eretz Israel, 1938-1948." *LBIY* 57 (2012): 105-117.

Kaelter, Wolli, and Gordon Cohn. *From Danzig: An American Rabbi's Journey.* Malibu, CA: Pangloss, 1997.

Kahn, Ava F., and Adam Mendelsohn, eds. *Transnational Traditions: New Perspectives on American Jewish History.* Detroit: Wayne State University Press, 2014.

Kaplan, Edward K. "Coming to America: Abraham Joshua Heschel, 1940-1941." *Modern Judaism* 27 (2002): 129-145.

---. *Spiritual Radical: Abraham Joshua Heschel in America.* New Haven, CT: Yale University Press, 2007.

Kaplan, Edward K., and Samuel Dresner. *Abraham Joshua Heschel: Prophetic Witness.* New Haven, CT: Yale University Press, 1998.

Kaufmann, Irene. *Die Hochschule für die Wissenschaft des Judentums (1872-1942)*. Berlin: Hentrich & Hentrich, 2006.
Kaźmierska, Kaja. *Biography and Memory: The Generational Experience of the Shoah Survivors*. Boston: Academic Studies, 2012.
Kieval, Hillel. "The Lands Between: The Jews of Bohemia, Moravia and Slovakia to 1918." In *Where Cultures Meet: The Story of the Jews of Czechoslovakia*, edited by Natalia Berger, 23-51. Tel Aviv: Beth Hatefutsoth/Ministry of Defence, 1990.
Kingsley, Ralph P. "How Henry Kissinger Became My Cousin." *AJA* 33 (1981): 166-169.
Kisch, Guido, ed. *Das Breslauer Seminar: Jüdisch-Theologisches Seminar (Fraenkelscher Stiftung) in Breslau 1854–1938*. Tübingen: Gedächtnisschrift, 1963.
Kisseloff, Jeff. *You Must Remember This: An Oral History of Manhattan from the 1890s to World War II*. Orlando: Harcourt Brace Jovanovich, 1989.
Kober, Adolf. "150 Years of Religious Instruction." *LBIY* 2 (1957): 98-118.
Kohler, George Y. "Platzmachen für Gott: Else Lasker-Schüler, Rabbiner Kurt Wilhelm und der religiöse Liberalismus in Palästina." *Aschkenas* 21 (2013): 179–199.
Kohli, Martin. "Die Institutionalisierung des Lebenslaufs." *Kölner Zeitschrift für Soziologie und Sozialspychologie* 37 (1985): 1-29.
Kohli, Martin, and M. Szydlik, eds. *Generationen in Familie und Gesellschaft: Lebenslauf—Alter—Generation*. Opladen: Leske & Bucrich, 2000.
Krah, Markus. *American Jewry and the Re-Invention of the East European Jewish Past*. New Perspectives on Modern Jewish History 9, edited by Cornelia Wilhelm. Berlin: De Gruyter, 2018.
Kranzler, David. *Holocaust Hero: The Untold Story and Vignettes of Solomon Schonfeld*. Jersey City, NJ: KTAV, 2004.
Kranzler, David, and Dovid Landesman. *Rav Breuer: His Life and Legacy*. New York: Feldheim, 1998.
Kraut, Benny. *German-Jewish Orthodoxy in an Immigrant Synagogue: Cincinnati's New Hope Congregation and the Ambiguities of Ethnic Religion*. New York: Markus Wiener, 1988.
———. "Towards the Establishment of the National Conference of Christians and Jews: The Tenuous Road to Religious Goodwill in the 1920s." *American Jewish History* 77 (1988): 388-412.
Küng, Hans, and Walter Kasper, eds. *Jews and Christians*. New York: Seabury, 1975.
Künzl, Hannelore. *Islamische Stilelemente im Synagogenbau des 19. und frühen 20. Jahrhunderts*. Frankfurt a. M.: Verlag Peter Lang, 1984.
Kulka, Otto Dov, and Eberhard Jäckel. *Die Juden in den geheimen Stimmungsberichten 1933–1945*. Düsseldorf: Droste, 2004.
Landau, Maximilian. "Samson Raphael Hirsch und Unsere Zeit." *Nachlaß Z'wi: Eine Monatsschrift für Judentum in Lehre und Tat* 7, no. 1 (October 1936): 27-35.

Landesmann, Peter. "Die Geschichte der Ausbildung von Rabbinern in Wien bis zur Gründung der Jüdisch-Theologischen Lehranstalt (ITLA)." In *Wien und die Jüdische Erfahrung*, edited by Frank Stern and Barbara Eichinger, 143-153. Vienna: Böhlau, 2009.

Laqueur, Walter. *Geboren in Deutschland*. Berlin: Propyläen, 2000.

———. *Generation Exodus: The Fate of Young Jewish Refugees from Europe*. London: Bloomsbury, 2003.

Lässig, Simone. "How German Jewry Turned Bourgeois: Religion, Culture, and Social Mobility in the Age of Emancipation." *Bulletin of the GHI* 37 (2005): 59-73.

Lässig, Simone, and Swen Steinberg. "Knowledge on the Move: New Approaches toward a History of Migrant Knowledge." *Geschichte und Gesellschaft* 43 (2017): 313-346.

Lazarus, Paul. *Gedenkbuch: Beiträge zur Würdigung der letzten Rabbinergeneration in Deutschland*. Jerusalem: Jerusalem Post, 1961.

Lee, Helen. *Ties to the Homeland: Second Generation Transnationalism*. Cambridge: Cambridge Scholars, 2008.

Lehman, Robert. "Herzl's Zionist Ideology." Rabbinic thesis, HUC Cincinnati, 1954.

Lehmann, Hartmut, and James Sheehan, eds. *An Interrupted Past: German-Speaking Refugee Historians after 1933*. Cambridge: Cambridge University Press, 1991.

Lehrer, Erica. *Jewish Poland Revisited: Heritage Tourism in Unquiet Places*. Bloomington: Indiana University Press, 2013.

Lengyel, Gabor. *Moderne Rabbinerausbildung in Deutschland und Ungarn*. Berlin: Hopf, 2012.

Levinson, Nathan Peter. *Ein Ort ist, mit wem Du bist: Lebensstationen eines Rabbiners*. Berlin: Edition Hentrich, 1996.

———. *Ein Rabbiner in Deutschland: Aufzeichnungen zu Religion und Politik*. Gerlingen: Bleicher Verlag, 1987.

Lidji, Eric. *The Seventeenth Generation: The Lifework of Rabbi Walter Jacob*. Pittsburgh: Rodef Shalom, 2018.

Liebman, Charles S., and Asher Cohen. "Synagogue and State: Religion and Politics in Modern Israel." *Harvard International Review* 20 (1998): 70–73.

Living Legacy: Essays in Honor of Hugo Hahn. New York: Congregation Habonim, 1963.

Lorge, Michael, and Gary Zola. "The Beginning of Union Institute in Oconomowoc, Wisconsin, 1952-1970: Creation and Coalescence of the First UAHC Camp." In *A Place of Our Own: The Rise of Reform Jewish Camping*, edited by Michael M. Lorge and Gary P. Zola, 52-71. Tuscaloosa: University of Alabama Press, 2006.

Losego, Sarah Vanessa. "Überlegungen zur 'Biographie.'" *BIOS* 15 (2002): 24-47.

Lowenstein, Steven. *Frankfurt on the Hudson: The German-Jewish Community of Washington Heights, 1933-1983, Its Structure and Culture*. Detroit: Wayne State University Press, 1989.

———. "The German-Jewish Community of Washington Heights." *LBIY* 30 (1985): 245-254.

Lowenthal, David. *The Past Is a Foreign Country*. Cambridge: Cambridge University Press, 1985.

Marcus, Jacob Rader, and Abraham J. Peck, eds. *The American Rabbinate: A Century of Continuity and Change, 1883-1983*. Jersey City, NJ: KTAV, 1985.

Mausbach, Wilfried. "Auschwitz and Vietnam: West German Protests against America's War during the 1960s." In *Coping with the Nazi Past: West German Debates on Nazism and Generational Conflict, 1955-1975*, edited by Philipp Gassert, 279-298. New York: Berghahn Books, 2006.

Meisner, Marian. *A History of Milburn Township*. Milburn, NY: Milburn Short Hills Historical Society, 2002. https://millburnlibrary.org/wp-content/uploads/2021/05/HistoryMillburnTownshipEbook.pdf.

Mendes-Flohr, Paul. "Knowledge as Service: An Appreciation of Nahum N. Glatzer." *Jewish Studies* 31 (1991): 25–46.

Meyer, Michael A. "A Centennial History." In *Hebrew Union College—Jewish Institute of Religion at One Hundred Years*, edited by Samuel Karpf, 1–284. Cincinnati: HUC Press, 1976.

———. "Denken und Wirken Leo Baecks nach 1945." In *Leo Baeck 1873-1956: Aus dem Stamme von Rabbinen*, edited by Georg Heuberger and Fritz Backhaus, 21-40. Frankfurt: Jüdischer, 2001.

———. "Jakob J. Petuchowski (1925-1991)." *Proceedings of the American Academy of Religion* 58 (1992): 27-31.

———, ed. *Joachim Prinz, Rebellious Rabbi: An Autobiography—The German and Early American Years*. Bloomington: Indiana University Press, 2008.

———. "Modernity as a Crisis for the Jews." *Modern Judaism* 9 (1989): 151-164.

———. "The Refugee Rabbis: Trials and Transmissions." *LBIY* 57 (2012): 87-103.

———. "The Refugee Scholars Project of the Hebrew Union College." In *A Bicentennial Festschrift for Jacob R. Marcus*, edited by Bertram Wallace Korn, 359-375. New York: HUC Press, 1976.

———. *Response to Modernity: A History of the Reform Movement in Judaism*. New York: Oxford University Press, 1988.

———. "Scholarship and Worldliness: The Life and Work of Fritz Bamberger." *LBIY* 58 (2013): 143-158.

Meyer, Michael A., Mordechai Breuer, Michael Graetz, Michael Brenner, Stefi Jersch-Wenzel, Steven M. Lowenstein, Avraham Barkai, and Paul Mendes-Flohr, eds. *German-Jewish History in Modern Times: Renewal and Destruction, 1918–1945*. Vol. 4. New York: Columbia University Press, 1998.

Moscowitz, John, and Nathalie Fingerhut, eds. *A Rabbi of Words and Deeds: Essays in Honor of the 90th Birthday of W. Gunter Plaut*. Toronto: Holy Blossom Temple, 2002.

Nadell, Pamela S. *Conservative Judaism in America: A Biographical Dictionary and Sourcebook*. Westport, CT: Greenwood, 1988.

Nattermann, Ruth. *Deutsch-jüdische Geschichtsschreibung nach der Shoah: Die Gründungs- und Frühgeschichte des Leo Baeck Institute*. Essen: Klartext, 2004.

Neuberger, Herman N. *Neuberger Memorial Dinner*. Baltimore: Ner Israel, 2006.

———. *Treasuring His Legacy, Perpetuating the Mission*. Baltimore: Ner Israel Rabbinical College, 2006.

Niethammer, Lutz. "Die letzte Gemeinschaft: Über die Konstruierbarkeit von Generationen und ihre Grenzen." In *Historische Beiträge zur Generationsforschung*, edited by Bernd Weisbrod, 13-38. Göttingen: Wallstein, 2009.

Niewyk, Donald L. *The Jews in Weimar Germany*. New Brunswick: Transaction, 2001.

Nikou, Lina. *Besuche in der alten Heimat: Einladungsprogramme für ehemals Verfolgte des Nationalsozialismus in München*. Frankfurt: Neofelis, 2020.

———. *Zwischen Imagepflege und moralischer Verpflichtung und Erinnerungen: Das Besucherprogramm für jüdische ehemalige Hamburger Bürgerinnen und Bürger*. Hamburg: Dölling and Galitz, 2011.

Novick, Peter. *The Holocaust in American Life*. Boston: Houghton Mifflin, 1999.

Nussbaum, Max. "Kantianismus und Marxismus in der Socialphilosophie Max Adlers." PhD diss., University of Würzburg, 1931.

———. "Ministry under Stress." In *Gegenwart im Rückblick*, edited by Herbert Strauss and Kurt R. Grossmann, 239-247. Heidelberg: Lothar Stiehm, 1970.

Nussbaum, Ruth, and Lewis M. Barth, eds. *From Berlin to Hollywood: A Mid-Century Vision of Jewish Life*. Malibu, CA: Pangloss, 1994.

Ophir, Nathan. *Rabbi Shlomo Carlebach: Life, Mission, and Legacy*. Jerusalem: Urim, 2014.

Osten-Sacken, Peter von der. "Institut Kirche und Judentum (1960–2005): Geschichte, Ziele, Perspektiven. Bilanz und Perspektiven des christlich-jüdischen Dialogs." *Epd-Dokumentation* 9/10 (1 March 2005): 7-16.

Ottensoser, May, and Alex Rohberg. *Israelitische Lehrerbildungsanstalt Würzburg, 1864-1938*. Detroit: Harlo, 1982.

Paucker, Arnold, ed. *Die Juden im Nationalsozialistischen Deutschland*. Tübingen: Siebeck, Mohr, 1986.

———, ed. *The Jews in Nazi Germany, 1933-1943*. Tübingen: Siebeck, Mohr, 1986.

Peck, Jeffrey. *Being Jewish in the New Germany*. New Brunswick, NJ: Rutgers University Press, 2006.

Penkower, Noam. *The Holocaust and Israel Reborn: From Catastrophe to Sovereignty*. Urbana: University of Illinois Press, 1994.

Petuchowski, Jakob. "Abraham Geiger and Samuel Holdheim: Their Differences in Germany and Repercussions in America." *LBIY* 22 (1977): 139-159.

———, ed. *When Jews and Christians Meet.* Albany: SUNY Press, 1988.

Petuchowski, Jakob J. *Das Buch vom Volk des Buches: Jüdische Gedanken zur Buch- und Lesekultur.* Freiburg: Herder, 1982.

———. "The Development and Design of a German-Jewish Prayerbook." In *The Jewish Legacy and the German Conscience*, edited by Moses Rischin and Raphael Asher, 1711-1787. Berkeley, CA: Judah Magnes Museum, 1991.

———. *Ferner lehrten unsere Meister...: rabbinische Geschichten.* Freiburg: Herder, 1983.

———. *Mein Judesein: Wege und Erfahrungen eines deutschen Rabbiners.* Freiburg: Herder, 1992.

Petuchowski, Jakob, and Clemens Thoma, eds. *Lexikon der christlich-jüdischen Begegnung.* Freiburg: Herder 1997.

Pfeiffer, Klaus, and Joachim Rott, eds. *Die erste Ausbürgerungsliste vom 25. August 1933.* Berlin: Hentrich & Hentrich, 2016.

Plaut, W. Gunther. "Contributions to the History of German Jewry in the Eighteenth Century, from Hebrew and Missionary Sources." Rabbinic thesis, HUC, 1939.

———. *Deuteronomy: Commentary.* New York: Union of American Hebrew Congregations, 1983.

———. *More Unfinished Business.* Toronto: University of Toronto Press, 1997.

———. *The Torah: A Modern Commentary.* New York: CCAR, 2005.

———. *The Torah: The Five Books of Moses.* Philadelphia: Jewish Publication Society of America, 1963.

———. *Unfinished Business: An Autobiography.* Toronto: Lester & Orpen Dennys, 1981.

Prinz, Joachim. *Der Freitagabend.* Berlin: Brandus, 1935.

———. *Die Geschichten der Bibel.* Berlin: Erich Reiss, 1934.

———. *Helden und Abenteuer.* Berlin: P. Baumann, 1930.

———. *Jüdische Geschichte.* Berlin: Verlag für Kulturpolitik, 1931.

———. "The Right to Be Different." In *Best Jewish Sermons of 5714*, edited by Rabbi Saul I. Teplitz. New York: Jonathan David, 1954.

———. *Wir Juden.* Berlin: Erich Reiss. 1934.

———. "Zum Begriff der religiösen Erfahrung: Ein Beitrag zur Theorie der Religion." PhD diss., University of Giessen, 1927.

Raim, Edith. *Nazi Crimes against Jews in German Post-War Justice.* Berlin: De Gruyter, 2015.

Rheins, Carl J. "Deutscher Vortrupp, Gefolgschaft deutscher Juden, 1933-1935." *LBIY* 26 (1981): 207-229.

Richarz, Monika, ed. *Jüdisches Leben in Deutschland: Selbstzeugnisse zur Sozialgeschichte, 1918-1945.* Vol. 3. Stuttgart: DVA, 1982.

Richter, Karl. "A Refugee Rabbinate." In *The Jewish Legacy and German Conscience*, edited by Moses Rischin and Raphael Asher, 205-218. Berkeley, CA: Judah L. Magnes Museum, 1991.

Rinott, Chanoch. "Major Trends in Jewish Youth Movements in Germany." *LBIY* 19 (1974): 80-83.

Rischin, Moses. "The German Imperative and the Jewish Response." In *The Jewish Legacy and German Conscience*, edited by Moses Rischin and Raphael Asher, 1-10. Berkeley, CA: Judah L. Magnes Museum, 1991.

Rischin, Moses, and Raphael Asher, eds. *The Jewish Legacy and the German Conscience: Essays in Memory of Rabbi Joseph Asher*. Berkeley, CA: Judah L. Magnes Museum, 1991.

Rock-Singer, Cara. "A Prophetic Guide for a Perplexed World: Louis Finkelstein and the 1940 Conference on Science, Philosophy, and Religion." *Religion & American Culture* 29 (2019): 179-215.

Röder, Werner, and Herbert Strauss, eds. *Biographisches Handbuch der deutschsprachigen Emigration 1933-1945*. 3 vols. Munich: Saur, 1980-1983.

Rohde, Saskia. "Die Zerstörung der Synagogen unter dem Nationalsozialismus." In *Verdrängung und Vernichtung der Juden unter dem Nationalsozialismus*, edited by Arno Herzig and Ina Lorenz, 153-172. Hamburg: Christians, 1992.

Rosenstock, Werner. "The Jewish Youth Movement." *LBIY* 19 (1974): 97-105.

Rosenthal, Gabriele, and Artur Bogner. *Ethnicity, Belonging and Biography, Ethnographical and Biographical Perspectives*. Münster: Lit-Verlag, 2009.

Rosenzweig, Franz. *On Jewish Learning*, edited by Nahum Glatzer. New York: Schocken Books, 1955.

Rozenblit, Marsha. "Jewish Identity and the Modern Rabbi: The Cases of Isak Noa Mannheimer, Adolf Jellinek and Moritz Güdemann." *LBIY* 35 (1990): 103-131.

———. "The Seminary during the Holocaust Years." In *Tradition Renewed: A History of the Jewish Theological Seminary of America*, edited by Jack Wertheimer, vol. 2, 283-304. New York: Jewish Theological Seminary, 1997.

Rupprecht, Nancy, and Wendy König, eds. *Holocaust Persecution: Responses and Consequences*. Newcastle: Cambridge Scholars, 2010.

Rürup, Miriam, and Doerte Bischoff, eds. *Ausgeschlossen: Staatsbürgerschaft, Staatenlosigkeit und Exil* (Exilforschung, 36). Munich: Edition text + kritik, 2018.

Sabrow, Martin, and Norbert Frei, eds. *Die Geburt des Zeitzeugen nach 1945*. Göttingen: Wallstein, 2012.

Sarna, Jonathan. *American Judaism*. New Haven, CT: Yale University Press, 2004.

Schenderlein, Anne Clara. *Germany on Their Minds*. New York: Berghahn Books, 2020.

———. "Ties of Belonging: A Transnational History of German Jewish Identities." MA thesis, University of California at San Diego, 2014.

Schochow, Werner. *Deutsch-jüdische Geschichtswissenschaft: Eine Geschichte ihrer Organisationsformen unter besonderer Berücksichtigung der Fachbibliographie.* Mit einem Geleitwort von Guido Kisch. Berlin: Colloquium, 1969.

Schorsch, Emil. "The Rural Jew: Observations on the Paper of Werner J. Cahnman." *LBIY* 19 (1974): 131–135.

Schorsch, Ismar. "German Anti-Semitism in the Light of Post-War Historiography." *LBIY* 19 (1974): 257–271.

———. "Jewish Reactions to German Anti-Semitism, 1870-1914." PhD diss., Columbia University Press, 1972.

———. "The Leo Baeck Institute: Continuity amid Desolation." *Leo Baeck Institute Year Book* 25 (1980): ix–xii.

Schrafstetter, Susannah. "The Diplomacy of Wiedergutmachung: Memory, the Cold War, and the Western European Victims of Nazism, 1956-1964." *Holocaust and Genocide Studies* 17 (2003): 459–479.

Schröder, Wilhelm Heinz. "Kollektive Biographien in der historischen Sozialforschung. Eine Einführung, in Lebenslauf und Gesellschaft: Zum Einsatz von kollektiven Biographien in der historischen Sozialforschung." In *Lebenslauf und Gesellschaft: Vom Einsatz von kollektiven Biographien in der historischen Sozialforschung* (Historisch Sozialwissenschaftliche Forschungen 18), edited by Heinz Wilhelm Schröder, 7-17. Stuttgart: Klett-Cotta, 1985.

Schulz, Andreas. *Generationswechsel und Historischer Wandel.* Historische Zeitschrift Beiheft 36. Munich: Oldenbourg, 2003.

Schulzinger, Robert D. *A Time for War: The United States and Vietnam, 1945-1975.* New York: Oxford University Press, 1997.

Schwab, Simon. *Heimkehr ins Judentum.* Frankfurt: Hermon, 1934.

Schwarzschild, Maimon. "A Note from Steven Schwarzschild and the Letters from Berlin." *LBIY* 60 (2015): 243-247.

Schwarzschild, Steven. "Franz Rosenzweig's Anecdotes about Hermann Cohen." In *Gegenwart im Rückblick: Festgabe für die Jüdische Gemeinde zu Berlin 25 Jahre nach dem Neubeginn*, edited by Herbert A. Strauss and Kurt R. Grossman, 209-218. Heidelberg: Lothar Stiehm, 1970.

———. "Germanism and Judaism—Hermann Cohen's Normative Paradigm of the German-Jewish Symbiosis." In *Jews and Germans from 1860 to 1933*, edited by David Bronsen, 129-172. Heidelberg: Universitätsverlag C. Winter, 1979.

———. "Report on Berlin on World Union for Progressive Judaism Conference in London, July 14-19, 1949." *LBIY* 60 (2015): 249-256.

———. *The Tragedy of Optimism: The Writings of Herman Cohen.* Albany: SUNY Press, 2018.

———. "Two Modern Jewish Philosophies of History: Nachman Krochmal and Hermann Cohen." DHL diss., HUC, 1955.

Schweitzer, Joszef. "Das Budapester Rabbinerseminar: Der Platz des jüdischen Rabbinerseminars in der jüdischen Wissenschaft." In *Wissenschaft des Judentums: Anfänge der Judaistik in Europa*, edited by Julius Carlebach, 74-85. Darmstadt: WBG, 1992.

Segev, Zohar. *The World Jewish Congress during the Holocaust: Between Activism and Restraint*. Berlin: De Gruyter, 2014.

Shapiro, Marc. "Torah im Derekh Eretz in the Shadow of Hitler." *Torah u-Maddah Journal* 14 (2006/2007): 84-96.

Shaprio, Marc B. *Between the Yeshiva World and Modern Orthodoxy: The Life and Works of Rabbi Jehiel Jacob Weinberg, 1884–1966*. Oxford: Littman Library of Jewish Civilization, 1999.

Sheppard, Eugene. "'I Am a Memory Come Alive': Nahum Glatzer and the Legacy of German Jewish Thought in America." *Jewish Quarterly Review* 94 (2004): 123–148.

Sheramy, Rona. "'Resistance and War': The Holocaust in American Jewish Education, 1945-1960." *American Jewish History (AJH)* 23 (1991): 287-313.

Sherman, Moshe. *Orthodox Judaism in America: A Biographical Dictionary and Sourcebook*. Westport, CT: Greenwood, 1996.

Shlomo Shafir. *Ambiguous Relations: The American Jewish Community and Germany since 1945*. Detroit: Wayne State University Press, 1999.

Sinn, Andrea. "The Return of Robert Raphael Geis to Germany: One of the Last Witnesses of German Jewry?" *European Judaism* 45 (2012): 123-138.

Sklare, Marshall. *America's Jews*. Waltham, MA: Brandeis University Press, 2006.

Slobin, Mark. *Chosen Voices: The Story of the American Cantorate*. Urbana: University of Illinois Press, 2002.

Slomovitz, Albert Isaac. *The Fighting Rabbis: Jewish Military Chaplains and American History*. New York: New York University Press, 1999.

Smith, Timothy L. "Religion and Ethnicity in America." *American Historical Review* 83:1155-1185.

Spalek, John, ed. *Deutsche Exilliteratur seit 1933*. 2 vols. Bern: Francke, 1976.

———, ed. *Deutschsprachige Exilliteratur*. 8 vols. Bern: Francke, 1989-2005.

Spillman, Lyn. "When Do Collective Memories Last? Founding Moments in the United States and Australia." *Social Science History* 22 (1998): 445-477.

Steckel, Charles W. *Destruction and Survival*. Los Angeles: Delmar, 1973.

Steidle, Hans. *Jakob Stoll und die Israelitische Lehrerbildungsanstalt: Eine Spurensuche*. Würzburg: Israelitische Kultusgemeinde, 2002.

Steinweis, Alan. *Kristallnacht 1938*. Stuttgart: Reclam, 2011.

Strauss, Herbert. *In the Eye of the Storm: Growing Up Jewish in Germany, 1918-1943*. New York: Fordham University Press, 1999.

———. "Jewish Emigration from Germany: Nazi Policies and Jewish Responses." *LBIY* 25 (1980): 313-361.

———. *Jewish Immigrants of the Nazi Period in the USA.* 7 vols. Munich: Saur, 1981.
Strauss, Herbert, Kurt Düwell, and Tilman Buddensieg, eds. *Emigration: Deutsche Wissenschaftler nach 1933.* Berlin: Technical University Berlin, 1987.
Strauss, Herbert A., and Kurt R. Grossmann, eds. *Gegenwart im Rückblick: Festgabe für die Jüdische Gemeinde zu Berlin 25 Jahre nach dem Neubeginn.* Heidelberg: Lothar Stiehm, 1970.
Sudfeld, Peter. "Reclaiming Heimat in Memories: Journal of Austrian Refugees." *Holocaust and Genocide Studies* 17, no. 2 (2003): 366-368.
Sussman, Lance, Kerry M. Olitzky, and Malcom H. Stern. *Reform Judaism in America: A Biographical Dictionary and Sourcebook.* Westport, CT: Greenwood, 1993.
Taubitz, Jan. *Holocaust Oral History und das lange Ende der Zeitzeugenschaft.* Göttingen: Wallstein, 2016.
"Teachers Seminary for Girls." *Mitteilungen* 24 (June/July 1963): 1.
Thelen, David. "The Nation and Beyond: Transnational Perspectives on United States History." *Journal of American History* 86 (1993): 1045-1077.
Tomaszewski, Jerzy. *Auftakt zur Vernichtung: Die Vertreibung der polnischen Juden aus Deutschland 1938.* Osnabrück: Fibre, 2002.
Trepp, Leo. *Die Oldenburger Judenschaft.* Oldenburg: Heinz Holzberg, 1973.
Turan, Tamas, and Carsten Wilke, eds. *Die Wissenschaft des Judentums in Hungary: An Introduction.* Berlin: De Gruyter, 2016.
Turner, James, and Paul Bernard. "The 'German Model' and the Graduate School: The University of Michigan and the Origin Myth of the American University." *History of Higher Education Annual* 13 (1993): 69-98.
Unfried, Berthold, Jürgen Mittag, and Marcel van der Linden, eds. *Transnational Networks in the 20th Century: Ideas and Practices, Individuals and Organizations.* Vienna: Akademische, 2008.
Van de Mark, Brian. *Into the Quagmire: Lyndon Johnson and the Escalation of the Vietnam War.* New York: Oxford University Press, 1991.
Voges, Wolfgang, ed. *Methoden der Biographie und Lebenslaufforschung.* Opladen: Springer, 1987.
von Wahl, Angelika. *Zwischen Heimat und Holocaust: Das Deutschlandbild der Nachkommen deutscher Juden in New York.* Frankfurt: Peter Lang, 1992.
Webb, Clive. *Fight against Fear: Southern Jews and Black Civil Rights.* Athens: University of Georgia Press, 2001.
Weczerka, Hugo. "Die Herkunft der Studierenden des Jüdisch-Theologischen Seminars zu Breslau 1854–1938." *Zeitschrift für Ostforschung* 35 (1986): 88–138.
Weinberg, Norbert. *Courage of the Spirit.* Pensacola, FL: Indigo, 2014.
———. *A Time to Tell: Stories and Recollections of a Rabbi from Kristallnacht to the Present.* Bloomington, IN: Author House, 2004.

Weitz, Martin M. *Interview with Mrs. Karl (Trudie) Rosenthal: Concentration Camp Survivor, Given in 1976.* Greenville, NC: Pambrit Publishers, 1993.

Wertheimer, Jack, ed. *Tradition Renewed: A History of the Jewish Theological Seminary.* New York: Jewish Theological Seminary Press, 1997.

White, Lyman Cromwell. *300,000 New Americans: The Epic of a Modern Immigrant Aid-Service.* New York: Harper, 1957.

Whitfield, Stephen. "Brandeis University at the Beginning: Judaic Studies." *European Judaism* 45 (2012): 112-122.

Wiese, Christian. "Auf Deutsch nach Amerika: Über den Transfer der Wissenschaft des Judentums im 19. und 20. Jahrhundert." In *Sprache, Erkenntnis und Bedeutung. Deutsch in der jüdischen Wissenskultur*, edited by Arndt Engelhardt and Susanne Zepp, 57-86. Leipzig: Leipziger Uni-Verlag, 2015.

———. "The Philadelphia Conference 1869 and German Reform: A Historical Moment in a Transnational Story of Proximity and Alienation." In *American Jewry: Transcending the European Experience?*, edited by Christian Wiese and Cornelia Wilhelm, 136-158. London: Bloomsbury Academic, 2016.

———. "Translating Wissenschaft: The Emergence and Self-Emancipation of American Jewish Scholarship, 1860–1920." In *American Jewry: Transcending the European Experience?*, edited by Christian Wiese and Cornelia Wilhelm, 185-211. London: Bloomsbury Academic, 2016.

Wiesemann, Falk. "Die israelitische Lehrerbildungsanstalt Würzburg (1864-1938): Ein Beitrag des fränkischen Landjudentums zum jüdischen Bildungswesen in Deutschland." In *Wissenschaft—Bildung—Politik: Von Bayern nach Europa. Festschrift für Ludwig Hammermayer zum 80. Geburtstag*, edited by Wolf D. Gruner, 341-359. Hamburg: Reinhold Krämer, 2008.

Wilhelm, Cornelia. *Bewegung oder Verein? Nationalsozialistische Volkstumspolitik in den USA.* Stuttgart: Franz Steiner, 1998.

———. "German Refugee Rabbis in the United States." *European Judaism* 45 (2012): 78-89.

———. *The Independent Orders of B'nai B'rith and True Sisters: Pioneers of a New Jewish Identity, 1843-1914.* Detroit: Wayne State University Press, 2011.

Wilhelm, Cornelia, and Tobias Grill. "The German Rabbinate Abroad." *Leo Baeck Institute Yearbook* 57 (2012):1-6.

———. "German Rabbis Abroad as Cultural Agents?" *European Judaism* 45 (2012): 2-7.

Wilhelm, Kurt. "The Jewish Community in the Post-Emancipation Period." *LBIY* 2 (1957): 47-75.

Winkelbauer, Thomas. *Vom Lebenslauf zur Biographie.* Waidhofen: Waldviertler Heimatbund, 2000.

Winstel, Tobias. "'Healed Biographies?' Jewish Remigration and Indemnification for National Socialist Injustice." *LBIY* 49 (2004): 137-152.

Wolffsohn, Michael. *Eternal Guilt? Forty Years of German-Jewish-Israeli Relations.* New York: Columbia University Press, 1993.
Würzburger, Walter. "Brentano's Theory of a Priori Judgments." PhD diss., Harvard University, 1951.
Wyman, Eva Goldschmidt. *Escaping Hitler: A Jewish Haven in Chile.* Tuscaloosa: University of Alabama Press, 2013.
Yadgar, Yaacov. *Secularism and Religion in Jewish-Israeli Politics: Traditionists and Modernity.* London: Routledge, 2011.
Zafren, Herbert. "From Hochschule to Judaica Conservancy Foundation: The Guttmann Affair." *Jewish Book Annual* 47 (1989/90—5750): 6-26.
Zajdband, Astrid. *German Rabbis in British Exile: From "Heimat" into the Unknown.* Boston: De Gruyter, 2016.
Zloch, Stephanie, Lars Müller, and Simone Lässig, eds. *Wissen in Bewegung: Migration und globale Verflechtungen in der Zeitgeschichte seit 1945.* Berlin: De Gruyter, 2018.
Zola, Gary, and Michael Lorge, eds. *A Place of Our Own: The Reform Jewish Camping.* Tuscaloosa: University of Alabama Press, 2006.
Zolot, Marvin. *Mensch: Biography and Writings of Manfred Eric Swarsensky.* Madison, WI: Edgewood College Press, 2009.
Zuroff, Ephraim. *Response of Orthodox Jewry in the United States: The Activities of the Vaad Ha-Hatzala Rescue Committee, 1939-1945.* Philadelphia: KTAV, 2000.

Digital Resources

"11. Verordnung zum Reichsbürgergesetzt vom 25." November 1941. http://www.ns-quellen.at/gesetz_anzeigen_detail.php?gesetz_id=4410&action=B_Read.
Baron, Salo. "Israelitisch Theologische Lehranstalt." *Encyclopedia Judaica.* https://www.encyclopedia.com/religion/encyclopedias-almanacs-transcripts-and-maps/israelitisch-theologische-lehranstalt.
Biography of Simon Schwab. https://web.stevens.edu/golem/llevine/rsrh/bio_r_s_schwab.pdf.
Brachear Pashman, Manya. "Rabbi Herman Schaalman, an Interfaith Pioneer, Dies at 100." *Chicago Tribune,* 1 February 2017. https://www.chicagotribune.com/news/obituaries/ct-herman-schaalman-obit-met-20170201-story.html.
Elsby, Liz. "I Shall Be What I Shall Be—The Story of Rabbiner Regina Jonas." *Yad Vashem.* https://www.yadvashem.org/articles/general/rabbiner-regina-jonas.html.
Enoch, Vivien. "A Holocaust Story Searching for Family Roots in a Photo on PBS." *My Jewish Detroit.* http://myjewishdetroit.org/2015/03/in-search-of-family-roots/.

"Die erste Synagoge, die den Nazis zum Opfer fiel." *Süddeutsche Zeitung*, 8 June 2018. https://www.sueddeutsche.de/muenchen/juedische-geschichte-wie-muenchen-vor-80-jahren-seine-synagoge-verlor-1.4004815-2.

"Dr. Alfred Gottschalk, z"l, Former President and Chancellor Emeritus of HUC-JIR." Hebrew Union College-Jewish Institute of Religion, 14 September 2009. http://huc.edu/news/article/2009/dr-alfred-gottschalk-zl-former-president-and-chancellor-emeritus-huc-jir.

Heschel, Susannah. "God Talk, Friendship and Activism: The Theological Affinity and the Relationship between Abraham Joshua Heschel and Martin Luther King, Jr." The Jewish Federations of America. https://www.jewishfederations.org/page.aspx?id=13296&print=1.

Institut für Zeigeschichte München. NSG-Datenbank "Die Verfolgung von NS-Verbrechen durch deutsche Justizbehörden nach 1945." https://www.ifz-muenchen.de/das-archiv/benutzung-und-service/nsg-datenbank/.

"Ismar Schorsch." Jewish Theological Seminary. http://www.jtsa.edu/ismar-schorsch.

Jünger, David. "Prinz and King." *Frankfurter Allgemeine Zeitung*, 25 August 2013. https://www.faz.net/aktuell/politik/die-gegenwart/vor-50-jahren-prinz-und-king-12546288.html.

Jureit, Ulrike. *Karl Mannheim. Das Problem der Generationen.* http://www.1000dokumente.de/pdf/dok_0100_gen_de.pdf.

"Justin Fränkel 1896-1984." Aufstehen Gegen Vergessen und Unrecht. https://www.bllv.de/index.php?id=11296.

King, Lyndsay Alissa, and Dana Smith. "AAJR Responds to Nazism: The Refugee Research Fellowship Program, 1933–1945." AAJR. http://aajr.org/centennialexhibit/exhibits/show/exhibitionhome.

"Leopold Neuhaus." Neue Deutsche Biographie. https://www.deutsche-biographie.de/sfz71416.html.

Lewis, Morgan. "Report of Investigation into Allegations of Misconduct at Hebrew Union College-Jewish Institute of Religion, Cincinnati 2021." https://huc.edu/wp-content/uploads/HUC-REPORT-OF-INVESTIGATION-11.04.21.pdf.

"The Luxembourg Agreement between Israel and the Federal Republic of Germany, 10 September 1952." Treaties, the United Nations. https://treaties.un.org/doc/Publication/UNTS/Volume%20162/volume-162-I-2137-English.pdf.

Martin, Douglas. "Alfred Gottschalk, Reform Rabbi, Dies at 79." *New York Times*, 15 September 2009. https://www.nytimes.com/2009/09/16/us/16gottschalk.html.

Narvaez, Alfonso. "79 Year Old Leader of Orthodox Jewry." *New York Times*, 8 February 1990. https://www.nytimes.com/1990/02/08/obituaries/rabbi-s-r-weiss-79-year-old-leader-of-orthodox-jewry.html.

Oliver, Myrna. "Alfred Wolf, 88; Noted Rabbi Started Jewish Youth Camps." *Los Angeles Times*, 2 August 2004. https://www.latimes.com/archives/la-xpm-2004-aug-02-me-wolf2-story.html.

Ostrowski, Jens, and Oliver Volmerich. "'Reisst ab den Judentempel'—Dortmunds NSDAP—Chef vor Gericht." *Ruhr Nachrichten*, 28 October 2018. https://www.ruhrnachrichten.de/dortmund/dortmunds-nsdap-chef-vor-gericht-als-friedrich-hesseldieck-die-synagoge-verschwinden-liess-plus-1341012.html.

"Our History." OSRUI. https://osrui.org/about/history/.

Prinz, Joachim. "Civil Rights." http://www.joachimprinz.com/civilrights.htm.

"Rav Shimon Schwab, zt"l, Recollections of His Years in Baltimore on the Occasion of This 13th *Yahrzeit*." Adapted by Yitzchok Levine. *Hamodia Magazine* 14 Adar 5768 (20 February 2008). http://personal.stevens.edu/~llevine/recollections_r_schwab.pdf.

"Restoration of German Citizenship." Consular Services, German Missions in the United States. https://www.germany.info/us-en/service/03-Citizenship/restoration-of-german-citizenship/925120Trepp, Leo. www.leotrepp.org/en/.

"Rev. Herbert Walter Langford (1919-1992)." Winthorpe. http://www.winthorpe.org.uk/Rev.-Herbert-Walter-Langford-1919-1992.

Steinberg, Jacques. "Rabbi Alexander Schindler, Reform Leader and Major Jewish Voice, Dies at 75." *New York Times*, 16 November 2000. https://www.nytimes.com/2000/11/16/nyregion/rabbi-alexander-schindler-reform-leader-and-major-jewish-voice-dies-at-75.html.

Tyrell, Ian. "What Is Transnational History?" https://iantyrelol.wordpress.com/what-is-transnational-history.

Weisbrod, Bernd. "Generation und Generationalität in der Neueren Geschichte." *APUZ* 8 (2005). Bundeszentrale für Politische Bildungsarbeit. http://www.bpb.de/apuz/29215/generation-und-generationalitaet-in-der-neueren-geschichte?p=all.

Wilhelm, Cornelia, ed. "German Refugee Rabbis in the United States, 1933-1990." http://mira.geschichte.lmu.de/.

Woo, Elaine. "Alfred Gottschalk Dies at 79; a Leader of Reform Judaism." *Los Angeles Times*, 13 September 2009. https://www.latimes.com/local/obituaries/la-me-alfred-gottschalk13-2009sep13-story.html.

Yitzchok Levine. *Hamodia Magazine* 14 Adar 5768 (20 February 2008). http://personal.stevens.edu/~llevine/recollections_r_schwab.pdf.

Zacharias Frankel College. http://zacharias-frankel-college.de.

„Zentralrat der Juden empört über neuen Träger von Rabbinerschule." *Der Spiegel*. 13 January 2023. https://www.spiegel.de/panorama/bildung/abraham-geiger-kolleg-in-potsdam-streit-ueber-liberale-rabbinerschule-in-potsdam-hoert-nicht-auf-a-eea89ec6-4e38-477c-a783-19607569ef9e

Zimet, Erwin. "1933: The Beginning of the End of German Jewry." *Jewish Museum Berlin.* https://www.jmberlin.de/1933/en/05_18_student-identification-card-issued-to-erwin-zimet-by-the-friedrich-wilhelm-university-of-berlin.php.

Films

"Der letzte Rabbiner: Die Geschichte des Leo Trepp." Director Christian Walther. RBB Fernsehen. Rundfunk Berlin Brandenburg, DVD, Germany: 2010 (shared with me by Christian Walther).

"Nahum N. Glatzer and the German-Jewish Tradition." Director Judith Wechsler, USA: 2011.

List of Archival Holdings

Political Archive of the German Foreign Office, Auswärtiges Amt, Berlin

B 11: 1951–58, Länderabteilung
B 32: 1958–1969, Referate 305, II A 6,
   1970 ff. ebenfalls B 32, Referat 204, here, record nos. 754-04 (1951–58), 305-82.23 bzw. IIA6-82.23 (1958–72) und 322.36 (1972 ff.)
B 92: Referate 602, IV 3 und 641, religion in foreign relations

Agudath Israel of America Archives, New York

Folder "Jewish Refugee War Internees, Canada 1941."
Folder Rabbi Dr. Joseph Breuer.
Mitteilungen—Organ der K'hall Adass Jeshurun und der K'hall Agudath Jeshorim, 1939–1964.

Jacob Rader Marcus Center of the American Jewish Archives, Cincinnati, Ohio, at americanjewisharchives.org (AJA)

Picture Collection

Manuscript Collections

MS-5 Hebrew Union College Papers
MS-26 Kivie Kaplan Papers
MS-30 Julian Morgenstern Papers, 1900–1974
MS-34 Central Conference of American Hebrew Congregations Records, 1885–2007
MS-78 Fritz Bamberger Papers
MS-110 Ismar Elbogen Papers
MS-165 Wolli Kaelter Papers
MS-171 Hugo Schiff Collection

MS-210 Jacob Rader Marcus Papers, 1907–2000
MS-260 Guido Kisch Papers
MS-663 Alexander Guttmann Papers, 1908–1988
MS-673 Rabbi Joachim Prinz Papers
MS-708 Max Nussbaum Papers, 1928–1974
MS-825 Milton Grafman Papers
SC-15217 Manfred E. Swarsensky Letters, 1939
SC-12426 Leo Trepp, autobiographical sketch
SC-12008 Ulrick B. Steuer eulogy, 21 October 1973
SC-1184 B'nai B'rith Hillel Foundation papers, 1915–1945
SC-5215 Isaac Aaron Holzer
SC-5203 Jakobovits, Immanuel: Holocaust, Religious Responses
SC-626 Baeck, Leo, article written by Dr. Fanz Landsberger "Memories of Leo Baeck"
SC-13834 Mansfield, OH, Records of the Congregation specifically concerning the hiring of Karl Rosenthal of Berlin as Rabbi, 1938–39
SC-11104 Schwarz, Joseph, Correspondence with Joint Distribution Committee

Nearprint-biographies

    Appel, Ernst
    Asher, Joseph
    Carlebach, Shlomo
    Cohn, Hillel
    Fackenheim, Emil
    Gruenewald, Max
    Hahn, Hugo
    Hamburger, Wolfgang
    Jakobovits, Immanuel
    Kisch, Guido
    Klappholz, Kurt
    Krauss, Samuel
    Landau, Moses
    Landsberger, Franz
    Lehmann, Robert
    Levinson, Nathan
    Lewy, Julius
    Lichtenberg, Leo
    Schiff, Hugo
    Schorsch, Ismar
    Schwarz, Joseph

Siegman, Henry
Sonne, Isaiah
Sperber, Alexander
Trepp, Leo
Weitz, Martin
Wolf, Alfred

Bancroft Library, The University of California, Berkeley

Mss. 2010/783: Rabbi Joseph Asher Papers

American Jewish Historical Society (AJHS)

I-66 Union of Orthodox Jewish Congregations records

Archive of the Institut für Zeitgeschichte, München (IfZ)

MA 1500 Biographische Dokumentation der deutschsprachigen Emigration 1933–1945 in Kooperation mit der Research Foundation for Jewish Immigration, Microfilm Series A and B.

"Die Verfolgung von NS-Verbrechen durch deutsche Justizbehörden nach 1945." Institut für Zeitgeschichte. https://www.ifz-muenchen.de/das-archiv/benutzung-und-service/nsg-datenbank/.

The Leo Baeck Institute New York (LBI)

AR 25385 Research Foundation for Jewish Immigration, oral histories
    Breuer, Jacob
    Cohn, Bernhard
    Gruenewald, Max
    Schwab, Simon
    Würzburger, Walter
AR 25376 Steven Schwarzschild Papers
AR 66 Leo Baeck Collection, 1885–2001
AR 3156 Hans Kronheim Papers
AR 3070 Julius Galliner Papers
AR 3677 Leo Baerwald Collection
AR 7188 Rabbi Adolf Kober Papers
AR 25598 Robert L. Lehman Collection
AR 7204 Max Gruenewald Collection
AR 25446 Emil Schorsch JTS Collection
AR 25103 Emil Schorsch Collection
AR 12030 Rabbi Kurt Metzger, Speeches and Sermons, 1931–2005

AR 6544 Rabbi Wilhelm Weinberg Collection, 1928–1938
AR 25206 Rabbi Gunter and Ruth Hirschberg Collection
AR 1693 Max Nussbaum Collection, Temple Israel of Hollywood
AR 3464 Isaak Holzer Collection
AR 787 Guido Kisch Collection
AR 7084 George Vida Collection
AR 25322 Helmut Frank Collection, 1939–1945
AR 796 Alexander Altmann Collection

Jewish Theological Seminary (JTS), Special Collections, Ratner Center (RC)

Jewish Theological Seminary of America Records

> General Records, RG 1, Series A (1902–1942), Series B (1943–1944)
> Faculty Minutes, RG 3, Faculty Meetings
> Finkelstein Archive (unprocessed), Correspondence, 1920–1939
> General Files
> Sol Landau Papers

The New York Public Library. Astor, Lenox, and Tilden Foundations. Manuscripts and Archives Division (NYPL)

Emergency Committee in Aid of Displaced Foreign Scholars Records.

United States Holocaust Memorial Museum (USHMM)

Dr. Enoch Kronheim Collection, Accession no. 2008.292
Jacob Wiener Papers, Accession no. 2012.182.1
Kurt Rosenthal Family Papers, Accession no. 1994.A.0029 (RG-10.087)
Rabbi Manfred Swarsensky Letters, 1939–1941: Accession no. 1995.A.0260
Wilhelm Weinberg Collection, Accession no. 1999.A.0163 (RG-10.238)

Oral Histories

Eva Angress (daughter of Rabbi George Kantorowsky), Accession no. 1999.A.0122.390 (RG-50.477.0390)
Helmut Frank, Accession no. 1997.A.0441.80 (RG-50.462.0080)
Ib Nathan Bamberger, Acession no. 2011.177.6 (RG-50.677.0006)
Jacob Wiener 1994: (RG-50.030.0249)
Jacob Wiener 1998: (RG-50.106.0112)
Jacob Wiener 2008: (RG-50.999.0217)
Jacob Wiener 2009: (RG-50.999.0245)
Karl Richter, USC Shoah Foundation

Manfred Fulda, Accession no. 2014.65.15 (RG-50.639.0015)
Manfred Gans, Accession no. 2004.563 (RG-50.030.0489)
Samuel Graudenz, Accession no. 1999.A.0122.946 (RG-50.477.0946)
Theodore Alexander, Accession no. 1999.A.0122.508 (RG-50.477.0508)
Emmie Vida, Accession no. 1995.A.0658.1 (RG-50.184.0001)
Emmie Vida, Accession no. 1995.A.0658.2 (RG-50.535.0001)
Emmie Vida, Accession no. 1999.A.0122.652 (RG-50.477.0652)
Trudie Rosenthal, Accession no. 1995.A.0872 (RG-50.174.0001)

Yeshiva University (YU), Special Collections, Gottesman Library

Bernard Revel Papers (including his correspondence on/with students and supplemental files)
Congregation Beth Hillel-Beth Israel
Dr. Erich Gutkind
Dr. Leo Rosenzweig
Emergency Committee in Aid of Displaced Foreign Scholars
International Student Service, 1937–1941
Jacob Hartstein Papers (JHP)
Leo Jung Collection
Press Releases
Vaad Hatzalah Collection
YU Graduate School Administration

Hebrew University, Avraham Harman Institute of Contemporary Jewry, Oral History Division, Holocaust Collection

Interview 13 Ernest Lorge
Interviews 18 A and B with Herman Dicker
Interview 24 George Vida

Private Collections and unprocessed interviews taken by the author

Papers pertaining to Rabbi Erich Löwenthal shared with the author from the Dr. Abaraham Lowenthal private collection
Interview Dr. Cornelia Wilhelm with Dr. Ismar Schorsch, taken by Cornelia Wilhelm on 15 November 2013, (shared with the LBI).
Interview Dr. Cornelia Wilhelm taken with Dr. Eli Faber, taken by Cornelia Wilhelm on 17 and 19 April 2019, (shared with the LBI).

INDEX

Abahams, Joseph B. 77, 79
Aber, Felix 130
Abitur (German degree) 40, 69, 73, 120
Abraham-Geiger-Kolleg (founded in 1999, Potsdam) 8, 16, 168, 206–07
adaptation 105, 121, 209,
Adass Jisroel (community) 185
Adass Jisroel School (Berlin) 120, 200
Adenauer, Konrad (chancellor, FRG) 194
Adler, Cyrus 47–49, 51, 56–57, 77, 79, 91–92, 94, 101–02
Adler, Leo 153, 173
Adler, Max 27
Adler, Nathan 85
Adler, Oscar 72
affidavit 57–58, 60–61, 66, 68, 86, 88, 97–98, 107, 118
Agudah Israel 18, 41, 185–86
AIDS 165
Aish Dosh 63
Algiers 124
Alien Registration Act (Smith Act) 58
alienation 146, 148, 155, 161
Aliyah (youth movement) 96
Altmann, Alexander 24, 162, 170
American Academy of Jewish Research 49, 56, 58
American Friends of Hebrew University 118
American Friends of the Union of Progressive Jews in Germany, Austria, and Switzerland 26
American Jewish Committee 12, 45–46, 56, 163, 172
American Jewish Congress 12, 45–46, 81, 158, 160, 176, 193, 194, 196
American Jewry 2, 37, 45, 62, 100–03, 106, 111, 137–38, 142, 146, 149, 156, 159, 166, 205, 211, 213
American Jews 5–7, 44–46, 105, 126, 141–42, 147–49, 155–56, 159–63, 166, 168, 180, 190, 192, 196, 208, 211, 216
American military government (in postwar Germany) 183
American rabbi 2, 4, 12, 45, 49, 83, 100, 103, 106, 111, 121, 126–27, 131, 166, 193, 199
American rabbinate 72–73, 93–94, 99–100, 103, 105, 108, 111, 118, 127, 129–30, 208, 212
American South 112, 126, 147, 158
Americanization 16, 105 106, 112, 118, 122, 132, 156, 211
Amsterdam 87, 121, 124
antisemitism (see also persecution, exclusion, degradation, humiliation) 10, 19, 21, 25, 36, 45, 89, 134, 142, 149, 162, 170, 171, 173, 181, 182, 184, 189, 192, 193, 198, 210, 213–14

Appel, Ernst 36, 72, 88
Appel, Martha 88
Arab-Israeli peace process 169
arms race 165
Arndt, Curt 75–76
Arzt, Max 103
Asher (Ansbacher), Joseph 19, 71, 109–11, 130, 139, 143, 158–159, 162, 177, 186–87, 196–98
assimilation 5, 25, 27–28, 30, 32, 34, 46, 111, 113, 119, 130, 141, 148–49, 154, 161, 208, 210, 212–13
Atlas, Samuel 24, 55–56, 112–14, 163
Auerbach, Selig 130
Australia 17, 18, 71, 110, 158, 186
Australian Army 71, 110, 186
Austria 24, 26, 70, 74, 76, 89, 91, 98, 104, 134, 184, 205, 206, 210
autobiography 16, 18, 32, 85, 92, 97–98, 107, 135, 141, 143–44, 158, 170, 175, 189
Axis 75, 134

B'nai B'rith 12, 46, 56, 88, 104, 144, 154, 198
Babad, Josef 74
Bachelor of Arts (degree) 69, 70, 72, 73, 130
Baeck, Leo 8, 11, 13, 18, 29, 42–43, 67, 71, 73, 99, 110, 138–39, 140–41, 144, 156, 162, 170, 183, 186, 199, 201, 203
Baerwald, Leo 24, 89, 121, 169
Baltimore 45, 60, 64–66, 81, 85–86, 120, 130, 135, 211
Bamberger, Ib Nathan 81–82
Bamberger, Seligman Baer 82
Bancroft Library (UC Berkeley) 19
Barzel, Rainer 194
Bavaria (German kingdom/state) 2, 85, 90, 195, 205
Beis Medrash Elyon 63
Beis Yaakov School for Girls (see also Beth Jacob Schule) 66
Bergen-Belsen 124

Berger, Anna 59
Berlin 3–5, 8–9, 14, 16, 19, 24–27, 29, 31, 33, 38, 40–43, 50–51, 55, 60, 62, 67, 69, 70–74, 76, 78, 84, 86–87, 89, 96, 98–99, 106–08, 113, 115, 118, 120, 124–25, 126, 128, 131, 139, 140–41, 143, 150, 153, 155, 157, 159, 161, 168, 173, 182–89, 194–96, 198, 200–03, 206, 207, 210, 214
Bernardine, Joseph (archbishop of Cincinnati (1972–1982), and Chicago (1982–1996) and cardinal after 1983)
Berney, Arnold 39
Beth Jacob School (see also Beis Yaakov School) 63
Biberfeld, Philipp 63
Bielefeld 97
Bildung 39, 61, 65, 212
biography (see also prosopography) 17, 32, 174
Birnbaum, Bruno 60,
black market 186, 189
Blau, Ernst 73
Blau-Weiss (youth movement) 149
Bluhm, Arthur 131
Bochum 90
Bodenheimer, Ludwig 82
Böhm, Franz 191
Boston University 163
Bournemouth 75
Brandeis University 162, 195
Breger, Marcus 24
Breslau 3–5, 9, 14, 16, 24, 26–27, 31, 38, 40, 43, 53, 57, 72, 74, 77, 84, 86, 99, 118, 121, 128, 129–30, 151, 201, 210
Breslauer, Jehuda Leo 121
Breuer Edith 97
Breuer Yeshiva (see also Yeshiva Samson Raphael Hirsch) 30, 98, 110
Breuer, Jacob 97
Breuer, Joseph 24, 37–38, 60–61, 63–64, 81, 84–85, 97–98, 110, 119, 122–123, 212
Breuer, Meta 97

Breuer, Samson 97
Breuer, Sophie 97
Briar Lodge (Oconomowoc, WI) 151
Brickner, Balfour 198
Brumach, Ernst 39
Buber, Martin 39, 150, 161, 162, 163
Buchdahl, Gustav 109
Buchler, Joseph 151
Budapest 3, 74
Bukovina 14, 26
Bund (Jewish socialist organization) 26
Burnstein, Alexander 75–76, 94, 100–03

Cadbury, Henry J. 50
Cahn, Leo 59
Cambridge (UK) 43
Cambridge University (UK) 43
Camp Hess Kramer 153, 174
Camp Munk 153
Camp Saratoga 152
Camp Swig 153
Carlebach, Alexander 170
Carlebach, Ephraim 80
Carlebach, Hartwig N. 98, 123
Carlebach, Leni 65
Carlebach, Naftali Henry 82
Caro, Friedrich 39
Carter, Jimmy (US-president) 177
Catholic Church 26, 172, 173, 174
Catholics 172
Cavert, Samuel 172
Central British Fund for German Jewry 100, 185, 189
Central Conference of American Rabbis (CCAR) 45–46, 49–50, 83, 92, 166, 199, 205
Central Yeshiva Beth Joseph, Brooklyn 131
Cernauti (Ukraine) 27
challenge of Nazism 5, 9, 21, 32, 37, 40, 88, 96, 103,
challenge of starting over 9, 37, 49, 55, 103, 106, 117, 126, 127, 142, 149, 155

challenges (general) 5, 7, 10, 50, 116, 121, 146, 164, 171, 174, 181, 189, 213
challenges for American seminaries 72
Chamberlain, Perkins Joseph 101
chaplain (*Seelsorger*) 13, 22, 32, 39, 58, 71, 110, 128–31, 176, 180–81, 186, 189
Charles University, Prague 74, 77, 130
Chicago 103, 151, 152, 174
chief rabbi 43, 62, 77, 80, 92, 96, ,99–100, 102, 134, 184, 188–189, 199, 205
Christian Democratic Union (CDU, German political party) 194
Christian theology 4, 9, 198, 199, 206
Christianity 172, 173, 175, 187, 214
Christians 49, 129, 162, 171, 172, 173, 174, 175, 199, 201
church and state 169, 171
Church of the Holy Sepulchre 174
Cincinnati, Ohio 13, 18, 36, 42, 47, 51, 54–56, 67–72, 106–10, 113–14, 118, 132, 138–40, 144, 146, 150, 163, 165, 168, 173, 175, 183, 186–87, 189, 191, 197, 201–02,
citizenship 14, 24, 33, 68–69, 88, 91, 99, 105, 108, 132–35, 171
civil rights 15, 133, 146–147, 158–62, 15, 172, 174, 213
civil rights movement 15, 146–47, 158–62, 172, 214
clergy 43, 44, 65
Cleveland, OH 103, 126
Clinchy, Everett 49, 172
Clinton, Bill (US-president) 169
Coblenz 86
Cohen, Herman 114, 163
Cohen, Judah 151
Cohen, Samuel M. 92, 93, 101, 125
Cohn Affair 25,
Cohn, Bernhard N. 109
Cohn, Emil Moses (pseud. Cohn, Emil Bernhard) 25, 28, 36, 87, 123, 127
Cohn, Hillel 110
Cohn, Mort 106
Cohn, Sally 106, 107

Cohon, Samuel 113
Cold War 157, 168, 179, 192, 193, 202
collective 15–16, 33–34, 136, 141–42, 145, 175, 190
Collegio Rabbinico, Rome 75
Columbia University 121, 130, 164
Committee in Aid of Foreign Students of the Rabbinical Assembly 72, 77
Committee on Refugee Jewish Ministers (CRJM) 99, 100, 101, 103
congregation (see also *Gemeinde*) 4, 7, 10–12, 27–28, 32, 37, 44–45, 49–50, 54–55, 57–59, 62–64, 66, 72, 76, 81, 85–88, 93, 94, 96, 100–03, 105, 110, 118–32, 135, 146–49, 151, 153–58, 164–65, 173–74, 184, 191–92, 196, 203, 205, 211, 213
Congregation Agudass Achim, Zurich 96
Congregation Agudath Achim, Philadelphia 131
Congregation Anshe Shalom, Kew Gardens, NY 129
Congregation Emes Wozedeck, New York City (Washington Heights) 86
Congregation Gemiluth Chassodim, Detroit 184
Congregation Habonim, New York City 54, 123–24
Congregation New Hope, Cincinnati, OH 132, 191
Congregation Ohav Zedek, New York City 154
Congregation Shaarey Shamayim, Philadelphia, PA 129
Congregation Shaarey Tikvah, Cleveland OH 125, 191
Conrad, Ernst 70, 138
Conservative movement in Judaism 9, 61, 72, 80–81, 124, 127–128, 130, 166, 169, 207, 211
consulate (German) 190, 191
consulate (US) 54–55, 69, 75, 78
conversion 135, 157, 173, 186, 187, 205

critical inquiry 3, 14
Cuba 58, 69, 78, 86, 88, 108
cultural transfers 1, 6, 7, 147, 210
culture 3–5, 8–9, 11, 14–15, 24–25, 27, 33, 41, 49, 55, 77, 87, 111–12, 114, 116, 121, 136, 144, 146, 149, 177, 180, 182, 186, 200, 210, 214, 216
curriculum 39–40, 49, 56, 63, 113, 144, 154
Currik, Max 101
czarist 24
Czechoslovakia 24, 77, 89, 102, 104, 134

Dachau 76, 81, 96–97
Danzig 68, 72, 146
Database German Refugee Rabbis after 1933 (MIRA) 5, 17–18, 20, 35, 126, 130, 185, 212, 216
De Sola Pool, David 59, 101, 103
degradation 53, 73, 117, 158
degree (BA, MA, doctorate) 11, 22, 35, 42, 43, 45, 46, 50, 67, 69, 70, 72, 76, 77, 145, 146, 211
deicide 173
democracy 12, 25, 46, 114, 190-95
Department of State 52–55, 58, 65–66, 103–04, 158
Deppe, Klara 59
dialogue 8, 16, 172–75, 177, 190–92, 194–95, 199–200, 214, 216
diaspora 146, 147, 149, 156, 159, 176, 190, 211
Dicker, Hermann 80, 119, 130, 180
Dienemann, Max 23, 99,
Diner, Hasia 250
discrimination 21, 50
displaced persons (DPs) 99, 104, 178, 181
displacement 8, 15, 105, 110, 122, 125, 136, 177, 209, 216
doctorate (degree) 2–3, 15, 27, 31, 35, 38, 55, 72, 74, 110–111, 118, 127, 145–46, 162–64
Dolina (Galicia) 98
Dolins, Peter 93
Dortmund 36, 88, 90

Dothan, AL 173
Dropsie College (Philadelphia) 13, 47–48, 50–51, 92
Drury College 205
Drury, Betty 64
dual-track education 3, 38
Dublin 55
Duggan, Stephen 47–48
Duke University 155
Dünner, Joseph Hirsch 80

education 3, 13–14, 16, 22–23, 26, 30, 35, 38–40, 42, 47, 63–64, 66, 69, 81, 84–85, 110–11, 114, 121, 123, 128–32, 146, 148, 153–54, 164, 169, 181, 183–184, 187, 189, 194–95, 198, 200, 211–13
Egypt 34, 204
Ehrentreu, Chanoch 207
Ehrentreu, Jonah Ernst 207
Ehrlich, Ernst Ludwig 43
Eichmann Trial 157
Eidenbaum, Julius 76
Einstein, Albert 48, 60, 88
Elbogen, Ismar 13, 16, 24, 39, 42, 50–53, 57, 60, 67–68, 78, 99, 108, 137–38, 144
emancipation (Jewish~) 2, 10, 20, 22, 30, 85, 141, 152, 170
Emanuel Federated Employment Service 102
Emergency Committee in Aid of German Scholars (ECAGS) 47–51, 56, 59, 64–65, 71
Emergency Council of the Chief Rabbi (UK) 80, 96, 100
emotions 26, 140
employment 23, 47–49, 51, 59–61, 65, 75, 80, 83, 102, 105, 125, 131, 151–152, 154, 189
Enemy Aliens 134–135
England (see also Great Britain) 54–55, 71, 75, 97, 141, 175, 185–86, 198, 204
English (language) 4, 49, 58–59, 69, 77, 85, 93–94, 97, 103–04, 107, 108, 110, 112, 121, 124, 138–39, 162, 212–13

Eppstein, Paul 39
equality 150, 158, 162, 172
Erlangen 36
Essen 123
ethnic brokers 8
ethnic identity 25–26, 30, 34, 122, 127, 130, 148, 208
Europe (general) 2–3, 5, 8–12, 24, 26–27, 31, 37, 41, 44–47, 55, 57, 61, 66, 71, 73–74, 76–77, 83, 85, 87, 92, 98–99, 104–05, 109, 112, 119–20, 137–38, 142, 144, 146–49, 162–63, 170–72, 177–78, 180–84, 186–187, 198, 202, 205, 209–15
Europe, central 3, 9, 12, 24, 37, 41, 55, 57, 6- 62, 66, 74, 76–77, 83, 99, 104, 112, 119, 171, 177, 184, 186–87, 205, 214, 215
Europe, eastern 5, 24, 27, 31, 45–46, 85, 98, 137, 147, 162, 170, 178, 182–83
Europe, western 137
exchanges 8, 45, 101, 119, 145, 173, 192–193, 195, 214
expatriation 133
Ezra (youth movement) 64, 149, 153

Faber, Eli 99, 128–29
Faber, Salamon 99, 128–29
Fackenheim, Emil 98, 143, 176
Fairmont, WV 54
faith 15, 129, 155, 160–61, 165–66, 171, 174, 199
Falk, Gustave 92–93, 101
Fargo, ND 188
fascism 84, 162
Feldheim Publishers 131
Feldman, Leon Aryeh 81, 120, 163–64, 167, 200–01
Fest, Joachim 193
Festschrift 143
film 18, 106, 143, 162
Finkelstein, Louis 51, 57–58, 75, 78–80, 113, 118
First World War 5, 13–14, 24–26, 50, 84, 115, 128, 148, 210

Fisher (Fischer), Frank 109, 129, 155
Fiume (Rijeka) 38, 84
Fleishman, Ludwig 82,
Flexner, Abraham 47
flight 1, 4–5, 7–8, 15, 19–20, 37, 44–45, 51, 62, 95, 98, 108, 125, 127, 134, 175, 177–79, 184–85, 200, 204, 216
Florence (Italy) 102
Forum on behalf of Greensboro's civil rights activists 159
Foxwell, William 49
Frank, Helmut 130–31
Fränkel, Justin 36
Frankfurt am Main 30, 37–38, 54, 60, 62-63, 73, 84–85, 93, 97, 99, 154, 161–62, 170, 183–84, 187, 191, 199, 212
Frankfurt Kehillah 38, 60, 62–64, 122, 123, 212
Franklin and Marshall College 68
Fredericksburg, MD 125
freedom 11, 28, 37, 141, 147, 152, 158, 162, 171
Friedenwald, Harry 60
Friedlander, Albert 109, 138, 162, 201
Friedländer, Hans 39
Friedman, Elisha 77
Friedmann, Kalman 102
Friedrich-Wilhelms-Universität Berlin 115, 128
Fulda, Manfred 81, 120
future 2, 8, 16–18, 23–24, 28, 37, 41, 68, 71, 73–74, 80, 87, 90, 94, 105, 109, 111, 113–14, 136, 138, 142, 144, 148, 154, 159–60, 162–63, 165, 168, 170, 177, 184, 187, 189, 191, 193, 195, 198, 200–09, 214

Galliner, Helmut 73, 78–80, 118
Galliner, Julius 73, 78
Galut 34
Gate Club (Cincinnati) 107
gay 168, 205
Geiger, Abraham 9, 206
Gemeinde 10–13, 22, 27–28, 30, 32, 36–37, 84, 87, 93, 121, 127, 132, 203, 215

generation 1–5, 11, 14–18, 22–23, 25–28, 31–32, 34, 36, 44, 63, 67, 81, 109–11, 119–24, 127, 130, 132, 136, 141–43, 146–47, 149–51, 154, 156, 163, 166, 168, 170, 175, 177, 179, 180, 184, 193, 196, 198, 201, 203–04, 207–08, 210–14
generation-building 12, 15–16, 143–145, 180
German (language) 2–3, 15, 26, 36–37, 60, 70, 77, 86, 93–94, 99, 107, 119, 122, 143, 162, 186, 191, 201, 204–05, 209, 215
German Army 115,
German culture 8–9, 14–15, 24, 136
German Foreign Office (FRG) 19, 190, 192, 196
German Jewry 1–2, 6, 8, 21, 23–24, 28, 30–31, 34, 38, 43, 48, 50–51, 61, 83, 87, 100, 102, 111, 138, 140–42, 148, 169, 171, 178, 182, 184–85, 189, 206
German Jews 1, 4–5, 21- 22, 24–26, 28, 30–31, 33–34, 38, 43, 48, 50–51, 57, 61, 73, 83, 87, 100, 102, 111, 122, 124, 129, 138, 140–142, 148–50, 169, 171, 178, 182- 186, 188–89, 202, 206, 208–09
German modern Orthodoxy (see also Breuer Gemeinde, Breuer Yeshiva, Yeshiva Samson Raphael Hirsch, Hildesheimer thought, Orthodox Rabbinerseminar Berlin) 9, 11, 30–31, 43, 60–62, 64, 80–81, 86, 123, 130–32, 153, 203, 212
German rabbinate 1–2, 4–5, 12–15, 17–18, 21, 34, 44, 61–62, 66–67, 91, 94, 99, 128, 136–38, 141, 143–46, 168, 177, 179–80, 193, 208, 210, 212–15
German rabbi 1–5, 8, 11–12, 14, 36–38, 44, 72, 93, 98, 100, 102, 126–28, 134, 136, 143, 146, 169–70, 175, 185, 208, 212, 215
German Research Foundation (Deutsche Forschungsgemeinschaft, DFG) 19
German society 8, 10, 21–22, 24–25, 91, 95, 142, 149, 171, 175, 182, 214
German-American Bund 134
German-Jewish experience 8

German-Jewish history 1, 169–71, 208
Germans (non-Jewish~) 8, 15, 95, 107, 111, 117, 133–35, 138, 147, 175, 178–79, 181–83, 192–96, 198, 205, 211, 214
Germany (general) 1–11, 13–19, 23, 24–25, 31–33, 35, 37–51, 54–55, 57, 60, 62, 64–69, 71–78, 80–91, 93–109, 111–12, 115–16, 120, 122–24, 126–27, 130, 133–34, 136–39, 141, 143, 146, 148–49, 153, 156–62, 168, 170, 175–216
Germany under Allied occupation (1945–49) 181, 184, 186
Germany, Democratic Republic of (East Germany, 1949–1990) 188, 202
Germany, divided (1949–1990) 8
Germany, Federal Republic of (West Germany, 1949–) 8, 14, 17, 19, 176, 179, 181–82, 188–89, 190–96, 198, 201–02
Germany, Nazi era (1933–1945) 4, 5, 8, 17, 23, 37–46, 48–51, 54–55, 60, 66–69, 72, 75–77, 80, 83–105, 133–34, 190, 212, 215
Germany, Weimar Republic 25, 148, 149
Gesamtarchiv der deutschen Juden 43
Gindling Hilltop Camp 153, 174
Ginsburg, Leo 72
Glatzer, Nahum 143, 162–63, 169–70
Glazer, Benedict 101, 103
Glueck, Nelson 106, 145
Goldhagen, Moses 39
Goldman, Felix 27
Goodman, H. A. 185
Gottschalk, Alfred 109–10, 166–68, 177, 206
Gottschalk, Walter 54, 163
graduates 7, 12–13, 16–17, 35, 44, 52, 62, 69, 70–72, 74, 76, 86, 91–92, 107, 112, 120, 128, 130, 143, 164, 166, 170, 187–88, 211, 215
Great Britain 17–18, 37, 80, 138, 185, 216
Greenberg, Simon 92
Greensboro, NC 158–59
Grinstein, Samuel 92–93, 101

Grodzensky, Chaim Ozer (Rabbi of Vilna) 41
Gruenewald (Grünewald), Max 26, 28, 36–37, 57–59, 119, 134, 169–70
Gruenewald, Hans 73
Gruner, Wolf 89
Grynspan, Herschel 95
Guggenheim Foundation 48
guilt (German) 190
guilt (Jewish, survivor guilt) 158, 159
Gutkind, Ernst 59
Guttmann, Alexander 13, 24, 52, 56, 112, 114, 170, 201–02
Guttmann, Henry 24
Guttmann, Julius 170

Haberman (Habermann) Joshua 70, 107, 109, 206
Hahn, Hugo 123, 124, 145
Hallein (Austria) 99, 184
Hamburger, Wolfgang 43, 71, 138, 140, 170, 183
Hanover, Siegmund 121, 184
Hartstein, Jacob 59, 80, 113
Harvard Divinity School 50, 120, 164
Hassidim 114, 128, 160
Havana, Cuba 69, 78, 79
Haverford College 50
Hebrew Bible 160, 161
Hebrew Immigrant Aid Society (HIAS) 104, 131
Hebrew Sheltering and Immigrant Aid Society of America 58
Hebrew Union College 13, 18, 42, 47, 50–54, 56, 67–71, 74, 106–14, 117–19, 124, 136–39, 145–46, 150, 152–53, 163, 165–66, 168, 175, 186–87, 189, 197–98, 201–02, 205–06, 211
Heidelberg 16, 115–16, 189, 198–200, 202–03
Hertz, Joseph (Chief Rabbi UK) 43, 62, 77, 80, 92, 96, 100
Herz, Reinhold 73

Heschel, Abraham Joshua 24, 35, 52, 54–56, 73, 91, 108, 112–14, 140, 160–62, 172–73
HICEM 77
Hildesheimer school of thought (see also Orthodox Rabbinerseminar, Berlin) 30
Hildesheimer, Esriel Erich 41, 60, 118
Hildesheimer, Meir 41, 207
Hillel Campus Organization (Hillel Foundation) 129, 154–55
Hirsch, Samson Raphael 30, 37–38, 63, 80, 84–85, 97, 131, 212
Hirschberg (Silesia) 86
Hirschberg, Hans 97
Hirschfeld, Erwin 59
Hirschian school of thought (see also Breuer Yeshiva, Yeshiva Samson Raphael Hirsch) 30, 38, 63, 84, 212
history (Jewish Europe) 120
history (American Jewish) 1, 120, 179
history (German-Jewish) 1, 120, 169, 170, 171, 175, 206, 208
history (Jewish general) 32, 33, 34, 137, 147, 149, 157, 163, 164, 168, 175, 180, 207, 210
Hitler, Adolf 36, 84, 90, 115, 168, 187, 194, 196,
Hochschule für die Wissenschaft des Judentums (1872) in Berlin 3, 13, 16, 19, 23, 38–43, 49–53, 67, 69, 70–72, 76, 91, 98–99, 106–07, 112, 114, 118, 140, 144, 146, 152, 155, 160–61, 170, 173, 184, 200, 203
Hoffman, Jacob 13, 24, 92, 93, 134, 146, 154
Holborn, Hajo 115
Holocaust 1, 4–7, 16, 18–19, 61, 76, 104, 124–25, 131–32, 136, 141–42, 144, 146–47, 149, 158–59, 161, 172–73, 175–83, 190, 193, 196, 202, 204–06, 209, 213–16
home (*Heimat*) 55, 94, 99, 112, 124, 129, 132, 141, 158, 166, 190, 214–15
Horovitz, Eugene 103
Horovitz, Saul 57, 118
House of the Wannsee Conference (*Haus der Wannseekonferenz*) 198

human relations 177, 196
humiliation 73, 88–89, 97–98, 105, 135, 181, 210
Hungary 14, 24, 26, 84, 128, 134, 154
hybridity 116, 144, 179, 214
Hyde Park Congregation, Chicago, ILL 174

Ichenhausen 85
immigration 19, 28, 37, 44, 53, 55, 65–66, 75, 80, 83, 85, 93, 97, 102, 108, 153, 184–85, 200
immigration authorities and bureaucracy 42, 52–53, 55, 58, 100, 103, 184
immigration law (USA) 37, 44, 78, 97, 134
immigration status (change of status) 48, 68, 78, 88
immigration visa 54, 58, 68, 69, 78, 84
Indiana University, Bloomington, IN 155
inequality 158
Information Center of the City of Berlin 194
Institut für Zeitgeschichte (IfZ) Munich 12, 9, 95, 185, 120, 132
Institute of International Education 47
integration 2, 6, 9, 11, 17, 21, 31, 66, 89, 106, 108, 109, 111–11, 122, 126, 130, 172, 203, 211
interfaith 15, 165, 171, 174, 196, 199, 214, 216
International Migration Service 102
Israel (state of~) 10, 41, 148, 168, 187, 188, 190, 191, 195, 202
Israelitische Lehrerbildungsanstalt (ILBA), Würzburg 31, 65, 81, 153, 212
Israelitisch-Theologische Lehranstalt, Vienna 3, 70, 74

Jacob, Ernst 96, 176
Jacob, Walter 96, 109, 111, 163, 164, 165, 166, 168, 176, 203–06
Jacobs, Alfred 80
Jamestown, NY 97, 125
Japan 62, 189
Jerusalem 40, 43, 166, 168, 169, 174
Jewish Chautauqua Society 192

Jewish civilization 160, 186
Jewish ethnic pride 4, 25, 27, 107, 135, 156, 181, 201, 208
Jewish Institute of Religion (JIR) New York City 13, 15, 109, 113, 124, 146, 166
Jewish knowledge 31, 34, 46, 61, 64, 74, 120, 127, 142, 148, 156, 161, 210, 211, 213
Jewish law 30, 49, 129, 154, 157, 180
Jewish minority 8
Jewish people 6, 30, 33, 34
Jewish philosophy 48, 55, 59
Jewish Rabbinical Seminary, Budapest 3
Jewish revival 148
Jewish Social Service Association of New York City 102
Jewish Studies 3, 4, 16, 35, 38, 39, 43, 46, 47, 48, 51, 52, 71, 121, 131, 137, 153, 161, 164, 168, 170, 177, 201, 205
Jewish substance 149, 150
Jewish teacher 23, 170, 200
Jewish Theological College, London (precursor of Leo Baeck College, London) 138
Jewish Theological Seminary (JTS) in New York City 6, 13, 18, 37, 47–51, 56–58, 60, 69, 70–80, 92, 94, 112–14, 117–20, 127, 130–31, 168–69, 211
Jewish theology 9, 15, 170, 175, 206
Jewish Welfare Society 131
Jewishness 4, 22–23, 26, 32, 126, 154, 161, 202, 204
Jews see German Jews, American Jews
Johns Hopkins University 49
Johnson, Alvin 48
Joint Distribution Committee (JDC) 46, 56, 185
Jonas, Regina 23
Jospe, Eva 155
Jospe, Raphael 155
Judaism (see also Orthodox Judaism, Reform Judaism, Conservative Judaism, Liberal Judaism, German Judaism, American Judaism) 3, 8–9, 11, 15, 17, 22, 24, 26–34, 40, 43–44, 51, 61, 67, 71, 108–114, 119, 124, 130, 132, 136–39, 141–44, 147–150, 152–54, 156, 159–61, 163–70, 172–76, 186–88, 196, 198–99, 202–16
Jüdisch-Theologisches Seminar in Breslau (1854) 3, 24, 27, 38, 40, 43, 53, 57, 72–73, 76, 87, 99, 128, 151
Jung, Leo 62–63, 83–85, 92–93, 101, 103
Jünger, David 159, 160

Kadimah (youth movement) 149
Kaelter, Hans 68
Kaelter, Robert Raphael 68
Kaelter, Sarah (nee Shapiro) 108, 152
Kaelter, Wolli 67–68, 106–08, 112, 146, 151–53
Kahal Adass Jeshurun (see also Breuer-Gemeinde, Breuer Yeshiva, Yeshiva Samson Raphael Hirsch) 62–64, 122–23, 212
Kahn, Shlomo 120
Kaiserslautern 90
Kameraden (youth movement) 149
Kaminka, Armand (Vienna) 91
Kant, Immanuel 27, 60
Kaplan, Edward 172
Kapustin, Max 80,
Kaufmann, Fritz 39
Kayser, Rudolf 60,
kehillah 10, 27, 37, 60, 62, 84
Kempner, Fritz 76
Kieffer, Melvin 58
King, Martin Luther, Jr. 159, 161
Kingsley (Kissinger), Ralph 109
Kisch, Guido 49, 52, 56–57
Klappholz, Kurt 74, 80, 131
Klatzkin, Jacob 48
Knappstein, Heinrich 195
knowledge transfer 44, 48, 61, 120, 162, 212–13
Kober, Alfred 96, 170
Kohler, Kaufmann 137
Kohs, Samuel C. 93, 101

Köpenick (Berlin) 87
Koppel, Max 86
Krah, Markus 141
Kramer, Ruth 66
Kraus, Heinrich 76
Krauss, Samuel 70, 91
Krochmal, Nachman 163
Kronheim, Hans Enoch 24, 36, 97, 125, 126, 191
Kronstein, Heinrich 57
Kushelevsky, Elihu 76

Lampel, Werner 76
Landau, Ezekiel 24,
Landau, Max 60
Landau, Sol 119
Landman, Max
Landsberger, Franz 52, 54, 56, 112
Lanner, David 70, 74
Lasdun, Tuvia 131
last generation 1, 14, 16–18, 44, 67, 136, 141, 143–46, 156, 168, 175, 177, 179, 180, 193, 208, 213–14
last rabbi of 4, 17, 137, 143, 144, 145, 159, 170, 176, 193, 195, 209, 213
Law for the Restoration of the Professional Civil Service (Gesetz zur Wiederherstellung des Berufsbeamtentums) 21, 46
Law on the Redesign of German Cities (Gesetz über die Neugestaltung deutscher Städte) 89, 90
Law on the Revocation of Naturalizations and the Deprivation of German Citizenship (Gesetz über den Widerruf von Einbürgerungen und die Aberkennung der deutschen Staatsangehörigkeit) 133
leadership 1–6, 11–12, 22–23, 31, 34, 36, 39, 41, 44, 49, 51, 62, 64–65, 69, 77, 79, 83–84, 86, 88, 91, 95, 99, 113, 115, 120–23, 126–27, 134, 138, 142, 144, 147–48, 150–52, 155–56, 163, 166, 176, 188–89, 203, 205, 208–11, 213, 215

legal expert 3
Lehman, Robert 109, 138
Lehranstalt für die Wissenschaft des Judentums (see Hochschule für die Wissenschaft des Judentums) 38, 39, 42
Lehrhaus 34, 43, 73, 136, 150, 161, 162, 170
Lehrman, Cuno 24, 192
Leipziger, Michael 119
Leo Baeck Institute (LBI) 18, 144, 200
lesbian 168
Levi, Eric 81,
Levinson (Levinsky), Nathan Peter 43, 70, 107, 109, 138–41, 143, 189, 198–99, 201, 203
Levinson, Helga 189, 199
Levor, Hilde 108
Levy, Felix A. 101
Lewin (rabbi of Turka) 73
Lewkowitz, Albert 52, 53
Lewkowitz, Hans 72, 74
Lewy, Immanuel 80
Lewy, Julius 48–49, 51, 56–57, 112, 115–16
Liberal Judaism 8–10, 17, 30, 33, 36, 43, 51, 57, 70, 108, 112, 122–25, 138–39, 142, 144, 152–53, 174, 186–89, 195, 198–99, 203, 205–06, 211, 214, 216
Lichtenberg, Leo 67–68, 106, 108–09, 155
Liebeschütz, Hans 39
Liepmann, Klaus 59
life cycle 179
Loewe, Herbert 43
Loewenstein, Egon 74
London 75, 92, 96, 97, 100, 108, 110, 114, 169, 185, 186, 188, 199, 201, 203, 205
London School for Jewish studies 71
Long Island 58, 97
Lorge, Ernst 69, 109, 110, 151, 152, 180
Lorge, Moritz 69
Löwenstamm, Arthur 110
Lowenstein, Steven 122
Löwenthal, Eric 80, 96, 204
Ludwig-Maximilians-Universität München (LMU) 5, 20
Luxembourg Agreement (1952) 188, 191

INDEX

Magen David (Star of David) 180
Magnus, Dora 77
Maney, Edward S. 103
Manhattan Jewish Day School 154
Mann, Louis 103
Mannheim 28, 57, 189, 198
March on Washington 159
Marcus, Jacob Rader 117
Marx, Alexander 51, 60, 62, 73, 79, 118
Marx, Karl 27
masculinity (of the rabbi) 11
Maslow, Will 194
Master (degree) 69
Mauthausen 124
May, Harry 77, 130
Mayer, Irwin 82
Mayfield Temple, Cleveland OH 125
McKeesport, PA 152
memoirs 16, 18, 37, 88, 140, 143–44, 189
memory 1, 7, 8, 10, 14–15, 18, 20, 139, 142–43, 145, 157–58, 169–70, 175, 179, 204
Mendelssohn, Moses 162, 205
Mesifta Talmudical Seminary 64, 81
Messersmith, George 53
method 7, 14, 17, 112, 137, 150, 155, 161, 209, 210
Metzger (nee Scharff) Lore 207
Metzger, Arnold 39
Metzger, Kurt 192
middle class 14, 21, 22, 23, 26–27, 125
Midrash 78
milieu 110, 131, 186, 189
military chaplain 110, 129–30, 181, 189
military police 187, 189
Millburn, NJ 58
Milwaukee 46
Mittwoch, Eugen 49, 78
Mizrachi 185
Montagu, Lily 139, 186
Montreal 75
Morgenstern, Julian 42, 47, 50–56, 69–70, 101, 106, 108, 114–17, 139
Mülheim (Ruhr) 183

Müller, Nachum Norbert 70, 74
Munich 18–19, 55, 68, 89–90, 95, 120, 164, 181, 185, 205
Munk, Elie 185
Munk, Marie 59
Munk, Michael (Yehiel) 131–34, 153, 185–86
Murray, Gilbert 54
Muskogee, OK 126, 157

Nachlas Zwi 63
Nachmann, Werner 199
Nadelman, Ludwig 119, 120, 130
Naples 75
National Committee in Aid of Jewish Ministers 69, 75
National Coordinating Committee for Aid to Refugees and Emigrants Coming from Germany (also National Coordinating Committee, NCC) 77, 92, 93, 99, 101, 102, 103–04
National Council of Jewish Women 12, 102, 104
National Council of Young Israel 153
National Foundation of Temple Youth (NFTY) 151
National Refugee Service (NRS) 104, 131
National Socialism 4–5, 7, 12–13, 15, 17, 19, 21–22, 28, 30–32, 34–35, 38–40, 50–51, 61–62, 90, 98, 120, 133–34, 137, 141, 146–48, 158, 159, 162, 171, 174–76, 179, 180–82, 184, 207–08, 213, 215–16
National Socialist (Nazi) 1, 4–5, 8, 15, 21–23, 32–33, 35–36, 38, 45–46, 48, 50, 52, 60–61, 65, 67, 73, 75, 77, 83–95, 97–98, 100, 102, 105, 115, 127, 133–34, 136–37, 157, 159, 161, 176, 180, 184, 187, 190–95, 208, 210, 212, 215
nationalism 25, 45
nationality 105, 132–33, 135
Nationalsozialistische Betriebszellenorganisation (NSBO) 22
naturalization 91, 107, 133–35
Nazi past 8, 15

Nellhaus, Dagobert D. 170
Ner Israel Rabbinical College 64–66, 81–82, 120, 130, 211
Netherlands 53, 87, 88, 198
networks 5–7, 41, 44, 46, 105, 209, 212
Neuberger, Herman Naphtali 65–66, 81, 120, 211
Neuhaus, Ralph 24, 129, 131, 183–84
Neumann, Ernst 82
New School for Social Research 41, 121, 164
New York City 51, 54–57, 59–60, 71, 76, 78, 88, 94, 98, 102, 104, 109, 113, 118, 123–124, 127, 131, 134, 145, 195, 200, 212
Ney, Hans 81–82
Nostra Aetate 172–73
Novick, Peter 142, 216
Nowy Sacz (Poland) 128
Nuremberg 36, 68, 76–77, 89–90, 133
Nuremberg Laws 68, 76, 77, 133
Nussbaum, Max 24–27, 33–34, 99, 126–27, 156–58, 160, 176, 192–93, 195–96, 199, 206
Nussbaum, Ruth (Offenstadt-Toby, Ruth) 99, 158, 206

Office, Miriam Jean 108
Oldenbourg 96
Olin Sang Ruby Union Institute (OSRUI) 151
Olympia, WA 174
Oppeln (Opole) 27, 97
Oppenheimer, Franz 39
ordination 3, 24, 27, 31, 35, 42–43, 64, 67–68, 77, 85, 98, 108, 110, 120, 128, 165, 168, 197, 201, 205–207
Orthodox Judaism 9–11, 14, 30–32, 35, 37, 41, 43, 45, 50, 57, 59, 61–64, 71, 81, 84–86, 91–93, 96, 98, 107, 110, 119–20, 122–23, 130–32, 149, 153–54, 162–64, 168, 182, 185–86, 188, 191, 199–200, 202–03, 207, 211–12, 214
Orthodox Rabbinerseminar (2009-), Berlin 207
Orthodoxes (Orthodox) Rabbinerseminar (1873–1938), Berlin (see also Hildesheimer Seminar) 3, 9, 10, 24, 38, 39, 41, 60, 62, 73, 74, 80, 84, 118, 119, 120
Ottawa 75
outsider 28, 198
Oxford University (UK) 54

Palestine 17, 28, 36–37, 40–43, 48, 54, 57–59, 80, 84–87, 115, 126, 137, 148, 170, 216
Parzen, Herbert 71, 77, 92–94
passport 86, 91, 125, 134
past/history 7, 8, 15–18, 28, 33, 66, 109, 133, 137, 140–44, 147, 152, 157, 159, 171, 176–178, 180, 192–94, 196–97, 204, 211, 213–14, 216
pastor 3, 10, 13
Pater Dr. Stephan Schaller 194
peoplehood (Jewish~) 25, 30, 34, 148
persecution 4–5, 8, 17, 20–21, 34–36, 46, 50, 55, 60, 83, 86, 93, 135–36, 147, 159, 171, 175, 177–79, 202, 209, 211, 215–16
Petuchowski, Elizabeth 206
Petuchowski, Jakob 109–11, 130, 132–33, 139, 143, 164, 175, 200, 206
Philadelphia 47, 50, 124, 129, 131
Philipson, David 106
philosophy 3, 27, 32, 38, 39, 48, 54, 56, 59, 60, 63, 114, 161, 164
piety 30, 160
Plaut, W. Gunther 67–70, 106–109, 143, 155, 163–164, 166, 168, 180, 206
Plaut, Walter 69–71, 107, 109, 110
Plötzensee 87
pluralism 9, 11, 147, 164, 171, 203
pogrom of November 9, 5, 11, 35, 42–43, 70, 74, 81, 89, 90, 94–97, 99, 126, 129, 176, 209
Poland 5, 14, 24, 26, 54, 55, 61, 62, 72, 73, 90, 91, 94, 95, 128, 179
Polenaktion (Polish action, 1938) 24, 90–91
Pope John Paul II 174
Pope John XXIII 172, 173
Posen 26

post-Holocaust 6, 131, 141, 147, 159, 161, 178, 180, 206, 209, 213, 215–16
postwar era 4–5, 7–8, 15–18, 61, 67, 71, 81, 95, 99, 110, 128, 140, 144, 146–147, 155, 166, 173, 176, 178–88, 190–91, 193, 199, 208–09, 213–14
Prague 31, 74, 77, 102, 130
preacher 27 32, 33, 71, 174, 183
prejudice 196
Priesand, Sally 168
Prinz, Joachim 25–28, 30, 32–33, 36–37, 83, 86, 89, 119, 126, 134, 150, 158–60, 162, 176, 189, 193–95
Project Judaica (JTS, NY) 168
prosopography 7, 18
Prussia 14, 26–27, 52–53, 94, 115

Rabbi Isaac Elchanan Rabbinical Seminary (RIETS) of Yeshiva University in New York City 59–60, 80–82, 119–21, 164
Rabbinical Assembly 45, 72, 77, 92, 128
Rabbinical Council of America 50, 164
rabbinical training 2–4, 9, 12, 14, 38, 40–41, 44, 81, 84–85, 93–94, 101, 113, 118, 126, 130, 156, 160, 164, 166, 168, 173, 200, 204–06, 211, 214
Rabenstein, Aaron 120, 132
Ramah youth camps (JTS, NY) 169
Ranke, Hermann 115
Rath, Ernst Eduard von 95
Rathenau, Mathilde 157
Rathenau, Walther 157
rationalism 22, 34, 155, 160
Rawidowicz, Simon 162,
Razovsky, Celia (correct) 69, 93, 101, 104
reconciliation 179, 192, 195
reconstruction 16, 61, 141, 142
Reconstructionism 130, 160
Reconstructionist Rabbinical College, Wyncote, PA 130
Reform movement in Judaism 3, 6, 8, 10–12, 46, 67, 70, 72, 83, 108, 111, 118–20, 122–24, 126, 130, 132, 136, 144, 148, 151, 153, 163–66, 171, 174, 199, 203–04, 211, 213, 216
refugee rabbi 1, 5–6, 8, 13–14, 17–19, 35, 44, 62, 67, 80, 83, 92, 94, 99, 100, 102, 105, 118, 121, 126, 130, 135, 136, 142, 147–48, 150, 152–53, 158, 162–64, 168–71, 173–74, 176, 178–80, 184–86, 190–93, 195, 199–200, 207, 210–12, 214–15
Reich Association of Jews in Germany (*Reichsvereinigung der Juden in Deutschland*) 23
Reinitz, Hermann 74
Reka Breuer Teacher's Seminary 63
religion 7, 9, 11, 26, 32–34, 37, 51–52, 54, 121, 132, 155–56, 158, 160, 163, 166, 168, 171–72, 175, 216
religious feeling 11, 30, 161
Religious Society of Friends (Quakers) 50
renaissance 7
renewal 7, 25–26, 31–32, 147, 154, 161, 195, 202, 207, 209–10, 216
reorganization 1, 23, 38, 104
representative 3, 10, 12, 92–95, 123, 137, 172, 176, 185–186, 190
rescue 2, 5–7, 13, 15, 18, 41–45, 47–48, 50, 52, 57, 60–61, 64–67, 83, 92, 103, 107–110, 117, 119, 123, 127, 129, 184, 208, 212, 215
Research Foundation for Jewish Immigration 19, 85, 131, 153, 185, 200
resilience 35, 83, 88, 95, 150, 156, 207, 210
restitution 132, 147, 184, 187, 188, 190, 191, 193, 202
return from the concentration camp (during Nazi period and after Nov. 9, 1938) 42, 75, 87–88, 96–98, 99
return to Germany (or formerly German places of birth) 8–9, 17–19, 37–38, 42, 57, 67–68, 75, 77, 84–86, 88–99, 115–16, 138–39, 140, 144, 177, 179–86, 188, 189, 191–93, 196–98, 201, 204, 207, 209, 214
return to Judaism 9, 16, 30, 33–34
return to Palestine 58

return to the United States 58, 68, 79, 86, 119, 129, 131, 185, 188, 193
Revel, Bernard 59–61, 80, 98, 119, 164
Richter, Karl 77, 146, 152, 206
Riepl, Christian 20
Rockefeller Foundation 47, 49
Romania 14, 24, 26, 33, 99
Römer, Gernot 176
Rösel, Isaak 73
Rösel, Manfred 73
Rosenau, William 45–46
Rosenthal, Franz 39, 52, 55–56, 112, 124–26
Rosenthal, Georg 124
Rosenthal, Karl 124, 125
Rosenthal, Klaus 124
Rosenthal, Trudie 124
Rosenzweig, Franz 22, 150, 161–63
Rosenzweig, Leo 48, 59
Rotary Club 129,
Rubinstein, Yitshack 62
Ruderman, Yaakov Y. 64, 66
Russia 14, 24, 47, 61, 169
Rutgers University 121, 164, 200

Sachar, Abraham 195
Sachsenhausen 54, 96, 98
Saint Joseph, MI 176
salary 49, 53, 79–80, 85, 114, 125–26
Salomon, Felix 59
Salomon, Jacob 60
Salzburg 99, 184
Samuel, Jacob A. 98
San Antonio 129
Schaalman, Herman 67–69, 106–09, 151–52, 163, 166–67, 174, 206
Schechter Institute of Jewish Studies, Jerusalem (JTS, NY) 168
Schechter Schools (JTS, NY) 169
Scheiber, Alexander 74
Schiff Warburg, Frieda 47, 80
Schindler, Alexander 109, 138, 163, 164, 165, 166, 167, 168, 180, 181, 206

Schindler, Pessach 119
Schneemann, Heinz 68
Schocken Publishing Company 163
scholar 1, 3–4, 7, 12–13, 16, 19, 21, 30–31, 35, 39, 43, 47, 49–50, 52, 54, 56–57, 59–61, 78, 107, 113, 116, 127, 162–64, 170, 173, 201
scholarship 2, 4, 10, 13, 14, 15, 16, 24, 44, 62, 67, 78, 79, 110, 111, 113, 121, 127, 131, 137, 144, 160, 162, 163, 169, 175, 209, 212, 213, 214
Scholem, Gershom 162
Schön, Gerhard 20
School of Jewish Youth 150
Schorsch, Emil 170
Schorsch, Ismar 97, 119, 128, 163, 168, 170
Schwab, Simon 30, 36–37, 66, 85–86, 89, 135
Schwalbe, Hanna 97
Schwarzschild, Steven 70–71, 109, 138–39, 163, 187–88
science 3, 34, 207
Seattle, WA 70
Second World War 8, 15, 43, 54–55, 61, 75, 98, 104–05, 112, 115–16, 123–24, 126–27, 134, 136, 149, 170, 175, 177, 180–82, 202, 214, 216
Second World War Powers Act (1942) 135
Sedalia, MO 77
segregation 15, 90, 147
Seligman, Edwin 48
Selma, AL 189
seminary rabbi (*Seminarrabbiner*) 113
sermon 26, 33–35, 87, 103, 121, 150, 157
settlement 41, 105, 148, 190
shabbat 31, 34, 125, 140, 154
Shanghai 98, 153, 212
Shapiro, Sarah 108
Shatzkes, Moses 62
Shavuot 33, 34
Shearith Israel Congregation, Baltimore 59, 66, 85, 86
Shluwass, Victor Moses 80
Siegman, Henry 81

INDEX

Sifre 57
Silberman, Lou 68, 107
silence 87, 142, 216
Silver, Abba Hillel 103
Silver, Eliezer 120, 132
Sister, Moses 91
Slobodka Yeshiva 114, 120
Smicha (see also ordination) 64, 120, 128, 205
Smoller, Phineas 152
social justice 159, 161
socialism 26, 150
Society for Christian-Jewish Cooperation 191
Society for the Advancement of Judaism 130
Soloveitchik, Joseph 62
Sonne, Isaiah 112
Soviet Army 182
Soviet Union 62, 98, 169, 182, 182, 202, 203
Spanier, Arthur 52, 53
Special Committee Meeting to Consider Problems of Refugee Jewish Religious Functionaries 93
Special Committee on World Jewry (CCAR) 45
Sperber, Alexander 48–49
spirituality 150, 159, 161
Springer, Axel 195
Springfield, Illinois 125
Springfield, Missouri 77
statelessness 132, 133
status 21, 33, 38, 44, 48, 58, 64, 69, 70, 73, 76, 78–79, 88, 91, 97, 105, 108, 112, 114, 125, 128, 131, 133, 135, 156, 172, 183, 189, 195
Stein, Fred 47
Steinbeck, John 141,
Steinharter, Meir 81
Steinhaus, Heinz 59
Steinhouser, Lou 82
Steltzer, Werner 194
stereotypes 23, 171, 196
Stern, Lotte 108

Stern-Taeubler (Täubler), Selma 55, 112, 189
Stockholm 193
Stoll, Jakob 81
Strauss, Elizabeth 108
Strauss, Herbert 19, 43, 66, 108, 200
Stroginetz 26
Stuttgart 54
Sud, Ira 134
Sumner Wells, Benjamin 56
Swarsensky, Manfred 96, 99, 174
Swig, Ben 152–153
Switzerland 36–37, 85, 124, 205–206
synagogue (see also congregation, *Gemeinde*) 9, 12, 14, 27–28, 32–33, 36, 72, 75–76, 87–88, 90, 93, 96, 98, 101–02, 106, 123, 125, 127, 140–41, 146, 148, 151, 158, 173, 176, 184, 199, 201, 204, 210–11
synagogue on Hiltropwall 90
Syracuse, NY 54
Szobel, Sigmund 73, 80

Taeubler (Täubler), Eugen 39, 43, 52, 55, 112, 115, 116, 117
Taft, Robert A. (Congressman Ohio) 53
Talmud 26, 31, 55, 66,78, 114, 120, 128
teacher (*Lehrer*) 3, 13, 23, 27, 28, 36, 40, 65, 66, 108, 140, 152, 163, 170
Teacher's College of Columbia University 103
Tel Aviv 41, 58, 92, 207
Temple B'nai Abraham, Newark NJ 126
Temple Brith Sholom, Springfield, ILL 125
Temple Emanu-El (New York City) 102
Temple Israel, Hollywood, CA 127, 157
Temple Israel, Tallahassee, FL 155
temple sisterhood 151
theology 4, 9, 110, 113, 121, 160–61, 170, 172, 175, 198, 200, 206–07
Theresienstadt (ghetto) 138, 140–41, 183, 186
Theshow (Tessier), Werner 157
Toeplitz, Otto 24, 39–40

Torah 9, 30, 33, 34, 41, 123, 141, 146, 164, 204
Torah im Derech Eretz 9, 30, 63
Torah scrolls 146
Torah U'mesorah 63, 131, 154
Torah University, Los Angeles, CA 131
Touro College, New York 131
tradition 2–3, 5–6, 9, 10, 15–17, 22, 25–26, 28, 30–31, 33–34, 37, 41, 61, 65, 74, 85, 108, 111, 114, 119, 120, 122–23, 128, 132, 136–38, 143–44, 148, 154, 156, 158, 160–61, 163–64, 168–70, 175–76, 182, 185, 193, 203, 207–08, 210, 212–14, 216
transition 16, 37, 103, 105, 108, 111, 122, 127, 144, 213
transnationalism 1, 6, 74, 106, 137, 178, 209, 212, 215
trauma 97, 124–125, 136, 141, 209
Tree of Life Congregation, Morgantown, WV 110, 155
Trepp, Leo 96, 130, 143
Tuscaloosa, FL 159

UAHC Social Action Committee 159
Union Institute (see also Olin Sang Ruby Union Institute, OSRUI) 151, 152, 155
Union of American Hebrew Congregations (UAHC) 93, 146, 151–52, 159, 164, 166, 174, 196, 205–06
Union of Orthodox Jewish Congregations 45, 93, 131
Union of Orthodox Rabbis 92
Union Theological Seminary 51
United Jewish Youth Movement 69
United Kingdom 43, 120
United Palestine Appeal 86, 126
United States Holocaust Memorial Museum 19, 177
United Synagogue of America 92, 93, 97, 102, 125
University in Exile 41, 48, 50, 53, 41, 48
University of Amsterdam 121
University of Berlin (see Friedrich-Wilhelms-Universität Berlin) 115

University of Bonn 39, 48
University of California 19, 123
University of Dorpat (Estonia) 31, 64
University of Giessen 28, 48, 51, 116
University of Munich (LMU), see Ludwig-Maximilians-Universität München
University of Potsdam 8, 168, 205–06, 214
University of Toronto 177
US-Army 59, 119, 123, 127, 129, 131, 174, 180–81, 189, 199

Va'ad Hayeshivot 41
Vaad Hatzalah 61, 212
Vadakin, Royale (*Msgr.*)
Valley Forge Army Hospital 129
Vassar College 155
Via Dolorosa 174
Vienna 3, 43, 70, 74, 75, 83, 91, 134, 203, 205
Vietnam War 147, 162
visa 43–44, 50, 52–56, 58, 60–61, 64–66, 69–70, 74, 75–78, 80, 83–84, 86, 88, 93, 97–98, 100, 103–04,
Vogelstein, Max 36, 86
Vorspan, Albert 159

Wallach, Luitpold 76, 130
Wanderbund (youth movement) 149
Warburg Wyzanski, Gisela 96
Warburg, Felix 172
Warburg, Max 77
Warren, Ava 53, 56
Warren, OH 130
Warsaw 54, 60, 108, 114
Wasaw Ghetto 108, 155
Washington Heights (Manhattan, New York City) 7, 63, 86, 119, 122–23, 153, 212
Washington, DC 19, 53, 55, 104, 155, 160, 174, 177, 193, 195–96
Wechsberg, Bernard 119
Weinberg, Jehiel Jacob 60
Weinberg, Norbert (born 1931) 120
Weinberg, Norbert (son of William Weinberg) 119

Weinberg, William (Wilhelm) 184
Weiner, Karl 74, 151, 152
Weiss, Samson Raphael 30–31, 64–66, 120, 130, 153–54
Werner, Eric 52, 56, 112
whiteness 147
Wiener, Jacob 120
Wiener, Jacob 81
Wiener, Max 52, 54
Wiesbaden 71, 189, 196
Wilensky, Michael 112
Wilhelm, Kurt 170
Wilkes-Barre, PA 103
Wilmington, NC 125
Wilshire Boulevard Temple, Los Angeles, CA 153, 173, 174
Wind, Leon 72–73
Wise, Jonah 53, 172
Wise, Stephen 46, 52, 83, 86–87, 127, 158, 172
Wissenschaft des Judentums 2–4, 9, 16, 21, 23, 38, 42, 156, 201–02
Wolf, Alfred 67–68, 89, 106, 108, 110, 144, 151, 153, 173–74, 206
Wolf, Arnold 151
World Jewish Conference 45
World Jewish Congress (WJC) 46, 118, 158, 193, 195
World Student Service 69
World Union for Progressive Judaism (WUPJ) 71, 138–39, 186–88, 198, 200, 203, 205
Woythaler, Bert 72, 119
Würzburg 27, 31, 33, 65, 120, 153, 184, 212
Würzburger, Walter 81, 120, 121, 164

yeshiva 13, 18, 30–31, 38, 59–65, 71, 74, 80–82, 84–85, 97–98, 110, 114, 117, 119–21, 123, 130–31, 153, 164, 167, 211
Yeshiva College of Yeshiva University in New York City 13, 59, 62, 74, 119, 120, 130

Yeshiva Etz Chaim 71
Yeshiva Grodna 62
Yeshiva in Exile 62
Yeshiva Mir 64–65, 85, 98, 120
Yeshiva Samson Raphael Hirsch (see also Breuer Yeshiva) 85, 131
Yeshiva Torah Vodaas 61–63, 81
Yeshiva University (New York City) 18, 59–62, 80–82, 98, 113, 117, 119–21, 130, 164, 167, 211
Yiddish 3, 27, 93–94, 154
Yiddishkeit 154, 166
Yishuv (see Palestine, see Land of Israel) 41, 57, 148
Young Israel Institute for Jewish Studies 131, 153
Young Men's Hebrew Employment Service 102
youth 25-26, 28, 32, 64, 69, 73, 85, 96,112, 149, 150–52, 155–56, 198, 210–11
youth bible 28, 149
youth camp (see also individual youth camps) 28, 151, 169, 174
youth movements (*Jugendbewegung*) 25–26, 28, 64, 69, 149–52, 155, 198, 210–11
youth rabbis 28, 149, 150–51

Zacharias Frankel College (2013) in Potsdam 9, 207
Zbaszyn 91
Zentman, Avraham 81
Zimet, Erwin 91, 129, 155
Ziona (youth group) 26
Zionism 11–13, 22, 25–27, 30, 32, 36, 46, 48, 64, 83–84, 86–87, 96, 98, 104, 106, 148–49, 160, 208, 210
Zionist Organization of America 12, 104, 158, 160
Zunz, Leopold 170
Zurich 31, 96, 98

CORNELIA WILHELM is Professor of Modern History at Ludwig-Maximilians-Universität München. Her work focuses on comparative and transnational aspects of (Jewish) history and on race, ethnicity, migration, and religion. She is author of *Bewegung oder Verein? Nationalsozialistische Volkstumspolitik in den USA* (1998) and *Pioneers of a New Jewish Identity: The Independent Orders of B'nai B'rith and True Sisters* (2011). Currently, she works on a digital research portal highlighting the cultural transfers related to the emigration of the German rabbinate after 1933.

For Indiana University Press
Tony Brewer, Artist and Book Designer
Dan Crissman, Acquisitions Editor
Anna Francis, Assistant Acquisitions Editor
Brenna Hosman, Production Coordinator
Katie Huggins, Production Manager
David Miller, Lead Project Manager/Editor
Dan Pyle, Online Publishing Manager
Pamela Rude, Senior Artist and Book Designer
Stephen Williams, Marketing and Publicity Manager

www.ingramcontent.com/pod-product-compliance
Lightning Source LLC
Chambersburg PA
CBHW021345300426
44114CB00012B/1093